The Strange Death of the Liberal Empire
Lord Selborne in South Africa

Part political biography and part study of imperialism, *The Strange Death of the Liberal Empire* is an examination of Lord Selborne's career as high commissioner for South Africa from 1905 to 1910. David Torrance examines Lord Selborne's conception of empire and, by implication, the nature of British imperialism, focusing on the Chinese labour controversy, the self-government issue, the development of racial segregation and the creation of the Union of South Africa. He also reassesses the role the imperial factor played in shaping the state, economy, and society of twentieth-century South Africa. Behind the debate over imperial policy, Torrance shows, were deep and bitter divisions inextricably linked to domestic tensions within Britain itself.

The Strange Death of the Liberal Empire provides a clearer understanding of British imperial policy and of a crucial period in South African history.

DAVID E. TORRANCE is assistant professor of history, Mount Allison University.

Lord Selborne, High Commissioner for South Africa, in 1905.
(Photograph from Praagh, ed., *The Transvaal and Its Mines*)

The Strange Death of the Liberal Empire

Lord Selborne in South Africa

DAVID E. TORRANCE

Liverpool University Press

© McGill-Queen's University Press 1996
ISBN 0-85323-970-3 (cased)
ISBN 0-85323-980-0 (paper)

Legal deposit first quarter 1996
Bibliothèque nationale du Québec

Printed in the United States on acid-free paper

Published simultaneously in the European Union
by Liverpool University Press

This book has been published with the help of a grant from the Social
Science Federation of Canada, using funds provided by the Social Sciences
and Humanities Research Council of Canada. Publication has also been
supported by a grant from the Marjorie Young Bell Faculty Fund, Mount
Allison University.

McGill-Queen's University Press is grateful to the Canada Council for
support of its publishing program.

British Library Cataloguing-in-Publication Data

A British Library CIP record is available

This book was typeset by Typo Litho Composition Inc.
in 10/12 Baskerville.

To Mom, Dad, and Elizabeth, and to my late Grandma

Contents

Acknowledgments

Many people assisted me in this project, but space only permits mention of a small fraction of those to whom I am indebted. I must begin by expressing my deep appreciation to Alan Jeeves for his incisive criticism, thoughtful insight, and constant encouragement. I am also grateful for the kind coaching I received from so many other history professors at Queen's University; I am especially grateful for the support and guidance that George Rawlyk has extended to me over the years. In addition, I must make mention of the undergraduate professors who stimulated my interest in imperial history: Drs Sanders, Porter, Jarrett, Jenks, and Futch. At Mount Allison I have been fortunate to have had congenial encouragement from my colleagues: Bill Godfrey, Eugene Goodrich, Graham Adams, Peter Penner, Jack Stanton, David Beatty, Wayne Hunt, and Carolyn Smith.

The manuscript was greatly enriched by the scholarly advice tendered by colleagues at Queen's University. Of these, Ronald T. Ellsworth and Greg Marquis must receive special mention. I am also grateful for the suggestions which William Roger Louis, of the University of Texas at Austin, made on parts of the manuscript.

Needless to say, this project would have been impossible without the kind assistance of the staffs at the following libraries and archives in England: the Bodleian Library, Rhodes House, the British Library, the Public Records Office at Kew, the University of Birmingham, the India Office Library, and the Salisbury collections at Hatfield House. In Canada, I am much obliged to the documents library of Queen's University and to the staff of the Ralph Pickard Bell library at Mount Allison.

I would also like to thank the 4th Earl of Selborne for permission to cite the papers of the 2nd Earl and for furnishing the photograph of Lady Selborne. I also appreciate Lord Selborne's kind advice on matters of aristocratic usage.

The help I have received from Mount Allison University, especially from the Marjorie Young Bell Faculty Fund, is most appreciated. I am also indebted to Professor Leonard Thompson for permission to reproduce a map of South Africa. The title of this book alludes to George Dangerfield's work, *The Strange Death of Liberal England.*

I deeply appreciate the great assistance I have received at all stages of the publishing process from the staff of McGill-Queen's University Press. I am especially grateful to Don Akenson for his strong encouragement over many years, and to Diane Mew for her incisive editing.

I owe my greatest debt to my wife, Elizabeth, without whose creative insight, compassionate support, and long hours of typing and editing this project would have been indefinitely delayed.

Preface

This is a book about British imperialism – more particularly, about British imperial policy towards South Africa during the critical period from 1905 to 1910. To understand the "imperial mind" which formulated this policy, I have focused on the high commissionership of William Waldegrave Palmer, the 2nd Earl of Selborne. In doing so, I sought to comprehend what imperialism meant to its practitioners and how it operated in southern Africa. My study complements the classic work of George Dangerfield, who argued in *The Strange Death of Liberal England* that one of liberalism's most dangerous antagonists was Britain's new plutocratic elite which South African gold did much to create. My study shows how Britain's high commissioner in South Africa promoted the gold mining industry and in the process undermined the Liberal government he was supposed to be serving.

Two generations ago, the study of a British high commissioner for South Africa following the Boer War would have possessed self-evident significance. Though in decline, the British Empire still appeared formidable, and its past proconsuls seemed worthy objects for scholarly inquiry. But since 1945, as the Empire diminished in power, it faded from memory, and intellectual attention shifted to the indigenous histories of the areas which had recently won independence from European rule. Of course, the British Empire still evoked interest, and no amount of historical rethinking could obliterate the Empire from the historical map, but its historiography began to balkanize into regional studies. A decade ago D.K. Fieldhouse likened the field of imperial history to Humpty Dumpty and advised scholars to relinquish grandiose, but futile, attempts to depict the Empire as a whole.[1] Instead, he enjoined, they should limit their focus to the "area of interaction" between the metropole and the periphery.

Some theorists, however, have remained oblivious to Fieldhouse's caveat, and have presented imperialism as a coherent process which, although emanating from Europe, affected the entire world. Many years ago, such metropolitan assumptions provided the theoretical foundation for a wide variety of interpretations – diplomatic, economic, or sociological. Currently, underdevelopment theorists attribute imperialism to First World capitalism and blame the imperial experience for the stunted development, political instability, and general poverty which has afflicted the Third World since 1945. Critics of this school, however, charge that recent attempts to reassemble Humpty Dumpty on such lines have produced no empire recognizable to history (or historians), but a grotesque monster of marxist imagination. Imperial historians, it would seem, may choose between two very different characterizations of Empire: a feeble Humpty Dumpty, or a villainous Mr Punch.

These contrasting pictures come from two different but equally distinguished traditions which might be labelled multi-causal-peripheralist and radical-metropolitan.[2] The pioneers of the peripheral school were Robinson and Gallagher, who disputed that the "new imperialism" of the late Victorian period represented a significant break with previous policy.[3] In *Africa and the Victorians* they investigated the official mind of imperialism – the beliefs, hopes, and fears of ministers, permanent or political, who made policy. They concluded that what informed the judgement and animated the decisions of those in power were strategic and geopolitical considerations, which remained unchanged during the nineteenth century. Driven neither by economic calculation nor ideological fervour, late Victorian statesmen were preoccupied with national security and had no desire to expand but rather an obsession to preserve what Britain already had.

How then do the authors account for the formal acquisition by Britain of huge tracts of the African continent? Here, the scholars introduce the notion of local crisis. The growth of nationalism – whether African or settler – on the circumference of empire undermined the system of collaboration through which Britain had ruled informally. It was the Egyptian nationalism of Urabi Pasha and his followers which drove Britain's Khedival collaborator from power in 1882 and saddled Gladstone with direct responsibility for Egypt's governance. At the opposite extremity of the continent, the discovery of gold in the Boer-ruled Transvaal transferred power away from Britain's "collaborating" colonies on the coast and so rendered the imperial position precarious. Instead of signifying the high-water mark of Britain's imperial activity, the conquest of Egypt and later of South Africa represented desperate measures to retrieve the metropole's deteriorating situation on the periphery. And these frantic efforts ended in failure.[4]

At the risk of simplifying Robinson and Gallagher's work, one can summarize their thesis by reference to two complementary points: continuity at the metropole and dynamism on the periphery. These are the two sides of the "R & G" coin. Without entering into a full critique, it might still be useful to single out certain problematic issues. One might, for example, question the generalizations which Robinson and Gallagher make about the official mind. Was there such a thing and, if so, had it received no new ideas in half a century? And was it really impervious to shifts in public opinion or to changes in government? One might also wonder how sharp the distinction was between metropole and periphery. These difficulties notwithstanding, the influence of Robinson and Gallagher has been immense. By shifting scholarly attention away from the hub to the various spokes of the imperial wheel, they have encouraged the fragmentation of academic effort and the dissolution of the Empire as a conceptual unit.

The metropolitan-radical school is both older and newer than the multi-causal-peripheralist. J.A. Hobson presented his classic theory of imperialism about a century ago. This owed much to his earlier analysis of the crisis in South Africa where he served as a correspondent for the *Manchester Guardian* during the Boer War. In a series of articles, he argued strenuously that the war was being waged in the interests of the Witwatersrand gold-mining magnates, who found President Kruger's Boer republic a major hindrance to the profitable operation of their mines. Hobson attributed British expansion to surplus capital, which could not be profitably invested in England because of underconsumption resulting from the uneven distribution of wealth. The more equitable allocation of wealth at home would remove the incentive to export capital abroad.[5]

Building on Hobson, but far less optimistic about the possibilities of reform, Lenin saw imperialism as an inevitable development in capitalism, which had finally reached its last stage (i.e., monopoly) before collapsing from its own rot. Every facet of each nation's economy had fallen under the monopolistic ownership and control of the country's financiers. In all western countries finance capital (as opposed to commercial or industrial capital) had taken over the state. The financial interest in each nation then turned abroad. As "backward" countries offered higher returns on investment than the home economies which they monopolized, the financiers exported their capital and called the metropolitan government in to protect their investment. Once these monopoly capitalists had devoured the world, they fought amongst themselves to redivide the spoils. Lenin believed that this titanic struggle among rival blocks of capitalists explained not only imperialism, but also World War I.[6]

Though Hobson and Lenin wrote half a century before Robinson and Gallagher, the radical tradition has continued to develop throughout the century. One strand of Lenin's thought matured in the 1970s – the underdevelopment theory. This was formulated by such scholars as A. Gunder Frank and Immanuel Wallerstein to explain Third World economic stagnation. In the sixteenth century, so the theory runs, Europe brought the rest of the world into a global capitalist economy, marked by metropolitan dominance over and exploitation of the periphery. Through the system of unequal exchange, the metropole sucks wealth from the periphery, which is left not simply undeveloped but underdeveloped, its growth stunted, its economy distorted. For four centuries, the First World has shaped the Third World in accordance with the needs of metropolitan capital, and it does so still. Imperialism, therefore, has merely changed its form since 1945 and continues to operate through nominally independent states.[7]

The issue of underdevelopment has sparked a lively debate within the radical camp. Some, such as Bill Warren, have countered that imperialism pioneered capitalist development around the world and "acted as a powerful engine of progressive social change ..." Despite this debate, Warren, Wallerstein, Frank, Lenin and Hobson would all agree that, whether as pioneer or underdeveloper, Europe, especially Britain, was formative in shaping the rest of the world.[8]

We can now highlight the differences between the multi-causal peripheralists and the radical metropolitanists. The obvious distinction concerns the greater relative power that the latter confer on the metropole vis-à-vis the periphery. Secondly, the metropolitan radicals eschew multi-causal explanations and see instead an economic dynamic as the driving force in imperial expansion. More specifically, most radicals attribute imperialism to the imperatives of capitalism. Thirdly, they would argue that rather than conform to a continuous pattern, Europe's overseas activity since 1600 passed through several distinct stages, reflecting the changing nature of capitalism. Finally, unlike the peripheralists, the radicals tend to subordinate ideas and ideology to what they consider material reality. Thus, Lenin does not concern himself with policies or an official mind but devotes considerable attention to monopolies and capital flows. Though modern Marxists admit that human consciousness plays an active part in history, they confer primacy to the material forces which, they believe, shaped minds. Thus the distinguished historian Shula Marks cited approvingly

Geoffrey Barraclough's denunciation of historians' "almost neurotic absorption in questions of motivation."[9] The historian of empire thus finds him/herself in a quandary between two incompatible conceptions of imperialism. Worse still, there seems little common methodological ground on which to work out differences.[10]

The discrepancy between imperial mind and capitalist matter underscores the intractability of the historiographical divide. All historians agree that the export of British capital reached unprecedented heights in the late Victorian and Edwardian periods. True, little of this went to the Empire, but whatever the final destination of British investment, the United Kingdom was increasing its financial commitment overseas prodigiously.[11] Moreover, as the tariff reform campaign attests, there were some currents of opinion which profoundly feared industrial and commercial competition from the United States and Germany. One would think that such considerations would figure into the geopolitical calculations of British policy-makers, whether imperial or diplomatic. And yet, according to Robinson and Gallagher, the official mind of Empire took no notice of these trends. If these historians are correct, then we are facing an imperial version of the mind-body problem, for the Empire's head seemed oblivious to the global action of its economic sinews.[12]

Recently the debate between metropole and periphery has re-emerged with an interesting twist. In 1980 two scholars, P.J. Cain and A.G. Hopkins, introduced a new theory of imperial history which attempted to reintegrate the field by "putting the metropolitan economy back at the centre of analysis." In their 1993 two-volume study, *British Imperialism: Innovation and Expansion, 1688–1914*, they propounded their thesis of "gentlemanly capitalism."[13] According to this, what drove Britain's economic growth and its expansion overseas were the interests of non-industrial capital. From the late seventeenth century until the middle of the nineteenth, the landed interest predominated, but it bolstered its pre-eminent position by allying with the City, that collection of commercial and financial interests concentrated in London. This economic alliance was solidified by common public school backgrounds, by marriage, and by a shared "gentlemanly" ethos. Despite the growing wealth and importance of manufacturing after the industrial revolution, this sector never gained ascendancy. Though the landed aristocrats lost influence after free trade, their gentlemanly cousins in finance inherited their commanding heights and dominated the British economy for the next century until 1945. According to Cain and Hopkins, both land and then finance promoted overseas expansion. In their words, "The imperial mission was the export version of the gentlemanly order." Thus, the rise and fall of British industry was irrelevant to imperialism, which remained a gentleman's affair from the 1600s until 1945.[14]

Not surprisingly, many recent scholars have tried to knock this gentlemanly Humpty-Dumpty off the wall. In 1990, Andrew Porter subjected the concept of gentlemanly capitalism to close scrutiny, claiming that the interests covered by the term were too diverse to fit the pattern which Cain and Hopkins laid out. The "fundamental difficulty," Porter charged, "lies in the lack of bridges between the gentlemanly capitalist outline and the complexity of the calculations and circumstances involved in major episodes of Britain's expansion." Finally, "historians of empire must surely lodge a methodological protest against any suggestion that their explanations 'ought' both to begin with the metropolitan economy and to assume its priority throughout."[15]

In this exchange of ideas, we can see the minefields awaiting historians of the British Empire. After negotiating the metropolitan-peripheral divide, the imperial scholar must then confront the controversy surrounding change and continuity in imperial policy. Then, he or she must analyse the balance of forces – economic, political, and ideological – to assess the relative importance of each and the interaction of all in the evolution of British imperialism. It is surprising that the ideological factor has not played a larger role in the debate over gentlemanly capitalism, which, after all, refers to a set of values and attitudes, as well as a mode of production. Perhaps a deeper analysis of the consciousness of imperial statesmen might enable the historian to reconcile metropole with periphery, politics with economics, and the mind of empire with its material context.

These considerations inform the present study of Lord Selborne, whose role in South Africa has received little scholarly attention. As radicals do not usually discuss personalities, the few Selborne references that have appeared have been made by scholars in the multicausal-peripheral school. He is portrayed as an imperialist of Unionist stamp who sought to uphold British paramountcy by maintaining the power of the imperial factor on the periphery. In this losing battle, he opposed the Liberals, whose policy, especially regarding self-government, he viewed as likely to restore the political power of Afrikanerdom. In the late 1960s, a Cambridge scholar, Ronald Hyam, concluded that on this, as on most issues, Selborne was overruled. Summarizing Liberal policy, Hyam remarked: "If for any reason, a colony was attracting public attention, it was much harder for the governor to impose his will. Because of this, Selborne in South Africa never stood much chance of getting his way with the Liberal government. Almost every recommendation which he made was turned down, though

Elgin was careful to show that he appreciated Selborne's sense of frustration."[16] This view accorded well with that of another prominent historian, Leonard Thompson, whose work on South African unification, which came out in 1960, has yet to be superseded. Despite his warm advocacy of closer union, Selborne, in Thompson's opinion, played little part in the movement; he was merely "kept informed" of the proceedings.[17]

It is clear that Selborne has deserved fuller treatment from historians. He performed important work in South Africa, but most of this has remained hidden in the peripheral shadows. This book seeks to bring his achievements to light. A broader objective is to elucidate the mind and operation of British imperialism in the Edwardian period.[18] The relation between Lord Selborne and the mining magnates might illuminate the meaning of gentlemanly capitalism. The Chinese labour controversy and the intercolonial conflict over rail rates forced Selborne to confront the issue of business-state collaboration. The dealings of a Unionist high commissioner with a Liberal government will test the contention of some scholars that there existed a continuity in policy over time and between parties. Also, the facts relating to Selborne's involvement in the closer union movement must be brought to light. An examination of the relative significance of Britain vis-à-vis local factors in the formation of the Union might make us sceptical about the validity of the metropole-periphery distinction – a distinction which undergirds much of the writing on Britain's experience overseas. And finally, Selborne's attitudes, motives, and values might seem at variance with the official mind which Robinson and Gallagher depict.

Though this work treats ideas seriously as important stuff of history, it seeks to avoid the solipsistic tendency of biography to see the world through its subject's eyes. Indeed, this study relies heavily on the many secondary works which delineate the objective conditions which would have faced any imperial statesman in Britain or South Africa. Of course, Selborne's perceptions of these conditions will be emphasized. By so humanizing impersonal factors, this book hopes to join in the work of restoring life and wholeness to imperial studies. With diligent effort, we might yet put Humpty Dumpty together again.

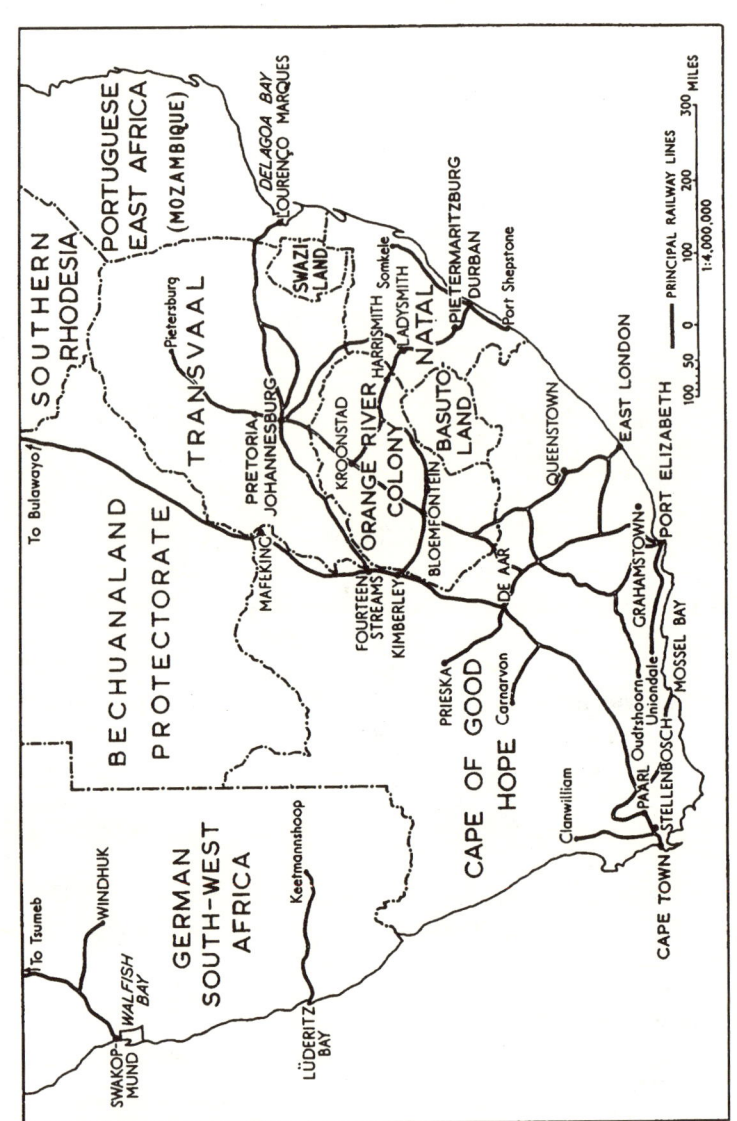

SOUTHERN AFRICA, 1908
Reprinted, by permission, from Thompson, *The Unification of South Africa, 1902–1910*

The Strange Death of the Liberal Empire

1 Introduction

When William Waldegrave Palmer was born in 1859, British wealth and British power dominated the world. At the time of his death in 1942, England was in the process of liquidating its assets to finance its struggle for survival against Hitler's Germany. In his lifetime Palmer had witnessed the displacement of Britain from its position as the centre of industrial progress, international trade, and the world's greatest modern empire; he had seen it decline to the status of a small, economically troubled country on the fringe of Europe. In the posts he occupied from 1895 to 1910 in the Colonial Office, the Admiralty, and as high commissioner of South Africa, Lord Selborne (as Palmer had become in 1895) could discern the slippage in Britain's international footing. Though he bravely attempted – and to no small extent helped – to keep the Empire on its feet, neither he nor anyone else could arrest the slide.

Yet despite its retreat from power, Britain and the Commonwealth played a leading role in thwarting German militarism twice in this century. Whatever the malaise in British industry, productivity increased prodigiously during the period of so-called decline. And though the pound is no longer the world's currency, London has remained an important centre of international finance. Too sharp a focus its on decline obscures the real power that Britain and its economy continued to exert throughout the world and within the Empire during the late Victorian and Edwardian eras. Diplomatically, Great Britain shaped the configuration of international power as much as it was shaped by it. Moreover, British imperialism before the First World War conditioned the socio-economic transformation which much of Africa and Asia endured in the early twentieth century. These contrary tendencies of exhaustion and vigour appeared in South Africa, where the economic dynamism of British capitalism shook southern Africa even as Britain's formal rule receded.

This is not to deny that Edwardian statesmen had reason for alarm. The mounting deficit in the balance of visible trade caused considerable concern. The average annual shortfall climbed from £84.9 million during the 1870s to £97.1 million for the 1880s, £133.4 million for the 1890s, and £159.7 million for the first decade of this century.[1] That German and American trade was increasing more rapidly than British seemed vexing indeed, for Britain depended, far more than they, on overseas commerce. While in 1880 British goods accounted for 23.2 per cent of world trade, its share had shrunk to 14.1 per cent by the First World War. More disquieting still, the old staple industries continued to predominate in British trade, textiles alone accounting for 36.3 per cent of total exports in 1913.

England's commercial difficulties stemmed from the relative decline of its industrial base. From a healthy 4 per cent in the period from 1820 to 1840, its industrial growth had shrivelled to 1.5 per cent by 1875.[2] In 1880 22.9 per cent of the world's manufacturing capacity lay in Britain. Thirty years later, Britain's share had dropped to 14.7 per cent, while Germany's reached 15.9 per cent and that of the United States bounced to 35.3 per cent. In the heavy metals, German progress was remarkable. While British steel production jumped impressively from 3.6 million tons in 1890 to 6.5 million tons in 1914, in this same period Germany's had increased more dramatically from 2.4 million to 14 million tons. Another worry was England's backwardness in industries such as chemicals and optics – new fields in which Germany excelled.[3]

Britain's sluggish performance has been attributed to various factors: bad management and industrial organization, the decline of entrepreneurial spirit, poor labour relations, deficient training in modern technology, cultural hostility to business, and England's early industrial start which committed it to primitive techniques and forms of organization. More contentiously, some scholars have blamed the rivalry between the financial and service sectors on the one hand and the manufacturing sector on the other.[4]

Banking and financial enterprise flourished in the City of London well before the industrial revolution and remained crucial to British capitalism well after it.[5] The City interest emerged in the late seventeenth century, stimulated by the government's enormous call for loan funds. As the nation's debt ballooned to over £800 million in 1815, growth in the City burgeoned to match. In the nineteenth century overseas fields of investment found increasing favour among City financiers. By 1870 more capital left Britain each year than remained at home. In the last quarter of the nineteenth century the inflow from these investments abroad exceeded the outflow, making them important sources of British income. No other country was as deeply committed to the world economy as Great Britain, which accounted for 75 per cent of all international capital movement in 1900.

By 1913–14 one-third of all British wealth lay outside the British Isles. In the fifty years from 1865 to 1914, 42 per cent of Britain's capital flowed to foreign countries, one-third remained at home, and only one-quarter went to the Empire; and of that, only one-third went to the dependent Empire. Especially important as a growing field for English funds was Canada, which took one-third of all British loans between 1900 and 1914. Another attractive investment, and one increasingly important for monetary stability, was South African gold.[6]

Sterling was the world's currency and London the centre of international finance. The banking and mercantile services which the City provided its international customers became increasingly important to the British economy itself. Although the deficit in Britain's visible trade grew from £58.2 million in 1865 to £134.4 million in 1913, the surplus on its balance of payments increased from £21.8 million to £187.9 million. What accounted for this was the rising income from financial, insurance, and shipping services – the so-called invisibles, which swelled from £80 million to £340 million.[7]

Despite these figures, many scholars question the City's contribution to Britain's economic strength. Eric Hobsbawn, in his classic study, *Industry and Empire*, portrays the City as a vampire sucking the economic life out of England. Overseas investments, he claims, drained off funds which might have been more fruitfully deployed at home to revamp the nation's decaying economic infrastructure. Geoffrey Ingham argues that the cosmopolitan financiers have had few relations (business or social) with the nation's industrialists, and that, operating in distinct spheres, the two sectors often promoted antithetical policies. The implication is that, as the City gained, industry suffered.[8]

Most recently, Sidney Pollard has argued that London financiers not only diverted funds abroad, but also used their privileged backgrounds and gentlemanly connections to persuade their friends in politics to pursue policies which favoured finance and injured industry. Free trade and the gold standard, for example, benefited the City but could and often did impede productive growth. Moreover, according to Pollard, the increasing inflow from overseas investments created an import surplus which undermined British manufacturing. Thus the City's financial power sustained the established elite; power, wealth, and privilege all reinforced each other. Whereas the growth of industry in the United States led to the rise of an entrepreneurial class, in Britain the ascendancy of finance favoured the existing ruling class with its established social network, common public school background, and gentlemanly ethos. It seems clear that the interests of the British elite were not necessarily those of industrial capitalism.

Having discussed the British economy and its component sectors, we can now take up the question of imperialism and its importance to Great Britain economically, strategically, and ideologically. The economic impact of imperialism on Great Britain has furnished a subject of hot debate. Recently, Davis and Huttenback undertook a quantitative analysis of the Empire's costs and benefits to the United Kingdom. In their judgment, the small proportion of capital absorbed by the Empire, especially by the dependent colonies acquired after 1880, suggests that British capitalism owed little to the "expansion of England." Costly to maintain, the Empire gave little back, and the regions most directly controlled gave back least. As the authors conclude, "The evidence indicates that probably at no time, and certainly not after the 1870s, were Empire profits sufficient to underwrite British prosperity."9

The circumscribed parameters of their study, however, cause Davis and Huttenback to understate the global orientation of England's economy. Moreover, the quantitative methodology of their study ignores essential qualitative aspects of Britain's economic situation. In the minds of statesmen, a region's potential wealth figured more prominently as a consideration than the actual riches it currently produced. A quantitative analysis also fails to account for commodities or enterprises whose strategic importance in Britain's economic structure far outweigh the actual returns on investment. As the basis of the world's monetary system, gold possessed a value which greatly exceeded the price of bullion. The importance of South Africa to Britain's position in the international economy, therefore, eludes Davis and Huttenback. Finally, as the authors themselves acknowledge, the English elite did tend to invest heavily in the Empire.[10] Thus, a stark measurement of capital flows might hide imperialism's full importance to the British economy, and it certainly ignores the economic significance that the ruling class attached to Empire.

Perhaps the British economy would, in the long run, have grown more healthily without its far-flung responsibilities overseas. When all costs are taken into account, the Empire undoubtedly consumed more capital than it paid back. But, whatever the absolute importance of Empire to industry, it proved a vital support to "gentlemanly capitalism" in the late Victorian age.

Economic motives were never far behind imperial activities. For example, in the last quarter of the nineteenth century India had become an important market for British textiles, taking 45 per cent of British cotton goods. Hobsbawm expressed the point emphatically: "In India, the formal Empire never ceased to be vital to the British economy."[11] Finally, Britain's position as the world's banker depended on the strength and stability of the pound, and until 1931 this depended on gold. As Ian Drummond explained the operation of the gold standard:

The system could readily accommodate real economic growth at stable or rising price levels only if the quantity of monetary gold, both for coin and for reserves, was rising as well. If the several countries had all been trying to stay on gold, and also to grow in real terms, while competing for an unchanging stock of gold, great stresses would have appeared almost at once. Kitchen has estimated that between 1880 and 1914 the international gold standard required the accumulation of monetary gold worth nearly a thousand million pounds – an immense sum at the time.[12]

The gold discoveries in the United States, Australia, and especially South Africa were vital in guaranteeing the sterling-based system of international exchange and in facilitating world economic growth.

Of course, the Empire cannot be depicted in merely material terms, for it was also a system of power and the embodiment of values, beliefs, and sentiments which, together, comprised the "British spirit." By 1900 this spirit contained a heavy dose of Social Darwinism. Fusing economic strength with military might, this doctrine, in its geopolitical garb, conceived of the world as an arena of competing empires "struggling for existence." With the relative weakening of Britain's economic position vis-à-vis Germany and the United States, many statesmen feared that Britain would have to scramble to maintain its integrity and independence. In 1898 Lord Salisbury, the prime minister, made a speech which exemplified this view of international affairs. He told his audience: "Nations may roughly be divided between the living and the dying ... For one reason or another – from the necessities of politics or under the pretence of philanthropy – the living nations will gradually encroach on the territory of the dying, and the seeds and the causes of conflict among civilised nations will speedily appear. These things may introduce causes of fatal difference between the great nations whose mighty armies stand opposite threatening each other."[13] Thus, in 1905 the Empire appeared not only profitable but vital for Britain's existence.

To such stark considerations of power, all British politicians infused a strong moral element into their geopolitics. Christianity was still a potent force in Britain. At the great public schools religious values were instilled into the nation's future leaders. When this religiosity was combined with romanticism, also pervasive in the nineteenth century, the result was a profound sense of mission, which Corelli Barnett has described as "evangelism in the red coat of imperialism."[14] The imperial elite carried with it a strong sense of purpose and duty. To paraphrase the words Lord Randolph Churchill used in a different context, English imperialists believed that, if necessary, Britain should fight and that it would be right! Wealth, power, and culture were but three facets of the same imperial diamond.

As the Empire rose in importance to British security, so did the European challenges to it. In 1882 Britain's occupation of Egypt incurred French hostility, which intensified until the Fashoda crisis of 1898, when a French climb-down narrowly prevented war. Two years after the bombardment of Alexandria, London felt the force of the newly united German nation when in 1884 Bismarck launched his colonial bid. British interests also clashed with those of Russia – over central Asia, India's northern frontier, China, and the Dardenelles. Anglo-Russian tension constituted a persistent feature of nineteenth-century diplomacy, and after 1878 crises flared up with increasing frequency.

Conditions on the continent of Europe after 1890 also worked against British diplomacy. As European relations solidified into the alliance system, London lost the leverage it once enjoyed over the continental powers. Britain now found it difficult to isolate a competitor. For example, by presenting the possibility of a joint naval threat, the Franco-Russian Alliance of 1894 rendered precarious Britain's hold on the Bosphorus and the Dardanelles. In 1895 Lord Salisbury, the British prime minister, decided to abandon these straits as a route to the East and rely instead on the Suez and, as a secondary route, on the Cape. The former, of course, brought Britain into further conflict with France. As for the Cape, Germany's friendly overtures to the anti-British South African Republic occasioned considerable anxiety at Whitehall. When in 1895, after the Jameson Raid fiasco, the kaiser sent Paul Kruger, the republic's president, a congratulatory telegram, Britain's anxieties turned to outrage. Germany's empty threat of ranging a continental league against Britain merely stiffened English resolve to keep the rest of Europe away from its sphere of influence in South Africa, where its economic, diplomatic, and strategic imperatives seemed to converge.

The threat to the Empire came not only from diplomatic rivals but also from within. The Congress movement in India and the emergence of nationalism in the dominions presented a challenge to London's hegemony over its colonies and to the imperial order itself. And in South Africa, after the Jameson Raid, Britain faced considerable resentiment and hostility from the Boer or Afrikaner population not only in the Transvaal and Orange Free State but also in the Cape. As the Empire loomed larger in Britain's fortunes, imperial ties seemed to weaken dangerously, and all the while European rivals appeared close at hand to snatch up the fragments as soon as the bonds of empire had dissolved.

Not all British statesmen viewed the situation in such bleak terms. Though few wished to liquidate the Empire, many argued that it should not be held together forcibly. On the left, various groups – especially those with a labour orientation – denounced the new imperialism as a capitalist expedient to exploit the rest of the globe. The Liberal party had always shown a certain ambivalence towards imperial ventures. Although it was Gladstone's government that had brought Egypt under direct control, it was this same government whose dilatory tactics had left General Gordon to the mercy of the Mahdi in 1885. The following year the unsuccessful introduction of Gladstone's Home Rule bill drove Joseph Chamberlain and ninety-two others out of the party.

The next twenty years witnessed the ascendancy of the new imperialism as personified by Joseph Chamberlain. When the Conservatives and their Liberal Unionist allies came to power in 1895, Chamberlain became colonial secretary. Determined to uphold British paramountcy in South Africa against the claims of the two Boer republics, he and his high commissioner, Sir Alfred Milner, pursued an aggressive policy, which in 1899 precipitated the Boer War. Though generally popular, the war did spark criticism from certain groups on the left, known as pro-Boers.[15] While labour groups denounced the conflict as a capitalist war, a substantial section of the Liberal party charged that the forcible annexation of the two Afrikaner states vitiated the liberal spirit of Britain's Empire, which was bound together by reciprocal consent and ties of sentiment. By 1901 the appalling condition of the concentration camps into which Kitchener's prosecution of the war had driven Boer women and children convinced the Liberal leader, Sir Henry Campbell-Bannerman, to throw his weight behind the doves in his party. Although the Liberal imperialists (dubbed Limps) continued to support the war throughout its duration, peace brought the two wings of the party together again. Campbell-Bannerman spoke for a united party when he urged generous peace terms and the speedy conferment of self-government on the conquered Boer states.

Joseph Chamberlain, however, considered that his work had just begun. Worried about the centrifugal tendencies within the Empire and about commercial competition from without, he proposed a measure which was designed to solve both problems at once: tariff protection against foreign competitors with exemption for Empire states. Thus, Chamberlain would supplement ties of sentiment with more material inducements for the countries of the Empire to remain within the imperial fold. When Arthur Balfour, who in 1902 replaced Salisbury as prime minister, refused to commit the party to this program, Chamberlain resigned from the cabinet to publicize the cause.

The tariff reform campaign damaged the Unionist government in two ways. Besides splitting the party, it led the public to associate all Unionists with high prices and dear bread. The approval given to the importation of Chinese labour into the Transvaal seemed to confirm, in the public mind, that Balfour's government was in league with ruthless capitalists who would reduce people to starvation or slavery to make a profit. This shift in public attention from imperial to social issues was registered at the polls in 1906 when the Liberals won a landslide victory. Shortly after their accession to power, they conferred self-governing institutions on the Transvaal and Orange River Colony (as the two republics had been renamed) and then turned from imperial matters to social reform.

Chamberlain, whose earlier radicalism had not completely left him, hoped that tariff reform would at once save British jobs and provide revenue to defray the costs of various social reforms. The Liberals, on the other hand, tended to place social improvement first and would finance it through higher taxes. This, many Liberals argued, would create a vigorous race fit to rule others. During the domestic crises before the First World War, imperialism and socialism did come to signify opposing policies; people lost sight of their possible complementarity and viewed the two as inversely related.

Thus, the pre-1905 mutual commitment to empire should not obscure the very different priorities which lay behind each party's policies. Edwardian politics tended to polarize into a struggle which resembled the class conflict of marxist prognostication. Political discourse rang with the rhetoric of class warfare, and political action gave force to the rhetoric. The political mobilization of the working class, made manifest by the great expansion of unionism and the emergence of political groups representing labour, moved the Liberal party to the left, but this drove much of its middle-class constituents to the Tories. Though unlikely revolutionaries, the Liberals led the attack on privileged property with such measures as the People's Budget of 1909 and the Parliament Act of 1911. How it would have treated the intensified labour militancy in 1914 must remain unknown, for the First World War intervened. What is clear is that England in 1914 verged on the edge of a dangerous social crisis.[16] This confirms the classic study of George Dangerfield, who wrote of the intensifying struggle between capital and labour.

The gold discoveries in South Africa had flowed to England and corrupted the landed elite.

Indeed, that tide of gold, rolling up out of South Africa, had deposited in the board rooms and drawing rooms and palaces of England a preposterous and powerful flotsam, which, arriving casually like seaweed, established itself with the instinctive adroitness of a barnacle. The new financier, the new plutocrat, had little of that sense of responsibility which once had sanctioned the power of England's landed classes. He was a purely international figure, or so it seemed, and money was his language, like a loud and glittering Esperanto; it was a language, moreover, which England's upper classes seemed unable to resist. Where did the money come from? Nobody seemed to care. It was there to be spent in the most ostentatious manner possible; for its new masters set the fashion, and the fashion they set was not likely to be a reticent one. Society in the last pre-war years grew wildly plutocratic; the middle classes became complacent and dependent; only the workers seemed to be deprived of their share in prosperity.[17]

Though the First World War might have saved Britain from a social revolution, it could not rescue British liberalism. Although exaggerated, Dangerfield's account captured the social tumult and chaos which blighted Edwardian England. For present purposes, it is interesting to note the financial importance which Dangerfield attached to South Africa. One might add that the crisis which South African gold had caused in England reverberated back to the Cape from where it shook and shaped the subcontinent.

While South Africa's fortunes and misfortunes affected England and the Empire in many ways, Great Britain exercised a decisive influence on the subcontinent. After a half-century of light and liberal rule, southern Africa felt the more vigorous application of imperial power after the diamond discoveries of the late 1860s. As early as 1872, when the Cape Colony received responsible government, Britain envisioned a South African federation which would include the two British colonies (the Cape and Natal) and the two Afrikaner republics in the interior (the Transvaal and the Orange Free State). This was expected to stabilize white rule, consolidate British power, and allow the imperial factor to withdraw in safety from the interior.

The confederation issue in the 1870s was closely linked to the subjugation of the African polities. Indeed in 1875, Lord Carnarvon opened the question of confederation by calling a conference of white South Africans to formulate a common policy towards the region's black population. Sensitive about imperial interference with colonial prerogatives, Prime Minister Molteno of the Cape rejected the overture. Carnarvon then turned to the Transvaal, a bankrupt Boer state which could not control its own burghers much less defeat the formidable Pedi tribe within its borders. London chose Sir Theophilus Shepstone, Natal's secretary for native affairs, for the delicate task of persuading the republic's burghers to accept British "protection." Shepstone, unhappily, exceeded his instructions and, without consulting the Transvaal legislature (or Volksraad), annexed the state to Britain in 1877.

By this time the forceful Sir Bartle Frere had taken up his post as high commissioner to carry Carnarvon's project forward. Shortly after his arrival, the Xhosa broke out in rebellion on the Cape's eastern frontier. The conflict provided occasion for a major confrontation between Frere and Molteno, as a result of which the high commissioner dismissed the Cape prime minister and replaced him with Gordon Sprigg. This high-handed act of dubious constitutionality did little for the cause of confederation.

What decisively defeated the project were the Zulus. The destruction of Zulu military power would, Frere calculated, remove a standing threat to the colonial polities and make them more confident in entering a federation. The resultant boon to imperial prestige would also help this objective. Frere's calculations went badly awry. After he provoked war with Cetshwayo, the Zulu king, British troops suffered a shattering defeat at Isandhlwana in 1879. The British soon recovered and, in time, conquered the Zulu warriors, deposing their king and dissolving his kingdom. Despite Britain's ultimate triumph, the Zulu War greatly damaged imperial prestige and did nothing to stem the growing Afrikaner hostility towards British rule.

In 1880 the Transvaal Boers rebelled and defeated imperial forces at Majuba Hill. Resigning himself to Britain's withdrawal from the interior, Gladstone came to an agreement with the new Boer leader, Paul Kruger. Signed in 1881, the Pretoria Convention conferred internal self-government on the Transvaal (now the South African Republic) but acknowledged Britain's "suzerainty," an ill-defined term designating some vague British overlordship. The convention explicitly gave Britain control over the republic's foreign affairs and its relations with Africans. Three years later, the London Convention modified these terms in Kruger's favour; no mention was made then of suzerainty. The republic's foreign affairs and native policy, however, remained under imperial jurisdiction.

Thus, Carnarvon's plans not only failed but also damaged Britain's position on the continent. But if this crisis over confederation was a setback for England, it was a catastrophe for the Zulu, Xhosa, and Pedi.

Soon few independent African kingdoms would remain. Worse than formal conquest were the colonists' despoliation of African lands and increasing control of their persons. Subjected to new colonial regulations and onerous taxation, Africans began to feel the pinch of land pressure. Though some peasant communities continued to thrive, most Africans moved to (or found themselves on) white-owned land. If they were lucky, they might be allowed to work the land as sharecroppers or cash tenants, The trend, however, was towards labour tenancies or, worse, the direct employment of Africans as landless farm labourers. Blacks had no political rights, except in the Cape Colony, where a minority enjoyed the franchise. Even this colony was growing less liberal. In 1892 it raised its franchise qualifications in response to the white fear of being swamped at the polls by the recently incorporated black territories on the eastern frontier. The Cape government also attacked the traditional communal system of African tenure. The Glen Grey Act of 1894 parcelled out land to Africans in small blocks on the basis of individual tenure. Reserved for blacks, these allotments would not count towards the franchise requirement. In addition, the act provided for local representative councils, and it imposed a tax on all adult males in the district who had not worked outside the region for at least three months out of the year. The act was designed to protect whites from cheaper African peasant farming and, of course, to push black people into mine or farm labour. The Glen Grey Act became a model of sorts for the rest of southern Africa.

The exploitation of South African blacks intensified significantly after 1886. The discovery of gold in the Witwatersrand that year initiated a chain of developments that revolutionized southern Africa. At first, prospectors flocked to the gold fields just as they had to the Kimberley diamond diggings nineteen years before. And, as with the diamond industry, small-scale prospectors soon gave way to huge capitalist companies. The magnitude of the gold industry, however, and its impact on the country far exceeded anything in South Africa's previous history.

The gold industry was built on the backs of exploited African labourers. Whereas the mine owners attracted skilled white workers from Europe by offering high wages, they depressed the African pay scale to a level well below the market price and, in some cases, below subsistence. Why did Africans accept such miserable wages? Land pressure and repressive tax policies helped to push them to the mines. Also, the migratory pattern of labour, whereby African workers returned home to rural areas for several months a year, made a stint on the Witwatersrand less distasteful to blacks; in addition, it enabled the mine owners to eliminate from their unskilled wage bill the cost of maintaining a black labourer's family.[18] The Randlords adopted the compound system from the Kimberley diamond mines, which forced the unskilled workforce to reside in concrete barracks under prison-like discipline. Working conditions undergound were nothing short of horrific.

Despite the ultra-cheap cost of African labour, the mining magnates remained dissatisfied. They sought to lower black wages even more but were frustrated by the heavy competition for labour between the mining and agricultural sectors and among the mining companies themselves. The mineral revolution had placed many thousands of Africans under the power of such men; as the industry developed, so did the subjugation of the African population. South African blacks had little reason to celebrate the year 1886 – unless to commemorate it as the inauguration of a human tragedy.

If gold mining dislocated African life, it also destabilized the South African Republic, which soon swelled with mostly English-speaking immigrants. Afraid that their enfranchisement would overturn his regime, President Paul Kruger refused to give the vote to the new arrivals (or Uitlanders, as they were known). The unrest which this generated among the Uitlanders proved especially dangerous, with imperial authorities ready to stoke and aid it. Equally unhappy with the South African Republic (SAR) were the gold magnates, for whom the Boer oligarchy constituted a major obstacle to progress. Kruger's policy of awarding government monopolies for rail service and dynamite production greatly increased mining costs. And for all the repressive features of the labour system, the state had proven itself a feeble instrument for recruitment and control. It offered little help in procuring labour or in regulating the workers who had come to the Witwatersrand. It could not stem the growing rate of desertion and, with its own interests in the liquor trade, it would not take adequate measures to prevent worker drunkenness. The gold industry required a stable polity, efficient enough to provide support for mining needs and willing to do so. Kruger's regime fell short on both counts. It soon became apparent that there was not room in the Transvaal for both a progressive modern industry and a backward frontier state. With heavy long-term investments in deep-level mining, the Randlords were there to stay.

The effects of gold mining stretched well beyond the Transvaal. The Witwatersrand's enormous demands for all manner of supplies sparked a commercial boom throughout southern Africa and set off a railway race to the area. From £493,991 in 1880, imports to the SAR skyrocketed to £10,632,895 in 1898. By 1899 there were more than three thousand miles of rail, two-thirds of which had been constructed since 1890. Not surprisingly, the coastal states of the Cape and Natal became increasingly dependent on the Witwatersrand. Indeed, most of the governmental revenue of the Cape and Natal came from railway receipts and custom duties. The Transvaal seemed to control the destiny of the entire region.

The mineral revolution affected Britain in two ways, one of which proved favourable to British interests, the other quite detrimental. First, it increased the world's supply of bullion. By 1898 the SAR produced 27.55 per cent of the world's gold, making it the world's largest source for the precious metal.[19] Thus, the Witwatersrand had become crucially important to the City. Second, the discovery of gold had shifted power from the British coastal colonies to the Boer states in the interior. The more reliant they became on the South African Republic for their economic survival, the more they slipped from Britain's grasp and into Kruger's. Soon, English pundits predicted, the Boer republic would dominate South Africa – with its enormous gold deposits and its strategic position on the route to India.

By 1895 the continent had become more than a matter of strategic or economic advantage. To Whitehall, it had become an imperial question, upon which the fate of the Empire hinged. Once secured within the imperial fold, it could be used as a keystone around which a cohesive imperial structure could be grafted. With southern Africa safe, plans to forge the Empire into an integrated economic and political unit could proceed. In the words of Sir Alfred Milner, despatched to South Africa in 1897 as high commissioner to retrieve the situation: "All this about South Africa, because that is the corner I know and where I can help. But don't suppose that I care for it *supremely for itself.* I care for it because of the vital importance of a real and permanent success there to the whole future of the nation; alike in its position in the world, and in its internal development."[20] In Africa, England could arrest the centrifugal tendencies within the Empire and bring the colonies into a unified superstate that could face European and American competitors with confidence.

The problem in 1895 was to secure the South African Republic for the Empire. Germany's friendly attention to Kruger disturbed Britain. So did the completion in 1894 of the rail line from Johannesburg to the Mozambiquan port of Lourenço Marques, for this removed the SAR's dependence on the ports in the British colonies. The next year when, in an attempt to draw traffic away from Mozambique, the Cape lowered its rail rates to the Transvaal, Kruger slapped on countervailing rates at the border. The Cape thereupon sent its goods from the border railhead to Johannesburg by ox wagon. Escalating the conflict, the Boer president closed the border by blocking the drifts across the Vaal River. At this point, the Cape turned to London, which sprang to its defence, issuing an ultimatum so strong that Kruger backed down.

At the end of 1895, Great Britain suffered great humiliation as a result of Dr Jameson's disastrous raid into the republic. According to the plan which Cecil Rhodes and his co-conspirators hatched, the Uitlanders in Johannesburg would rise in revolt, whereupon troops of Rhodes's British South Africa Company would invade from a jumping-off point along the railway strip that the Colonial Office had recently transferred to the company in the Bechuanaland Protectorate. Although the Johannesburg rising never materialized, Jameson impetuously bolted across the border, only to be captured ignominiously by Transvaal burghers.

The motives of the conspirators were mixed. Rhodes no doubt wished to overthrow a powerful threat to the Cape and one which stood in the way of his ambitions for a federation organized along colonial, not imperial lines. While attempts to attribute the Johannesburg plot solely to mining interests have foundered, some linkages did exist. Alfred Beit, George Farrar, Lionel Phillips, and Rhodes himself were active conspirators, and all had long-term commitments to deep-level mining.[21] Despite the lingering suspicions concerning Chamberlain's part in the proceedings, scholars have established that the imperial government's role was limited and defensive. It neither originated nor participated in the plot but, rather, watched on anxiously, dreading Rhodes's possible failure as well as his potential success. It nervously prepared to assert some degree of control if the conspirators prevailed yet to avoid complicity in case of failure.[22]

Although the Raid poisoned relations between Boer and Briton in South Africa and toppled Rhodes from the Cape premiership, imperial interests survived intact. The kaiser's congratulatory telegram to Kruger provoked a stern British protest, punctuated by a naval demonstration at Delagoa Bay. This rallied British public opinion and, faced with such hostility, the Germans backed off. And in his relations with Kruger, Chamberlain appeared not repentant but indignant. Taking up the Uitlander grievances, he forcefully pressed Kruger to reform. He even tried unsuccessfully to coax the Boer leader to London for discussions. This marked a significant change in British policy, for, before the Raid, London officially took the view that, while it might legitimately resist a violation of the Pretoria or London Conventions, the Uitlander complaints constituted an internal matter for the Boer republic. Thus, Chamberlain moved from a policy of legalistic circumspection to one of active involvement to uphold the rights of British subjects. This appeal to democratic principle would, he hoped, hit the nerve of the British public and awaken its imperial instinct.

The appeal to the public was essential in 1895, since by this time successive reform acts had expanded the electorate enormously. Chamberlain's approach signalled a new type of diplomacy, one which attempted to democratize the conduct of foreign affairs by educating the public about Britain's vital interests abroad.[23] Of course, this new focus did not turn Britain's attention away from the Pretoria and London conventions, and Kruger was held to strict account for violations. When, in late 1896, the Transvaal Volksraad passed a restrictive immigration law, Chamberlain forced Kruger to retract the law.

Kruger was at the time involved in political difficulties at home. First, there was his dispute with Chief Justice Kotze over the testing right. By opposing Kotze's claim that judges could pronounce on the constitutionality of Volksraad law, Kruger made himself unpopular with the growing body of liberal opinion in the SAR. It was Britain's hope that the progressive element would defeat him in the next election, which was slated for early 1898. For this reason, Britain eased its pressure on the republic in 1897.

Although Chamberlain despatched an ardent imperialist, Sir Alfred Milner, to South Africa in 1897 as high commissioner, Sir Alfred decided to leave the SAR alone in the hope that it would reform from within. Events, however, were moving towards confrontation. Since the Raid, Kruger had imported vast amounts of armaments – rifles, Maxim guns, and artillery – to defend his state from the British threat. Within the republic's borders, the Uitlanders had formed the South African League to air their grievances. The growing acrimony between the Uitlanders and Boers created a tense atmosphere in which minor incidents could burst into fire; Milner hoped for precisely such an event. One soon occurred when a Boer policeman shot a Uitlander by the name of Edgar for resisting arrest after beating another man in a drunken brawl. Unfortunately for Milner, the incident occurred while he was visiting England, and the acting high commissioner, Sir William Butler entertained considerable scepticism towards the Uitlander cause. He not only refused to work this episode into a crisis, but also rejected a petition of protest from the South African League. In London the exasperated high commissioner sighed that he had paid dearly for his holiday. Even more troubling developments occurred on his return. In March negotiations between Kruger and the mining magnates produced a provisional settlement known as the "great deal." According to this, Kruger would put the republic's fiscal and tax policies on a sound footing and would extend the franchise to Uitlanders after five years' residence. In return, the capitalists were to use their influence to dampen Uitlander agitation and to assist the SAR in securing European loans. The agreement worried imperial officials. Should Kruger succeed in squaring the magnates, Britain would lose crucial leverage over the republic. The disapproval of Chamberlain, expressed to the mining companies' principals in London, helped to undermine this agreement. So did the gold magnate Percy FitzPatrick, who prematurely published sensitive information, the secrecy of which was essential for the negotiations. By the end of March the attempt by capitalists and Boer officials to reach a settlement had foundered amid mutual recrimination.

Shortly after this, Uitlander agitation commenced again, resulting in another massive petition to the queen, and this time Milner was on hand to accept it. Chief among Uitlander grievances were the stringent franchise provisions which prevented them from voting. As matters stood, an immigrant could not vote until he had been resident in the SAR for fourteen years. On receipt of this petition the Colonial Office worked out a reply, but the cabinet could not agree on the suitable tone or the appropriate degree of menace which its answer should carry. On 9 May 1899 Milner tried to prod his superiors with a bellicose despatch which stressed the urgency of action to help thousands of British subjects who were being treated as "helots." Unsure how to respond to the deepening crisis, Chamberlain eagerly snapped up the overture by President Steyn of the Orange Free State offering to host a conference at Bloemfontein. At this, Milner resolved that he would either wreck the negotiations or insist on a Uitlander enfranchisement so massive and sudden as to overturn the Boer oligarchy currently in charge.[24] When it became clear that Kruger would not grant a five-year franchise retrospectively, Milner abruptly terminated the discussions.

In the wake of the Bloemfontein conference, certain bodies in Britain and South Africa pleaded for peace. On 17 June 1899 the Natal government presented London with a minute urging a peaceful solution to the crisis. Although the Cape never officially sent such a minute, many of its ministers disapproved of Milner's belligerent policy. In England Chamberlain felt that the public needed to be convinced that a resolute policy in southern Africa was imperative. During July and August the SAR continued to make franchise proposals, but none found favour in London. The last offer, which prescribed a five-year retrospective franchise, came close to acceptance, but the condition attending this offer – that Britain thereafter relinquish all right to interfere in the republic's internal affairs – proved unacceptable. Meanwhile, sentiment in Britain and in South Africa was hardening, as arms shipments flowed to Pretoria and the British mobilized their forces. Certain that imperial forces planned to attack, the SAR and its Orange Free State ally decided to strike first. After issuing an ultimatum, Boer troops invaded the Cape on 11 October 1899, inaugurating the Anglo-Boer War.

Britain's victory over the Boers two and a half years later gave Sir Alfred Milner the opportunity to impose his imperial vision on South Africa. An imperial consolidationist, he saw the region as a keystone around which an imposing imperial edifice could be built, without which the Empire would fall apart. Central to Milnerism was, in the words of Eric Stokes, "the Germanic conviction in the creative role of political power." Specifically, Milner believed that political action could transform the Transvaal government into a powerful, highly regulated, and well-administered state which would solidify Britain's position in southern Africa. Similarly, the Empire itself could be consolidated along statist lines.[25] The first step was, of course, to oust the Afrikaners from power.

The high commissioner soon discovered, however, that removing the Boer oligarchy by force did not ensure British preponderance in the conquered states. Indeed, intelligence reports conveyed the alarming information that, even after Kitchener's troops and concentration camps had whittled down Boer numbers, their population still exceeded the British. As serious as the problem was, it seemed susceptible to a statist solution, and the proconsul soon devised a 'grand design' to ensure British dominance. The plan was simple. Industrial expansion would attract enough British immigrants to swamp the Boers at the polls. Milner estimated that his plan would require five years to take effect. Only then could the Transvaal and Orange River Colony be entrusted with self-government. Until that time, the conquered territories would be ruled autocratically as crown colonies.

Milner's plans backfired badly. First, a serious labour shortage stalled industrial recovery. Not only did the anticipated British immigrants fail to materialize, but those English-speakers already in the Transvaal were divided among themselves. Indeed, it was from a section of the English colonists that the cry for self-government first arose. Faced with opposition from the disaffected British as well as from the Afrikaners, the Unionist government in London was forced to concede a measure of self-government prematurely in 1905. The promulgation of the Lyttelton Constitution in that year signalled the failure of Milner's grand design. South African realities had compelled him to surrender his autocratic powers or risk having all influence wrested away.

To be sure, his policies had helped to produce this result, but Milner was attempting a task of such complexity, dependent on so many variables, that the chances of success were minimal. Conflicting interests in South Africa and Britain made impossible the establishment of a multilateral network of ties between the two. All Milner could do was to sustain a bilateral relationship between the Unionists in England and the gold-mining interests in the Transvaal. With this single strand holding together the periphery and metropole, the imperial connection was thin enough to snap at any moment. In 1905 it seemed only a matter of time before Britain's discomfiture in southern Africa would be complete.

With his policies in tatters, Milner left South Africa in political disarray and economic distress. The country's malaise was not all his making, but he had done little to assuage discontent. Part of the reason for his failure to mobilize general support among the British element was the favouritism he showed to one section of it – the gold interests. He treated solicitously the Randlords , for his imperial project depended on the rapid expansion of the mining industry. Especially favoured were Sir James Percy FitzPatrick, Sir George H. Farrar, Sir Lionel Phillips, and Sir Francis Drummond Chaplin. Percy FitzPatrick and Lionel Phillips were partners in the firm of Eckstein and Company, which had joined up with Wernher, Beit, and Company to form the Corner House group, the largest mining concern on the Rand. Drummond Chaplin headed Consolidated Goldfields, the second-largest group, while George Farrar chaired the Anglo-French Exploration Company and the East Rand Proprietary Mine, both prominent mining enterprises. Farrar, FitzPatrick, and Phillips had all joined the conspiracy against Kruger's republic during the Jameson episode. All four men had, at one time, served as president of the Chamber of Mines, Chaplin enjoying the honour in 1905–6. During reconstruction, these men actively allied themselves to the crown colony government.

FitzPatrick and Farrar sat in Milner's Legislative Council, and all four individuals worked actively for the Progressive party, founded in 1904 to represent mining interests. Though the high commissioner could rely on substantial support from the Johannesburg crowd, some magnates opposed the imperial regime. Yet, while Milner's objectives and those of the Randlords overlapped, the high commissioner did not subordinate his interest to those of Johannesburg. Indeed, he took some measures, such as doubling the profits tax on gold mining, which aroused great resentment among the Randlords. Nevertheless, as the labour shortage affected government policy as much as mining profitability, the state offered its full assistance. In 1901 Milner had agreed to give favourable treatment to Portuguese rail lines in return for recruiting privileges in Mozambique. As Mozambiquans refused to come out in sufficient numbers, the high commissioner and the Chamber of Mines decided in 1903 on a desperate expedient – Chinese labour. With London's reluctant permission, the Transvaal started importing Chinese in 1904.

While Chinese labour split the British community in the Transvaal, it unified the Afrikaners under the leadership of two ex-generals: Louis Botha and Jan Christian Smuts. Well before the war, land pressure had divided the largely agrarian Boer population. By the 1890s the tradition of partible inheritance had reached the point where the land inherited could not sustain a farming family. This and the incentive for commercial agriculture provided by the Johannesburg market led to the consolidation of Afrikaner landholding into fewer and fewer hands. By 1899 the Boer population was becoming increasingly stratified, with progressive farmers such as Botha and Smuts at the top and a growing class of *bywoners* or landless labourers at the bottom. The latter's ejection from the land in the decade after the Boer War and their concentration into overcrowded urban areas created what became known as the poor white problem. It is significant that the Afrikaners who surrendered early (the *hands-uppers*) and those who actively assisted British forces came mostly from the *bywoner* class; more prosperous Boers were more likely to be holdouts or *bitter-enders*. The war, thus, deepened the schisms in Boer society.

Milner, with his ethnic prejudice against all Afrikaners, failed to exploit these divisions. Instead, he hoped that generous British expenditure for war compensation and resettlement, coupled with increasing prosperity from economic growth, would satisfy the Boer rank and file, however irreconcilable the Boer leadership might be.[26] Britain's war payments did not satisfy the Boer population, which had been ruined by the war; the persistence of drought for three years afterwards did not ease their plight. Milner's unsuccessful attempt to introduce British settlers into the countryside inflamed the Afrikaners, as did his policy of anglicization. The English-speaking schools which the reconstruction regime established were boycotted, as Afrikaners set up their own Dutch-language "Christian National" schools. Thus, instead of weakening Boer resistance, Milner's policies created deep resentment which found expression in a virulent Afrikaner nationalism.

Boer leadership took shrewd advantage of Milner's mistakes. They welcomed the *hands-uppers* back into the fold. Despite their refusal to serve in the crown colony administration, Botha and Smuts proclaimed their loyalty to Britain and gave an appearance of moderation that was certain to impress the Liberals waiting in the wings at Westminster. The Afrikaner leaders astutely took advantage of the Chinese labour issue to attack the crown colony regime. After a protest meeting in 1903, Botha and Smuts formed the Het Volk party the following year to represent Afrikaner interests in the Transvaal. Milner was now confronting an Afrikanerdom which was organized, unified, and hostile.

What had defeated the grand design more than anything else was the refusal of Africans to provide cheap labour for the mines. Alternative employment during the war and increased access to land as, for example, squatters on crown lands had made Africans less vulnerable to the mines' labour touts. The horrific conditions and high death rates on the compounds repelled most blacks from mining jobs. There were, however, ominous signs that the relative improvement in black well-being would prove short-lived. First, contrary to their expectations of more humane treatment under British rule, Africans found the new order just as harsh as the old one. Not only did the crown colony regime take over the republic's constrictive system of pass laws and heavy taxation; it enforced these repressive measures with a vigour and efficiency unknown before. And soon white pressure for anti-squatting measures would squeeze Africans from the land. The South African Native Affairs Commission, which Milner had set up in 1903, condemned squatting in forcible terms in its final report of 1905. In addition, the commission urged territorial segregation as well as separate and limited political representation.

The Treaty of Vereeniging withheld political rights from blacks in the conquered republics until the white colonists there had received self-government. This provision drew sharp criticism from the black petty bourgeois, which had organized itself into Native Vigilance Associations in the new colonies. The political disabilities of South African blacks was fully brought to light by the Cape's John Tengo Jabavu in his newspaper, *Imvo Zabantsundu*. Also prominent in the struggle for African political rights was Abdullah Abdurahman. While his African Political Organisation (APO) represented the country's coloured population, he enjoyed a broader appeal among other non-white groups. Although Milner asserted that any differential laws should be based on civilization rather than "the rotten and indefensible ground of colour," he had done nothing to lift the disabilities which South Africa's non-whites had endured on account of their race.

The tighter control which constricted Africans even more under the crown colony regime owed much to the bureaucratic apparatus with which Milner endowed his state. All blacks were placed under the administrative control of a new Native Affairs Department headed by Sir Godfrey Yeatman Lagden. To assist rural areas Milner established the Department of Agriculture, and to foster industry he set up a mining commission. Chinese importation necessitated the creation of the Foreign Labour Department.

In the autocratic crown colony system, Milner, as governor, worked through his Executive Council, which included the heads of the major departments, as well as the lieutenant-governor, Sir Arthur Lawley. Milner was fortunate to have as his attorney general Sir Richard Solomon. From the Cape Sir Richard brought considerable legal and political experience, which was seriously scarce in the Transvaal. Advising the Executive Council was the Legislative Council, which by 1903 included fifteen officials and fourteen appointed unofficial members. To administer matters of joint concern to the Transvaal and the Orange River Colony, Milner constructed the Intercolonial Council (ICC) and appointed to it both official and unofficial members. Under the rubric of the ICC was the Central South African Railways, which operated the combined rail lines of both colonies. The ICC also bore responsibility for the South African Constabulary (SAC) and for administering the £35 million imperial loan fund. The high commissioner hoped that this agency would form the nucleus for the future amalgamation of the entire region. Thus, Milner drew his crown colony staff from the imperial service, the Oxbridge circuit, the mining industry, and from selected local politicians. Although the Afrikaner leaders had received invitations to join the Legislative Council, they refused the offer for fear of compromising their anti-imperial position. Needless to say, no black was represented in Milner's government.

In addition, Milner drew talent from England's young intelligentsia. Inspired by a strong sense of duty and by Milner's imposing character, a dozen or so idealistic and able young men came to southern Africa to assist in reconstruction. They were not recruited systematically, but were selected on the basis of personal contacts or their Oxford connections. With Milner, they formed a tight coterie derisively dubbed the Kindergarten. They embraced Milner's ideas about imperial union and Britain's civilizing mission with passionate idealism. Their ranks included Lionel G. Curtis, who served an Johannesburg's town clerk and in various other capacities; William L. Hichens, who, among other posts, was treasurer of the Intercolonial Council; and Patrick Duncan, who rendered solid service in many positions, most notably as colonial secretary of the Transvaal.[27]

Despite all this administrative talent, the machinery of government did not operate smoothly. Officials on the executive fell out amongst themselves and with Milner. Several of the unofficial members in the Legislative Council became dissatisfied with autocratic imperial rule and began to advocate responsible government. The lawyer, H.C. Hull, and the Pretoria businessman, R.K. Loveday, were among the first to call for change. These councillors were soon joined by E.P. Solomon, the head of Hull's law firm and the brother of the Attorney General. In December of 1904, these men and other English-speaking dissidents coalesced into the Responsible Government Association.

The fact that the first call for responsible government came from the English element rather than the Afrikaners was especially ominous for Milner's plans. Even before the formation of the association, the governor realized the necessity of some concessions to placate the Transvaal English, but rather than concede full self-government at once, he proposed representative government as a half-way house. This was embodied in the Lyttelton Constitution, which provided for a thirty to thirty-five person legislative assembly, with six to nine official members, who would all be appointed. This, it was hoped, would guarantee a British majority in the house. Though modest, the property qualifications required for the franchise were sufficiently high to bar poor whites from voting. Needless to add, Milner's constitution completely ignored the political claims of the colony's non-white population. Though promulgated in March of 1905, the Lyttelton scheme could not come into effect until a delimitation commission had laid out electoral boundaries, a process involving months of work. How smoothly this constitutional arrangement would function remained an open question, especially since, in the same month that letters patent were issued, Het Volk and the Responsible Government Association concluded a pact to resist the representative scheme and agitate for full self-government.

Whatever the demographic balance in the Transvaal, the Boers far outnumbered the British in the the Orange River Colony. The ex-president of the Orange Free State, Marthinus T. Steyn, still enjoyed a distinguished reputation throughout South Africa. His protégé, Abraham Fischer, seemed an able successor, helping to form in 1905 the Orangia Unie to articulate Boer grievances. With overwhelming numbers against them, British moderates such as Sir George Fraser, who enjoyed prominent positions in the crown colony regime, would have little influence once the colony had regained self-government. For this reason, Milner offered no constitutional concession and planned to keep the colony under the benign autocracy of Lieutenant-Governor Sir Hamilton Goold-Adams.

Natal, on the other hand, presented no problem of loyalty. Governor Sir Henry McCallum found his ministers cooperative on imperial issues. Other matters, however, sparked more controversy. Especially vexing was the increasing share of Witwatersrand traffic that Natal was losing to Mozambique. African affairs presented even more serious difficulties. The paternalistic despotism of Sir Theophilus Shepstone had been rigidified into an impersonal and irresponsible system by the Natal Native Code of 1891, and successive white ministries used their power to pressure blacks into the labour force. The Delimitation Commission of 1905 worsened the African land shortage by setting aside 2.6 million acres of Zululand for white settlement. The following year the Natal government touched off a major rebellion by instituting a £1 poll tax on every African male not subject to the hut tax. By this time, Natal's African policy had distinguished itself as the most incompetent and oppressive in all of southern Africa – a rare achievement given South African standards.

The Cape Colony, with its colour-blind franchise, was far more liberal than Natal but, alas for Milner's purposes, less reliable in other respects. In 1900 the administration of W. P. Schreiner balked at the high commissioner's proposal to disenfranchise all Cape citizens who supported the Boers when they invaded the colony's northern districts. Supported by Jan H. Hofmeyr, the leader of the Afrikaner Bond, and by John X. Merriman, a staunch liberal, the Schreiner government decided to resign rather than accede to Milner's measure. The high commissioner thereupon installed John Gordon Sprigg as prime minister in order to pass the controversial disenfranchisement. By the end of the war, Milner had become so exasperated with the Cape that he urged Chamberlain to suspend the colony's constitution; fortunately, the secretary of state refused. Though in 1904 that notorious imperialist Dr L.S. Jameson secured election as prime minister, he faced many problems and many opponents. As with Natal, the Cape was losing railway business to Mozambique, and as a result the colony's financial base shrank. Liberals and Afrikaners were quick to exploit any opportunity to criticize Jameson in particular and imperialism in general.

More ominous for the long term were informal discussions among liberal and Afrikaner politicians concerning future federation. While the Boer War still raged, Merriman had proposed making the Transvaal and the Orange Free State self-governing within a South African federation. In 1905 Merriman initiated a three-way correspondence with Smuts of the Transvaal and Steyn of the Orange River Colony, on the subject of union. They all agreed that no closer union movement should be inaugurated until non-imperialists had come to power in all three colonies. Then negotiations could commence for a union or federation that, it was hoped, would free South Africa from Downing Street interference.

Ironically, Milner too looked forward to union in the distant future, but his would be created not by the sentiment of local nationalists but by material bonds forged through economic development. He had attempted to bring the four colonies more closely together in 1903 by establishing an intercolonial customs union. To safeguard development projects after representative government, he sought unsuccessfully to secure borrowing powers for the Intercolonial Council. This agency became the last refuge for imperial interests, and Milner's failure to enhance its powers left it and those interests vulnerable to the Afrikaners once they had regained power in the old republics.[28]

This emphasizes the enormous difficulties which faced Milner's successor. On Sir Alfred's resignation in 1905, he left many critical problems behind: industrial depression, African discontent, Afrikaner hostility, and political instability. The imperial position was imperilled from all sides. The new high commissioner did, however, have one key asset: the support of most of the mining magnates, who controlled the wealth on which the destiny of the Transvaal, South Africa, and the Empire's gentleman capitalists depended.

2 Lord Selborne's Early Life and Career

By 1860 Great Britain had emerged as the richest, most powerful, and most productive nation in the world. While its fleets controlled the seas, its industry, commerce, and capital ruled the world economy. The devolution of imperial authority to colonial legislatures in North America, South Africa, and Australia had not diminished Britain's world standing. In southern Africa, for example, so long as London was guaranteed a naval base at the Cape, it had little interest in ruling white settlers on the coast and no interest at all in the doings of the two Boer republics in the desolate interior. It seemed, in fact, as if there was an inverse relationship between Britain's direct authority over its colonies and its international influence. Never had Britain's formal Empire appeared so irrelevant to Britain's real power in the world. The French Empire of Napoleon III approximated Marx's description of it as farce;[1] the Russian Empire had recently suffered humiliation in the Crimean War; the United States would shortly tear itself apart in a great civil war; Germany was just a figment in the imagination of ineffectual Frankfurt liberals; and the Austrian Empire exhorted itself with the inspiring toast, "Onward to a happier yesterday." For an Englishman born at this time, however, Britain's best days still seemed to lie ahead.

Domestically, Selborne's birth antedated Gladstonian liberalism and the formation of the party that embodied it. Despite the ascendancy of the middle class, the hereditary elite still dominated politics. The world which William Waldegrave Palmer viewed as a child had not yet grown into "liberal England." As for the working class, it could not form legally recognized unions, much less vote in elections.

Though William was not born into the aristocracy, his father, Roundell Palmer, was soon to enter its ranks. Indeed, in 1882 Gladstone made him the Earl of Selborne for his service as lord chancellor. Young William's social background, therefore, was both bourgeois and aristocratic. As the most recent authority of the aristocracy explained, "Roundell Palmer was another lawyer from a middle-class family; but he ended his career as Lord Chancellor and Earl of Selborne, and both he and his eldest son married into the heart of the peerage."[2] It was the sort of mixture that produced gentlemanly capitalists.

William, by his own account, enjoyed a happy childhood. Later in life he expressed deep gratitude for being blessed with the best of parents, brothers, and sisters. At the age of ten, he left the happiness of home for Waterfields School. There he endured rigorous discipline from the schoolmasters and rough bullying from the boys. Four years later he went off to Winchester public school, where he was "blissfully happy all the time." Rarely did he misbehave, but on some occasions, as when he let a schoolmate copy his answers, he was caned. He nursed no ill-feeling about corporal punishment at school. "It seems to me," he wrote later, "the limit of nonsense to suggest that there is anything degrading in being flogged for the breach of a necessary school rule." For his last two years at the school William served as head of his house.

After Winchester he entered Oxford, where, despite a regimen of cards, cricket, and tennis, he took a first in history. He confessed later that, though many at college discussed such questions as the meaning of life, "I can safely say that I was not troubled that way and that such discussions, at that time, would have simply bored me." He qualified his academic indifference by adding that the "only intellect that I possess or any power of thinking, as distinguished from cramming up facts, was subsequently developed in me by contact with Maud's wonderful mind." This was a reference to the eldest daughter of the 3rd Marquess of Salisbury, Lady Beatrix Maud Cecil, whom he married in 1883. Theirs was a wonderful marriage, a companionship of mind as well as heart. In his "Reminiscences" Selborne entered a touching prayer that in death he and Maud would not be severed through eternity.[3]

The year before his marriage, Palmer became an assistant private secretary to Hugh Childers, Gladstone's secretary of state for war. Two years later he joined his father's office staff. (In the meantime when his father became an earl, Palmer assumed the courtesy title, Lord Wolmer.) In 1885 he decided to run for Parliament. He secured election to a seat in east Hampshire and entered the Commons that year on Gladstone's side of the House. He did not remain a Liberal for long. The next year the Home Rule Bill for Ireland split the party and sent Wolmer to Joseph Chamberlain's camp in the opposition. Chamberlain and his followers coalesced into the Liberal Unionist party, for which Wolmer served as whip. In 1895 the Unionists decided to associate themselves with Lord Salisbury's Conservative government. This was fortunate for Wolmer, as he was chosen to serve as Chamberlain's undersecretary of state in the Colonial Office.

By this time Wolmer had become the 2nd Earl of Selborne. He accepted the title after his father's death but, honouring an agreement he had made with St John Brodrick and George Curzon,[4] decided to test the rule that prohibited peers from serving in the House of Commons. When Selborne entered the House, the radical Henry Labouchere protested at "the presence in the House of a nobleman ... who has since become a Peer of the Realm."[5] A House committee decided against Selborne and sent him to the House of Lords.

It was in the upper chamber that he spent his mature political life. His experience in the Commons had provided good training and had introduced him to the key questions that he would face throughout his career. As D. George Boyce noted, "The great domestic issues which confronted his mature political career: Ireland, the House of Lords; social reform; and the character of the Unionist party – were all foreshadowed or defined in the ten years of his political apprenticeship."[6]

As undersecretary for the colonies Selborne found that South Africa absorbed most of his attention. His views on this situation accorded well with those of his superior, Joseph Chamberlain. Throughout his tenure, Selborne showed a keen awareness that Britain's position in southern Africa depended on its local supporters in the Transvaal, Cape, and Natal. Often these allies required more support than they gave back. Moreover, there was always the danger that they would compose their differences with the Boer states and turn their backs on the imperial factor. This seemed to be the danger in the late autumn of 1895 when the railway tension between the Cape and the Transvaal culminated in the drifts crises – so named because Paul Kruger, the president of the South African Republic, blocked the Cape's access to his state by closing the drifts across the Vaal. With his superior away on holiday, the undersecretary bore the immediate responsibility for Britain's policy, although he kept Chamberlain fully informed by telegraph.

Imperial objectives were complex. First, Britain felt obliged to uphold the Convention of London, which Kruger's action had violated, in spirit if not in letter. Then the imperial government had to assist the Cape and dissuade it from succumbing to Kruger's pressure. The oldest colony had not only to be supported but bound more tightly to Britain. In light of these objectives, the undersecretary urged that "the S.A. Republic and King Kruger must be made to open the drifts at once."[7] At the same time Selborne and his Colonial Office colleagues, with the prime minister's approval, approached Kruger tactfully, even offering to investigate the Transvaal side of the question, once the drifts had been opened. The failure of gentle persuasion led Britain to adopt more forceful measures. On 5 November 1895 it issued an ultimatum to Kruger, who reopened the drifts within twenty-four hours.[8]

Britain did not enjoy this diplomatic triumph long, for, within six weeks, it suffered the débâcle known to history as the Jameson Raid. This time, it was the Uitlander population in Kruger's republic which, as a buttress for Britain's position, proved to be a slender reed. The half-hearted Johannesburg rising sputtered out and Jameson and his band were captured. As a consequence Kruger gained enormous prestige and Britain's covert association with the plotters brought it great humiliation. The evidence in the Selborne Papers, however, suggests that imperial officials were innocent of any involvement with Rhodes or impropriety in the matter. Selborne, for his part, "believed that a bona fides, purely internal, revolution was imminent at Johannesburg."[9]

Nonetheless, Britain found its prestige and influence diminished as a result of the Raid. Surveying the situation in 1896, Selborne, in an important state paper, expressed his anxieties about the imperial position in South Africa. He observed that the mineral discoveries of the 1880s had thrown economic power to the government of the Transvaal, which would increasingly dictate the fortunes of the British colonies over the coast. Unless brought under imperial influence, the South African Republic would, even if controlled by a British majority, attract the rest of the region into a United States of South Africa – outside the Empire. To preserve Britain's leverage over the SAR, Selborne advised the purchase of Delagoa Bay from Portugal, whose financial difficulties would make it likely to sell the port.[10]

Beyond this, however, the undersecretary advised caution and tact, which the ambivalent pressures on the imperial government made necessary. Recognizing the need to defend the interests of British subjects to retain their loyalty but to do this without alienating the Afrikaners, he advised taking up the Uitlander cause but not as assiduously as Chamberlain wished. Britain's position as paramount power made it perfectly proper for the imperial government to make "friendly representations" to Kruger on behalf of the Uitlanders. At the same time, the imperial government should, he believed, insist on full compliance with the London Convention, which, while giving Britain certain controls over the SAR's foreign and African policies, also guaranteed the republic's internal autonomy. The undersecretary would thus steer British policy between the inconsistent objectives of Uitlander rights and the Convention.[11]

In the next year Selborne grew more confident of Britain's position, as Kruger took a series of controversial measures. Responding to the republic's immigration law, Selborne set out the firm policy that his superior endorsed. On this issue, events proved the undersecretary correct when he wrote that the Boer president "will always give way on the Convention at the very last moment."[12]

When Selborne learned that Sir Alfred Milner was to become high commissioner of South Africa, he rejoiced that, "we have the best man in the British Empire for the toughest job in the British Empire."[13] The Kotze controversy later in the year gave Selborne hope that if Britain kept its involvement in South Africa to the bare minimum of upholding the Convention against blatant violations, Boer opinion would turn against Kruger. As he wrote to Chamberlain: "The worst thing we could do would be to reconsolidate Kruger's power by imitating in however small a degree Jameson's mistake – we must not seem to be interfering beyond the point recognised as our right under the Convention. It is for his reason that I think the allusion to the quarrel with the Supreme Court in our despatch must be most carefully scanned. As long as we confine ourself to the maintenance of our rights under the Convention we can only make Kruger's position more difficult and embarrass him the more."[14]

While Selborne was urging that British policy in South Africa keep a low profile, he worked behind the scenes to restrict the SAR's access to the European money market. Alfred Beit and Lord Rothschild, prominent financiers, agreed to use their powers to deny loans to Kruger, but their influence did not extend beyond London or Paris.

Early in 1898, certain ominous developments in South Africa disturbed the complacency in the Colonial Office. Kruger's re-election in February cast doubt on the likelihood that the Transvaal would reform itself. So shaken by this was Milner that he forecast renewed friction with the SAR and warned that it might reach perilous proportions.[15] This prompted Chamberlain and Selborne to stress the importance of a peaceful policy. Writing to Milner, the undersecretary stated that: "Peace is undoubtedly the first interest to South Africa, but not peace at any price. Our object is the future combination of South Africa under the aegis of the Union Jack, and I think we all feel that, if by the evolution of events this combination can be achieved without a rupture, or war, of any sort between the two white races in South Africa, it will have a more durable and valuable result than it would have if the same result were achieved by means of war."[16] Only a definite denunciation of the conventions would constitute sufficient *casus belli* for Selborne.

Milner was not convinced. The essential difficulty was the intractable conflict between two different societies: "Two wholly antagonistic systems – a mediaeval race oligarchy, and a modern industrial state, recognizing no difference of status between various white races – cannot permanently live side by side in what is after all *one* country. The race-oligarchy has got to go, and I see no signs of its removing itself."[17] Milner seemed belligerent indeed.

Selborne stoutly countered that, for Britain to take decisive actions, "The general case against the SAR must be glaring, patent, and actual." Any British action must carry with it the almost unanimous support of British public opinion. A policy which lacked such wide support was liable to be overturned when a new government came to power, and "no greater calamity could befall the British Empire and South Africa than that once again one political party in the U.K. should reverse action taken by the other in respect of the Transvaal." Selborne, in fact, remained more optimistic that natural causes were working in Britain's favour.[18]

Nevertheless, he continued to urge Rothschild and Beit to do all in their power to block funds to Kruger. He also promptly took up the grievances of non-white British subjects who were ill-treated in the republic. Finally, he forcefully pressed his government to secure Delagoa Bay; he even suggested its armed occupation if Portugal seemed likely to sell it to Britain's European rivals. By the end of 1898 Britain came to an agreement with Germany whereby, in the event of Portuguese bankruptcy, its eastern possessions in Africa would be divided by Germany and England; Lourenço Marques fell to the latter. In the event, Portugal remained solvent and retained full possession of Mozambique and its port on Delagoa Bay.[19]

Selborne's patience and that of his government eventually gave way in 1899. The year started off violently with the Edgar incident. Viewing this as a case of police brutality against a British subject, he sympathized with Milner's rage and assured the high commissioner that any future complaints against General Butler, Milner's temporary replacement who refused to send a massive Uitlander petition forward, would be supported by the Colonial Office. When, shortly afterward, the republic entered into negotiations with the Rand magnates, Selborne watched with a wary eye. He advised Wernher and Beit, two of his financial contacts in London, to exercise caution and to show imperial authorities the details of any agreement. Once he saw the terms, he condemned it as a "disastrous one for the Uitlanders and pregnant with mischief for us." Towards the Randlords he entertained great suspicions, exclaiming, "I do not trust them a bit."[20]

As relations deteriorated between the imperial government and the SAR, Selborne came to accept the view Milner had expressed in his "helot despatch," that the case for intervention is overwhelming. It was not solely a matter of the conventions, or even of Uitlander grievances, but of British supremacy. In early May the undersecretary wrote to Curzon that "the Transvaal carbuncle is ripening to the picking point."[21]

Selborne saw that the situation was urgent. Ready for action, the Uitlanders turned for support to Britain, which could not disappoint them without relinquishing its position in southern Africa. As for Natal's peace minute, Selborne would treat the ministers' concerns tactfully but would not allow the little colony to veto the policy of Her Majesty's Government.[22]

At the same time Selborne appreciated, as Milner did not, that imperial policy could not outrun public opinion at home. He assured the high commissioner that he and Chamberlain were making progress in educating the nation but that public opinion was not yet convinced that the republic's shortcomings justified war.[23] He also cautioned the high commissioner from attempting to rush the cabinet. "While the policy adopted is yours, you must allow the Cabinet to regulate the pace. At the present moment my sole and emphatic advice to you is do not allow the least appearance of excitement to appear in your telegrams, letters, despatches."

While restraining Milner, Selborne proselytized his policies. In the aftermath of the Bloemfontein Conference, he dissuaded Chamberlain from pushing for Johannesburg municipal autonomy as an alternative to the general enfranchisement of the Uitlander population. In late July he assured Balfour that Milner had not exaggerated "the absolute utmost unctuousness of the Kruger regime." The press was, he declared, "sound as bells." He also gained his father-in-law's adherence to a firm policy which would secure, as a minimum, Milner's Bloemfontein demands. The real object, as Salisbury put it, was to show "that we not [the] Dutch are Boss." The prime minister added testily that "I will go my own pace – I will not be hurried by anyone, not by all the English in South Africa."[24]

Selborne, in short, functioned as a pivot, who pushed his Unionist colleagues ahead as he kept Milner from advancing too far beyond British opinion. Keenly alive to public sentiment, he, like Chamberlain, practised the "new diplomacy." In October 1899 the Transvaal carbuncle finally burst, and the Empire went to war with the republics.

This gave Selborne occasion to reflect on the nature of any postwar settlement. Like Milner, he anticipated a short conflict which would resemble more an expedition than a war.[25] His war aims were, accordingly, light and liberal. He agreed with Salisbury on the government's three war aims: British paramountcy, equal rights for Boer and Briton, and philanthropy towards Africans. Although he acknowledged the temporary necessity of a military government for the conquered republics, he anticipated its speedy termination and replacement by a civilian government that "must be an absolutely democratic one." Rather than annex the two territories, he would declare them both protectorates and confer full rights to any British subjects within them. Aside from certain prerogatives that Britain would enjoy as suzerain power, the old republic would enjoy considerable autonomy and would even retain its old institutions of government. If, however, Her Majesty's Government did decide to annex the regions, this would present great difficulties, for Britain had more limited power over self-governing colonies than over protectorates. If annexed, the two territories must soon enjoy responsible government which would leave the imperial government with little leverage. In that case, it would be crucial to ensure a British victory at the Transvaal polls.

But here the difficulties deepened, for the English-speaking element, largely male, was concentrated in the Witwatersrand. Even if the Uitlanders outnumbered the Boers, the fact that the latter were scattered throughout the country would entitle them to a certain territorial representation which would probably give them the edge. "I know of no precedent," Selborne mused, "where population and taxable capacity even when combined are allowed to outweigh territorial area to the extent which would have to be the case in the Transvaal to give a majority in the Legislature to the British majority in the country." Rather than risk an Afrikaner victory in a Transvaal that would be self-governing shortly after annexation, Selborne commended Balfour's suggestion to divide the old SAR into two discrete parts, separating the Witwatersrand. As for federation, he viewed this as the ultimate objective but did not consider that the pro-imperial element yet possessed sufficient strength to make the experiment a safe one. He would, therefore, "let the question slumber" but, at the same time, encourage the consolidation of postal, customs, and railway services in the hopes of advancing the economy of the whole region. Prosperity would, in turn, provide "a great impulse" to British immigration, which would eventually make confederation safe.[26]

This minute contains several interesting features. First, though its author advocated a "revolution in the spirit of Government," he did not suggest erecting a completely new polity in the Transvaal; he did not acknowledge that the region's economic transformation necessitated far-reaching changes in the organization of the state. Second, in contrast to his 1896 state paper which forecast a United States of South Africa with a British majority, his 1899 minute related British interests to the size of its population in the Transvaal. As the number of British settlers increased so, it was believed, would British power. This view makes economic development simply a means of attracting English immigrants for the sake of British hegemony. And finally, a corollary of this is the racialist distrust which Selborne exhibited towards the Boers. It seems that Milner's missives had persuaded the undersecretary to accept some of the racialist assumptions which underlay the "grand design."

In late 1900 Lord Selborne turned his attention from South Africa to naval affairs when he took up a cabinet appointment as first lord of the Admiralty. The offer came as a welcome alternative to the Cape governorship, which Milner was trying to press on him.[27] At the Admiralty Selborne initiated several crucial policy changes. First, he modified the two-power standard so that instead of maintaining a fleet as large as the next two most powerful fleets combined, Britain would merely keep sufficient strength to deal with her two most likely enemies, which in 1902 he identified as France and Russia.[28] Maintaining this standard became increasingly expensive, and between 1898 and 1905, Britain increased its naval expenditure from £20.9 million to £36.8 million.[29] Not surprisingly, Selborne encountered persistent criticism from the chancellor of the exchequer for these ballooning estimates. In late 1901 Selborne contended in a lengthy memorandum that Britain's economic strength and its naval power were interdependent: "Its [Britain's] Credit and its Navy seem to me to be the two main pillars on which the strength of this country rests, and each is essential to the other. Unless our financial position is strong, the Navy cannot be maintained. Unless the Navy is fully adequate for any call which may be made upon it, our national Credit must stand in jeopardy." Not only did Britain's naval preponderance protect its trade, it also deterred foreign rivals from escalating their disagreements into war. The memorandum concluded with a stark reminder: "To us defeat in a maritime war would mean a disaster of almost unparalleled magnitude in history. It might mean the destruction of our mercantile marine, the stoppage of our manufactures, scarcity of food, invasion, disruption of Empire."[30] The first lord was not, however, unmindful of the billowing Admiralty estimates. In early 1901 he had strongly urged an alliance with Japan, which the two countries consummated in 1902.[31]

The prospect of cutting naval expenditure, however, appeared dimmer than ever; as early as 1901 Selborne noticed the disturbing growth of the German fleet. In his memorandum of 16 November 1901 he observed that "The [German] Empire seems determined that the power of Germany should be used all the world over to push German commerce, possessions and interests." The following year he told Balfour that he had begun to realize "the intensity of the hatred of the German nation to this country." By 1903 Selborne began advocating that British naval construction exceed the two power standard. To Curzon, he wrote: "We must have a force which is reasonably calculated to beat France and Russia and we must have something in hand against Germany. We cannot afford a three Power standard but we must have a real margin over the two Power standard and this policy the Cabinet adopted." The destruction of the Russian fleet in the Russo-Japanese War in 1904 allowed the Admiralty to concentrate more fully on the German menace. By February of 1904 study and thoughtful consideration had led Selborne "to the conviction that the great new German navy is being carefully built up from the point of view of a war with us."

Lord Selborne was one of the first British statesmen to perceive the German Empire as a threat to the British. Under Selborne's administration the Admiralty prepared for a deadly naval race with Germany. As Britain increased the quantity of its vessels, it also improved the quality of its battle fleet. It was during Selborne's tenure that Admiralty experts drew up the designs for the Dreadnought. Selborne did not see its launching, for, by that time, he had been called back into colonial service.

Though crucial, fleet construction was only one of Selborne's many responsibilities at the Admiralty. The First Lord also instigated many reforms in personnel and training, by which he sought to eliminate social privilege as a criterion for promotion. The Selborne Scheme, as these reforms were known, went far to professionalise the navy. An authority has concluded that "Despite modifications, the system justified the faith of its warmest advocates." Selborne also played a part in the creation of the Committee of Imperial Defence, established to coordinate the Empire's military policy. As chief of the Admiralty, he demonstrated his concern for economy and efficiency, proving himself an able administrator.[32]

Selborne's years at the Admiralty also enabled him to develop the vision of Empire he had articulated earlier at the Colonial Office. We would do well to pause at this juncture and analyse more fully Selborne's idea of imperialism before it was modified by his South African experience. In his famous 1896 memorandum, he was optimistically enthusiastic about material progress. He welcomed the modernization of the backward continent, and he believed that this would, if not obstructed by political obstacles, favour the Empire. The danger in South Africa, he felt, lay in obsolete political arrangements which encouraged each colony to consider only its own short-term advantage. A United States of South Africa would signify, to Selborne, the triumph of peripheral parochialism.[33]

A little over a year after penning his memorandum, Selborne expounded on his vision of the Empire to the Bradford Chamber of Commerce. To those who denigrated the importance of colonial trade, he declared: "Let them think of what the trade of the colonies would be when our Australasia and Canada and South Africa had extended, not perhaps, in the same huge magnitude of the United States, but on the same lines." As for black Africa, "there was no reason why all that country should not fill up with a teeming population and become a market for our goods." Colonial consumers, he forecast, would assume increasing importance as home markets became saturated.[34]

With his confidence in material advancement, Selborne believed in state action, not to stem the tide of economic progress but to channel and encourage it. The war against the South African Republic would not, in his view, resurrect an illusionary status quo of the past but would obliterate the political boundaries that stood in the way of progress. Not surprisingly, Selborne endorsed Chamberlain's tariff reform program in the optimistic faith that it would solidify the Empire and make it self-sufficient.[35] While he admitted that polity and economy might work at cross purposes, he sought to mesh the two and firmly believed that political power could and should engender economic growth. Less than two years after he had composed the 1896 paper, he minuted on another document: "I think one of the most wonderful things of this century has been the creation of German commerce and the German marine by the persistent and unwearying application of the German Govt. to this end. No point is too small for them."[36] It was clear that Selborne wished to make the Empire a potent political force for progress.

This suggests a third aspect to his imperialism. Nowhere in his 1896 state paper did he conceive of imperial relations in terms of British metropolitan power versus colonial (or dominion) power.[37] To Curzon, Selborne stressed the imperative need of "enlarging our mind from the UK to the Empire." He conceived of the geopolitical world not in terms of metropole or periphery but in terms of competing empires: "My mind is clear that in the years to come the UK by itself will not be strong enough to hold its proper place alongside US or Russia, and probably not Germany. We shall be thrust aside by sheer weight. But the British Empire could hold its own terms more than equally."[38] Even in the 1896 memorandum, Selborne vented his fear that the consciousness of all South Africans – whether Natalians, Cape colonists, or Transvaalers – was too blind and narrow to understand the great danger which Germany posed to them. A weak Empire would imperil the Cape and the SAR as well as England. Finally, it might be noted that the peripheral pressures whose workings the 1896 document discerned in

Southern Africa were not really peripheral at all. What threw regional power to the Transvaal was the Witwatersrand's development by largely European capital.

These strands in Selborne's imperialism – his enthusiasm for material progress, his belief in state action to direct and promote this progress, and his holistic vision of empire which effaced the metropole-periphery divide – were given force after 1905 when he became high commissioner for South Africa. These three components would be developed during his tenure there, and they would be augmented by other considerations emerging from his experiences at this post.

Selborne's appointment to this post was a disinterested act of high policy. Anticipating the imminent downfall of his government, Balfour, the Unionist prime minister, contemplated despatching Lord Selborne to South Africa, where, as high commissioner, he might survive the change of ministries to carry on the work of reconstruction. When asked for his views, Milner suggested as his replacement either Selborne or Arthur Lawley, the Transvaal's lieutenant-governor. Sir Alfred Lyttelton, Chamberlain's successor at the Colonial Office, warmly described the qualities which made Selborne perfect for the post. The political, administrative, and economic instability of the region, as well as the serious discontent which this engendered among both Boer and Briton, required "a sagacious and experienced politician versed in the conflicts of political forces and parties." As Lyttelton explained, "To deal with the situation we certainly require a first rate man, if possible of proved strength and capacity and I think that our high reputation as Imperialists rather than party men in the matter of appointments is involved in such a man." Sir Arthur Lawley's limited administrative experience and poor health made him far less qualified than Selborne. There were, admittedly, a few Unionist politicians more prominent than Selborne, but these men had attracted considerable hostility from the Liberals. By contrast, as Lyttelton noted, Selborne had made few enemies. "As a peer without constituents and in a great comparatively speaking Administrative office, he has had less conflict with the opposition than most ministers."[39]

All of these considerations led the colonial secretary to recommend formally that Lord Selborne be asked to assume the high commissionership of South Africa. Included in his commission would be the governorship of the Transvaal and Orange River Colony. Although responsible for the Orange River Colony, the day-to-day operations of government there would be conducted by the lieutenant-governor, Sir Hamilton Goold-Adams. Despite the colonial secretary's glowing recommendation, it took over a month to secure Selborne's appointment. The delay was not Selborne's fault, for, though unenthusiastic about the post, he accepted it out of duty. As Lyttelton explained to Milner, "The difficulty of getting him arose not on his side, but in our very weakened condition not unnaturally from my colleagues who did not at all wish to lose him. It was only by repeatedly hammering into A.J.B.'s head that S. Af. was more important just now than almost any place in the Cabinet that we gained the day." Milner greeted Selborne's appointment "with the greatest possible relief."[40] In April of 1905 Lord Selborne set sail for South Africa.

Milner briefed his successor on the South African situation by letter. He first warned Selborne about the Afrikaner danger. "Perfectly charming in their duplicity," the Boer leaders were secretly striving to win back in peace what they had lost in war – an independent state. They sought "a separate Afrikander nation and State, comprising, no doubt, men of other races, who are ready to be 'afrikanderized', but essentially autochthonous, isolated and un-British." The Afrikaner politicians worked up a virulent anti-English resentment among their rank and file, who would otherwise have come to accept British rule. The means by which such hostile sentiments were engendered included "monstrous lying" and "the vigorous squelching of schemes of material development." Milner advised Selborne to assist the country Boers by continuing the various projects for agricultural improvement. As for the Boer elite, no imperial official should be taken in by then. Milner did not explain how to deal with the threat that these Afrikaner politicians would pose to the Transvaal polity once the representative constitution came into operation.

Lamenting that commercial and industrial questions divided the British element, Milner urged his replacement to try to unite the English-speakers in the Transvaal and throughout South Africa. Some of the mining magnates, he assured Selborne, could be relied on to help; so could the engineering and "professional men." He urged the new high commissioner to provide the leadership that the British lacked. In all events, he must retain the confidence of the loyalists. How precisely Selborne could unite the divisive and truculent British community remained unanswered in Milner's missive.

In his letter Milner confessed that the greatest mistake he made as high commissioner, which he bitterly regretted, was in acceding to the sweeping exclusion of all non-whites from the franchise. Though he would never put black and white on an equal political footing, he did consider that both Boers and British in South Africa were too rigid and absolute in their discrimination of non-whites. Their prejudice he also considered foolish and unjust, for it made colour rather than civilization the basis for political rights. "The whites will see nothing but colour, and refuse to recognise the enormous gulf, wh. separates one coloured man from another in respect to civilisation." Milner also warned Selborne that "many Europeans *would like a native war*," for this would enable them to despoil the blacks of all their land. Again, Milner did not explain how to reconcile a benevolent policy towards Africans with the exploitative demands of his Randlord allies, nor did he suggest how a high commissioner or governor could, in terms of practical politics, overrule the combined prejudices of Boer and Briton.

Finally, Milner described the dangerous intercolonial friction over customs and railways, which the *modus vivendi* exacerbated by directing such a large share of the Transvaal's rail traffic through Portuguese territory. Milner lamented that the long-standing ideal of federation must be postponed indefinitely. "Everybody clamours for union, everybody recognises, in the abstract, its desirability, yet everybody kicks violently against the inevitable sacrifice of local self-containedness which it involves." All Milner could advise was to attempt to keep the Intercolonial Council beyond the reach of the elected legislatures in the two new colonies. Selborne must try especially hard to maintain the amalgamated railway system which the ICC administered. Unfortunately, as Milner admitted, his failure to secure borrowing powers for the council sealed its doom as an autonomous agency. How, then, was Selborne to prevent the fissiparous tendencies of the region from dissolving South Africa into regional particles?[41]

The South Africa which Milner depicted in his letter appeared in sombre colours indeed. Its industry depressed, its political system destabilized, its black people oppressed, and its white population divided along ethnic and intercolonial cleavages, South Africa seemed a land of intractable difficulties. Milner's letter presented it to Selborne as one big problem with no solution. And, once the Liberals ousted the Unionists from power in 1905, Selborne lost a crucial asset that Milner had enjoyed throughout his tenure – the support of a sympathetic government at home. In the dismal conditions of 1905, it was questionable how much Selborne could salvage from the South African wreck. Glimmering through the wreckage, though, were still the gold mines.

3 Abandoned by London: Selborne and the Chinese Labour Controversy

When Sir Alfred Milner sailed from South Africa in 1905, he left the Transvaal mining industry with a full stock of labour and the foundations for a new state to control it. Milner could not, however, have created these favourable conditions for industry without the acquiescence, in fact support, of the imperial government. London did more than simply sanction the high commissioner's policies, especially in regard to the labour question. The Unionist ministry not only defended the importation of Chinese labour against vehement critics in Parliament, it also provided the diplomatic influence necessary to secure Chinese approval for the measure. A recent authority has concluded that "the ability of the gold-mining industry to draw on the full force and historic weight of British Imperialism in China and South Africa was a *sine qua non* of the whole project's success."[1] Without imperial support, it was an open question whether Milner's state could alone serve the Rand's titanic needs.

In the same year that Milner resigned, the Unionists fell from power in England, and the enormity of their subsequent defeat at the polls in January 1906 owed much to the Chinese labour issue. The full extent of Milner's intimacy with the industry was exposed the following year when it was revealed that he had condoned the illegal flogging of Chinese labourers in the mines. This revelation discredited the proconsul, who barely escaped a censure from the House of Commons. The mining industry needed friends in high places, but in Liberal England, friendship with such a dubious enterprise carried with it a political liability which ensured that its friends would not remain in high places for very long.

The requirements of the gold mining industry were considerable. The geology of the Witwatersrand, with its extensive reefs of low-grade ore, made mining there a capital- and labour-intensive operation. The full exploitation of the gold fields necessitated deep-level mining, and consequently the deployment of sophisticated technology, expensive machinery, and an enormous quantity of labour. The internationally fixed price of gold made it impossible to transfer the costs of production onto the consumer; yet this same factor encouraged increasing production, for there was no limit to the world's consumption of gold. Indeed, as the average grade of ore declined, the Rand interest found expansion imperative. After the war the Randlords committed themselves to finance major new development works. This necessitated a great expenditure, which would have to come either from fresh capital investments or from cost reductions. As capital was in short supply after the war, the gold magnates directed their efforts to cutting expenses.

The cost structure of the industry included machinery, technological services, and labour, both skilled and unskilled. As the costs of equipment and technology were relatively inflexible, the Randlords devoted their efforts to lowering labour costs. The workforce was divided along racial lines, with whites doing the skilled work and non-whites the unskilled. Although less that 10 per cent of the workforce, the white labour bill represented twice that paid to non-whites and amounted to one-quarter of industry's total costs. This was an obvious target for cost-cutting, either by wage reductions or replacement by the cheaper non-whites. Several considerations, however, made the magnates think twice before adopting this alternative. For one thing, white skills were necessary and scarce. A more important consideration was the fact that whites were heavily unionized and possessed of political rights, which gave them access to the levers of power. As productivity depended on industrial peace and political stability as much as on low costs, the sword which slashed the white wage bill might cut profitability as well as expenditure. For these reasons, it took an exceptional opportunity or crisis to move the magnates in this direction.

The non-whites enjoyed no such political advantages and were therefore eminently exploitable. So it was on this group that industry's imperatives were ruthlessly exercised.[2] But the moment was inopportune to attempt wage reductions, for there was a serious shortage of African unskilled labour after the war.[3] In effect, the Africans were conducting a "strike" against horrid mining conditions in general and the Chamber of Mines' recent wage reductions in particular. In the short term, the boycott was successful. It forced the mine owners to increase the wage scale from the wartime rate of 30 to 35 shillings per month to

45 to 60 shillings. Not even this, however, could attract a sufficient number of Africans to the mines.[4] However, by raising costs in this way, the labour shortage diminished the existing supply of capital, thus further alarming the European investor and ensuring that fresh capital would not be forthcoming. Without sufficient labour or capital, there could be no expansion, and without expansion it was questionable whether Rand gold mining could continue as a going concern.

Lord Milner, the British government, Chinese authorities, and tens of thousands of Chinese workers were "persuaded" to come to the rescue. There is little question that Chinese labour rescued the gold industry from a serious crisis. The labourers were recruited and shipped from China by the Chamber of Mines' Labour Importation Agency (LIA), which enticed its victims by misleading accounts of the genial conditions on the Rand. By the provisions of the Labour Importation Ordinance, which the imperial government had approved, the labourers signed on for a three-year term, during which they were limited to unskilled work but guaranteed a monthly wage of 50 shillings after six months. Though they could extend their terms by an additional three years, they were obliged to return to China on the expiry of their contracts. Subject to close regulation, the "coolies" were housed in prison-like compounds, from which they emerged each day to proceed down the shafts to labour underground. They were not permitted to leave their compounds without a pass. The maintenance of discipline was entrusted to the infamous Chinese police, whose ruthless methods could not stop opium-smoking, gambling, homosexuality, or desertion. Witwatersrand profits were built on considerable human suffering.

It is estimated that 53,828 Chinese were eventually employed in the mines, amounting to one-third of the unskilled labour force. The benefit of the Chinese labour system, however, cannot be measured by numbers alone. The three-year contract stabilized the workforce and permitted better labour management. Furthermore, mine owners could maximize Chinese productivity through the wage system. The widespread extension of piece-work and the establishment of a "fair day's work" standard ensured that as much labour as possible was squeezed from the workers at a cost below the contract price. In this way, Chinese importation allowed employers to undercut the Africans' bargaining position.[5] In part because of their diminished leverage, Africans came to the mines in increasing numbers after the arrival of the Chinese. By 1907 the African supply had doubled from what it had been four years before. Finally, the Chamber of Mines could decrease its dependence on white labour. From a ratio of 5.6 to 1 in 1903–4, the non-white to white ratio rose to 7.2 to 1 the following year.[6]

As soon as Lord Selborne arrived in South Africa, the *Rand Daily Mail* laid out the task of the high commissioner: "He has, in the interests of the well-being of the State, to encourage the efforts of those who devote capital to its development, while seeing that the investment of such capital shall not create monopoly or grant complete control of administration to the investor. In this connection, too, the rights and interests of the State must be safe-guarded, so that while the men who risk their money have fair return for their enterprise, the country has an adequate share of what is primarily its own property."[7] This was a tall order indeed, yet it accurately described the conflicting demands which would confront any high commissioner seeking to promote Transvaal prosperity. To encourage capital investment, he would have at once to maintain political stability and at the same time to preserve a labour system which had produced disruption within South Africa and political hostility without. And in fulfilling these disparate objectives, he could not compromise the integrity of the state. This required either a local polity of Leviathan proportions or powerful imperial support abroad.

Lord Selborne took up the challenge and dedicated his efforts to the colony's material development. South Africa, he enthusiastically reported in 1909 to a former Admiralty colleague, Ernest Pretyman, had magnificent economic prospects. Its soil would produce abundant quantities of maize, citrus, tobacco, tea, sugar, and coffee. One day South Africa would become a leading sheep exporter. And beneath the turf lay a vast mineral treasure of gold, coal, copper, tin, and asbestos. The exploitation of the region's natural bounty had just begun and could not be halted. Kruger's obscurantist regime had tried to block progress and had failed. With the republic vanquished, "It [progress] might be obstructed in its pace by obstacles put in its way, or its flow might be quickened by removing obstacles from its path, according as to this or that Government wished to check or accelerate the speed, but nothing could stop it. Milner's work was imperishable."[8] Though this exudes the Union optimism of 1909, Selborne was dedicated to material advancement before he even landed in South Africa.[9] In 1905 he saw it as his duty to quicken the pace of progress.

Few Liberals would have denied the desirability of economic development, but they would not have permitted it at any cost. Their denunciations of Chinese labour were sharp and widespread. Fearing what their advent to power might mean for the Transvaal's economic future, Selborne sent a barrage of arguments to Liberal leaders in support of the imported labour system. Through these, his perceptions of the Transvaal's economic needs emerge clearly.

In November 1905, even before the Unionist government fell, the high commissioner sent Sir Edward Grey, soon to become foreign secretary in the Liberal Cabinet, a letter explaining the economic position. He pointed out that the Witwatersrand was the source of all South African prosperity, future and present. Railway revenues as well as colonial budgets depended on the gold industry, as did commerce, not only in the Transvaal but in the other colonies too. Moreover, "it is on the mining industry that the Boer farmer depends," in the way of capital for railways, the land bank, and irrigation schemes, and in the way of markets. It also furnished a common form of investment and savings throughout South Africa. If the Chinese left, the entire economy would shrink proportionately.[10] For this last assertion, Selborne no doubt relied on a memorandum he had received from the Chamber of Mines. He sent this on to Lord Elgin, the new colonial secretary, in December 1905 with his full endorsement, adding in his cover letter that the departure of the Chinese would bring on a grave financial crisis in which "the amount of human distress would be terrible."

In a further memorandum, the Chamber of Mines added an interesting twist to the theme of economic interdependence. Penned by F. Perry, the chairman of the Witwatersrand Native Labour Association, the memorandum contended that all sectors of the regional economy – agriculture, commerce, and mining – were in dangerous competition for non-white labour. As mining work was relatively unattractive and poorly paid, other sectors had the first call on local labour. Why then had African labour in the Witwatersrand increased from 135,954 in September of 1904 to 185,681 in April of 1905? The explanation, claimed Perry, lay in the depression which had freed labour from other sectors. Thus, Chinese labour was vital if general prosperity was to accompany mining progress.[11]

Selborne accepted this thesis, passing it on to Elgin in these words:

If, therefore, the mining industry were to be dependent on African labour alone, it seems probable that it would continue to dwindle through lack of labour due to the successful competition of private employers, but that the diminution of the general prosperity, which would inevitably follow from the dwindling of the mining industry, would, in time, release a larger proportion of the native labour for employment of the mines. It would be impossible that the mining industry and private business should both enjoy the steady expansion which they may reasonably expect.[12]

Through these despatches, Selborne's central assumption emerges clearly: despite sectoral rivalry, South Africa was an economic unit with mining its foundation. Though an obvious point, he emphasized it to defuse Radical politicians' rhetoric, which often obscured the fact that not only the magnates depended on gold. When Elgin referred to the

Rand industry as speculative, Selborne retorted sharply: "The Stock Exchange in London and here is speculative but I do not believe that there is any industry in the world less speculative in so far as the raw material is concerned."[13] For Selborne, gold was not just a millionaire's game but a sure and respectable basis for a permanent economy.

While mining's importance to the regional economy was easily demonstrated, it was more difficult to explain why so much labour was needed so soon. In his November 1905 letter to Sir Edward Grey, Selborne argued obscurely that the Chinese laboured primarily on crucial development work which could not be easily cut back once initiated.[14] If the Chinese were repatriated, all development projects, so essential for the future, would be halted and the millions invested therein sterilized.

Unconvinced, Grey protested that indentured labour was a bad foundation on which to build an industry, and "that it would be much better for the mining industry to develop slowly on a healthier foundation than to develop rapidly with the help of the Chinese." In his attempt to refute Grey's contention, Selborne came to the heart of the matter: without cheap labour, the Transvaal could not profitably exploit its mineral wealth. Chinese labour 'enables vast resources in the country to be developed, which would otherwise remain absolutely useless.' More impatient than Grey, he added: 'It is not a question of slow development with local labour. The slowness would be such that it would not be developed generations hence. Compared with the possibilities of the country, all development will be slow, considering its size and wealth. To say that the employment of 130,000 miners altogether is rushing the pace seems to be an odd standard when compared with the development of other countries.'[15] By development Selborne was not referring specifically to gold but to all the unexploited wealth of the country – animal, mineral, and vegetable.

To Lord Elgin Selborne produced the further argument that the Transvaal government was organized in expectation of industrial expansion. Therefore, "the existing machinery of Government can only be justified by the anticipation of a steady and reasonable expansion of the industry."[16] Fuller proof of his commitment to progress could not have been offered. Economic expansion was not merely a high priority; it was the state's raison d'être.

In South Africa the theme of economic expansion was well rehearsed. Speaking before the General Mining and Finance Corporation, the magnate George Albu urged his audience to work on the biggest scale possible, for this would reduce working costs, make lower-grade ore profitable, and in doing so increase the life of the industry. *South African Mines Commerce and Industries* extolled the advantages of the "big-mill, low- grade" policy in January of 1906. Six months later, it argued that expansion was not simply desirable but urgent to offset the fall in grade which had scared off European investors.[17]

The high commissioner was certainly in touch with local opinion. But although Selborne understood and supported the industry's need for expansion, it would be misleading to cast him simply as a magnate in official dress. He did not ally with the magnates to encourage their prosperity but rather to encourage South Africa's. Selborne wanted to keep on the Rand an industry profitable enough to spark progress and permanent enough to keep it burning. Thus he sought to convince the European investor that the future outlook in South Africa was bright, and he encouraged every effort to make it so. He worried not about profits per se, but about continuous, long-term profitability. This is why development was so important to him. It also explains why he so vigorously disputed Lord Elgin's claim that the industry was specula-tive. He had found in the Randlords capitalists who, for their own rea-sons, had committed themselves to a long-term venture, and he did not wish to disappoint them.

The next argument in Selborne's brief was much more contentious. He asserted that there was no substitute for imported labour. To Win-ston Churchill, the colonial undersecretary, he cast doubt on Elgin's hope that labour-saving devices might compensate for the loss of the Chinese. "In respect of native labour," he advised Grey, "unless com-pulsion were used, which of course is altogether abhorrent to our ideas and impossible, there will be no native labour forthcoming to take the place of the Chinese. It simply does not exist." The perpetual scarcity of farm labour underscored this point.[18]

There was still the white alternative. The racial division of labour was "a deeply rooted traditional custom in South Africa." White "in-eradicable prejudices" against "Kaffir work," he informed Grey, car-ried on this tradition. He did admit, however, that the restriction of whites to skilled work was a convenient, indeed essential, custom for the mining industry. The white standard of living was so high that the white miners demanded at least 10 shillings a day and "at that price of course most of the mines could not possibly work."[19] It followed from his contentions that the position of white skilled labour depended on the unskilled supply. Far from displacing whites, the Chinese provided Europeans with jobs. Echoing the Chamber's of Mines' memoran-dum, Selborne warned that Chinese repatriation would cost five thou-sand white positions.[20] The last point, of course, nicely reinforced his general thesis that every sector of South Africa depended on gold mining which in turn depended on the Chinese. There was no divi-sion of interest.

Opinion in South Africa was, however, far from unanimous. Though many white labourers did support Chinese labour, many others embraced the ideas of F.H.P. Creswell, mining engineer and owner of Village Main Reefs. It was his contention that, with full use of labour-saving devices, white unskilled labour, at white man's wages, could profitably work the mines.[21] Churchill warmly supported Creswell's efforts. If it [the white labour experiment] failed it would give Chinese labour at least an economic justification, while "If it succeeded you [Selborne] would I am sure rejoice at the prospect of a white working class community in Johannesburg, settling as it would for once and all the question of British supremacy."[22] Churchill obviously did not understand what "British supremacy" meant to Selborne. Unlike Creswell and unlike the Liberals, the high commissioner wanted a prosperous Transvaal, even if it was built on a non-white foundation. The prospect of an English-speaking South Africa carried no appeal to him if such a vision stood in the way of progress.

In the House of Commons, the Radicals questioned Selborne's economic analysis. Questions were frequently asked regarding the displacement of skilled whites by the cheaper Chinese. Sir Brampton Gurdon went so far as to claim that, "If ever was a mandate given to a Government in this country it was that at the last general election [1900] the British Government was to find a new field for the British workman." The subsequent introduction of Chinese and the exodus of white men from the Transvaal proved to the speaker that the Boer War was a "Stock Exchange" war after all. British supremacy certainly meant different things to different people.

The divergence between Selborne and the Liberal government can also be seen in their ethical judgments about Chinese labour. Though few Liberals sincerely believed that it was as evil as slavery, there was, as Elgin noted, a genuine belief that indentured labour, involving as it did, restrictions on liberty, was immoral.[23] Selborne, on the other hand, told Grey, "I, who have been six months on the spot, who have devoted hours, days, and weeks, to the study of this question, to investigating the conditions of these Chinamen on mine after mine and on mine after mine, say with the most honest conviction in my heart that the system is not an immoral or wicked one." He declared to Elgin that the Chinese were free agents who signed voluntarily for an arrangement which was beneficial to them. If Chinese labour was so wrong, then how, he asked Grey, could Liberals tolerate African labour? After all, "the *only* difference between the conditions of Chinese coolie labour and Kaffir labour is that the former contracts for a longer period of service than the latter does, which is a detail in no way affecting the principle."[24]

On 18 December 1905 the Colonial Office prepared a cabinet memo for Elgin. This recommended that, rather than repatriate all the Chinese immediately, which could precipitate an industrial collapse, the matter be left to an elected local legislature. It cited the suggestion made on 27 October by Sir Alfred Lyttelton, then colonial secretary, that the Chamber of Mines voluntarily suspend recruiting operations as evidence that the Unionists too envisioned an end to the system.[25] Selborne's advice was fully considered by the government, and his letter to Grey circulated through the cabinet. Herbert Asquith, the chancellor of the exchequer, found his assertion that one-third of the economy would shrink "very unconvincing," while Grey still contended that imported labour was a bad foundation for the industry. In December the cabinet decided to suspend further importation pending a final judgment by the people of the Transvaal in a "really representative" assembly.[26]

Not indifferent to the fate of the mining industry, the Liberals had no wish to precipitate an economic crisis which, Elgin appreciated, would ruin the entire Transvaal community – small-scale investors, honest workers, and magnates alike. The colonial secretary, however, refused to believe that there were no alternatives, such as white labour or labour-saving devices.[27] Moreover, Radical pressure exercised a powerful influence on the cabinet.[28] Having to juggle various considerations, the Liberals hoped to satisfy the Radicals without damaging the mining industry. "But crash or no crash," Churchill declared, "the policy will have to go forward and the sooner this is realised, the better for all concerned."[29]

On 20 December 1905 Elgin cabled the government's decision to Selborne and told him to prevent the shipment of the 14,700 Chinese for whom licences had already been issued but who had not yet left China.[30] Though unhappy with Liberal policy, the high commissioner was not completely pessimistic about the fate of Chinese labour if the decision was to be left to the Transvaal. As he confided to his lieutenant-governor, Sir Arthur Lawley, "Everything will be smooth so long as the question is really referred to the elected representatives of the people in July."[31] In his estimation, the only implacable opposition was a section of British miners. "The Boers," he told Churchill, "have not an ounce of principle in their composition [opposition?] against Chinese labour. Their only real objection to Chinese labour in its present form is that it is not servile enough, that is, that the Chinese are not shut up in compounds."[32] The Afrikaners were, the high commissioner surmised, simply using the issue to secure responsible government.[33]

The magnates themselves worried more about Liberal interference than about what a local legislature might do. *South African Mines Com-*

merce and Industries declared: "The Transvaal, therefore, is not afraid to submit this question to the decision of its own Parliament. It knows that such opposition as is offered will come from the least enlightened and the least progressive section of the community. For our part, we believe, as we have said before, that the Colony can be relied on to vote for industrial expansion and increased prosperity."[34] It is clear the gold industry did not equate self-government with Chinese repatriation. For this reason, it accepted with equanimity the Liberal decision to entrust the Transvaal with the final say.

The revocation of licences already issued, however, evoked a storm of indignation in the Transvaal. Three days after receiving these instructions, Selborne telegraphed home that, according to his attorney general, Richard Solomon, the governor had no legal power to prevent the shipment of labourers already authorized to proceed.[35] On January 2 1906, the Colonial Office prepared a memorandum which confirmed Solomon's opinion that the existing licences could only be revoked by an order-in-council which, if issued, would inflame Transvaal opinion and make its government liable for compensation.[36] Before this even circulated, the prime minister, Sir Henry Campbell-Bannerman, had written Asquith that "it will be ticklish and may appear small to meddle in any wholesale way with the new Licenses." Consequently, Elgin informed Selborne that the licences in question could stand.[37]

The Transvaal press made of this controversy, castigating the imperial government's high-handed and unconstitutional interference. The high commissioner, on the other hand, earned praise from the *Johannesburg Star,* which thanked him for championing the colony's cause.[38]

The Liberal government found itself in the unenviable position of administering a system it abhorred. In late 1905 Herbert Samuel, a Liberal politician, prepared a memorandum which offered a way of assuaging Radical criticism. Specifically, he proposed that every "Chinaman" discontented with the work be allowed to terminate his contract and return home. The expense of this scheme could be defrayed from licence fees and, if need be, by His Majesty's Government.[39]

Though favourable towards this proposal, Elgin emphasized the importance of first consulting the high commissioner. He broached the subject to Selborne by cable on 6 January 1906, citing Selborne's own admission that several labourers did not realize what mining work entailed when they signed up.[40] Selborne replied unenthusiastically that the policy proposed would admit a dangerous principle which might encourage African labourers to demand the same option. Moreover, many Chinese would take advantage of the scheme to get a free holiday to China. (Of course, they would return to the Rand, for working conditions were really quite satisfactory.)[41]

In March Elgin telegraphed that although he did not seek a mass exodus, he would insist that no man be kept on the Rand against his will. Privately, he told Selborne that the measure was designed to meet the general demand for wholesale repatriation.[42] Churchill also urged Selborne to make this scheme a success, if only in the interest of the mining industry. He hoped that between fifteen hundred and three thousand men would take advantage of it. In another letter he added, "I daresay you can make the path to freedom sufficiently stormy to prevent indecent crowding upon it."[43]

These reassurances failed to remove Selborne's misgivings, nor those of the Chamber of Mines which, Selborne reported, was very nervous about the proposal.[44] In a protest to London, the Chamber itself predicted that the Liberal initiative would produce a "considerable exodus" of Chinese.[45] George Farrar of the Anglo-French Exploration Company warned Selborne that the offer would evoke a "storm of indignation."[46] The magnate Sir Frederick Eckstein, of Hermann Eckstein and Company, received a letter from his partner, Lionel Phillips, who privately doubted that many Chinese would leave, especially as the notice advising them of the offer was framed so obscurely. The real mischief he feared, "lies in the blow it will strike at discipline." Whenever coolies became discontented in the future, they could threaten to leave. The capitalist press, represented by *South African Mines Commerce and Industries*, dubbed Elgin and Company "the wreckers."[47]

The procedure adopted to give effect to Liberal policy was that suggested by Selborne to Elgin at the end of March.[48] By early May notices conveying the repatriation offer had been printed in Chinese and posted throughout the compounds. At the end of the month, Selborne reported that only twelve coolies had applied for state-aided repatriation.[49]

Radicals soon found an explanation for this meagre turnout when, in June, the *Manchester Guardian* published a literal translation of the poster. At the bottom of the obscurely worded notice the Chinese were instructed to "tremble and obey."[50] Churchill angrily wrote Selborne that the whole policy had turned into a fiasco and had discredited the government, especially in the eyes of the Radicals. The wording of the notice had "rendered it ridiculous." The high commissioner retorted that the poster had been drawn up in good faith and that the words "tremble and obey" were a formality in official Chinese literature, just as the coat of arms in British official documents. He added, "If you had informed me that what HMG desired was not a proclamation, which should be intelligible to the Chinese coolies but to the H. of Co. I would have drawn one up in the best style of the Daily *News*."

A revised notice, carefully scrutinized by Elgin, was posted on 18 July. Less than a month after this, six hundred Chinese had applied for state-aided repatriation. Selborne complained that applicants with sufficient funds often feigned destitution to avoid contributing to the cost of their repatriation. He would empower the superintendent of foreign labour to search all suspected of this fraud and, on confirmation, to reject their applications. With reservations, Elgin approved this procedure. He would not, however, approve Selborne's proposal to post a notice advising Chinese who applied after October 1906 that logistical difficulties would delay their repatriation by several months and that during that time, they would not receive full rations. By the end of 1906, 766 of the 1,550 applicants had been accepted for repatriation. Between January and July of 1907, however, only fifth-three applicants secured approval out of 359.[51] The Foreign Labour Department, especially after self-government, was able to make the path to freedom "stormy" indeed.

Though there was no mass exodus to China, the Chinese provided other proof of their dissatisfaction with conditions on the Rand. Weeks before Selborne had arrived in South Africa, the North Randfontein mine was shaken by a violent disturbance, which ended in the arrest of fifty-three Chinese labourers. Faced with cost restraints typical of low-grade mines, North Randfontein kept wages below the daily 1s. 6d. required by the ordinance six months after importation. Chinese discontent took various forms, culminating in a deliberate go-slow. When the police came in to arrest the ringleaders, mass violence broke out. Significantly, the mine management made its decisions without recourse to the Foreign Labour Department, which the government had established for the control, supervision, and "protection" of the Chinese. Though suppressed, the strike did induce the mine owners to raise day wages to the contractual minimum. To keep wage levels low without provoking another disturbance, North Randfontein decided on the widespread extension of the piece-work system. In its wage policy, this mine set the model for the entire industry.[52]

Well before the North Randfontein incident, the mining industry had been designing a wage strategy to squeeze the most work out of the Chinese for the least cost. This entailed, among other things, erecting a minimum daily performance level, euphemistically called a fair day's wage, below which pay would be deducted. In a despatch to Lyttelton penned while the Unionists were still in power, Selborne fully supported the Chamber's wage policy. Defending the fair day's work standard, he argued that "it is clearly impossible in practice to compel a Mining Company to pay a wage of 1s. 6d. a day to a man who has not done a day's work fairly equivalent to that wage." He also praised the piece-work system as of mutual benefit to employees, who would, he predicted, earn more thereby, and to employers, who would profit by the increased productivity.[53]

Though considerably more critical of industrial wage policy than their predecessors, the Liberals were only inclined to rectify the more obvious abuses. They fully realized that, contrary to assurances given to the House of Commons, the Chinese were being used to undercut the Africans.[54] When Elgin pressed Selborne, the governor reported that the Foreign Labour Department enforced the ordinance's wage clause but that its provisions were ambiguous. Not inclined to offer a legal challenge, Elgin let the matter drop and the Chamber continued to exploit the clause's loose wording to violate its spirit.[55] In the main, Selborne successfully fended off imperial obstruction, Liberal and Unionist, to the Chamber's sovereign control over wage determination.

There were other disturbances besides North Randfontein and other sources of grievance. A major source of trouble, according to a contemporary report, was abusive treatment of Chinese by white miners. The Foreign Labour Department claimed that white overseers, frustrated by their inability to make themselves understood by the Chinese, conveyed their message by "a blow or the application of a heavy boot."[56] It is clear that the underlying tension between the two groups sprang from more than communication problems. The Chinese were subjected to a repressive system of discipline, which manifested itself to them in the form of white supervisors who exacted as much work as possible and who, no doubt, occasionally administered rough justice. For his part, the white labourer had reason to resent his potential ultra-cheap competitor.

Discontent did not always express itself in violence. Less dramatic but equally indicative were the minor responses which occurred every day. The Chinese resorted to such tactics as desertion, "loafing," drug use, or belief in other worldly solutions.[57] It was known that they smoked opium in the compounds. With the Chamber's tendency to exaggerate, it is difficult to ascertain how prevalent loafing was, but it is clear from industry's constant concern that the Chinese did not give their best effort willingly. Desertion also constituted a serious problem and was identified as such by the Foreign Labour Department. In January of 1906, 809 coolies voted with their feet.[58] In time, desertion became more than an employer's concern; it grew into a major community problem.

Selborne did not see compound living conditions as a cause for dissatisfaction. Shortly after assuming his post, he inspected sixteen Chinese compounds. Reporting to Lyttelton, he considered the accommodation clean and far superior to that provided for Africans, the food of excellent quality and plentiful, and the hospital facilities modern and efficient. Not unduly restricted in their movements, the Chinese could "wander at will" over the vast mine premises.[59] No doubt Selborne was sincere in his report, for he wrote to his wife in similar terms, though he admitted to her that he would have to bring about some improvement in hospital conditions. (Obviously, Selborne had not seen the conditions of work underground, much less witnessed the disciplinary system in action.) Once the Liberals assumed power, they too received these glowing accounts.[60]

More suspicious of Chinese conditions, the Radicals at home searched for abuses in a system they condemned as slavery. Before and after the Liberals took power, critical questions were frequently fired at the government of the day, which was always sensitive about this political issue. As a result, Selborne found himself constantly answering hostile questions concerning the mining industry. He constituted himself both defence attorney and public relations person for the Chamber.

In late 1906 he found himself replying to the report of Mr Bucknill, who alleged that the all-male compound system had spawned rampant homosexuality. Elgin instructed the governor to investigate and to telegraph his findings in terms suitable for presentation to Parliament. In a telegram, Selborne assured the colonial secretary that he was doing all in his power "to stamp out this execrable crime," by repatriating all suspected of this unnatural vice. He was certain that Bucknill's report was a gross exaggeration and that those repatriated for this reason would be "a small but vile suspected minority."[61]

Privately, Selborne refused to believe that compound conditions fostered this practice. Typical of his combination of cultural arrogance and individualism are his comments to Grey on this issue:

The Chinese are not Christians, and therefore, I think it is probable that in all these questions their standard is even lower than that of the white who does not observe the rules of his religion. I have no reason whatever to suppose that the Chinaman in the Transvaal is a more immoral man than the Chinaman in China. I must confess that I feel much more sympathy with our own soldiers … who … for periods of eight to ten years in India, are entirely separated from their homes and families, than I do for the Chinese who are separated from theirs a maximum period of three years. If it is wrong to bring the Chinese labourers into the Transvaal under these conditions I am quite sure it is much more wrong to send our soldiers to India. But I do not think either act is wrong. The State cannot deprive the individual of his individual responsibility as a man.[62]

This was not simply for political consumption; it was a statement of conviction.

There is evidence that Selborne genuinely considered the Radical attacks on Chinese labour not simply reckless economically but also untrue and self-serving. In November 1905 he suggested to Grey that a commission be appointed to investigate these allegations. As late as 1909, he complained bitterly to his old colleague, Ernest Pretyman of "Radical mendacity."[63] In a private letter to Elgin, he warned of another effect of Radical rhetoric:

In all my political experience I have never known lies so profuse, so malignant, so wicked, and so dangerous. The only way in which the British, commercial and industrial and professional classes in Johannesburg differ from those classes in England and Scotland is in being superior in every way to the average of those classes in England and Scotland. The mines are managed by men of these classes, and the resentment, the bitter intense resentment, which they feel about the foul lies told about their treatment of the Chinese during the general election constitutes a real political danger.[64]

Selborne worried about alienating the upwardly mobile colonial professionals.

In South Africa the Randlords were leading a public campaign against the Liberals. In April 1906 Lionel Phillips spoke out against the Liberal "campaign of calumnies," while two months later, three thousand persons attended a meeting at Wanderer's Hall protesting against Liberal charges. There, Mr Quinn, mayor of Johannesburg and formerly an opponent of Chinese labour, cast the Liberal charges as an attack on the working man.[65] The *South African Mines Commerce and Industries* chimed in:

How long are the misdeeds of the Rand to be served up each morning as pungent tit-bits to the readers of British radical dailies? How, in fine, can we expect any revival of confidence in this country when there are those in our midst whose life-work is to chronicle our every failing, to quench every spark of returning belief in our industrial possibilities by querulous reiteration of our shortcomings or worse; to ruin the Rand economically, past praying for out of sheer political prejudice?[66]

Selborne's main concern was to retain the support of the Transvaal bourgeoisie, which, in terms of influence, was indeed a factor to be reckoned with. Elgin, on the other hand, had to worry about placating the radical elements in Britain. Acknowledging the political dangers that Selborne had noted in South Africa, he nevertheless protested that in England, "There is a genuine dislike of Chinese labour, and the conditions under which it has been introduced: and I cannot even if I wished, cut aloof from that."[67] Imperial connections were frayed indeed.

Yet somehow Selborne had to account for the very visible disturbances which had taken place and which Liberals such as Herbert Samuel were casting as "the inevitable outcome of the system of attempting to govern people after depriving them of their liberty."[68] Well before the Unionists left office, the high commissioner offered his analysis of the situation. Publicly, he minimized the outbreaks of violence, treating them as simply the initial difficulties of launching a great experiment.[69] Officially, he offered three reasons for the troubles. To his Unionist boss, Alfred Lyttelton, he cited language as the chief difficulty and one which inflated "simple misunderstandings" into full-blown disturbances. In Selborne's opinion, every compound should have at least one white official conversant with the North China dialect. In addition, five inspectors so qualified should be added to the Foreign Labour Department to raise the total number to ten. Secondly, there were certain "bad characters" among the Chinese. Thirdly, echoing the report of the Foreign Labour Department, he cited "the improper exercise of authority by individual white men."[70] He saw none of these problems as serious or insurmountable, and he assured his Liberal friend, Sir Edward Grey, that the matter was well in hand, adding, "I do not believe that a similar aggregation of human beings of any race could have been collected in one spot and less crime have ensued."[71]

Privately, Selborne was not so glib. In a despatch he informed Lyttelton that the cumulative effect of the outbreaks could not be treated with "indifference." Though he mentioned bad characters, both white and yellow, as well as the language difficulty, he saw these as symptoms of a larger problem; insufficient government control. He admitted that the Chinese had grievances, foremost of which was white abuse. "The mine owners," he assured the colonial secretary, "have done all in their power to secure the well-being of the coolies, but neither they, nor the mine, nor the compound managers can exercise immediate supervision over the action of the white miners (styled overseers) placed in charge of groups of coolies underground." The Randlords, to Selborne, seemed incapable of keeping order in the compounds. The government, he urged, must intervene to maintain effective discipline.

Later in the same despatch he specified the abuse of authority which had taken place. In late March 1905, before Selborne had arrived, the superintendent of the Foreign Labour Department, William Evans, had informed the lieutenant-governor, Sir Arthur Lawley, that he had, with Milner's permission, delegated certain powers of punishment to compound managers, who were thereupon authorized to inflict "slight corporal punishment" for minor offences.[72] In a letter to Lyttelton, Evans explained that, finding it impossible to deal with every breach of discipline, he considered that this delegation of power was "the only practicable way" to control the labourers.[73] Selborne's inquiries revealed that this power had been much abused, that white supervisors had indiscriminately flogged labourers. He identified this as the principal cause of the recent disturbances. On 13 June, Lawley sent a telegram to the Chamber cancelling this permission. The high commissioner assured Lyttelton that he had absolutely abolished this practice.[74]

After receiving this account, Lyttelton contacted Evans and Milner, both of whom confirmed Evans's story. As Milner reconstructed the situation from his admittedly hazy recollection, there had been a certain amount of "minor trouble with the Chinese in the compounds, insubordination and breaches of discipline too trifling to form the subject of proceedings in a Court, yet which, if not arrested, would have made things impossible." Not only did Milner admit that the government had lost control of the situation, he affirmed that his state was too weak to have even prevented the abuses of power. "Inspectors, being in fact, insufficient, they [illegal floggings] would still have occurred even if it had been proclaimed a capital offence to box a coolie's ears."[75]

After satisfying himself as to the facts, the colonial secretary despatched a telegram to Selborne on 24 October 1905. He commended Selborne's promptitude in eliminating the illegal practices and affirmed the high commissioner's determination to keep disciplinary powers in the hands of the government. In an oblique censure of Selborne's predecessor, Lyttelton added: "But I profoundly regret that corporal punishment, however slight, was authorised without the safeguards of the law, and that the matter was not brought to my notice as Secretary of State before it was authorised."[76]

Selborne expressed his private thoughts on the whole incident in a letter to Milner. Affirming his faith in "the chief," he refused to believe that Milner had given such wide powers to mine managers, many of whom were irresponsible. As a result of Evans's action, "Several of these Mine Managers delegated powers of every kind to subordinate and worthless white men and even to the Chinese police; a great deal of punishment was going on without any pretense of justice; and the Chinaman, who really has a very keen sense of justice, revolted: that is the simple fact."[77]

To Selborne, illegal floggings merely reflected a deeper and larger problem on the compounds: the breakdown of authority. The private sector had shown that it was incapable of keeping its labour force under control. The Randlords had bungled the job badly and, left to their own devices, promised to bring the whole system down. It was essential that the government take matters into its own hands.

As early as 8 June 1905, well before Lyttelton's probing, Selborne had determined to increase government control of compound conditions, especially as regards hospitals and sanitation.[78] He resolved to overhaul the entire system so that it would be an effective instrument for community stability and labour control. On 10 July 1905 Selborne laid out a scheme for the effective maintenance of discipline. In his August despatch to Lyttelton, he explained the details of the plan. "The principle," he declared, "which should be followed throughout is that power must be retained in the hands of the Government, on whom the responsibility for the security of the community rests."[79] All powers of punishment must reside "absolutely" in the state. To make this system effective, the authority of the administration would have to be extended. The existing arrangement whereby breaches of discipline were brought by the mine authorities to resident magistrates for trial by court was:

unsuitable to the peculiar circumstances of the case; unsuitable because it dislocated the mine administration if a number of the principal officials had to be absent all day at the Police Court in order to bring home the charge of riot to half a dozen Chinese; unsuitable because the supply of Chinese interpreters to the Courts had been necessarily inadequate and the Magistrates themselves have felt acutely the difficulties of administering justice under the circumstances; unsuitable because the accused Chinese had not the slightest idea of what was going on or what it all meant, and dissociated the whole proceedings from their previous conceptions of justice.[80]

Thus, Selborne did not intend to curtail the coercive features of the Chinese labour system but rather to rationalize them.

Accordingly, he would endow inspectors of the Foreign Labour Department with judicial authority so that they could try minor breaches of the law and violations of the ordinance or regulations. The officials of the department would be authorized to impose fines, collective or individual, and jail sentences. They could also approve flogging. The ordinance provided for the establishment on each mine of lock-ups, where accused labourers would await an inspector's judgment, which Selborne assured Lyttelton, would come within forty-eight hours after detainment.[81] In addition, the proposed Ordinance laid down stiff penalties for possession of opium. By early August this plan had received the approval of the secretary of state, who later expressed his hope that this would end completely the abusive treatment of the Chinese.[82] The Labour Importation Amendment Ordinance was certain to end illegal flogging in the compounds, for this could now be done legally. Selborne was attempting to make the state's coercive powers effective and accessible by bringing them to the compound itself.

Selborne's plan, however, entailed more than crude methods of enforcing obedience. It was a sophisticated design which sought to maintain order by defusing discontent as well as punishing disobedience. He praised the amendment ordinance for providing the Chinese with a more understandable and accessible legal system. He intended the Foreign Labour Department to stand between employers and employed, to investigate and address the grievances of both. The Chinese, Selborne believed, considered the compound managers employers, not authorities whose decisions were to be obeyed. On the other hand, "they look to the Government, as they should look, as the authority which is impartial between themselves and their employer, to whom they can appeal if they think they are not properly treated, and whose decisions they are prepared to accept without question."[83] Selborne's scheme called for the application of the carrot as well as the stick.

There was little doubt which would be utilized more, considering the needs of industry and the limited leverage that the state had over it. With only ten inspectors, the Transvaal government needed the co-operation of the mining managements. On 18 September, Selborne affirmed to Lyttelton his desire to support industry's mine managers, "on whom such great responsibility rests in connexion with the mines and all the labour on them." In July the lieutenant-governor asked Drummond Chaplin, president of the Chamber, for assistance in making the scheme a success.[84] For his part, J. W. Jamieson, superintendent of the Foreign Labour Department, sent all mine managers a circular letter in which he assured that "the Department will do all that lies in its power to render you every assistance in the management of your Chinese coolies." Three days later, he enjoined his inspectors to work with industry officials "in a sympathetic and friendly spirit." "It is only by cordial co-operation," he admonished, "that one can hope to attain the desired end, namely, an effective supervision and control of the coolies on the Rand." A few sentences later, however, he reminded his subordinates that "your primary duty is to *inspect*."[85]

Relations between the Foreign Labour Department and the Chamber of Mines did not always display the conviviality that Jamieson had hoped for. Indeed, he himself became unpopular with Walter Bagot, the head of the Labour Importation Agency, the organization the industry had established to recruit labour from China. In a letter to William Evans, whom we met earlier in connection with illegal flogging, Bagot explained his reason for leaving the Transvaal in 1907. "I don't think I could stand another 12 months of this drunken bounder

Jamieson who has been given a year's extension."[86] Nor did Selborne always get along smoothly with the magnates. He was most dissatisfied with industry's practice of taking the law into its own hands during disturbances. It had done this during the North Randfontein outbreak when police were called in before the Foreign Labour Department. In July 1905 Selborne discovered that the Chamber had recently issued a circular instructing mine managers that, in the event of a rising, they were not to negotiate with the labourers until the disturbances had been forcibly suppressed. The high commissioner considered this advice foolish in the extreme. An uprising was precisely when the government should step in. The Chinese, Selborne believed, seldom acted without a grievance, and it was the function of the government to provide redress. On 11 July he held a conference with representatives of the Chamber. There, he laid down his policy clearly and forcefully. In the event of an unarmed disturbance, the government would negotiate with the "strikers." If armed, the labourers would be asked to disarm and, once they did so, their complaints would be heard. Only if they refused to disarm should the police intervene.[87] The Chamber was forced to swallow this, and it retracted its circular.

This occasion gave the high commissioner an opportunity to vent his frustration with the industry and the disorderly administration of the Chinese labour system. He complained to Lawley:

The fact is there are too many cooks at work. There is the Chamber of Mines and the Foreign Labour Importation Agency, there is the Chinese Consul, and there is Showers and Jamieson, and they are all rather jealous of each other, including I am afraid Showers of Jamieson. These are all on the spot and can only be coordinated and kept in harmony by a permanent authority also on the spot. All the time there is only one real responsibility and therefore only one final authority, and that is myself ... I also object on principle to a private corporation like the Chamber of Mines issuing semi public instructions as to when or how a department of the government is or is not to act.[88]

In the event, the amendment ordinance did deflect Liberal attacks on the system of labour control, and it did help industry maximize labour productivity in the short run. Contrary to Selborne's wishes, however, it failed to satisfy Chinese grievances. It is an interesting statement on the operation of the ordinance that, while well over a thousand Chinese were convicted each month of various crimes, it proved virtually impossible to secure the conviction of one white compound manager who had admitted to Jamieson that he had illegally flogged coolies. Selborne himself inadvertently offered proof that his state was not powerful enough to ensure Chinese access to it. The Chinese police, on whom were cast many substantial charges of ill-treatment and brib-

ery, effectively obstructed their 'charges' from approaching government officials. Admitting that some of these police had become petty
tyrants, the governor nevertheless considered it unwise to interfere,
for undermining their authority would subvert order. Besides, 'Popular opinion is, as a rule, an adequate safeguard against the abuse of authority; moreover, in a compound, any serious abuse of authority by
the Chinese police would infallibly bring its own retribution at the
hands of the aggrieved coolies.' The last suggestion was an implicit admission that the system had failed to provide a safety valve for the
grievances of Chinese labourers. Their only remedy was to take the law
into their own hands, the very practice which the system set out to prevent. So feeble was the government's strength that the operation of its
ordinance was subverted not only by mining authorities but by the Chinese police. If any further proof of labour discontent was needed, the
booming desertion rates provided it.[89]

In fact, the series of incidents on the Rand since 1905 proved fatal
to the entire labour system. Chinese deserters broke into white, usually Boer, homes near the gold fields, robbing and sometimes killing
the inhabitants. These incidents intensified in the spring of 1906, ter-
rifying local Boer families and outraging the entire Afrikaner community.[90]

In September 1905 the lieutenant-governor met a Boer deputation,
which recounted several instances of robbery and murder. After hearing
their demand for protection, Lawley assured them that both the government and the mining authorities were devoting their attention to the
problem. Louis Botha, a prominent Boer leader, protested that he did
not want the magnates, "who never had the slightest sympathy for the
rest of the population," to present themselves as the protectors of the
general public. "We want protection from the Government and not from
the mines." Botha was clearly asking the impossible, as the government
proved by arming the Boer civilians and authorizing them to arrest without warrant any wandering Chinese. Dissatisfied with Lawley's response,
the deputation resolved on complete repatriation as the only solution.[91]

A year later, well after the adoption of the amended ordinance, the
problem had worsened. Resolutions poured in from distant Boer communities asking for protection. In May another Boer delegation met
Selborne. This time the delegates did not unanimously demand immediate repatriation, but they did condemn the mining industry and
urged that it pay compensation. The demand for white labour was also
raised. Selborne expressed his deepest sympathy and praised their for-
bearance. After pointing to such measures as the issue of arms to Boer
civilians and the deployment of the South African Constabulary around
the Rand, he assured the deputation that the government would continue to do all in its power to end the "outrages."[92]

On 16 May 1906 Het Volk sent a message to the governor which, while recognizing the efforts government had made, pointed to the meagre results that had attended these efforts: "The Transvaal Government have made every effort to stamp out these outrages but owing to a variety of causes, including the large amount of liberty allowed the coolies, and the remissness of many mine managements, they have failed to check the outrages or even to diminish the number of crimes perpetrated on the defenceless rural population. The result is a most lamentable state of unrest in the country, such as has not been known within the memory of man."[93] Het Volk warned that if this condition continued, it would have to send a deputation to Britain to demand immediate repatriation.

In forwarding this message to Elgin, Selborne claimed that the deserters were not fleeing repressive compound conditions but rather their creditors. Most of them were, he claimed, ruined gamblers. The recent troubles, he concluded, proved to him that control over the labourers had been too lax, not too strict.[94]

On hearing of the Boer deputation to the governor, the colonial secretary warned, "if causes are to be assigned to the want of confidence in rapid future expansion to which a depletion of the population bears testimony, one of the most important seems undoubtedly to be the lack of success in controlling the Chinese labourers, which has given rise to strong feelings and to agitation."[95] Elgin certainly appreciated the irony of the situation.

The high commissioner was fully alive to the serious threat the situation posed to the industry and in 1906 he appointed a committee to investigate. Privately, he tried to exhort the industry's leaders to take measures to sooth Boer wrath. In May he impressed George Farrar of the Anglo-French mining group with the gravity of the situation and with the industry's responsibility. "I say that the responsibility rests in this quarter [mining's] because the Chinese agitation had entirely died down at home and this possibly fatal second phase of it was fanned into existence by the outburst of Chinese outrages, and the outrages are, in my opinion, mainly, if not wholly due to this mismanagement."[96] Lionel Phillips responded very unenthusiastically to Selborne's suggestions. The mines could not afford to pay for police patrols of the Rand perimeter or for men to guard Boer homes, both of which Selborne had recommended. Fencing was also too expensive for Phillips to contemplate. Finally, the high commissioner's advice that the industry compensate victims could lead, Phillips warned, to serious legal complications, for it might be construed as admitting liability.[97] Three months later Selborne pleaded with de Jongh, the new Chamber president, to offer such compensation. "It was not a question of legal right; it is simply a question of common sense and wisdom."[98] Not even this appeal brought action.

The special committee which investigated the problem joined Selborne in attributing the desertions to gambling debts, "bad characters," and the opium habit. The lax control on the part of the mines compounded the problem. It recommended restricting the areas to which the Chinese could go on pass, tightening the issue of permits, and fencing the mines. It is doubtful that these measures would have solved the problem. If the Chinese had managed to evade the South African Constabulary, they almost certainly would not be impeded by fences or permits. In any case, the Liberal government refused to approve the committee's recommendations, for these imposed new restrictions on the Chinese.[99]

The crisis brought out the tension between industry and state. On the committee were both Jamieson and Bagot. Attached to its report were memoranda from both. Bagot blamed the outrages on the Foreign Labour Department, whose intermediary position between employer and employed "struck at the very root of discipline." It would be better, he urged, to have the Chinese express grievances to the mine managers. Jamieson, in rebuttal, reproduced a letter he had earlier written to Bagot, and in it he declared that "the coolie with a legitimate grievance stands a poor chance of having his wrongs righted if he is confined to making his representations through the chain of individuals placed in authority over him."[100]

For his part, Selborne let off steam to Milner. He asked rhetorically: "What do you think of mines that refuse to have a single white man who can speak a word of Chinese? What do you think of mines who issue passes absolutely wholesale, without dates, place, name of Chinaman, or anything on them? What do you think of mines who allow Chinese police to control everything, the so-called Chinese police being the biggest ruffians of the lot?"

The high commissioner was exasperated by the Chamber's shortsightedness.

But the longer I am here the more impressed I am with the amazing amount of inefficiency and incapacity there is among the mine managements. It all arises from this cursed absenteeism of the really responsible people. In many cases so long as working costs are kept down and no expenditure whatever takes place for which the return is not immediate and direct the officials on the spot are left to do exactly what they please and be as slack as they like; but if it comes to any expenditure, however necessary and wise, for which an immediate and direct dividend is not promised, then the most short-sighted and indefensible parsimony prevails.[101]

Selborne's diatribe was not without justification. There was little, however, he could do besides fume. The mining industry had injured its own interests for short-term gain. Before the Chinese housebreak-ings became an issue, the Boers had considerably softened their stance on Chinese labour. This issue helped to revive old antagonisms which, unlike before, would soon be given play in a responsible legislature.

Milner had been able to ignore colonial opinion because he had had imperial backing. There was no question where the Liberals stood on this issue. Indeed, as the anti-Chinese provision in the new respon-sible constitution showed, they were positively hostile to labour impor-tation. For his part, Selborne fully believed that the Transvaal could not count on the 'imperial factor,' especially when it was influenced by the Radicals. "They are a crowd of dangerous lunatics I say! The Em-pire cannot survive much of them."[102]

Without the backing of the imperial government, Selborne depended more than ever on the Transvaal state. But Chinese labour had exposed its deficiencies as well as its strengths. Selborne was able to moderate Liberal policy and in some cases (for example, wage policy) thwart it; he could assist the industry in controlling its labour force on the Rand mines and in maximizing their productivity when on the premises; and he could prevent the industry from extreme recklessness during actual disturbances. But the Transvaal government proved unable to exercise control over the labour force. It could not satisfy the immediate require-ments of industry and maintain, at the same time, the political stability so vital for investment. Moreover, the state lacked a mechanism for ab-sorbing Boer opposition, or at least containing its discontent. And, fi-nally, it failed to protect the mining industry from its own short-sightedness. There was no lack of trying or vision on Selborne's part. To control the Chinese, for example, he promulgated a sophisticated de-sign which could tolerate resistance but keep it within reasonable limits. He realized that if he were to foster progress, he would have to assist the mining industry, not simply by fulfilling its labour imperatives (which of course he did try to do), but also by remaining above it to guide it and to integrate its activities with the rest of the country. Selborne was a mod-ern leader, but his state was not quite up to the task. Despite its 'coercive apparatus,' his police state could not even police.

The situation was, however, far from hopeless, for Milner had laid foundations, which, if widened and reinforced, could support a power-ful polity. The withdrawal of imperial support forced the colony upon its own resources, which were not inconsiderable. Moreover, Transvaal politicians seemed more than willing to take command of the colony and force it to stand on its own two feet. A re-evaluation of the Trans-vaal's political status seemed a logical first step.

4 Bleak Prospects: Selborne and the Constitutional Settlement

The labour controversy served to focus the Liberal government's attention on the question of the Transvaal's future constitutional position. For Selborne, the labour question constituted the most important influence on his political views. The Liberals' apparent determination to terminate importation threatened the Rand's labour supply and, consequently, its economic health as well as its loyalty to Britain. These considerations drove Selborne to embrace self-government as the only way to eliminate in the future what he saw as baneful Liberal interference with the Transvaal economy.[1]

As we have seen, on the outbreak of war in 1899, Selborne prepared a minute summarizing his views on the political settlement. He put forward the traditional war aims which the prime minister, Lord Salisbury, had articulated publicly: British supremacy in South Africa and full political rights for the Uitlanders. Though he alluded to the "necessary revolution in the spirit of Government," he did not indicate how he would restructure the old polity to bring it into line with the revolutionized Transvaal economy.[2]

His thinking developed after his arrival in South Africa. Early in 1908 he reflected to his old mentor, Joseph Chamberlain, on developments over the past decade. He considered the war necessary for South Africa and the Empire. The South African Republic "was the embodiment of ignorance, stagnation, obscurantism, provincialism, and corruption, as well as of racial dominance and bitter hatred of every thing English."[3] Kruger had threatened progress as well as paramountcy. "The war, therefore, was really fought on two immense issues. Was South Africa to become an united, progressive, modern State? Was it to remain a part of the British Empire?"[4] The Treaty of Vereeniging had helped to settle the second question and reconstruction would resolve the first. Selborne saw it as his task to promote these twin objects, to keep South Africa on British tracks towards progress.

In Selborne's mind the two considerations were related, and giving political preponderance to the British element went hand-in-glove with promoting material prosperity. In regard to the Transvaal constitution, he identified four essentials: a wide suffrage to embrace British workers, an Upper House, the automatic redistribution of seats, and, most important, the voters' basis of representation. "If I had failed to get any one of these," he recounted to his former associate at the Admiralty, Ernest Pretyman, "I should have resigned."[5] The British settlers in the Transvaal tended to be single adult males, while the Boers tended to live in family units. Although the Boer population, counting women and children, was far larger than the British, the number of voters (that is, white males) was roughly equivalent between the two ethnic groups. If legislative seats were assigned on the basis of population, the Boers would dominate the Assembly, but if seats were assigned merely in proportion to the number of voters in a given area, then British representation might equal the Boer. The one-vote, one-value principle thus favoured the Rand, which was the centre of economic development as well as British political strength.

In 1905 conditions within the Transvaal seemed perilous indeed. The Afrikaners appeared as a united threat to all of Selborne's hopes, while the English-speaking population was split into various political factions. European divisions in the Transvaal confounded Milner. Though only a quarter of the colony's population in 1904, the white ruling caste fragmented sharply into a complex array of opposing groups: Boer versus Briton, town versus country, capitalist versus non-capitalist. In fact, the bourgeoisie itself divided into commercial and industrial sectors, whose interests, as we have seen, often diverged.

Except for the handful of settlers that Milner had managed to lure to the Transvaal countryside, the estimated one hundred thousand British resided in urban areas as merchants, mine owners, or skilled mineworkers.[6] With its high proportion of single men, the English-speaking community favoured a constitutional settlement which gave prominent representation to town dwellers and which made voters, as opposed to population, the basis of representation. It united on little else. The influential British colonists who opposed the Milner regime formed the Responsible Government Association in 1904; this was committed to promoting immediate self-government. Most of the

Rand capitalists, on the other hand, clung to Milner and established the Progressive Association to represent their interests.

The political position of white labour defies precise description. Soon after their arrival on the Rand, white miners organized into various associations and by 1902 had created a strong industrial union, the Transvaal Miners' Association, which a decade later boasted six thousand members. In addition, various political organizations, most notably the Witwatersrand Trades and Labour Council, claimed to represent the European proletariat.[7] Despite the radicalism of the political leaders, both Milner and Selborne doubted that these men really spoke the mind of the rank and file. It seems both proconsuls were correct, and Donald Denoon has concluded that the white workers on the Rand constituted a labour aristocracy which could cause trouble but which industry could usually buy off.[8] This does not, of course, make their political posture any more predictable. Though no hard data exist regarding their political preferences, it is not unlikely that white miners cast votes for all parties. And though docile in 1905, the European workforce might not always remain so, and Selborne, in particular, dreaded the importation of "Australian socialist tendencies."

The estimated 140,000 Afrikaners had their divisions too, though Milner did not appreciate this. Most of the Boers resided on the farms. War, drought, and pestilence had thrown the rural areas into dire poverty. Moreover, as capitalism infiltrated the countryside, certain notables accumulated land and reoriented production for the market.[9] These economic changes conspired with demographic trends against the lowest social strata of the Boer population, forcing countless young men and women off the land.[10]

Despite these tensions, the Afrikaner notables proved able to assert political control and prevent open schism. In January 1905, after Milner had announced his proposals for representative government, the Boers organized themselves formally into the Het Volk party. By April, the dissident British of The Responsible Government Association had concluded a pact with the Afrikaner leaders, with whom they issued a joint manifesto affirming loyalty to the imperial connection but urging full self-government. While they reached no agreement on the basis of representation (population or voters), they did agree that the Labour Importation Ordinance should remain operative for five years.[11]

Naturally, the new governor looked to the Progressives for support. Not only did he identify them as the dynamic element in the country, but he remembered the loyal support they had given the Lyttelton Constitution. Their political program, which included one man, one vote and automatic redistribution, accorded well with imperial interests and with Selborne's own thinking. These considerations made him receptive to Milner's exhortation to absorb the capitalists into the polity. As Sir Alfred had advised his successor in early 1905; "The material is there. What strikes me about the Johannesburg crowd is that, while there is a lot of frothy ambition on the surface, and certainly a most abominable and thick sediment, inter-national or denationalised scalawags of every kind in thousands, *the central body of the community* is of very good stuff."[12] For their part, the Progressives needed the cooperation of the state, especially in procuring labour. An ample basis therefore existed for a working partnership.

During his tenure, Selborne maintained close relations with certain magnates and secured the confidence of some, but by no means all, of the capitalist community. He described Drummond Chaplin as "a fine fighting man" and considered George Farrar and Percy FitzPatrick a valuable team together.[13] Selborne's efforts on the capitalists' behalf prompted Farrar to remark in gratitude, "I feel that wherever possible you have done your utmost for us. I know your sympathies are with us."[14]

One can, however, exaggerate Selborne's intimacy with the Randlords. Several magnates lacked the faith in Selborne that they had possessed in Milner. While some criticized his weak leadership, others charged that he did not assign a sufficient political role to Progressive men. In early 1906, FitzPatrick had complained to Sir Julius Wernher: "Lord Selborne, I think, has yet to learn, how enormously he would gain by allowing other people to speak for him more than he does. Apart from the effect of corroborative evidence, which is always strong, there is the other point that it stimulates the sense of loyalty and duty to him, and it even develops an enthusiasm, which, of course, you can never get from people who are deprived of all sense of responsibility."[15] Though most believed that Selborne was ultimately on their side, some even doubted this. In the view of G. G. Robinson, formerly Milner's private secretary, "Lord Selborne is plainly not *very* sympathetic to them [capitalists]."[16]

The feelings were mutual. Milner had warned that certain Randlords might prove unreliable.[17] Selborne's experience in South Africa confirmed this prognosis and, worse still, gave him little confidence in the political abilities of even trustworthy capitalists. "The real root of our trouble," he wrote his old cabinet colleague, St John Brodrick, in 1908, "is not the Boers but the British; by which I mean that the political incapacity of my beloved countrymen is a greater source of difficulty and a greater danger than all possible racial hostility on the part of the Boers."[18] He was referring here to the Progressives' political manoeuvrings before the National Convention, but his differences with them arose earlier and involved more than merely political tactics. He, unlike them, appreciated the need to establish a consensus among Transvaal whites for the political regime and its policies.

Milner's "phalanx" of Randlords was too thin, too top-heavy to prevail over the well-drilled, if unprogressive, political commandos lying in wait. Selborne eagerly devoted himself to completing Milner's unfinished state edifice, but, to ensure its permanence, he wished to widen its foundations. Though determined to fulfil capitalist imperatives, he was less inclined than his predecessor to entrust this task to the capitalists themselves. In 1908 Chamberlain commended his former undersecretary for having the wisdom "to keep well with the Boers and not to confine yourself entirely to the support of the mine owning British class."[19]

Selborne's attitude towards the Boers displayed a curious mixture of suspicion, arrogance, and sympathy. Shortly after his arrival in South Africa he conducted an extensive tour of country districts. This gave him a chance to learn more about the Afrikaners and to demonstrate his paternalistic concern for them.[20] In his person, he brought the state to country districts, emphasizing its presence there. To his close friend Sir Stafford Northcote he revealed his impressions. The average Boer, he asserted, was unprogressive and uneducated. Though they called themselves farmers, the Afrikaners knew little about agricultural methods and cared even less. The problem was largely racial, for extensive contact with blacks had caused the Boer stock to deteriorate. "But yet," he declared, "I believe they are capable of great things in the future, if contact with Britishers is substituted for contact with natives and above all if they get educated." Teachers in government schools had, in fact, attested to the Afrikaners' natural capacity to learn.[21] Selborne intended to develop the race.

The Boer politicians, however, presented a problem. As politically indifferent as Selborne considered the average Boer to be, the Afrikaner rank and file would, he predicted, slavishly follow their leaders. The Boer elite, he surmised, had abandoned the strategy of armed insurrection but not the aim of independence. However hostile the governor was towards this ideal, he understood the patriotism that produced it. As he confided to Milner, "My great protection against Boer slimness is that, baring [sic] the lieing [sic], I so thoroughly sympathise with their point of view. If I were a Boer I should be absolutely irreconcilable and I should spend my life in seeking for occasion to regain my independence by the use of any political opportunity which the folly of my enemies afforded me, or by arms, and I should with difficulty refrain from murdering anyone who talked to me of conciliation."[22]

Fearing that the Afrikaners would patiently bide their time until the moment came to strike for independence, Selborne resolved to deny them this chance. Unlike Milner, however, he did not see the Boers as simply an obstacle to the grand design. Instead, he would incorporate them into it. To Asquith he remarked, "The fact is that they are a very remarkable people, and they are far too good and valuable to lose for the British Empire."[23] To exploit this valuable resource, the leaders had to be tamed or thwarted and the Boer mass subjected to a new order which would prod them into modernity. This required both the carrot and the stick.

The governor was eager to use state power to relieve agricultural distress in the predominantly Boer countryside. To inject capital into rural areas, he proposed a land bank scheme. As he indicated to Alfred Lyttelton, a land bank "will tend to bind the mass of the farming community to the Government, by ties of material interest." The proposal, however, was more than a political strategem, for the farmers' plight caused Selborne great anxiety. When his proposal came into operation after self-government, it significantly restructured class relations in the countryside.[24]

The fusion of economic and political aims also appeared in Selborne's thinking on land settlement. To be sure, he believed, as Milner had, that British settlers would "leaven the Boer lump" in political terms, but Selborne was more concerned than his predecessor with the social ramifications of this policy. These immigrants would, he believed, modernize agricultural methods in a way which the unprogressive Boer farmers could not. Moreover, the land settlement scheme would erode racial differences and help to integrate the Afrikaners into a new social order. "The great misfortune hitherto has been," he observed to Lord Elgin,

that practically speaking, the British have been confined to the towns and the Boers to the country districts, and they have not been brought together in the habits of daily life, or as neighbours or in the exercise of their avocations. Now a double movement is going on, which I will do my utmost to foster. Many poor Boers are coming into the towns to work on the mines and in other branches of industry, while the younger sons of the more prosperous Boers are being trained in the Transvaal Technical Institute as mining engineers. This is the commencement of the Boers taking their proper place in the industrial and urban life in the country.[25]

Selborne's British supremacy exacted from the Boers more than a single oath of fealty to the king.

To the new governor in 1905, British supremacy did, of course, entail denying political power to Het Volk. The Lyttelton Constitution promised to do just this, and Selborne set about to implement its provisions as soon as he arrived. The political turbulence there, however, made his task exceedingly difficult and soon forced him to re-evaluate the Lyttelton scheme altogether.

In November 1905 he cabled home that the Progressives urged increasing the number of constituencies to forty-five or fifty. The astonished colonial secretary, backed by Colonial Office officials, urged the high commissioner to discourage the notion. On 22 November, Selborne reported that the Executive Council also wished to expand the Assembly, recommending an increase to sixty members.[26] Five days later he gave a more complete explanation for the Progressive proposal. Recounting an interview he had conducted with Farrar and Fitz-Patrick on the 21st, he observed:

The real point of their representations is that the advent of full self-government is not a matter of years but of months. Feeling confident of a majority in the new Legislative Assembly the rank and file of the Progressive party have no longer any cause to fear the advent of full self-government. If when the Legislative Assembly meets His Majesty's Government is not in sympathy with their political views it will, in Sir G. Farrar's and Sir P. Fitzpatrick's opinion, require only the slightest inducement to lead the Progressive Party into an immediate agitation for full self-government, a movement which these gentlemen will be obliged to lead as the only alternative to losing all influence over the members of their own party.

This demand, Selborne continued, would prove irresistible. In such a contingency an enlarged Assembly would ensure a smooth constitutional transition.[27]

At the Colonial Office, Sir Montagu Ommanney could not understand why the Progressives' confidence in a majority would induce them to advocate responsible government. After all, their majority would remain just as secure under the Lyttelton system.[28] Ommanney's perplexity was understandable, for Selborne had omitted to mention certain salient features of his interview with the Progressive leaders. FitzPatrick, according to his own account, told the governor that rank and file members of his association complained of his [Selborne's] high-handed indifference towards their views. In FitzPatrick's words, "Our people said to us at once. – 'Unsatisfactory as this [Selborne's educational policy] is in itself, it also throws an entirely fresh light upon the other two matters – the modus vivendi and Railway Unification. Anyday we may wake up and find that they are settled upon lines contrary to our interests and wishes. There is absolutely no safeguard except Responsible Government, and you know it.' "[29]

On 12 December, Selborne again urged the Progressives' proposals on the Colonial Office and gave them his personal support. His message, however, did not reach Unionist hands, for the Liberals had just assumed office. Winston Churchill, the new undersecretary, minuted that the controversies over the Lyttelton scheme made it desirable to reopen the entire constitutional question.[30] With the Liberal accession to power, the issues that had plagued Selborne receded as the larger question of responsible government came to the fore.

When the Unionist government fell in December 1905, Selborne became the servant of his political opponents. His old friends in the Liberal party immediately reassured him of their support. Especially kind, Richard B. Haldane, the incoming war secretary, called Selborne's continuing contribution to the Empire "a very great one, and as generous and high minded as it has been great."[31] The cabinet itself saw glowing praise of the high commissioner in a letter from Roderick Jones to Baron de Reuter. Jones remarked that "Liberals themselves could hardly get a man more after their own heart – he is very popular with the Boers, and is admired by the English. He is respected because he is quite independent of party, including the financial Houses, who certainly have not the influence with him that they exercised over Lord Milner."[32]

Lord Elgin, who had just become secretary of state for the colonies, met little objection when, for the sake of continuity, he decided to retain Selborne. For his part, Selborne resolved to stay at his post unless the Chinese were immediately repatriated or the voters' basis taken away.[33] His confidence that he could protect these vitals was bolstered by Milner, who wrote reassuringly that "To do something wh[ich] will look nice and 'pro-Boer' and especially wh[ich] can be represented as 'against the capitalists' but which will really not make very much difference – that is, I expect what would suit the majority of the Cabinet best." The government would, he predicted, content itself with insubstantial measures "to placate, or throw dust in the eyes of their more fanatical followers."[34] As time would tell, the fanatical followers were not easily placated.

In late 1905 Selborne still considered the Boers a more immediate threat to the Empire than was the House of Commons. At the end of November he expressed his dread of a Boer ministry to Sir Edward Grey, soon to be foreign secretary in the Liberal cabinet. No British would get any consideration except the magnates, who would buy it.[35] Elaborating on his fears, he painted a gloomy scenario to H.H. Asquith, chancellor of the exchequer, in which the Afrikaner leaders would slowly but inexorably diminish British influence until they had achieved their ideal of a Dutch Republic of South Africa. They would, he predicted, replace English officials with Boer ones, gerrymander constituencies, and, when the opportunity arose, take South Africa out

of the Empire. A Boer accession to power under a responsible government would mark the first step back to Krugerism.[36] In December the
colonial secretary received Selborne's formal memorandum reproduc-
ing these points in a milder form. Toning down his pro-British sympathies, Selborne argued blandly that the first elections would be
conducted on ethnic lines and that, whichever side won, it would govern the other badly. He further cited the education in parliamentary
methods which a representative constitution would provide.

Whatever the merits of this advice, it contained a danger which Selborne fully realized. Though representative government might protect
the Transvaal British from the Boers, it would also leave them vulnerable to the Liberal government. At the end of his memorandum to Elgin, the governor addressed this problem squarely:

If, however, His Majesty's Government decided to take action in respect of
such a matter as the importation of Chinese labour, which affects the industrial
and economical existence, and even the daily bread, of such a large proportion of the British population, irrespective of the opinion of the people of the
country, then I would run any risk inseparable from the immediate introduction of responsible government rather than that situation should arise, because, genuinely loyal as the majority of the British of the Transvaal are, they
would, rightly or wrongly, think they had been deeply wronged, and the conviction of wrong coming on top of the loss of employment, of the absence even
of daily bread, would excite a feeling which I should regard with grave apprehension.[37]

Better the Boers than radical fanatics.

One need not read too far between the lines to see the Chinese labour issue behind Selborne's political thinking. Besides alienating the
Progressives, the removal of the Chinese would, he considered, have
been ruinous to the South African economy. If forced to choose between the Lyttelton Constitution and the continuation of Chinese labour, he would clearly opt for the latter. As Liberal policy unfolded, he
came to believe that he faced precisely this choice. It became quite apparent that Liberal rule meant interference with the Rand's labour
supply. Responsible government might not. As the governor forecast to
Elgin, the Boers would not repatriate the Chinese, for it was not in
their interest to do so.[38] The provision in the Responsible–Het Volk
pact that would leave the importation ordinance operative for five
years confirmed Selborne's prognosis.[39] Citing the Chinese issue as an
important factor in his own advocacy of responsible government, Sir
Richard Solomon, the Transvaal attorney general, forthrightly told the
high commissioner:

I feel, whatever might be said against it, that Chinese labour in this Colony is a necessity ... His Majesty's Government have announced that there shall be no further importation of Chinese labour except with the approval of the people of the country. I am not afraid of the decision of a parliament under Responsible Government on this question. The responsibility of getting rid of Chinese labour will not, in my opinion, be undertaken by any Government here responsible to the people for the prosperity of the country, and that Government would get sufficient support in Parliament for continuing the policy of Chinese labour, with such safeguards as Parliament may deem necessary.[40]

In August 1906 Selborne confessed to his old boss, Alfred Lyttelton, his own preference for responsible government, given the recent course of Liberal policy.[41] When he tendered his political advice in December and January, however, he had yet to learn where Campbell-Bannerman and his Liberal government were going.

The transition in Selborne's thinking reflected, to some extent, currents of opinion in South Africa. He supported importation himself, but he also feared the alienation of the local British if the Chinese were withdrawn. On 13 January 1906, in response to Elgin's query, the high commissioner admitted that, while neither FitzPatrick nor Farrar favoured responsible government, the Progressive party would come out for it in the event of a conflict with the imperial government over the labour question, provided that a Progressive majority seemed likely.[42] The next month Selborne confided to his old friend Baron Northcote that if the Liberals proscribed indentured labour in the constitution, "This would mean Boston harbour over again."[43] The capitalist press confirmed his analysis. Though it feared industry's prospects under a Boer government, *South African Mines Commerce and Industries* confidently predicted that "the Colony can be relied on to vote for industrial expansion and increased prosperity."[44]

It was not only fear of repatriation which aroused the Transvaal British but also the aspersions cast on them by the Radical press. In February Selborne reported a mass meeting in Johannesburg repudiating Liberal allegations of Chinese mistreatment. A month later he warned Elgin of the "grave concern I feel at the growing estrangement between a large section of the Liberal Party and British Colonists throughout South Africa."[45] In a typically bitter editorial, *South African Mines Commerce and Industries* condemned the Liberal government for bringing on an industrial crisis by threatening the labour supply and by creating a political instability which frightened investors.

Whatever is the result of the present controversy, the new Liberal Government cannot escape the blame of having done lasting injury to the most progressive

Colony in the Empire. It has practiced calumny and cowardice to an extent unparalleled in the political history of the Mother-Country. It has told us that
there is an organised system of slavery on the Rand, and yet it allows the system
to continue! Hasten the day, we say then, when the Transvaal will be beyond
the influence of Downing Street.[46]

It seems that by February 1906 a substantial element of capitalist opinion came to see responsible government as the only way to save the labour supply, achieve political stability, and escape Liberal rule.

While most officials in the Colonial Office supported Selborne's December advice to retain the March Letter Patent, Liberal politicians
showed ambivalence on the issue. Elgin noted in a memorandum that
he could not address Selborne's proposal for an increase of seats until
the government had decided whether or not to retain the Letters
Patent. The government needed more information on local opinion.
On 20 December 1905 the cabinet established a small committee to
investigate the matter.[47] The imperial government remained undecided three weeks later when Elgin cabled Selborne that his proposals
were still under consideration. The colonial secretary requested information as to the views of the various local parties and instructed the
high commissioner to postpone the work of the Delimitation Committee, which had been appointed to demarcate constituencies for the
Lyttelton Constitution.[48]

The day after receiving this, Selborne telegraphed back his protest
at the proposed delay, which he warned might make it impossible to
convene an Assembly by year's end. This presented an alarming prospect in view of the mounting volume of government business which
the moribund Legislative Council could not appropriately address. A
week later, he singled out one issue which needed an Assembly's immediate attention: "The only subject on which anxiety is still being felt by
the members of the industrial and commercial community here is lest
the reconsideration by His Majesty's Government of the constitutional
arrangements of the Transvaal should lead to the final settlement of
the question of the importation of Chinese labourers being deferred
until after July next. The mining industry cannot afford to have the settlement of the question indefinitely delayed."[49] The deepening depression helps explain Selborne's sense of urgency. On 22 February,
he sent a desperate telegram to the secretary of state. In this he reported that, according to "one of the best men in Johannesburg," the
political uncertainty had caused widespread distress. His informer, a
principal worker in the Rand Aid Association, depicted a gloomy situation: banks were tightening credit and calling in loans; building operations had come to a standstill; and applications for relief had increased

by 30 per cent over the past six weeks. South Africa, Selborne warned, was treading on the brink of a financial collapse. The next day at the Chamber of Mines' general meeting, Drummond Chaplin charged that the present political suspense frustrated capital investment, which the Rand so desperately needed. Confident that a self-governing Transvaal would act sensibly on the labour issue, he called for some government, any government, as soon as possible. Throughout the next month, Selborne continued to send off resolutions from chambers of commerce, mayors, and various other public bodies condemning the political delay.[50]

Throughout January and early February, the Liberals studied the constitutional issue and moved steadily towards the responsible government solution. In his numerous minutes Churchill gave the best expression of Liberal reasoning. He predicted that the Lyttelton Constitution would prove an unworkable half-way house, producing deadlock after deadlock. By refusing supplies, the elected members of the Assembly would eventually wrench responsible government from imperial authorities and proceed to dictate constitutional terms: "What we might have given with courage and distinction both at home and in South Africa, upon our own terms, in the hour of our strength, will be jerked and twisted from our hands – without grace of any kind – not perhaps without humiliation – at a time when the Government may be greatly weakened and upon terms in the settlement of which we shall have only a nominal influence."[51] The imperial government could best retain influence by the concession of self-government now. Moreover, Britain must try to build a consensus of imperial support in South Africa. "British authority ... must stand on two legs." Under Unionist policy, it rested on only one – the Progressive party. By granting responsible government, the Liberals could create a broader base of support and provide the means for its articulation.[52]

Besides these strategic considerations, Chinese labour furnished a strong motive to transfer full authority to the Transvaal. So long as Britain controlled the executive, Churchill argued, it would bear responsibility for a policy which it found distasteful and for which it would face attacks in the House of Commons.[53] The lord chancellor, Lord Loreburn, considered it "intolerable that an Imperial Executive should be called upon to carry out a practice detestable to the great majority of our people in obedience to the vote of a Colonial legislature." The Chinese issue, he continued, made it imperative that self-government be implemented by July.[54] On 3 January 1906 the cabinet, though undecided on the political settlement, tied it to the labour question when it decided that a really representative assembly was needed to solve the Chinese problem. On 13 February the cabinet resolved definitely to recall the Lyttelton Constitution and to issue Letters Patent for full self-government. The government, however, would not draft these until it had the report of an official inquiry. Five days later, Selborne was advised by telegram of the Liberals' decision.[55]

On this issue, it is clear that the Liberals acted on the basis of their own consciences and calculations, since they overrode the advice of both the Colonial Office and their man on the spot. Neither the Progressives nor Smuts directly influenced their decision, though, of course, considerations of future Boer loyalty figured prominently in their thinking. The government was not, however, as free as Churchill had proclaimed.[56] Haldane explained the situation to the high commissioner:

The position has been difficult for us in a way which is hardly conceivable to you. Indeed, it cannot be conceived by anyone who was not through the late General Election. The country has swung violently over. Probably it will in course of time swing just as violently the other way; but, just now, parliament is dominated by a majority over which no minister can exercise control, excepting within very narrow limits. Our whole energies have been directed to averting catastrophies, which once or twice have been pretty near.[57]

The shifting political climate was noticed even at the Colonial Office, from where Fred Graham, a senior official, declared "never have I known such a complete reversal of policy, nor a House of Commons so meddlesome and difficult to satisfy."[58] Selborne came to see it as his primary duty to insulate South Africa from the Westminster gale.

Well before he learned the outcome of Liberal deliberations on responsible government, Selborne started pressing for the one-vote, one-value principle as the basis of representation, whatever the constitution. This, to Selborne, as to Progressives of the FitzPatrick stamp, was the essential political issue. He confided to both Lyttelton and Haldane that he would resign if overruled on this point.[59] Selborne, of course, embraced the voters' principle because it favoured the progressive (that is, British) element, and he prepared a variety of arguments supporting this basis. In December 1905 he had commended it to Elgin as simple, logical, and democratic. As to the Afrikaners' claim that their "permanence" entitled them to more representation, the high commissioner retorted that the British element, though individually fluctuating, was just as permanent in the aggregate. Moreover, the British population paid 90 per cent of the taxes.[60] Colonial Office officials divided on this question. While H.W. Just appreciated the last argument, A.B. Keith found it "dangerous."[61] In a personal letter to Elgin, Selborne expanded on this logic. Not only did the British provide the bulk of taxable wealth, they contained most of the colony's experience. He declared, "there is no forward movement in the country either intellectual or material which does not emanate from the British."[62]

To give additional force to his argument, the governor brought local pressure to bear on London. At the end of January he reported great unrest within the "loyalist" camp over the uncertainty of Liberal policy. The pro-British politician A. Woolls Sampson was organizing a mass meeting of veterans to promote the principles of one vote, one value, single-member constituencies, and automatic redistribution. Any deviation from these lines, Selborne warned, would produce "a convulsion of political feeling here."[63] Less than a week later Selborne returned to the charge, assuring Elgin that the voters' basis would not throw all power to the Rand. It would also give substantial representation to the moderate British.

After this bombardment of local British opinion, Elgin cautioned Selborne against identifying himself too closely with one particular point of view. Moreover, one cabinet member, the colonial secretary admonished, "was becoming a little anxious that you were pressing us too hard."[64] In response, the governor replied that he had only expressed his personal views confidentially to the colonial secretary. Moreover, "believing as I do that we are at the turning point which is going to decide whether South Africa remains British or not, I could not have said less than I have." The reason he only furnished British views, he wrote in a later letter, was that he had received no information himself on Boer opinion, at least since July. Indeed, he did not even learn of Smuts's visit to Europe until he read about it in the papers.[65]

Although the high commissioner gave little information as to Boer sentiment, he did report on labour's posture throughout the first half of 1906. In a long letter to Asquith he strenuously argued that, though dependent on the mining industry, the white workers were not the tools of the capitalists. Among the British population generally, "there is a natural and not unwholesome jealousy ... towards the capitalists."[66] When, however, labour organizations forwarded views so independent that they ran counter to his own, Selborne was quick to discredit them. Thus, he denounced the Transvaal Political Labour League, which came out for the population basis, as racist, sending Elgin a proposal by labour leader Peter Whiteside to exclude coloureds from white tram cars. The TPLL, Selborne remarked, had only eight hundred members. When the Witwatersrand Trades and Labour Council drew close to Het Volk, the high commissioner noted the council's scanty membership and observed, "Anything more incongruous than such an alliance can hardly be imagined." The leader of the Independent Labour League,

J.T. Bain, was, the governor advised, a professional agitator, formerly employed by Kruger to sow dissension between capital and labour.[67]

As Selborne's despatches formed the major source of information for the Colonial Office, not surprisingly it shared the high commissioner's views. After receiving Selborne's despatch on the TPLL, Graham saw no need to consider seriously the "ill-considered proposals of a dormant, perhaps moribund, body of 800 members in no sense representative of the white wage earners in the Transvaal."[68]

As to the voters' basis, a substantial body of Liberals favoured the principle and appreciated the dangers of delay which Selborne had depicted so vividly. In his first memorandum on the Transvaal Constitution, Churchill cited, as one advantage of responsible government, the fact that the imperial government could prescribe its basis. Advancing the principle of one vote, one value as symmetrical, logical, and democratic, he remarked, "It is not often that democratic principles are helpful in Imperial Administration. When they are they should be cherished." In a subsequent memorandum, he argued that, the refusal to adopt the voters' basis, which he observed (probably from Selborne's despatches) the entire British community in South Africa had declared for, would engender among the English-speaking population a sense of betrayal. In a February memo, he further cautioned that Selborne's loud advocacy for the voters' basis might make it politically impossible for him to accept anything less. The next month, after reading Selborne's urgent telegrams, Churchill warned that "the vexation, and, indeed, exasperation which is produced in an arrogant, highly excitable population by the feeling that their most vital interests are held in suspense from day to day, and even from month to month, may provoke a bitter hatred against His Majesty's Government." He advocated putting the voters' basis in the inquiry's terms of reference.[69] Even Elgin was impressed with the necessity of haste. He saw no reason for the committee of inquiry. Certainly the principles of the constitution could be better decided in Britain than South Africa. Indeed, "I can imagine nothing more directly calculated to increase political agitation and the dangers of the situation."[70]

Despite these sentiments, the cabinet refused to endorse explicitly the voters' basis. The telegram announcing the government's policy asserted that it would await the committee's report on this point.[71] Why the cabinet refused to declare itself is unclear, but one obvious reason was the desire to make the constitutional settlement appear as fair as possible.

However non-committal the February declaration appeared, Selborne received several assurances on the adoption of the voters' basis. In March Churchill wrote that, if he read between the lines, the governor would see that the committee's terms of reference tacitly presupposed the one-vote, one-value principle. In April Elgin telegraphed a summary of the undersecretary's speech in Commons where he came out strongly for this principle. Even Milner wrote that the government would probably preserve the Lyttelton basis of representation. Asquith too embraced the principle and on 11 April, Haldane told the high commissioner that he could take the voters' basis as settled in principle.[72] Less than a week earlier, the committee, chaired by Sir Joseph West Ridgeway, a distinguished veteran of the colonial service, had set sail for South Africa.

In contrast to Liberal suppositions as to Selborne's Progressive bias, the high commissioner, in fact, favoured the accession to power of a moderate, non-capitalist British party, under the leadership of Richard Solomon. As early as February, he wrote his attorney general that "such a ministry must be free from the dominating influence either of the Capitalists or of Het Volk and that it must command the confidence of the majority of born British subjects, colonial born and working men alike, whose opinions are very liberal and who are quite determined not to be dominated by either of these influences." He agreed with Solomon's suggestion that such a ministry should come into being before the elections, not after.[73] In a memorandum prepared later in the year, Selborne argued for the formation of a British coalition, which would include Progressives, Responsibles, and labourites. To effectively counterbalance Het Volk, he reasoned, the British would have to sink their differences and unify, preferably under Solomon's leadership. If so united, the Transvaal British could then consider a coalition government with Het Volk, for both parties could enter on an equal footing.[74]

The Randlords and their friends were not enamoured with any notion of coalition, nor were they pleased with Selborne's political posture generally. Geoffrey Robinson actually believed the governor was conspiring to put Richard Solomon in charge of an anti-capitalist alliance with Het Volk. He lamented the loss of Milner's leadership. In Chaplin's opinion, Selborne attached too much importance to the Responsibles. As he complained to Milner, "The unlucky thing about the Responsibles is that though they – or the leaders – are generally knaves, fools, or cranks, they make a great noise, and Lord Selborne has all along overrated their importance, advertised them, and doubtless conveyed to Ld. Elgin that they represent a great deal." In a letter to Wernher, FitzPatrick speculated that the governor favoured a British coalition, and he remarked in exasperation, "Was there ever anything more hopeless?"[75] However closely the Liberals identified Selborne with the capitalists, the Progressives themselves did not take him as their own.

On its arrival in South Africa, the West Ridgeway Committee went first to Pretoria to interview Het Volk leaders. After several days of wrangling, West Ridgeway persuaded the Boers to accept the voters' basis, modified by manhood suffrage and the retention of existing magisterial districts.[76] On 11 May, the committee then approached the Progressives and Responsibles, both of whom accepted this compromise, which, based on the 1904 census, stipulated the following allocation of seats: twenty-nine for the Rand, five for Pretoria, and twenty-nine for the country districts. The next day West Ridgeway telegraphed home this "highly satisfactory" result. The committee chairman anticipated that this arrangement would produce a British majority of from five to eight.[77] A copy of the agreement was immediately sent to Selborne, whom the committee proposed to interview on Tuesday the 15th, before making a formal offer to the Boers.[78]

The Progressive leaders met Selborne immediately after they had agreed to this compromise. To their surprise, he roundly denounced the arrangement which, he argued, took no account of the considerable British immigration since 1904.[79] After receiving this advice, the Progressives swung around completely. On Monday afternoon they told the committee that they wished to withdraw from the agreement. The following day, they sent West Ridgeway a memorandum asserting that, if immigration since 1904 were taken into account, the Rand should receive thirty-seven members and the rest of the Transvaal twenty-eight.[80] The inquiry's chairman reported the Progressives' withdrawal and Selborne's intervention to Elgin on the 15th. Within twenty-four hours the colonial secretary cabled the high commissioner for an explanation. Three days later the governor telegraphed a full account of the incident and his reasons for interfering. The committee, he charged, had been much too sanguine. The British would pick up no votes outside the Witwatersrand, Pretoria, and Barberton areas. Moreover, they would lose seats in the Rand itself, despite Botha's pledge not to run candidates there. According to Selborne's predictions, the proposed settlement would give the Boers a majority of one.[81]

Greatly disturbed at the governor's meddling, on 23 May the cabinet "unanimously decided that he had acted beyond his duty as High Commissioner." The government directed Elgin to send Selborne a rebuke, which was accordingly cabled to South Africa the same day. "It appears to me," Elgin chided,

that I might fairly have expected that, if you took exception to the proposals of the Committee appointed by His Majesty's Government, you would first state such objections to us, and meanwhile decline to advise the several parties on matters arising out of the actings of the Committee. That position would have safeguarded not only your impartiality and your right of independent judgment, but the freedom of action of the Committee within their instructions from us, and I am bound to say, from His Majesty's Government, that we regret that this course was not pursued by you on this occasion, and that we feel confident that, in further proceedings, you will see the advantage of adopting it.[82]

For his part, Selborne defended his action as necessary to avert an arrangement which was certain to produce a Boer majority. He considered his censure undeserved and corresponded less frequently with the colonial secretary.[83] He continued, however, to write freely to Churchill, who, after reading the governor's final explanation of the episode, minuted, "Lord Selborne's explanation ends this matter very satisfactorily."[84]

Colonial Office officials took the governor's advice seriously. H.C. Lambert and H.W. Just in fact blamed the committee for placing faith in Botha's promise not to contest Rand seats. In spite of Elgin's disapproval of Selborne's methods, he too was impressed by the substance of the high commissioner's criticisms. On the same day that he sent his telegraphic censure, he also cabled West Ridgeway that, in light of Selborne's advice, the government would find it difficult to approve the proposed settlement.[85]

Meanwhile, the Progressives' breach with the committee had widened, and relations between the two deteriorated quickly. The former rejected two further compromise agreements, the second of which generously accorded thirty-three seats to the Witwatersrand (excluding Krugersdorp-rural), six to Pretoria, and thirty to the rest of the country. The Progressives' truculence on this last occasion exasperated even Selborne who remarked to Milner, "Verily, the Johannesburg politician is a babe at politics, and a very foolish babe at that."[86]

In any case, the committee framed its proposals around this last scheme. The official report recommended the voters' basis, single-member constituencies, and automatic redistribution, as well as manhood suffrage and the preservation of existing magisterial districts in the country.[87] Pleased with the report, Selborne wrote Milner, "we could not possibly have done better for the British without bare-faced jerrymandering." He pointed out to Elgin that his intervention had made this result possible and asked that his censure be withdrawn. Sidestepping this request, the colonial secretary merely expressed his regret that they had differed.[88]

The substance of the Transvaal Letters Patent, transmitted to Selborne in late July, incorporated the recommendations of the West Ridgeway Committee. In addition, provision was made for a second chamber, as Selborne had advised since November, 1905.[89] The elections took place in February 1907 and produced an overall Het Volk majority largely because a substantial proportion of the British voted for Botha. This convinced Selborne that nothing could have kept the Boers out of power. It also proved to him that the Lyttelton Constitution could never have worked.[90]

At first glance, it would seem that Selborne's constitutional initiatives either stalled or backfired. Overruled on the responsible government issue, he had secured for the British the more essential principle of one vote, one value – only to have them vote for Het Volk. For all his efforts on their political behalf, the Transvaal British dealt the high commissioner a mocking defeat. His ethnic prejudice had obscured the class divisions which undermined his political calculations. Even Chaplin admitted that the Progressives had underestimated the strength of the labour movement[91] which elected three members to the Assembly.

Worse still, clause 34(b) of the Letters Patent seemed to make his failure complete, reserving as it did any legislation for the introduction of indentured labour.[92] The *Rand Daily Mail* in December 1906 castigated this insulting provision as an offence to both Boer and Briton, and, not unexpectedly, the Progressives sent Elgin a note of protest. Earlier, the governor had remarked sceptically to Lawley that all would be well so long as Britain left the Chinese labour question to the discretion of an elected Transvaal Assembly.[93] The Letters Patent even threatened to rob this one crucial benefit that self-government promised. Selborne's defeat was not, however, total. There was still Milner's state, with its modern bureaucracy, which might hold the Boers in check. So might the economic fact that the entire Transvaal depended on the mining industry. Despite his bias against the Boers, Selborne realized that the Rand could expect better treatment from the Afrikaners than from the "malignant lunatics" at home. However dark the situation seemed in 1907, the Transvaal had at least moved away from the Liberal shadow and, in doing so, had taken one large step towards a brighter future.

5 Brighter Prospects: the Labour Crisis, Imperial Obstruction, and Afrikaner Assistance

The course of events during Selborne's first year in South Africa was ominous enough for the gold mining industry, but as the next year wore on, the Transvaal's economic outlook grew dimmer still. Nineteen hundred and six witnessed the election of a hostile government in England as well as the promulgation of a constitution which could very well produce the same state of affairs in the Transvaal. Worse still, Liberal policy regarding the Chinese endangered the very foundations of mining prosperity – the supply and organization of its labour force. The lengthening shadows which this protracted controversy cast across the Rand soon enveloped the entire country.

In addition to Chinese repatriation, other labour crises beleaguered the mining industry and magnified its plight. In 1907 the mine owners faced a strike by their white workforce. Moreover, certain developments from 1906 to 1907 almost destroyed the industry's recruiting organization, as well as the racial division of labour itself.[1] Deeply concerned for the Witwatersrand's well being, Selborne made its problems his own. His concerns, however, extended beyond the purely economic, and he worried that Het Volk would, through incompetence or design, fail to provide the political support which the gold industry required. The Afrikaner leaders, Louis Botha and J.C. Smuts, would, Selborne feared, run the government to serve the interests of a backward Boer oligarchy instead of the needs of a progressive, industrial society.

The industrial crisis, therefore, involved not merely a labour shortage but structural dislocation as well. It threatened the cohesiveness of capital and the structure of labour deployment, both essential for capital accumulation.² With the additional prospect of an unsympathetic government, Selborne and the Randlords understandably feared for the survival of Rand mining as a going concern.

The crucial source for Rand labour was the Portuguese colony of Mozambique, which in 1906 supplied 65 per cent of the workforce.³ Since the days of Kruger, the Transvaal had enjoyed a special relationship with its eastern neighbour, whereby in return for recruiting privileges, it accorded Mozambique preferential treatment regarding railway traffic. This, compounded with its closer proximity to Johannesburg, gave the Portuguese port of Delagoa Bay a considerable advantage over its competitors in the Cape and Natal. While Kruger had strong political reasons for lessening his state's dependence on the British colonies, Milner, as high commissioner, had the duty of defending the interests of the Cape and Natal, and, before the Boer War, he took up their cause vigorously against the Transvaal. After the war, however, he shifted his policy – to the chagrin of the maritime colonies.

Milner predicated his grand design on the fortunes of the Witwatersrand and, to secure the labour which it desperately needed, he was willing to bargain away railway preferences, even at the expense of the Cape and Natal. Without prior approval from London, Milner renewed the prewar economic arrangements between the Transvaal and Mozambique.⁴

The ambiguity of this position would present any high commissioner with awkward problems created by competing demands. Responsible for the welfare of all colonies, Milner and later Selborne faced a situation where the welfare of the Transvaal could entail the ruination of the Cape. Charged with the promotion of British interests, each proconsul accorded more favourable treatment to a foreign state than to either of his own maritime colonies. Yet in the long run, the interests of all the British South African colonies were compatible and interdependent. Without sufficient labour, the Rand mines would suffer and so, as a consequence, would the carrying trade of the Cape and Natal. And intercolonial friction among the four colonies generated a political instability not conducive to investment in the Rand. Instead of trying to reconcile the short-term differences among the four colonies under their charge, both Milner and Selborne could, by virtue of their position after the war, choose and promote the interest which appeared most essential for the country's long-term future. They both selected the mining industry and fostered it with care. They devised their policy around the Witwatersrand's needs and carried it through in the teeth of maritime opposition. Neither proconsul was insensitive towards the plight of the older British colonies and each made strenuous if futile efforts to persuade Portugal to share more of the carrying trade with its competitors to the south. Both Milner and his successor would bend the *modus vivendi*, but neither would risk breaking it.

The Cape and Natal were in no position to take the long view. Contrary to their buoyant expectations in 1902, their fortunes declined steadily after the British triumph of arms.[5] Year by year the coastal colonies watched on, as Portuguese lines drained away their trade. It was no wonder that at the Bloemfontein Customs Convention of 1903 the Cape and Natal opened up a vigorous attack, forcing Milner to declare in unequivocal terms that the Transvaal's relationship with Mozambique was not open to discussion.[6] In the same predicament, Selborne attempted to enlist London's support in his struggle to wrench concessions from Portugal. Elgin, however, demurred, preferring to leave the matter for South Africa to solve after Transvaal self-government.[7] So the problem festered on.

Economic developments had produced in South Africa a welter of conflicting interests which jeopardized both intercolonial and imperial relations, not to mention the political stability of the region. Because of the Rand's economic imperatives, the fortunes of the country were, to a considerable extent, hostage to Mozambique. Try as he could, Selborne could not remedy the situation from the peripheral end. He required the forceful assistance which only metropolitan diplomacy could provide, and this the Liberals would not give.

In marked contrast to its reluctance to intervene in Lisbon regarding the railway clauses of the *modus vivendi*, the Liberal government bore down heavily on Portugal to modify the recruiting arrangements which had proven crucially important to the Chamber of Mines and to the Mozambique treasury. According to article 11 of the *modus vivendi*, all "collectors of labour" required approval from both the Transvaal and Mozambique governments.[8] Though not specifically mentioned, the Chamber's Witwatersrand Native Labour Association was understood by both parties to be the only authorized recruiting agency for the Transvaal mines. Run by J.F. Perry, this facilitated control over recruitment and eliminated the competition among mining groups that would have driven up black wages. Thus, the WNLA insured that labour costs would remain low. While its control over labour recruitment dissipated in South Africa after 1905, the association continued to enjoy a monopoly in Portuguese territory.

As essential as this monopsony was to the long-term interests of the gold industry as a whole, one notorious Randlord felt he could do better on his own. Having fared well by recruiting independently in the Cape, J.B. Robinson decided to do the same in Portuguese East Africa. But, with WNLA more firmly entrenched there, Robinson could not carry out his intentions without what one historian has called a "frontal assault" on the Chamber's monopsony itself.[9] In the Transvaal Mines Labour Company (TMLA), a new recruiting company headed by A.E. Wilson, Robinson found the instrument for his purpose. Wilson's unscupulous recruiting methods had earned him an unsavoury reputation throughout the region – no mean achievement given South African standards in this matter.

After approaching the Transvaal government, Wilson received in December 1905 a certificate of "no objection" from the Native Affairs Department. Less than two weeks later, Selborne explained to Governor General Coutinho of Mozambique that the Transvaal issued these certificates as a matter of routine and that he fully appreciated His Excellency's desire to confine recruiting to one organization. "It is recognised," he assured Coutinho, "that the grant of licenses is a matter which chiefly concerns the Portuguese Government," and that the Transvaal informed all applicants that it would exert no pressure on Portuguese authorities in these matters.[10] Not surprisingly, Mozambique refused to confer recruiting privileges on the TMLA.

In late March this agency approached Selborne for his personal endorsement, which he declined to give. Even when Wilson threatened to resort to Selborne's superiors the governor would not so much as grant an interview.[11] Before turning to London, Robinson's agent attempted to put leverage on the WNLA itself, which was opposing its potential rival in Lisbon. If the association did not stop its obstruction, Wilson warned, he would send the British cabinet a report which was certain to result in free recruiting in Mozambique. Better, he argued, to suffer one competitor from the Rand than to risk a free-for-all in which non-mining interests would enter the field and, because of mining's unpopularity among Africans, attract labour away from the Rand altogether. The friendly competition which Wilson envisioned would, he claimed, double the labour supply.[12] Neither argument nor threat could move the Chamber to abandon its monopsony.

Before Wilson's ultimatum had been delivered, British authorities, whether or not spurred on by Robinson, had begun sniping at the Chamber's recruiting monopsony. Addressing the House of Commons in mid-March, Churchill condemned the WNLA for its inefficiency. When the Chamber asked the undersecretary to substantiate his charge, he did not consider it his place to take up the challenge by answering the request. He added ominously, "Perhaps Mr. J.B. Robinson will oblige."[13] On 27 April, Robinson wrote directly to the Colonial Office for support in securing recruiting privileges in Portuguese territory. Perfectly seasoned to Liberal tastes, his letter charged that the Chamber was sabotaging his efforts because it did not want him to demonstrate the sufficiency of the African labour supply. It sought instead to curtail the supply of local labour and to prevent economic development. The mining establishment, he suggested darkly, wished to foist the Chinese permanently on the colony, so that they could take on skills and displace white workers. (He did not explain why the Chamber could not do the same with African workers, nor did he explain why capitalists would have as their aim economic stagnation.) The Chamber of Mines, he continued, was a political engine, through which Wernher, Beit, and Eckstein sought to dominate the entire colony. They already, controlled all the news agencies, as well as the high commissioner himself, who had the Chamber draft his correspondence home.[14] When, three months later, he heard of Robinson's last indictment, Selborne vehemently denied that his relations with industry involved anything more than proper consultation. For his part, he condemned Robinson as contemptible, and unleashed his feelings to Elgin: "I do not think that in this world you could find a greater incantation [sic.-incarnation?] of heartless selfishness."[15]

The Colonial Office, however, took Robinson's letter seriously. Though he considered the remarks about Selborne to be exaggerated, H.W. Just admitted that there had been excessive collusion between the mining industry and the Transvaal government. Sir Montagu Ommanney advised supporting the new recruiting agency, provided Selborne considered it a respectable body. On 7 May, Elgin cabled the high commissioner that, as the TMLA appeared a reputable agency, he had decided to support its request and would shortly ask the Foreign Office to deploy its diplomatic resources on Robinson's behalf.[16]

This disturbing development forced Selborne to show his hand. Three days after receiving Elgin's message, he sent a strongly worded telegram urging London to drop its support of Robinson. Acceding to Wilson's request would reintroduce the old order of free recruitment, when "there was a swarm of native labour touts who certainly competed against each other with a vengeance, but who were, speaking plainly, a crowd of ruffians." The number of recruiters in the field was a matter of "perfect indifference" to him but not to the Africans who would suffer from the abuse a free-for-all would engender. As for the TMLA's respectability, "the man who is the moving spirit in this matter rejoices in the name of Kaffir Wilson, and he has one of the most unenviable reputations in all South Africa." Hard pressed to explain how he had offered "no objection" to this "unenviable" man, Selborne feebly remarked that such approval was given out as a matter of course.[17]

Officials at the Colonial Office gave considerable weight to this advice. H.C.M. Lambert, for example, minuted, "However bad 'monopoly' may sound, the existence of one central and responsible body, run as it happens by a man who is an ex-official and thoroughly trustworthy, is an advantage which ought not I think to be thrown away when the risks of relapsing to such a state of affairs threatens us." Even Just, who had previously supported the TMLA, now cautioned against taking action against Selborne's views, at least until further information had been obtained. Fred Graham added that, while he was not convinced that "healthy rivalry" would lead to the disastrous anarchy depicted so vividly in the telegram, the British government could not support a company whose reputation seemed so tainted.[18]

Oblivious to the considered judgment of his officials, Churchill recommended overriding the high commissioner's advice. The British government should, he declared, follow through on its intention to back Robinson to the hilt. "I wonder," he minuted incisively, "what would happen to WNLA if *their* character and methods were exposed to a searching scrutiny." On 17 May Selborne was advised that, if he could not bring himself to support the TMLA, then His Majesty's Government would do so at its end by bringing its influence to bear on Lisbon.[19]

On receiving this, Selborne fired off a cable imploring the colonial secretary to defer action until London had received his long despatch detailing the situation. Lambert and Graham both considered this a reasonable request, but Churchill hoped that Elgin "will not consent to the long delay involved in awaiting mailed explanation."[20] To keep the government from waiting, Selborne sent off a long cable summarizing his even longer despatch. In this, he substantiated the aspersions he cast on Wilson by quoting extracts from the TMLA's threatening letter to the mining establishment. This, the governor castigated as a "barefaced attempt to blackmail [the] mining houses." In addition, he expanded on his concerns for Africans. He asserted that if Robinson secured independent recruiting privileges, other groups would demand the same and could not reasonably be refused. Thus, Robinson's success would entail free recruiting, and this would, Selborne assured his superiors, subject Africans to all manner of abuse. They would be lured into employment by pledges which recruiting agents had no intention of fulfilling. Touts would promise prospective workers the choice of employers and then, once the recruits had signed on, would sell them to the highest bidder. Moreover, Selborne added, independent recruiting would be difficult for the government to control. The only alternative, in his eyes, was a government monopoly. Though non-committal towards this option, the governor thought the entire question should wait until a self-governing Transvaal was able to express itself on the issue.[21]

Churchill remained unconvinced, and he took the occasion of Selborne's telegram to pen a full and thorough rebuttal of the case presented in it. As to the governor's concerns for Africans, Churchill pointed out that granting privileges to a few reputable organizations hardly constituted free recruiting. In fact, healthy competition would, he countered, benefit blacks by affording them some choice in the matter of employment.[22]

After broaching this question of recruiting practices, Churchill proceeded in his minute to offer a meticulous analysis of Wilson's blackmailing letter, defending it line by line. The Chamber of Mines, he agreed, did exercise a pervasive dominance over all South Africa and was attempting to constrict the labour supply to strengthen its case for Chinese importation. Alive to parliamentary opinion, he emphatically endorsed Wilson's prognosis that publicization of the dispute would injure the reputation of the entire mining industry. "I can conceive nothing more likely to damage the mining industry and to influence the H of C against it, than a hammer and tongs set to between two rival gangs of S. African financiers, both of whom probably know enough about each other to make their controversy extremely edifying." Churchill reserved his choicest words to refute the charge of blackmail. As he did so, he revealed a keen appreciation of the stratagems deployed by Selborne and the Chamber of Mines:

A firm has a license from Government to recruit. It is prevented from recruiting by the improper intervention of a rival firm. That intervention is indirectly but effectively sustained by the H. Commiss[ioner]. He cannot refuse the TMLA official recognition; but he allows the Portuguese authorities to continue to believe that his license was only a matter of form, was not meant in earnest, & that they will best please his wishes by ignoring it. The Portuguese authorities – stimulated perhaps by other more explicit and even more substantial arguments from the WNLA – decline to allow the TMLA to make use of its license. Wilson on their behalf then threatens to appeal to the British Cabinet and the public opinion in England, unless the WNLA do what? – give him money? No. Give him some special recruiting advantage? – No. Enter into any improper compact with him? – No. What then? Unless they cease to exercise all undue and perhaps illicit influence against his being enabled to recruit on equal terms with them. Merely that. And this is called 'black mail', solemnly and seriously by Lord Selborne and those who have minuted this paper.

Churchill ended by again urging that Robinson's request be granted post haste.[23] Elgin, however, refused to be carried so far. Though he would support any respectable rival, he would not, in light of Selborne's criticism, endorse "Kaffir Wilson."[24]

Throughout early June, Robinson bombarded the Colonial Office with letter after letter, providing Elgin with a sample of his pressure tactics. On 8 June he held out as bait the three thousand Chinese permits which he had not yet filled. Of course, he added, if he could not secure permits for Mozambique recruiting within a reasonable time, he would be compelled to resort to the Chinese. Three days later he provided the Colonial Office with a full list of the companies he represented to demonstrate that his request came from a substantial body. Three days after this, he conveyed the important news that he had dropped Wilson and was instead petitioning on behalf of the companies which he himself headed. On 18 June, Robinson began turning the screw. He gave the Liberals two days to produce results, or he would tell his mines to start filling their Chinese quotas.[25] The veiled threat of unfavourable publicity struck a responsive chord in Churchill, who on reading Robinson's first letter, recognized the danger he posed to the government's position in the House of Commons. "It will not be very convenient," the undersecretary minuted, "to have him stating publicly that we are forcing him to import Chinese, by refusing him [the] right to recruit perfectly recruitable Kaffirs." This possibility moved him to press Elgin to meet Robinson, who was currently in England.[26] Public opinion and parliamentary considerations constituted perhaps the most powerful influence on Churchill throughout the whole Robinson affair. As he wrote Selborne, "J.B.R." had high cards from a House of Commons point of view, for he was attacking "a recruiting monopoly in the hands of the hated ring of Financiers."[27] No doubt this factor loomed large in Elgin's mind when he agreed to meet Robinson on 20 June, the deadline date of the ultimatum. At this meeting, the magnate confirmed that he had dropped Wilson. After hearing that this major obstacle had been cleared, the colonial secretary agreed to give Robinson full support, political and diplomatic.[28]

In early July Selborne suggested another delaying tactic, which this time backfired badly. He advised that before pressing Robinson's claim, the imperial government should appoint a commission to investigate the recruiting situation, especially the dangers of a free for all. The colonial secretary outflanked the governor by agreeing to the commission without making Robinson's permit contingent on its appointment. He instructed Selborne in the meantime to employ all his influence to secure recruiting privileges for Mr. Holmes, Robinson's new agent.[29]

The Transvaal governor had been circumvented, but the Portuguese had not. In September the Colonial Office received yet another letter from Robinson, this time complaining that the Mozambique authorities had only issued Holmes one licence – a virtually useless concession. The high commissioner pressed Holmes's case half-heartedly and, not surprisingly, the Portuguese refused to budge. (The governor general cited as one reason for his intransigence the uncertainty of the Transvaal's real wishes.)[30]

Stonewalled by Mozambique, the British government next faced more obstruction from its own high commissioner, who warned that the WNLA would break up the moment Holmes secured full recruiting privileges. Every group would seek equal treatment, the WNLA would dissolve, and free recruiting with all its attendant evils would return. Elgin again outmanoeuvred Selborne by turning his own plan for a commission against him. To prevent the scenario which the governor feared, the colonial secretary instructed that no new requests for recruitment should be entertained until the commission had reported.[31] In late October the WNLA groups threatened to leave the organization if Robinson seceded, and each petitioned for the same independent recruiting rights Holmes was seeking. Selborne now overcame his fear of free recruiting and endorsed these requests, rationalizing his *volte face* with the specious argument that the WNLA had in fact ceased to exist. There was no use opposing free recruiting when it had become a reality anyway.[32] A Robinson victory would, of course, end the WNLA as a recruiting monopsony but not as a responsible body of control, and it was this last aspect which Elgin's instructions were designed to preserve. Not to be bludgeoned by the Chamber's stick, Elgin held his ground, even though he opened the Liberals up to charges of favouritism.[33]

At the beginning of 1907, then, the WNLA's monopsony stood on the brink of disaster, and it had barely managed to stay on the safe side of it. Elgin's refusal to sanction new licences made its dissolution impossible in the short run, but the Liberal government could not continue to deny to other groups the same privileges which Robinson might come to enjoy. The essential factor holding the association together was the fact that "J.B.R." had not yet succeeded in breaching the monopsony, and his failure can be attributed to Portuguese intransigence, bolstered by Selborne's tacit complicity. In short, a foreign state stood between industry and the complete dislocation of its recruiting structure in a vital area of supply. A more unstable state of affairs could not be imagined. The situation grew darker still when the governor general of Mozambique proposed taking over recruiting operations himself and entrusting them to the Mozambique government. This, Selborne recognized, would strengthen Portugal's hold on British South Africa through the *modus vivendi*. In addition, this arrangement could jeopardize the labour supply by giving Mozambique absolute control over it. When self-government was inaugurated, these issues still remained unresolved. J.B. Robinson and his Liberal allies had seriously destabilized industrial conditions. With the Rand's labour supply threatened from all directions, its recruiting apparatus, so essential for cost control, on the verge of collapse, and the political climate in which it operated more acrimonious than ever, it is not surprising that Selborne began to wonder if backward Afrikaners could be worse than the "malignant lunatics" in Westminster.

The day before the elected Transvaal Assembly opened, Selborne suggested that the Liberals defer appointment of the commission, so that the new self-governing colony might participate in its deliberations.[34] The British government reacted coolly towards this suggestion, but when six weeks later the Transvaal government announced that it was appointing a commission of its own anyway, the imperial government left the problem in local hands.[35]

The new Afrikaner government of Louis Botha approached Portugal and negotiated an arrangement which would come into force only if Robinson and the Chamber failed to compose their differences. Under this contingency plan, Mozambique would control the recruitment of labourers but the distribution would be undertaken by the Transvaal. Armed with this alternative, Het Volk was able to present Robinson with a no-win situation if he stood out of WNLA. Not unexpectedly, he yielded and rejoined. The WNLA became again the sole recruiting agency for Mozambique, though it would function under the general supervision of the Transvaal state, which took upon itself the responsibility and power of intervening in any future dispute that might jeopardize the monopsony. Perhaps H.C.M. Lambert at the Colonial Office summarized the situation best. "The T.V. Govt. have evidently come to the conclusion that nothing is to be gained by breaking up WNLA, whose monopoly is officially recognised."[36] The Afrikaner generals had rescued the Randlords from themselves, for, without the state's intervention, the monopsony might well have crumbled. Moreover, Het Volk provided the integrative machinery to prevent such serious problems from recurring. Most important, the generals saved industry from the home government.

The Botha government proved its worth to the industry in many other ways. It opened up negotiations on the *modus vivendi* with Mozambique in late December 1907. Warmly supported by Selborne, the Transvaal sought a twenty-five year treaty, which would add an important element of stability to the mines' labour situation.[37] Though the convention, as passed, guaranteed Mozambique 50 to 55 per cent of Rand traffic, as opposed to the 33 1/3 per cent which the Transvaal had pressed for, the other provisions of this treaty were highly satisfactory, especially its long life.[38] Het Volk had shown that the Transvaal could competently undertake delicate and difficult negotiations with foreign states and do so with the interests of the mining industry at heart. Botha and Smuts had accomplished what the Liberals would not.

Besides the controversies involving labour to the east, there remained the titanic Chinese controversy to resolve. The British government had officially entrusted the final decision on Chinese labour to the self-governing Transvaal. Yet the Letters Patent prescribed the repeal of the Labour Importation Ordinances one year from the formal inauguration of responsible government. And in March 1906 Churchill warned Selborne that, even if a responsible legislature re-enacted the ordinance, London would veto the measure. A month before the new Assembly convened Churchill offered some hope that renewals might be permitted, but he emphatically warned Selborne that under no circumstances would the imperial government sanction fresh importation: "Whatever is demanded, whatever is proposed, or by whomsoever it is demanded or proposed, we will not allow any more Chinese coolies under indenture, to enter South Africa. Everyone is resolved on that, – the most moderate members of the Government equally with the most extreme members of the party; and the resources of the Foreign Office, and if necessary, of the Admiralty, will be ruthlessly used to enforce that determination."[39] The day after Het Volk's installation, the undersecretary minuted that "The tug-of-war over Chinese labour is still to come."[40]

Although unlikely to fly in the face of Liberal opinion, the Botha government might possibly allow the Chinese presently on the Rand to renew their contracts. The governor certainly nursed such hopes. Sceptical about the feasibility of "repatriation and replacement," which Het Volk promised, Selborne remarked to his wife that, though his ministers were scouring all corners of southern Africa for substitutes, "every path they tread only brings them back to Chinese labour for a bit." If any added inducement were required to keep Botha on the right path, Selborne was confident that the capitalists could provide it. Earlier, he had confided:

The more I have seen of Ministers the more I am certain that they will want money, much money ... Now, Carl Meyer, late Rotheschild's [sic] Manager, and now a millionaire and financier in his own account and inter alia Chairman of De Beers, came to see me on Thursday and he gave me a message from Rotheschild that not one penny of money would the Transvaal get in London or Paris or Berlin until they had put the Rand Mines labour supply on a sure and permanent footing, but if they did that, they could have as much as they wanted at once and on easy terms. This is really the case in a nutshell.[41]

Though this may represent an empirical analysis of capital flow rather than collusion in an extortion attempt, it clearly reveals that Selborne had a keen understanding of the uses to which financial power could be put.

So too did the Liberal government. Shortly before Botha's visit to London for the Colonial Conference, Winston Churchill drew up a minute outlining his strategy for wooing the new premier. He presented the awkward situation which would arise if the Transvaal decided to let the Chinese on the Rand renew their indentures. To refuse the unanimous wishes of an elected legislature would land the imperial government "quickly into unfathomed waters." On the other hand, the Liberals had made definite pledges to the House of Commons concerning indentured labour, and the sooner the government could offer visible proof that a substantial number of Chinese were on ships back to China, the better. Churchill would obviate this dilemma by liberating the Transvaal government from the fiscal grasp of mining capital. At that moment, Botha was trying to float a £5 million loan from whatever sources he could find, and it was needless to specify what these sources were. Britain could rescue the Transvaal government from the Randlords by extending to Botha the guaranteed loan he required. Once free from capitalist pressure, the Transvaal would, Churchill hoped, make an "earnest effort" to repatriate at least ten thousand Chinese.[42] During his stay in London Botha held extensive talks with Liberal leaders, and when he departed, he came away with a £5 million guaranteed loan.[43]

Selborne had always nursed reservations about Botha's journey to the Colonial Conference, and, on hearing of the loan, surmised that it was "part of a sinister bargain with Botha about Chinese." When Het Volk decided to refuse renewals for the year, he became certain that some dark deal had been concluded. The exasperated governor exclaimed, "I hope that Jameson and H[ely]-H[utchinson] are thoroughly satisfied with the results of their uncalled for interference in getting Botha invited to the conference. No renewals this year! 16,700 Chinese to go!"[44] Het Volk laid the Chinese issue to a final rest in August with its decision to extend the ordinance only until the labourers had completed their present contracts. There probably was no actual bargain between Botha and the Liberals; nevertheless, certain considerations had been exchanged. Moreover, the Transvaal prime minister escaped the clutches of the Randlords by, quite literally, becoming indebted to the Liberals. The loan aside, there is little doubt that Het Volk policy regarding repatriation owed much to British pressure.[45] In sum, whether or not there was an informal bargain, Selborne and the Progressives were not far off the mark in attributing the final decision on Chinese labour to Downing Street interference.

When announcing his policy in June 1907, Botha made reference to his government's efforts to secure labour from the Cape Colony. The newly formed Native Labour Bureau would coordinate recruiting activities with the Cape government to facilitate the entry of labour into the Transvaal. This, combined with similar initiatives in Mozambique, Natal, and Zululand would, the prime minister confidently predicted, produce a labour supply sufficient to replace the departing Chinese.[46] Selborne did not share this confidence. Even should an increased labour supply result, it would merely signify that the depression had closed down non-mining jobs. Once the general depression lifted, the shortage would reassert itself in the mines. Moreover, Selborne reasoned, the investing public wanted the assurance of a continuous supply of labour; a sudden spurt which could dry up at any moment would not restore confidence. The financial outlook, he concluded to Elgin late in 1907, was decidedly grim.[47]

As it turned out, the high commissioner's prognosis was mistaken. The Cape Colony not only provided sufficient labour to compensate for the Chinese, it proved an adequate and continuous source of supply. To be sure, the depression was part of the reason, but the various recruiting strategies which developed after the WNLA's collapse in South Africa furnished the decisive factor. Also important were the initiatives of the Botha government. By mid-1908 even Sir Julius Wernher commended the government for its capable handling of the industrial crisis.[48]

The marked recovery of the mining industry took Selborne by surprise, but he remained sceptical of the government's success in solving the labour problem. The increased use of mechanical appliances afforded him some encouragement, but as late as December 1909 he still attributed the Rand's recovery to the general depression. The fact that this was lifting led him to believe that the mines' labour shortage would soon reassert itself.[49] Yet, despite his pessimism on this score, the high commissioner could, by 1909, at least rest assured that South Africa would shortly possess a unified and efficient state to deal with any labour difficulties that might arise and to guarantee the stability which investment required. More than this, by the time he left South Africa, Selborne had the secure knowledge that the future leaders of a united South Africa would have their hearts in the right place. This was more than he could say about the present House of Commons.

Closely related to the controversy over the labour supply was the structural question of its productive organization. Developments since 1906 have imbued the racial division of labour with an imperative logic and inevitability which it did not possess historically. Hindsight has in this case obscured the real choices which industry itself recognized as options from 1906 to 1907. An extensive debate emerged during the Het Volk years, both in and out of mining circles, as to whether and to what extent this division should be maintained.[50] With labour policy in a state of flux, gold mining confronted three broad choices. First, there was F.H.P. Cresswell's design to eliminate Africans completely from the work process. With better use of mechanical appliances, he claimed, the mines could run profitably with white labour alone. More efficient production by fewer hands would compensate for the higher average wages paid out. Representing "racialist Uitlander populism" more than trade unionism, Cresswell found support briefly from Milner in 1903 and then temporarily from Het Volk in 1907.[51] Most industrial leaders doubted that mines could run at a profit along these lines. Instead they adopted what might be called a centrist position, which prescribed migratory non-white labour for unskilled positions and white workers for skilled jobs. Though in a minority, some mining leaders advocated making fuller use of black workers by providing permanent living arrangements and higher pay. If stabilized, the African workforce, it was claimed, would develop efficiency and skill. This last viewpoint represented the non-white option and constituted one pole of the debate as against Cresswell's all-white alternative. Though most mining leaders clustered around the centre, there was some movement towards the non-white option after 1907. Few actually envisioned the imminent stabilization of African workers, but many members of the Chamber of Mines sought to employ Africans in skilled positions.

This tendency came out clearly in the evidence taken by the commission which the government appointed in 1907 to investigate the relative positions of white and black in mining development. The president of the Chamber of Mines, L.J. Reyersbach, condemned the debarment of Africans from any jobs they could undertake. The whites, for whom he saw a permanent need in supervisory positions, must look for security in the greater number of positions which industrial expansion would open up; this, in turn, depended on lowered working costs. "Any measure which pretends to increase the use of white labour by other than economic means, i.e., at the expense of an increase in working costs, will defeat itself by limiting the scope of the industry."[52] The Chamber president was advancing a policy which would deskill whites and leave them structurally vulnerable to displacement. Without the bargaining power which skills provided, they would lie at the mercy of management. The number of supervisory positions, after all, depended not on productive needs but on managerial discretion. For example, John Way, the consulting engineer for the New Kleinfontein Mines, would reduce white supervision to a minimum. More sensitive to the concerns of white workers, Drummond Chaplin of Consolidated Goldfields supported the maintenance of the present convention which divided the labour process into white skilled and non-white unskilled

employment. This convention he considered necessary "for the civilisation of the country."[53] Though the all-white option was rarely espoused
by the mining men who gave evidence, the commission, with its loaded
terms of reference, came out for this solution, although it had to distort
the evidence to compose a case. It was part of the general process of
reconciliation that the Botha government shelved these findings.

Beneath the complexity of this debate, two fundamental and contra-
dictory objectives emerge: mining profitability and white worker security. Although the Cresswellites were not unmindful of mining costs
and the John Ways were not without their racist prejudices, adherents
to the non-white option tended to give priority to profitability, while
the proponents of the all-white solution, of course, placed the welfare
of whites above other considerations. In one respect, however, the de-
baters all accepted the premise that the black man could develop the
skill to rival the white. Few would have disagreed with the majority report here: "The theory that the native is a 'mere muscular machine'
must be discarded. As will presently appear experience had shown that
he can no longer be looked upon as debarred by lack of brain and industrial training from interfering with the white man's opportunities
of employment and as merely an aid to enable the white man to earn
wages sufficient to keep him in contentment."[54] What industry welcomed, the commission dreaded.

Selborne's position in this debate is difficult to establish. In his policy proposals he lay between Chaplin and Way, but in his premises he
strayed completely outside the parameters of the discussion. Unsympathetic with the all-white solution, which Churchill favoured, the high
commissioner retorted, "There is no good proving that the gold can
be won from the ore by white labour if the cost of winning it is more
than the value of the gold."[55] Moreover, in his defence of Chinese labour, he echoed the arguments used by Reyersbach – that more black
labour would mean more white jobs.

Yet he did seek to foster the stabilization of the white workforce and
took special interest in the construction of family dwellings for it. In
early 1906 he prepared a memorandum for Lionel Phillips, in which
he pressed the magnate to undertake a substantial housing project so
that white families could enjoy a stable and comfortable living environment on the Rand. Not only would this lessen the costly changeover in
personnel, it would eliminate the drunkenness which saturated the
largely bachelor skilled workforce. He also claimed that his proposal
would weaken trade union influence on the reefs, for "constant birds
of passage from one group to another, are much more likely to be
amenable to Trades Union influence than the class of miners constantly working for one set of employers and with an ever increasing in-

terest in the mine." In addition, the presence of families would enable the workforce to pass on skills and reproduce itself. Phillips appreciated the advice but could not commit himself to any large-scale construction projects.[56]

Though Selborne considered white workers indispensable, he, like Reyersbach, would in no way limit the black man from undertaking any employment for which he was capable in the mines or in society at large. If his capabilities permitted it, a black man should be able to become a carpenter, or even a doctor. To block black opportunities by artificial impediments, such as colour bars, was tantamount to imposing slavery. "If any law exists in the Transvaal which is a bar to the native developing in any direction of civilised order or advancement, such law should," he declared, "be repealed."[57]

Unlike the commission majority, however, Selborne, as a social Darwinist, had no fear that the white man would lose the struggle for survival. "If the white man is ever out-rivalled by the black man, it will be entirely the fault of the white man. No one can have any experience of the two races without feeling the intrinsic superiority of the white man." Indeed, "the great danger to the white man in this country is lest he should lose those characteristics which have made him what he is by being pampered and coddled and insured against competition in the struggle for life, and by being allowed always to regard the black man as his hewer of wood and drawer of water."[58]

Besider white labour, Selborne also addressed the problem of poor whites. It could be expected that he would have little sympathy for the white unemployed, and none at all when the Unemployed Organisation, representing victims of the acute economic distress during these years, petitioned for increased relief. Smuts's rejection of this appeal elicited from the governor profound respect, for it showed that "Smuts has backbone."[59]

Not surprisingly, Selborne showed an open hostility to those white miners who, on 1 May 1907, came out on strike in response to the wage reductions and "deskilling" which had been proceeding steadily over the past two years.[60] Selborne considered the mine owners completely justified in reducing the number of whites supervising drill work. He confided to his wife, "It is really the old and ignorant struggle against machinery and the idea that you increase the number of men employed by obstructing the efficiency of machinery, worked on by scoundrels of the Outhwaite type." Contemptuous of worker grievances, he wrote Elgin, "I may say that it is the maddest thing that ever was done by any labour organisation. I do not suppose any workmen in the world are getting such magnificent wages for such a small amount of labour." The governor hoped that the mine owners would use this opportunity "to clean up a lot of existing mess connected with the inefficiency of the white labourers and subsequent high cost of production."[61]

The strike soon spread. On 23 May, at Botha's request, Selborne authorized imperial troops to suppress the strike. To Churchill, he declared that the troops were absolutely necessary.[62] Minuting on Selborne's report, R.V. Vernon, at the Colonial Office, regretted that the Transvaal had not deployed its own units, such as the town police or the South African Constabulary, as the use of imperial forces was certain to arouse "keen criticism here." The high commissioner deserved, he considered, a reprimand for not having sought prior permission from London. What Vernon did not know was that the Transvaal ministers had in fact planned to use local forces until their interview with Selborne, who recommended instead that British soldiers be deployed. He promised to supply them all the troops they asked for.[63]

The strike was soon broken, and the proconsul applauded what he anticipated as its results. The mines, he gloated, would be able to effect all sorts of cost reductions. They could now replace the more expensive British miners by cheaper Afrikaners, who would thereby acquire a greater stake in industry. Moreover, the mine owners could diminish the proportion of white to non-white labour. All of Selborne's predictions came true and the 1907 strike was a complete, if temporary, victory for the Randlords. Even the one demand granted to labour – arbitration machinery – came to operate more effectively against workers than on their behalf.[64]

One crucial result of the strike was to accelerate the process of rapprochement between industry and state. The capitalist Johannesburg *Star* commended the government for its firmness and stated that the country should be grateful that it had such responsible leaders at the helm of state.[65] To Churchill, Selborne defended his ministers, who, while they deplored the strike, had taken up an official posture of "strict impartiality," which he considered "absolutely correct."[66] This letter intimates the important shift which had been proceeding in terms of industry-state relations. Whereas eighteen months before the Liberals were preaching trust for the Transvaal government without any great evidence, Het Volk's handling of the 1907 strike earned Selborne's trust, and he gave force to his sentiments by defending Botha against possible sceptics in the Liberal camp. Though Churchill realized that the Liberal government could hardly repudiate the prime minister which their policy had put in power, he was anxious about Westminster opinion and bewildered about events in South Africa: "Fancy what a mixture of British party prejudice and antagonisms. A

Boer Government, ordering British cavalry, with the approval of a Liberal Ministry, to charge British strikers and protect Dutch blacklegs in the interests of Rand magnates!"[67] The confusing shift of loyalties which the colonial undersecretary depicted so sharply was part of a crucial realignment of political and economic forces on the subcontinent. Het Volk and the Chamber of Mines were drawing together into a partnership of mutual benefit. In the course of these developments, Selborne discovered who the real friends of progress were.

In February of 1906, Selborne did not realize the quality of Afrikaner friendship, and, in a letter to Asquith, expressed at length his fears regarding Boer rule. On a copy of this, he noted later that his gloomy predictions had been foiled by "the personality of one man, Louis Botha. He is a really big man desiring racial union and progress, and sincere in the allegiance he promised to the King and to the British Empire at Vereeniging."[68] By proving himself both loyal and progressive, Botha confirmed what in 1906 was only a hopeful glimmer – that the Boers would not bring on an economic catastrophe which would ruin themselves as well as the Rand. Under Afrikaner tutelage, Milner's state, and the interests it served, flourished. Het Volk had shown itself a more trustworthy guardian of Selborne's imperial objectives than the "wreckers" at home.

6 Exploitation, Protest, and Autocratic Rule: Selborne and African Policy

The Rand's rescue by Transkei labourers, who came out in sufficient numbers to replace the departing Chinese, took everyone by surprise – the Chamber of Mines, the high commissioner, and perhaps even Het Volk. Considering, however, the situation of Africans after Vereeniging, one might well be surprised at Selborne's surprise. There was certainly an abundance of African manpower in British South Africa itself, which contained in 1904 well over three million blacks, and four hundred thousand coloureds, as compared with approximately one million whites.[1] Moreover, the Africans' hold on the land was weak enough to slip them from it, at least long enough for a spell on the mines. Throughout South Africa the white minority had devoured most of the region's land resources.[2] Though the precise form of land allocation varied from colony to colony, for Africans the essential features of differential access, land scarcity, and insecurity of tenure remained universal aspects of their existence in British South Africa.

It was not merely their tenuous grip on land resources that made Africans vulnerable to capitalist exploitation. The Transvaal had an arsenal of legislation to control them at home and, more particularly, at work. For example, the pass law of 1895, which applied to specified labour districts, enabled the authorities to detect and punish deserters.[3] Politically, the Transvaal accorded blacks neither the franchise nor representation. Even the Cape had in 1892 imposed new franchise restrictions on its small black electorate. All four colonies used taxation and official pressure to induce Africans to work for whites, either in the mines or on white farms. It is not inaccurate to claim, as Sharon Stichter has, that South Africa's industrialization was based on a coerced labour supply.[4] At the same time, the Africans' unwillingness to abandon their rural holdings permanently was as responsible as capitalist imperatives for the system of migratory labour that developed. Africans would contract to work outside their homesteads for a certain number of months and return for the planting season. Although blacks were coerced into working for whites, they had some say about the terms on which they entered the workforce. This does not, of course, alter the fact that throughout South Africa, native policy came increasingly to mean deprivation, differentiation, and domination. It was no exaggeration to describe the position of Africans as ultra-exploitable.

Africans in the Transvaal were not unaware of their position, but they misjudged the intentions of the conquering British in 1900. Expecting that an English victory would signal their liberation from oppressive conditions, throngs of workers burned their passes when Roberts's soldiers appeared on the Rand. In the countryside, Africans generally thought that the war had freed them from their former landlords, whose land would fall into the tenants' possession. British authorities soon dispelled these hopes, though not without resistance on the part of Africans.[5] Also dashed was the expectation on the part of the African elite that imperial rule would bring the franchise or at least representation to educated blacks. At Vereeniging, Kitchener agreed to defer the question of African political rights until the European population had declared itself in a self-governing legislature.

The imperial regime not only took over the republic's laws, it enforced them more effectively. Taxes were collected and the pass laws rigorously applied.[6] Moreover, the imperial authorities erected a network of control which Kruger might have envied. To administer the black population, Milner established the Native Affairs Department and placed Sir Godfrey Lagden at its head.[7] The spirit behind the new administration was described by Lagden in 1903. Relations between the races, he claimed, could only be healthy, "if the two races share a feeling of useful dependence upon each other in promoting the development of this country, if the higher race recognises its obligations to the lower, and the lower race realises its true position, and, whilst claiming and receiving the fullest measure of justice, owns towards the higher race a becoming respect." The year before, Lagden had been more explicit about what useful dependence he wished to inculcate. "It was of paramount importance," he wrote, "to consider what regulations were necessary to place the condition of labour and the relations between labour and capital on a satisfactory footing."[8]

More ominous still for African interests was the South African Native Affairs Commission, which reported in 1905. Chaired by Lagden, the commission recommended, among other things, territorial segregation and the rigorous enforcement of anti-squatting laws. In addition, SANAC attacked the Cape franchise as "dangerous" and advised that voters there be placed on separate rolls.[9] For two decades, white hedges had been closing in on African turf from all sides. Their political rights had shrunk along with their access to land, while concomitantly the whites had increased both their control over Africans and their take from the land – whether in the form of vegetable or mineral. There certainly seemed an inverse relationship between white welfare and that of blacks.

Several historians have argued that the high correlation between industrial development and African emiseration was no mere coincidence.[10] Moreover, they have ably illustrated how capitalism elaborated upon racist ideology and put it to full productive use. Some scholars have attempted to establish more direct connections between state policy and mining needs. Colin Bundy, for example, argued that as commercial capitalism gave way to industrial capitalism, the peasantry, which had earlier thrived on market production, was dispossessed and driven to the mines. Marian Lacey has refined this picture somewhat. The mine owners, in Lacey's view, did not seek to impoverish the reserves altogether, for they wished to ensure that the area would be able to support a worker's family and the labourer himself when not on the mines. Migratory labour kept the wage bill to a minimum, and, to preserve the system, the Randlords favoured a land policy of territorial segregation which would turn the reserves into reservoirs of healthy labourers. It was an essential mining interest, therefore, that African areas contain sufficient land to reproduce the workforce but not enough to sustain an independent peasantry. Land bills whose parsimonious allocations threatened this delicate balance aroused keen opposition from the Rand.[11]

Scholars have not shown, however, that the capitalists themselves perceived their own interests so clearly or that the politicians did so. What can be stated with certainty is that imperial officials sought to establish and maintain white control – an essential prerequisite for black exploitation. It may also be suggested that the state provided a legal and ideological framework in which capitalist interests could flourish. One might even assert more boldly that government support for industry, though subtle, was deliberate.[12]

While dedicated to the Rand interest and keenly aware of its labour requirements, Selborne conceived of capitalist imperatives in broad terms and in the long view. His most pressing concern was to secure white rule over black. The vast majority of Africans he would consign to the "wise supervision" of administrative autocrats, though to absorb potential discontent, he would confer political rights on a small black minority. These institutional arrangements would not only preserve order but also facilitate the restructuring of South African society along lines conducive to capital accumulation. Most Africans would, Selborne envisioned, settle down to a proletarian future, though some might rise into bourgeois ranks. In one form or another, all would be incorporated into a stable capitalist order. He had not, of course, formulated such a clear design when he left England. As his subsequent proposals would reveal, the high commissioner's African policy developed gradually during his tenure in South Africa.

Shortly after his arrival in South Africa, Selborne sent his superior, Alfred Lyttelton, a dispatch which revealed the general direction his mind was taking on the so-called native question. While he fully subscribed to Rhodes's dictum of equal rights for all "civilized" men, he did not regard the franchise question as an urgent one, nor did he attach great significance to the black elite.

The civilised coloured persons or natives in these Colonies are, however, too prone to forget that they are but an infinitesimal portion of the community, and that from that very fact their special treatment presents a special difficulty and that generally the whole question is the reverse of simple and really most complicated. This leads them to dwell too much on the franchise, for which the vast mass of natives are wholly unfitted, and which might safely be left to the distant future if a consistent, firm, and just policy for the slow training of the black man towards civilisation under the guidance of the white man could be accepted and acted on by the whole white community.

The high commissioner, therefore, identified "civilization" as the essential aim of his African policy. The precise meaning which he gave to this term can only be illustrated by the actual policy he laid out during the course of his tenure.

Aware of the strong colour prejudice amongst both Boer and Briton, Selborne appreciated the importance of treading carefully. To be identified by whites as a 'negrophilist' would, he warned, destroy any influence he might have on African affairs. Rather, he would defer giving public expression to his views until later and would, in the meantime, "endeavour to lead people to clear and logical thinking on the subject." At the Colonial Office, A.B. Keith commended Selborne's despatch as "sane and statesmanlike."[13]

There was also African opinion to consider, and this factor imposed limits on the extent to which imperial authorities could direct the destiny of the country. Painfully aware that South Africa's industrial progress was taking place on their backs, Africans found various forms through which to vent their feelings. The Zionist or Ethiopian churches, which had recently seceded from missionary bodies, provided a religious medium for independent black expression. Fearing potential revolutionary implications in the separatist movement, SANAC treated it gingerly, advising non-interference, "so long as it remains unassociated with mischievous political tendencies."[14] Other Africans took a more worldly view. During the reconstruction period black discontent with industrial conditions found expression in a way which directly threatened white interests. In their refusal to come out to work on the mines, they precipitated an industrial crisis, which toppled Milner's grand design and sent shock waves into the current of British politics.[15] There was little that the British administration could do, for it had to tread warily, without seriously disrupting the internal fabric of African society. In Lagden's words, "all men who have directed the destinies of South Africa have realised the danger of interfering ruthlessly with native customs, lest it might give the aboriginals common cause against the white men."[16]

The African educated elite offered more explicit expressions of dissatisfaction with Milner's rule. Africans had been politically active in the Cape since its inception as a self-governing colony, but the northern states did not see the creation of African political associations until the reconstruction period. During the tenure of Milner and Selborne, a plethora of newly formed organizations persistently petitioned the imperial government for an extension of the franchise to educated blacks and coloureds in the new colonies. Just as persistently, their pleas met with disappointment, for London feared that forceful imperial intervention on behalf of Africans would alienate colonial whites. Only peripherally did these political groups mention as grievances the socio-economic hardships under which the black majority laboured. A recent authority has argued that the utopianism which the black elite absorbed through missionary education blinded it to the realities of white rule – economic as well as political domination. Detached from the black majority, the educated elite looked helplessly to the imperial factor for a salvation that never came.[17]

Not all school Africans waited patiently. Beyond the vision of the high commissioner, the African countryside in the Cape was undergoing great socio-economic change and a profound transformation in power relations. Whereas imperial authorities in the nineteenth century conferred special importance on mission-educated blacks, white politicians in the early twentieth century tended to shift their favour to the traditional rulers, thus renewing the power of the chiefs. Moreover, by reducing the need for collaborative agents, the bureaucratization of

African affairs further diminished the power and prestige of the west-
ern-educated classes in the Cape countryside. Along with the erosion of
the old mission-educated elite came the rise of more broadly based
movements, each possessing some sense of a widening identity. Informed by both traditional and Ethiopian currents as well as the common experience of migratory labour and colonial domination, this
rural Africanism bridged the distance between the chiefs and the now
disillusioned westernized Africans. Sometimes, dissident school Africans became popular leaders who mobilized resistance to European
rule by tapping this rural populism. At other times, such leadership was
taken by disaffected chiefs or by new persons altogether. Thus, in the
early twentieth century the Cape countryside was permeated by deep
currents of discontent which often welled up into potent resistance.
While such outbreaks often looked to the past, their broadening appeal
established new and wider unities which pointed to the future.[18]

These tendencies manifested themselves earlier and more visibly in
Natal, where thousands of blacks expressed themselves in violent terms
which Selborne could not ignore. In February of 1906 he learned that
twenty-seven armed Africans there had killed two white policemen.
The Natal government responded ferociously, quickly executing twelve
of the rebels under martial law. The troops which swept the disaffected
areas destroyed crops, seized cattle, and deposed chiefs. One of these
who lost government approval, Bambatha, led another insurrection in
April, which spread to serious proportions. It was not until July that active opposition to white authority ended. In the course of the rebellion, over three thousand blacks fell, along with two dozen whites.
Panic continued to grip the Natal authorities; in late 1907 they decided to arrest the paramount Zulu chief, Dinuzulu, whom they incor-
rectly believed had masterminded the entire revolt. The heir of
Cetshwayo was tried, convicted, and exiled to St. Helena. Though Britain insured that Dinuzulu received an adequate defence at his trial,
imperial authorities sat out the rebellion on the sidelines, disapprov-
ing of Natal's heavy-handedness but unwilling to intervene in what it
considered the affair of a self-governing colony. The fact that Natal
suppressed the revolt without imperial troops weakened Britain's leverage in the matter.

What sparked the conflagration was the poll tax which Natal's parliament imposed on Africans in 1905. The underlying causes, however,
can be located in the Africans' desperate land shortage and the colonists' rapacious appetite for labour. Land pressure in the reserves had
pushed more than half of the colony's blacks onto white farms, where
they were rack-rented remorselessly. Rand competition for labour
drove the colonists to stiffen pass laws, masters and servants acts, and

other coercive measures.[19] In light of these conditions, it is not surprising that Africans revolted.

The outbreak of the rebellion shook the high commissioner severely. In March he advised Lord Elgin that the seriousness of the situation had not been exaggerated but rather understated. He did not doubt the existence of a "concerted movement for rebellion," which would have involved the slaughter of whites on isolated farms. By August, Selborne could breath more easily, for the revolt had been extinguished before its sparks had lit resistance in the Transvaal or Swaziland. Natal's suppression of the rebellion would, he thought, have beneficial effects on white-black relations. As he explained to Elgin, "if the more ignorant natives are capable of learning anything, it must have an influence on them to have become assured that witch doctors can not charm warriors against white men's bullets."[20]

Several so-called expert witnesses offered Selborne their analysis of the Natal situation. A month before the disturbances broke out, Lagden warned that resurgent tribalism was creating a dangerous situation in Natal. Attempting to shore up his chieftaincy, Dinuzulu had been intriguing for years, even sending messengers outside the colony to Swaziland and Basutoland, neither of which would fall in with his plans. At the same time, the native commissioner cautioned that the chief's arrest would be a "fatal measure," likely to drive the Zulus to revolt.[21] Selborne was more circumspect. In a despatch sent on 13 August 1906, he discounted the notion that the Zulu king had instigated the revolt: "I have a strong instinct that some person, or persons, must have engineered the rebellions but not Dinuzulu. He has not the health, or intellect, or character to do it. Whoever has done it, has kept studiously in the background, though endeavouring to do his utmost to secure the co-operation of Dinuzulu, and failing that, to incriminate Dinuzulu. Dinuzulu, for his part, sat heavily on the fence; I doubt if he has in any way incriminated himself."[22] The next year, however, Selborne reconsidered the situation after the new Natal governor, Sir Matthew Nathan, had reported that investigation had left no doubt as to Dinuzulu's complicity. This finding alarmed the high commissioner, who now began to fear the Zulu king's influence in neighbouring territories such as Swaziland. The prestige of the Zulu royal family as well as the "close blood affinity" between the Zulus and Swazis increased his anxiety, and he asked Nathan to stay in close touch.[23] A year later, Selborne appeared completely convinced that the revolt had centred on Dinuzulu. To Balfour, he declared: "The Natal rebellion of two years ago was a feeler by Dinizulu. The people who rebelled were some of the tribes living in Natal most under Dinizulu's influence. He kept Zululand proper quiet til he saw whether the rebellion was going to be successful or not. From what I hear there will be no difficulty at Dinizulu's trial to prove enough abundantly to justify his arrest."[24] As the purpose of this letter was to persuade the Conservative leader to take up Natal's defence if attacked by Radicals in the House of Commons, Selborne might have been prone to exaggerate the Zulu king's culpability. Nevertheless, Nathan's report, along with the evidence of the Natal investigation, did eventually convince the high commissioner of Dinuzulu's guilt.[25]

Even when the revolt first broke out, however, Selborne refused to attribute it solely to conspiracies or to the "Ethiopian threat." Writing to Elgin shortly after the outbreak, he explained his thinking:

I fear the principal cause of the outbreak lies in the eternal truth of the adage, that "Satan finds some mischief still for idle hands to do." Almost everywhere the chiefs and elder men have said that they could not keep the younger men in hand. These are the younger men who do no work and whose only trade and only amusement has always been fighting. The great majority of them are not in any sense Christianised, but the teachings of the Ethiopian missionary had naturally upon them the effect of a spark upon timber.[26]

This diagnosis, conceived in the midst of the Chinese controversy, accorded perfectly with the industrial needs of the moment.

The Colonial Office received this despatch with warm praise. Lambert had "little doubt that Lord Selborne is right about idleness being the root cause of the trouble. British rule has suppressed war which is the natural outlet for the energy of the savage and it has substituted little else in the way of occupation." Other officials felt that perhaps the high commissioner had underestimated the importance of Ethiopianism.[27] No one in the Colonial Office contested Selborne's interpretation of the Africans' socio-economic situation.

Aware of the limits which self-government had imposed on metropolitan action, Selborne defended Natal throughout the crisis. In March 1906 he commended the colony for its "remarkable firmness and success" in handling the disturbances. "There has been," he reported, "no panic and yet no weakness; there has been stringent firmness, but no injustice."[28] During Dinuzulu's trial two years later, he feared that British criticism might alienate "loyal Natal," which would be "madness" in light of the union negotiations. Asking Balfour to stand up staunchly for the colony, he explained apologetically that Natal was too small to have enough material to form a competent government. Switching over to the offensive, he blamed the present state of affairs on the imperial government's refusal to accept responsibility for Zululand after the Zulu War.[29]

Through the lines of this defence of Natal, Selborne revealed that he considered its policy towards Africans incompetent. In his August despatch two years earlier, he expressed the hope that the rebellion would make "the Europeans recognise their responsibility for a wise native policy." And when the trouble first erupted, Selborne condemned the mediocre quality of the colony's magistrates and native commissioners. There were too many attorney's clerks and not enough civil servants knowledgeable about African affairs.[30]

The high commissioner thus faced the problem of reconciling imperial wisdom with local self-government. London could exercise no positive influence, and if it deployed its veto power it would arouse local resentment which might defeat the purpose. If Britain could not point out to Natal its mistakes, what authority could? This dilemma brought Selborne back to his earlier suggestion that a colonial upper house might be perfectly suited for this task. He noted that Natal's second chamber had indeed attempted to modify the infamous poll tax. It was essential, he believed, that the Transvaal constitution make provision for such a house, preferably nominated. An upper house composed of men appointed by the governor for their sympathy and wisdom regarding Africans would "have a great influence on the sane and impartial consideration of these matters." For example, it could attack the problem of African education, which no elected legislature would raise for fear of bringing blacks into competition with whites. Selborne had not yet decided on the usefulness of councils to represent African opinion, but he was certain that no white assembly would entertain the notion.[31] The high commissioner did not address the possibility of a constitutional deadlock, but neither had Great Britain at this time.

At the Colonial Office, Graham took up the proposal for an upper house, but Keith and Elgin preferred to wait until the West Ridgeway Commission had reported.[32] When Selborne had first brought his proposal before the Liberals in February, Churchill minuted, "Lord Selborne's anxiety about the natives seems to me a little too prominent in his argument. One would think 'native interests' was the only function of the second chamber."[33] To be sure, the Boer factor entered into Selborne's considerations here, but it was not the decisive influence Churchill thought. In the event, the West Ridgeway Commission took up the governor's proposal, and the Letters Patent provided for an upper house, nominated in the first instance but thereafter elected.[34]

As Selborne realized, it would take more than a sympathetic upper house to insulate Africans from unwise legislation, which, in arousing black discontent, might well destabilize white rule. Informed by the Natal experience, he suggested that, even in a self-governing colony, the governor could exercise a decisive influence on legislation affecting Africans. Specifically, he proposed that the Transvaal Letters Patent empower the governor, apart from his ministers, to act as the supreme authority in such matters by styling him the paramount chief of the colony. Governor McCallum occupied such a position in Natal and Kruger had done so in the South African Republic. At the Colonial Office, both Ommanney and Lambert observed that the governor of Natal was supreme chief in nothing but name. The deployment of such constitutional powers, Lambert continued, would merely spark white opposition. Keith, however, could foresee occasions when a governor should be able to disregard his ministers' advice. While Graham appreciated the objections which Ommanney and Lambert had raised, he believed that the Transvaal constitution should make Selborne supreme chief. Impressed with the high commissioner's views, Elgin stated that the despatch, along with Graham's minute "shall not be overlooked when the time comes for framing the Constitution."[35] As issued, the Letters Patent did confer on the governor the powers of paramount chief.

Even in theory, however, Selborne's constitutional position as regards Africans was somewhat obscure after self-government. Six months after Het Volk's installation, it passed a Native Administration Amendment Bill. This conferred wide powers upon the paramount chief and freed him from the jurisdiction of the colony's courts. It did not, however, free him from the cabinet, whose advice he was obliged to follow. After all, Botha ingeniously pointed out, a paramount chief according to native law could not act without the advice of his council.[36]

Selborne warmly praised the powers which the measure gave the paramount chief vis-à-vis Africans. Legislation was urgently needed to shore up the power of the chiefs, which, according to a recent test case, had no legal foundation. Selborne also considered it essential to free native administration from judicial review:

Native administration would be impossible if the Paramount Chief were not free to decide whether a given chief was or was not competent to rule a tribe, or whether the maintenance of peace within a tribe necessitated the removal of an individual chief to a different locality. Such questions are questions of State and cannot be subject to review by the Courts. It must be remembered that the great mass of the natives of the Transvaal are in a purely barbarous tribal state.[37]

Whatever his "civilising mission," this proconsul would leave Africans "without the law" – with neither their own, nor the white man's.

While enthusiastic towards the bill's legal provisions, Selborne vehemently condemned the constrictions on the governor's powers it prescribed. It was unjust and unwise to hand over the control of un-represented blacks to white politicians, whose constituents might demand repressive legislation. Though political considerations would animate Parliament, the governor, guided by the "expert advice" of his administrators, would act solely in the Africans' interest. As the ultimate security for the colony lay with imperial troops, the imperial government could reasonably demand that a British official have the final word on African policy. To be sure, the governor should always consult his ministers, who, after all, could resign if they took violent exception to his policy. But, while he admitted that the cabinet would have the final authority in any constitutional showdown, Selborne believed that, before matters ran to that extreme, the governor could exercise a useful check on hasty legislation.[38]

The High Commissioner also addressed Botha's interpretation of native law by citing the unanimous opinion of the Supreme Court judges that a paramount chief did in fact have arbitrary and absolute power over his subordinates. In 1905 the Executive Council had deposed Chief Amos Mathibe for drunkenness and profligacy. Mathibe appealed this decision, protesting that under traditional law, no paramount possessed the power which the crown colony's executive had appropriated. Rejecting this appeal, Chief Justice Richard Solomon reasoned that while African paramount chiefs had found it politic to consult their councils so as not to alienate the tribes, there was no legal requirement that they do so. Solomon declared, "Practically his power over his sub-chiefs is a despotic power, a power which he can exercise of his own free will."[39]

Selborne considered this finding an effective rebuttal to his ministers' claims, but the point is revealing for other reasons as well. For one thing, it exposes the flimsy judicial foundation of the Transvaal's African administration. The chief justice's eurocentric prejudices obscured his vision of African traditional societies, for in almost all cases, the council's consent gave not merely political force but also legitimacy to a chief's decision.[40] Solomon abstracted from its context the position of the paramount and embued it with powers it had never legitimately possessed. Thus, in endorsing the chief justice, Selborne predicated his system of native administration on misinformed, albeit convenient, anthropological assumptions. Secondly, the high commissioner's reasoning on this point lays bare the essence of his native policy – the maintenance of European domination – which, however benevolent or enlightened, amounted constitutionally to despotism.[41]

Selborne's objections convinced Johann Rissik, the minister of native affairs, to withdraw the substantial portions of the bill. Soon the matter became academic, for the National Convention had already convened and, as even Selborne had admitted in 1907, any union government must receive full control over its non-white people. Selborne never attempted to bolster metropolitan influence in African affairs but rather that of his administrators. Though Botha did not realize it, the issue at stake did not involve the relative powers of a British governor and South African ministers but those of the Transvaal Assembly vis-à-vis the Native Affairs Department. It was to this last that Selborne would confer absolute power. In his eyes, traditional authority should become a mere extension of the Transvaal administration. Here, he reflected not simply a South African trend towards differentiation but a modern world-wide movement towards bureaucratization.[42]

It was easy enough in theory to abstract Africans from South African life and file them away in the large folder labelled "native problem." In actual fact, African and white affairs intersected at innumerable points: land, labour, and politics. Indeed, the very movement of Africans throughout the colony became a subject which whites considered very much their affair. Selborne had to consider what the relations should be between black and white and on what terms, if any, Africans could be incorporated into white South Africa.

This problem arose in the question of property rights. Their exclusion from parliamentary participation rendered blacks vulnerable to white demands on them, and nowhere should this exploitability have been more marked than on the land issue. While Selborne was en route to South Africa, the Transvaal Supreme Court opened up this question by overturning the republic's prohibition against African land purchase. After the crown colony regime had refused to register the transfer of land to a certain Tsewu, the aggrieved person brought his case before the judicature, which decided in his favour.[43] This judgment brought on what Selborne described as "a rather absurd agitation" on the part of the white community. Sir George Farrar responded by hastily introducing into the Legislative Council an ordinance to restore the status quo (as he conceived it) before the Tsewu decision. He specifically proposed that all African land be registered in the name of the government, which would be empowered to restrict all black acquisitions to specified areas. When Richard Solomon pointed out the dubious constitutionality of any ordinance which took from Africans a right they presently enjoyed, Farrar dropped the overt restrictions from his proposal. The Legislative Council thereupon passed it, with only Solomon voting against it. The council's proceedings aroused sharp opposition from the African elite, which, through various bodies, sent emphatic protests to the Colonial Office.[44]

Reporting in July 1905, Selborne expressed little sympathy with Farrar's intentions but considered the ordinance harmless. It did not restrict African purchases and would give the Native Affairs Department the opportunity to tender advice so that black purchasers were not cheated by unscrupulous white hucksters. Moreover, though hollow, the concession to Farrar would calm white opinion, "which was becoming violent, mischievous and formidable." By October, however, the realization that the Tsewu decision might encourage the growth of communal tenure disposed the high commissioner more favourably to the ordinance. "This is *not* a simple question," he advised Lyttelton. "Most of the purchases are *not individual* but tribal, the chief taxing his tribe to purchase a farm to be added to the native Stadt."[45] Though no doubt exaggerated, Selborne's worries were not without foundation.

After reading Solomon's critique, the Colonial Office came out against the measure. Elgin explained that, in light of the protests from the black community, he could not endorse restrictive legislation emanating from a nominated legislature.[46] The Liberals could set aside the wishes of the unelected council with relative ease, but once the Transvaal received responsible government, such matters would involve considerable complications.

In 1908 the self-governing Transvaal passed a measure prohibiting non-white persons from acquiring mineral rights on land.[47] Taken up with closer union, Selborne was unable to address this specific bill, but he had advised Smuts generally that any legal infringement on a coloured person's right to undertake a mining enterprise constituted a disability which could not be defended "and the law ought to be altered." His views on this issue indicate that he was willing to incorporate within the capitalist classes some non-whites on certain terms. He did not explicitly include blacks and assured Smuts that "It will only be very exceptionally that a coloured man will be capable of embarking on any mining enterprise, and when he is so capable, it will only be when he is practically a white man."[48] The governor here came close to positing a social hierarchy based not on race but on class. To be a capitalist was almost the same thing, in Selborne's mind, as being a white man.

Whatever his respect for potential non-white entrepreneurs, Selborne showed little regard for squatter-peasants already working the land productively. In 1908 Selborne's ministry introduced a comprehensive land bill. Attempting to improve on the 1895 Squatter's Law, the new measure imposed on landowners a fine for every tenant-family in excess of five. It permitted any number of bona fide agricultural labourers. To discourage the growth of communal proprietorship, the bill prohibited the acquisition of land by more than five Africans. Fi-

nally, clause 10(2) made illegal the sale, lease, grant or transfer of urban property to Africans, except in locations set aside for them.[49]

The government's proposals sparked opposition from two very different quarters. Not surprisingly, the Transvaal Native Affairs Society
considered the legislation "unjust" and likely to "inflict hardship."
More surprising, in light of the Rand's long-term labour requirements,
was the opposition of certain magnates on this issue. The Transvaal
Landowners Association, with the mining interest well represented in
its ranks, strongly condemned the measure, arguing that its enforcement would displace a large number of Africans, who, given the inadequate allocation of reserve land, would be unable to find enough land
for subsistence. The class of large commercial farmers, from which
both Smuts and Botha came, stood to gain the most from the proposed law.[50]

When Selborne first perused the draft act, he did not see the urban
restrictions in section 10(2). Without this provision, the legislation appeared reasonable to him, and he gave it his qualified support. Not
surprisingly, he offered no criticism of the limitations on communal
purchase. Nor did he oppose the suppression of squatting, the nature
of which he misunderstood but roundly condemned nonetheless. Associating the practice with "Kaffir farming," he considered it injurious
to Africans themselves by subjecting them to unscrupulous whites who
charged extortionate rents. A "great evil and a growing danger," squatting, he surmised, furnished "one of the most potent causes of the recent rebellion in Natal."[51]

He did express concern that the act might discourage genuine tenant farming or market gardening and, recognizing that the legislation
did represent an attempt on the part of white farmers to force blacks to
labour for them, he castigated it as such. "But again," he equivocated,
"it is true that the more the natives are scattered among the white farmers, the more they advance in civilisation. Although I am not prepared
to say that there can be no progress in civilisation in a tribal reserve, it
is undoubtedly true that the progress there is much slower than when
the natives are living in close contact with white people."[52]

On reading the published version of the bill, however, the governor
was astonished to discover the urban restrictions embodied in clause
10(2). "No such provision," he chided Rissik, "was ever to be found in
any draft of the Bill which I had seen."[53] Selborne protested that this
provision took from Africans a right which the courts decided they possessed and one which they valued highly. He could not, for his part,
sanction the clause, nor did he expect the Liberal government to do
so. Though the high commissioner opposed communal tenure as retrogressive, he believed strongly that African individuals should be free

to purchase land wherever they chose, especially in urban areas. In a long memorandum to J.C. Smuts, the Transvaal's colonial secretary, he stressed this point, urging the general to show special consideration for urban blacks. "This is the class which, from the constancy of its contact with the white population, most quickly develops its civilisation." He did not favour uncontrolled African residence in towns and indeed considered sanitary regulations essential. But he did insist that "absolute fixity of tenure ought to be given to any native building his own house on such a location." And though to Smuts he did not question the principle of urban segregation, he forthrightly condemned it to Rissik when the land bill came up.[54] With Selborne's objections and the advent of closer union, which would permit white South Africa to address the land question on a comprehensive basis, the Transvaal government withdrew the bill.[55]

For rural areas, Selborne came to see territorial segregation as necessary. Though he favoured the creation and extension of reserves, he did not seem to appreciate these areas as a pool for migratory labourers. Instead, he commended reserves to Smuts for "sorting out automatically the less from the more progressive part of the population." Moreover, he considered them a "safety valve, an insurance of orderly progress." They constituted, for Selborne, an important instrument of control.

Closely connected with the land laws was the question of labour. While Selborne disparaged squatting, he praised government efforts to encourage the settlement of Africans on white farms as bona fide labourers. He would not, however, tie Africans to European farmers. As he told Smuts, "It is essential for the good of the white and the black alike that it should always be clearly understood that the native is free, consistently with the fulfilment of contractural obligations, to sell his labour whenever he can get the best market for it, and correspondingly that the farmer is not obliged to retain on his land, either as a labourer or as a tenant, any native that he does not so desire to retain."[56] Though theoretically the governor favoured the growth of a black bourgeoisie in town and country, the future he foresaw for Africans was a labouring one and the freedom he recommended for them was a free labour market. The absolute discretion he would confer on landowners, all of whom happened to be white, could and no doubt would be used to destroy any surviving African peasants. Given the distribution of land in 1908, the full exercise of private property rights would promote black proletarianization. Selborne's policy by itself would not directly cause this development, but it would create the framework which would make the displacement of peasant farmers a likely if not inevitable consequence.

As with the land question, it is difficult to link directly Selborne's concern for industrial development with his attitude regarding the pass laws or other disabilities under which Africans suffered. For one thing, his attitude shifted during his tenure in South Africa. In 1905 the Native United Political Association sent a petition of grievances to the high commissioner. Discerning a tendency towards "class legislation," the petitioners protested that the status of Africans had deteriorated under crown colony rule. In a point-by-point rebuttal, Selborne defended the existing network of municipal restrictions on non-whites.[57]

The Natal experience forced the high commissioner to re-evaluate the network of regulations which constricted almost every activity of non-whites, however educated. Even before the rebellion, he expressed to Elgin his anxiety on the subject.[58] Well aware of the general non-white disillusionment with imperial rule, he deplored what he described to Richard Solomon as the "great revulsion of feeling throughout South Africa in the attitude of the coloured people and educated natives towards the British." As incongruous as it might seem, the possibility that the Boers might woo these discontented people made Selborne decidedly uneasy. Not only had magistrates noticed this tendency in the Transvaal, but prominent black or coloured leaders in the Cape, such as J.T. Jabavu and Ismail Abdurahman, actively supported the Afrikaner Bond. The crown colony regime, he urged, should do all in its power to win back the loyalty of the black and coloured educated elite. He admitted that "there is not much that we can do; but anything we can do I say let us do it."[59]

As early as November 1905, Selborne had raised the question of African taxation with an eye to reform. He recommended to Lagden that the native tax be halved across the board from two pounds to one. The native commissioner took this proposal to the Executive Council, which refused to go as far as Selborne wished. It would, however, slash the tax to 10 shillings for urban residents who paid municipal rates and for permanent agricultural labourers, including squatters. Accepting the compromise, the governor prodded the cautious council to action. The Natal rebellion gave urgency to the matter, for as he warned Solomon, "If the trouble in Natal spreads, action or inaction in respect of taxes may just turn the balance in the mind of the foolish native in the Piet Retief District, or in Swaziland or in the Northern Transvaal." These tax reforms came into force as Ordinance 20 of 1906.[60]

As Selborne held up what he called civilization as the avowed end of his policy, education should logically have been of crucial concern to him. It certainly was to Africans. In 1903 the South African Native Congress observed to Chamberlain that, since all tribal resistance had been crushed, the white rulers no longer faced a native problem but rather a problem of rule: "How to govern and educate on those broad and impartial lines" which would promote justice and protect the weak.[61] Several Africans who gave evidence before SANAC argued more forthrightly for the expansion of black educational opportunities. The Reverend Mpela, for example, declared that "Boys, when they come back from school, must take a prominent place in the country."[62]

Selborne sympathized with these wishes. Moreover, he regretted that Africans received so little in return for the large contributions they paid into the Treasury. "No white man so far as I know contributes to the Revenue anything like so large a proportion of his earnings as the native." In June 1906, he discussed the matter with Lagden, who agreed that instead of merely granting aid to missionary schools, the government should start schools of its own where these did not already exist.[63] From 1905 to 1906 public expenditure on education increased from £5,800 to £6,500, and for the year 1906–7 the projected expenditure totalled £10,000.[64] Though this amounted to a pittance when compared with expenditures on white education, it did at least mark some small improvement.

In 1908 the high commissioner expounded his views on African education to Smuts. Selborne recommended that African education be run along the lines of agricultural training. Black men, he considered, should learn "how to plough a straight furrow," how to care for stock, how to mend fences and farm machinery. Besides reading, writing, and arithmetic, schools should teach Africans music:

The former would make him a more useful servant, and the latter a happier being; but the main lines on which I should like to see his education developed, are those of what in England I should call a first class agricultural labourer. The one thing which the farmers of the Transvaal most require is steady and efficient labour; the one work for which the native is most suited is agricultural work; and as an agricultural labourer he will never come into competition with the white man.

To finance this program, Selborne advised earmarking mineral royalties on government land. In addition, considering the African tax revenue, the state should generously extend supplementary grants. It would be in the white polity's interest to do so, for even if it granted no funding at all, Africans who wanted an education would get it anyway and would "probably get it under pernicious influences. Therefore I say that the Government itself must take this matter in hand."[65]

Selborne's attitude on this issue reveals the future he envisioned for Africans in a white South Africa and what he meant by civilization. Though his plans would not promise to produce mine workers, they would indirectly assist industry in the long run by promoting capitalist agriculture and, most important, industrial peace. While he claimed that blacks should be free to develop their full potential, Selborne's educational policy, whether deliberate or not, stacked the decks so that black inferiority and subordination would become a self-perpetuating prophecy.

In his minute of November 1905 Selborne had also suggested loosening the pass laws, but here he met opposition from Lagden, who feared that this might encourage malingering or desertion from work. The most Selborne could extract from his government was some reduction in penalties and the extension of the time permitted Africans to seek work without a pass from three days to ten.[66]

It is not surprising that these small gestures failed to mollify African opinion. In mid-1906 the Transvaal Native Congress appealed to Britain for protection against the arbitrary actions of the colony's government. The pass system, for example, not only infringed on their freedom of movement, it bred criminality by making outlaws of minor violators. The Congress anticipated even worse times after responsible government.[67] The high commissioner appreciated African grievances and was willing to travel a certain distance to redress them. His government, especially the commissioner for native affairs, limited the distance he could go. To be sure, the reforms which Selborne charted would have made for a short enough trip, but with Lagden in the front seat, he never really even got onto the road.

Once self-government had relieved him of responsibility in these matters, he articulated his sentiments more freely. In his long 1908 memorandum for Smuts, he roundly condemned the "pin-prick policy of the Municipalities," most notably the tram and walkway restrictions. Three years before he had described the Morality Law proscribing inter-racial intercourse as even-handed, but he now denounced it as "very unequal." He reserved his greatest fury, however, for the pass system. Exhorting Smuts to show more sympathy to blacks, he stated: "Now, if one wants to know how natives regard the Pass Laws, one has only got to ask oneself how one would regard it oneself. It is irritating to them in the highest degree." Selborne asked the Transvaal statesman to consider whether these laws were really necessary. Indeed, "they must militate seriously against the freedom with which natives leave their homes to seek work. After all, natives are very like other human beings in their essentials, and I say without hesitation that, if an English labourer had to get the passes which a native has to get in the Transvaal before he could leave his village, say, in Hampshire, to obtain work, say, in London, the circulation of labour would be enormously decreased in England."[68]

Mining prosperity remained as much a priority for Selborne in 1908 as it had been two years earlier. Contrary to what some historians might expect, this capitalist statesman did not consider the pass sytem as conducive to capital accumulation. Perhaps he had confidence that, in free competition for labour, the Rand would win, though his remarks about the attractiveness of farm work to Africans would seem to contradict this conclusion. It is more likely that Selborne was concerned here with the broader aspects of socio-economic development: integrating Africans into the capitalist system and, above all, preserving racial peace.

As crucial as land issues or pass laws were to most Africans, the most highly charged question which Selborne faced was the political status of educated non-whites, who represented, after all, a potentiality for all blacks. Though he could in 1906 write the majority of Africans off as "totally unfit to exercise any of the responsibility of a voter,"[69] he acknowledged the presence of coloureds and educated blacks who, without the colour bar, would indeed qualify for the franchise. If he needed reminding, a variety of non-white political organizations voiced their objection to political discrimination on the basis of race. Shortly after his arrival, the predominantly coloured membership of the African Political Organisation held a large meeting which denounced the franchise provisions of the Lyttelton Constitution as "a grave act of injustice unworthy of British traditions." The advent of the Liberals and the revocation of the Lyttelton scheme gave the APO new hope. In June of 1906, Dr Abdurahman of the organization suggested to London that coloureds did not come under the Vereeniging pledge to defer the native franchise question until a self-governing assembly could address it.[70]

To all these entreaties, Westminster replied that Vereeniging did indeed tie its hands, even in regard to coloureds. On this point Elgin, West Ridgeway, and Selborne all agreed, though not without anguish.[71] Despite his reluctance to exempt them from the Vereeniging pledges, the position of coloureds caused the high commissioner especially grave concern as early as 1906. He found it exceedingly difficult to locate these people in the racial order of society. Indeed, the existence of this group called into question the very notion of ordering a society along rigidly stratified lines. "I would observe," he wrote Elgin,

that in my opinion it is not the case that the sympathies of the so-called coloured persons are more with the aboriginal native than with their white fellow subjects. Much of the difficulty of dealing with the question of the treatment and status of coloured persons appears to me to lie in the fact that while it is as difficult to draw a clear distincion between the high-class coloured person and the white man at one end of the scale as it is to draw a distinction between the high-class aboriginal native and the coloured person at the other end of the scale, the broad distinction between the three classes is easily recognised, and the coloured persons as a whole are jealous of their superiority over the native as the white population as a whole are jealous of their superiority over the coloured persons. Similarly, the coloured persons are as ambitious of being recognised as the political and social equals of the white as the natives are of being recognised as the political and social equals of the coloured people.[72]

Race lay at the bottom of Selborne's analysis of South Africa's social organization, but he recognized that there existed no sharp stratification between racial groups. He posited instead a dynamic continuum with upwardly mobile individuals of different complexions shading into each other. This made the demarcation of colour barriers both artificial and arbitrary. In Selborne's mind, the clear racial lines along which industry organized its workforce were illusory. In 1906, however, he would not risk pursuing his logic in the face of white sentiment.

A year later, in 1907, the *Selborne Memorandum* initiated the movement for closer union. It cited as one advantage of unification the evolution of a uniform native policy instead of the present five or six. Though it did not address the franchise directly, it exhorted whites to "extend the hand of sympathy to the coloured people" and to the "educated native."[73] The high commissioner took the approach of union as an opportunity to make public his views on African affairs, especially the franchise question. He cultivated the friendship of well-known liberals such as J.M. Orpen and Theophilus Schreiner and encouraged their correspondence. More than this, he made speeches which warned white South Africa that if it denied "to natives those same elementary principles of justice which you have always claimed for yourselves, then the wheels of God will grind slowly your children and your children's children."[74]

On the eve of the National Convention for union, the high commissioner sent Smuts his expansive missive of 1 September 1908 offering his ideas on African affairs. He held up three aims of policy: the preservation of peace, the gradual destruction of tribalism, and the promotion of Christianity and civilization. "An important feature of this policy will be teaching the natives to work." His inducement, however, would not take the form of land measures or coercive acts. Rather, he would inculcate industrious habits gradually, by increasing African wants, especially the wants of the women. Contact with whites and education would engender these characteristics.

In his advice he stressed, as he had before, the necessity of insulating blacks from the white parliament. Responsibility for African affairs should be entrusted to a strong and permanent native affairs department, directly under the prime minister. This would provide "that personal, consistent, and continuous, government which is necessary for natives." While two years earlier he had condemned the formation of African advisory councils, he now considered that they could furnish a useful outlet for the expression of African grievances. He still, however, shied away from creating one large body, recommending instead the erection of district councils.

On this occasion, Selborne addressed the franchise issue squarely. Coloureds, he urged, must be integrated into the white order: "It seems to me sheer folly to classify them with Natives, and by treating them as natives to force them away from their natural allegiance to the whites and into making common cause with the Natives. If they are so forced, in the time of trouble they will furnish exactly those leaders which the Natives could not furnish for themselves." For the sake of stability as well as justice, coloureds should suffer no differential disabilities, though only those "civilised" should enjoy the franchise.

As for the vote, the high commissioner unequivocably declared that the criterion for the franchise must be civilization, not colour. The Cape franchise he considered too lenient in this respect, for property qualifications alone could not sift out "uncivilised" blacks. Carrying his logic through, he proposed a civilization test, administered and evaluated by three judges of the Supreme Court. The applicant would have to prove that "by his general standard of living and conduct, he was a civilised man." While coloureds could pass this privilege on to their sons, the heirs of "civilised" Africans would have to wait three generations before they could claim this right automatically.[75]

Vague as it is, Selborne's criterion is revealing in that it stressed not literacy or knowledge but standard of living. Selborne here was attempting to reorient the basis of South African society from race to class. The very ambiguity of the word "civilisation" left great discretion to the ruling caste in determining whom to admit into the club. Though restrictive, Selborne's scheme did burst the colour barrier. Moreover, he would probably have gone further in this direction if he thought he could have carried white opinion with him. This is not to suggest that Selborne was selling out the mining industry. On the contrary, he was too farsighted a statesman to tie capitalism to a socio-political practice he considered static, dogmatic, and possibly dangerous. He saw no reason why the gold industry could not continue to prosper on the less brittle lines of "civilisation," which would still leave the majority of Africans classified as uncivilized and therefore ultra-exploitable.

It might seem that Selborne was taking a risk by cracking a door which could in time be opened fully. The theoretical claim which Cape

Africans had to the franchise, even if only actualized in few cases, prevented Prime Minister Hertzog from implementing his segregationist land policy, which of course would have affected all non-whites. And Selborne would have extended this legal claim across the whole of southern Africa. Moreover, the existence of even a few black voters placed into jeopardy the order which, according to some historians, maintained both gold mining and agriculture. As Lacey put it:

Politicised, propertied, educated Africans not only exploded the myth of racial inferiority; they also stood outside the coercive system being built by the State. Cape Africans therefore had to be downgraded to the level of their Northern counterparts. Equally, as politicised Africans from the South settled in the main industrial towns in the North, the State believed they would contaminate the rest of the work force: soon all would demand the rights and privileges of the "civilised" voter in the Cape.[76]

How could Selborne assure Smuts that his proposals would not endanger white supremacy? The key lies in his social Darwinism, which left him in no doubt that "the black man is absolutely incapable of rivalling the white man." Selborne feared that, if coddled by discriminatory laws, the "white man" would lose those characteristics which made him superior. Any measure which prevented the African from developing his full potential amounted to nothing less than slavery.[77] Selborne's racial smugness enabled him to integrate Cape liberalism, industrial imperatives, and white supremacy. To this governor there was no contradiction, for civilization and capitalism went hand-in-hand.

White South Africa, however, was not so astute. It soon became apparent that the colonists would not concede the limited political equality Selborne advocated. Before the National Convention even assembled to draft a constitution for a united South Africa, Smuts and Merriman[78] agreed that the laws existing in the various colonies must remain in force, as no common policy could be hammered out without endangering closer union.

At the convention three outlooks were expressed: Cape liberalism, which made property and literacy the criteria for voting; the northern view, shared by Natal, that race should determine political qualification; and Selborne's civilization proposals as articulated by FitzPatrick. As a compromise, Merriman brought up a motion which suggested letting the Cape retain its franchise system and the other colonies theirs. This formed the basis of the final settlement embodied in the Act of Union.

This compromise protected the Cape's franchise system by requiring a parliamentary majority of two-thirds, with both Houses voting to-

gether, to remove it. Though the Cape delegates were decisive in producing the final settlement, Selborne's influence probably bolstered
their position, contrary to Leonard Thompson's wild speculation that
the proconsul weakened their hand by tarring it with the unpopular
imperial brush.[79] Though in retreat, the imperial government was still
a factor in the situation. It would accede to *almost* any settlement but,
as Sir Henry de Villiers, the convention president, realized, British tol-
eration did have its limits.[80] Through exhortation or veiled threat, Selborne deployed what influence he had effectively and contributed,
however modestly, to the final result.

The appeals which Selborne predicted would follow the act did not
take long to materialize. Numerous associations of African and coloured people sent emphatic protests to England.[81] Selborne himself
realized that the constitution represented a compromise which fell
short of his expectations for Africans and coloureds. Reckoning that
colonial opinion was also dissatisfied, he remarked, "the general feeling seems to be that the draft constitution, being the result of a series
of compromises not calculated to be entirely acceptable to anyone, is,
on the whole, as satisfactory a compromise between divergent aims
and aspirations as could have been expected."[82] He was most disap-
pointed with the entrenchment of the political colour bar, which could
in time prove dangerous. Excluded from political participation within
the South African polity, educated blacks and, more probably, coloureds would exercise their talents without – to the country's detriment. Shortly before sailing for home, Selborne delivered one last
speech which starkly revealed his fears on this score.

One day you may have to face some great concerted movement of the native
races of South Africa. Now I have said before, and I say it again here in one of
my last speeches, that I believe the statesmanship of the Union ought to save
you, and will save you, from any such catastrophe; and I do say this, that if ever
such a terrible catastrophe occurs, I make this prophecy: you will find the
leader of the native races to be a coloured man – a coloured man with the feeling, the character and the superiority of the white – if you have persisted in the
tendency to degrade him into the condition of the native.[83]

It is clear that the connections between Selborne's concern for industrial prosperity and his proposals on African policy were not direct but
subtle. He did not advocate territorial segregation to create a labour
pool, nor did he regard the reserves as a permanent or desirable feature of South Africa's human geography. Though he did oppose squatting, his opposition sprang from political motives. Indeed, he failed
even to recognize the existence of a productive peasantry. Moreover, he

attempted to stimulate the rise of an urban educated class of Africans and coloureds, who might in time strain the colour line to the breaking point. In urging the abolition of pass laws, he would have dismantled the coercive apparatus which controlled the labour supply. Finally, his political advice struck the racist underpinnings of the Witwatersrand and the rest of white South Africa.

What deflected the proconsul's policy from a narrowly economistic course was the intellectual baggage he brought with him from England and African actions in South Africa. His liberal individualism made pass laws and colour bars repugnant to him. And the Natal rebels convinced him that such measures were unwise. Throughout his tenure, Selborne's dominant concern was to prevent another rising, to preserve the peace in the country. This consideration overshadowed even the labour shortage in importance. In pursuit of this objective, he advocated removing blacks from the grip of white legislatures and consigning them instead to administrative experts, who would constitute their own law. Selborne was astute enough to realize that the black elite would not fit into this bureaucratic box. They must be placated, absorbed into the white polity before they destroyed it from outside. The governor would decapitate a concerted rebellion before it started.

This suggests that Selborne had far keener insight into capitalist interests than the capitalists themselves. His ideology legitimated the process of proletarianization, for his civilizing mission entailed the transformation of Africans into productive labourers. Though he spoke of developing African potential, his educational proposals reveal what he considered their potential to be, and, had they been adopted, would have hastened the creation of a proletarian workforce. In upholding the principle of individual property rights, he at once protected the European system of landownership from communal proprietorship and set out the terms on which non-whites could enter this system. And by controlling Africans, whether through regulation or co-option, he promoted the stability which investors required. He did more in this direction than merely keep the peace. With his ministers, he fashioned a thorough network of control, which would enable his successors to make efficient use of the country's black resources. In short, Selborne's African policy fostered dynamic stability in that it preserved peace and property relations while allowing for the incorporation of "progressive" non-whites into the ruling class.

During his tenure as high commissioner, he never saw his proposals put into action. In the face of white opposition, he could do little more than offer advice or check unwise legislation. He did succeed in keeping the peace. Moreover, future politicians would borrow his ideas, especially those prescribing tighter administrative control, to bolster the stability of white South Africa. The measures he took and those he advocated to ensure the subordination of Africans constitute an unfortunate contribution to South Africa.

This would have deeply grieved Selborne. When his successors borrowed his ideas, they borrowed selectively, taking the stick without the carrot. True, by placing such a premium on control, he helped to stabilize what was a differentiated order. He could not know, however, what grotesque dimensions this order would assume fifty years hence. He could not understand colonial illiberalism. His social Darwinism enabled him to reconcile liberalism with an economic order which amounted to coercion and repression. For him, civilization, white supremacy, and capital accumulation were all corners of the same triangle. He could not envision a world where white dominance was not tempered by reason, where ruling was not guided by justice. It would remain for later masters of South Africa to demonstrate how far white supremacy could diverge from liberal civilization.

7 South African Disunion: Selborne, the Railway Crisis, and Constructive Solutions

Although Selborne devoted great attention to African affairs, both within the Transvaal and without, the non-European population did not present him with the only problem of control. With four competing colonies, South Africa lacked political stability, without which it would never efficiently exploit the region's bountiful resources. European investors, would stay away so long as intercolonial chaos reigned supreme. The rivalries among the four colonies made the infrastructure which supported the gold-mining industry fragile indeed. In particular, the transportation network which served the Rand remained, in terms of cost and access, as unpredictable and unreliable after the Boer War as it had been before. As with non-European issues, Selborne found the solution to this problem in the extension of centralized state administration. And on this matter, he achieved considerably more success.

In the Intercolonial Council, Milner bequeathed not only an instrument for bureaucratization but also the institutional basis for unification. This nominated body controlled certain services common to both the Transvaal and the Orange River Colony, notably the railways and the South African Constabulary. It was created to administer the £35 million guaranteed loan which funded war compensation claims, the South African Constabulary, and, most important, railway development projects. From an imperial standpoint, the council's essential function was to promote material development by maintaining the existing communications network, extending it where needed, and rationalizing its operation. This included all aspects of rail policy, including not merely the upkeep of existing lines but the initiation of new construction where it would most benefit the local (primarily Witwatersrand) economy. Though nominally an advisory body, the ICC exercised virtually full control of the combined railways of the two new colonies. It set rates and decided routes over an integrated rail system and thereby furnished a certain degree of stability and uniformity. Under the crown colony regime, all rail lines in the two former republics operated according to ICC rules.[1] However efficient, this system would become anomalous after self-government.

Like his predecessor, Selborne attempted to save the ICC by securing borrowing powers for it, and like Milner he met insuperable opposition from the secretary of state.[2] Undeterred, Selborne moved on other fronts to salvage the ICC. Anticipating the imminent initiation of representative government, he feared for the future of the council. As he had admitted in his despatch of 16 September 1905, it was greatly unpopular in its appointive form, and was condemned by both the Responsible Government Association and Het Volk.[3] Selborne urgently sought some way to prevent the dismantling of the united railway system, which would prove both "retrograde and disastrous."[4]

In early August 1905, at a private interview, H.C. Hull of the Responsibles had warned Selborne that the ICC's only salvation lay in making it elective. A week later Selborne alluded to this possibility. By November he presented his superior in London, Sir Alfred Lyttelton, with a concrete proposal, which had emerged from a conference at his residence. Specifically, he recommended reconstituting the Intercolonial Council so that members elected from the colonial legislatures would possess a "commanding majority" over the officials. The council could then acquire borrowing powers and gain respect. If his proposals succeeded, "The charge that the Inter-Colonial Council rests upon no basis of popular consent will then have lost its force."[5]

This last contention was slightly misleading, for Selborne's scheme hardly made for democratic control. Out of a thirty-member council, he envisioned ten officials and twenty elected members (twelve for the Transvaal and eight for the ORC). The officials would not need many elected allies to check any retrograde parochialism on, say, the part of Het Volk. In any intercolonial dispute, the Transvaal could always swamp the ORC. Finally, the very existence of an intercolonial body controlling the railways prejudged the fundamental question of railway ownership and the united system. Under Selborne's plan, sectionalism would be excluded from the political process, at least on railway issues.

In any case, the advent of the Liberal government less than a month after Selborne tendered this advice and the subsequent decision to concede full responsible government rendered the governor's plan ir-relevant. By the Letters Patent, the ICC would continue, with its func-tions as assigned by the original order-in-council. It became, however, completely responsible to the governments of the respective colonies. The official members were appointed by the governments of the day and the unofficial ones elected by the assemblies. Either colony could withdraw after giving six months' notice.[6]

In August 1906 Selborne predicted privately to Elgin that, although the two governments would probably take individual control of certain ICC functions (such as the South African Constabulary), they would find it impossible to divide the joint railway system. To do so would in-jure ORC interests for, in the event of separation, the Transvaal would have no stake in its neighbour's lines. In December 1907 the Transvaal government gave notice of its intention to withdraw from the ICC. As Selborne had foreseen, however, the two new colonies subsequently came to a convention for the joint working and administration of their railways.[7] However narrow their outlook, the Boer politicians were un-willing to turn back the clock. They had, it must be noted, dissolved the agency which gave institutional direction, protection, and stability to the integrated transportation network which Milner had founded. A suitable substitute and one more compatible with representative poli-tics remained to be devised.

This highlights the central problem facing South African states-men. The Transvaal government had to foster material development without alienating the voters. The former aim required some central agency for integration and control. An autonomous bureaucracy, however, tended to stimulate public suspicion as much as economic growth. Political leaders could not resolve this dilemma by jeopardiz-ing economic progress. They therefore had to popularize the control of economic affairs. The erection of a state system economically effi-cient yet politically unobjectionable called for statecraft of the highest order. At the very moment the Transvaal tendered notice of the termi-nation of the ICC, certain political architects in South Africa were peddling the blueprint they had devised for just such an edifice. We will learn more about this in the next chapter.

Before responsible government, railway difficulties plagued Sel-borne not only in the new colonies but throughout Southern Africa. Dependence on Mozambique labour had forced the Transvaal to ac-cord to the Portuguese colony port privileges over the Cape and Natal, which as a consequence had to watch their rail traffic slip to Lourenço Marques. Facing financial ruin, it was no wonder the embittered coastal colonies complained loudly and vehemently denounced the Transvaal's bargain with Portuguese East Africa (Mozambique). Their discontent produced chronic instability, with a rate war perpetually either near or actually at hand. The inter-state rivalry for Rand traffic brought out both the Transvaal's pivotal importance in effecting any settlement and its vital interest in doing so. The strategic position of the ICC emerged clearly in every rail dispute, for its decisions could single-handedly boost or break the coastal treasuries. To be sure, the Transvaal depended on the maritime states, but, to a certain extent, it could choose among them. To say this in no way diminishes the importance of coastal traffic to the mining industry. Indeed, however much it might prosper by the efficient management and development of the Central South African Railway (CSAR) system, its very existence depended on overseas supplies. The cut-throat competition for Rand trade generated an intense hostility which poisoned relations among the British South African colonies and continuously dislocated the transportation network which fed the Rand. This instability proved harmful for business planning, capital investment, and, considering the agreement with Portugal, the labour supply as well. As the entire regional economy depended ultimately on the Rand's prosperity, it was in the interest of all colonies to bury their hatchets. Not surprisingly, however, local interests and short-term considerations prevailed in each colony.

So concerned was Selborne with this problem that, six months after his arrival, he issued a state paper which called for the amalgamation of the disparate South African railway systems.[8] In this important document, circulated in September 1905, he clearly outlined the divergent interests of the four colonies. The high rail rates which buoyed the government revenues of the Cape and Natal simultaneously inflated the already high cost of living in Johannesburg. The Delagoa Bay route to Lourenço Marques, on the other hand, was the cheapest for the Transvaal consumer and also the most remunerative for CSAR finances (since the Transvaal controlled more mileage along this route than along any other). While the Cape and Natal fought each other for Transvaal trade, they both joined together in common jealousy against Mozambique.

The situation seemed volatile indeed, for every new trunk line built by the CSAR would necessarily redistribute traffic and consequently create fresh discord. Thus, Selborne predicted that conditions would deteriorate further with each new line laid down: "In the near future there will be a considerable development of railway lines both East and West in the Transvaal and the Orange River Colonies, and, under the present condition of affairs, each of these developments will provide an occasion of jealous conflict between the coastal railway systems. No development of railways to the West or East can fail in some measure to redistribute trade and to give the Cape or Natal or the Portuguese railway systems respectively a share of that which is now enjoyed by one or other of them." It was impossible, of course, to stop development, for "South Africa has now reached the stage at which it cannot stand still: it must either advance or recede." As the Transvaal economy expanded, it would inevitably emit ripples which would rock, perhaps swamp, existing railway arrangements.

Intercolonial tension, therefore, would intensify and conflict become more frequent. "The economical and financial results of these quarrels," Selborne warned,

will be disastrous to the Cape Colony and Natal. They will in a certain, though probably not an immediate future, be equally disastrous to the Orange River Colony and to the Transvaal ... The result, to the cause of South African unity, would be fatal; indeed, it is probably not an exaggeration to say that on the manner and spirit in which the peoples and Parliaments of South Africa handle this railway question depends the eventual answer to the larger question, whether South Africa is to contain one great united people, like Canada and the United States, or a congeries of separate and constantly quarrelling little states, like the American states before the Union or the petty German Principalities prior to 1870.

The proconsul painted a bleak picture indeed.

The high commissioner did, however, discern a solution. He blamed these quarrels on archaic political boundaries, which obscured a deeper unity. In fact, he observed, the long-term interests of the various colonies complemented each other, for economically South Africa constituted an integral unit. However short the Delagoa Bay route, the Transvaal could not safely rely on a foreign power, whose friendship it could not always take for granted. Moreover, the Transvaal would gain by having as many lines as possible serve the Rand. Conversely, the coastal colonies' prosperity ultimately depended on the health of the gold-mining industry; they would therefore benefit in the long run if, in the short run, they sacrificed some revenue by lowering their rates.

Selborne presented the unification of the British South African railway systems as the only remedy. The consolidation of all railway assets would eliminate the parochial interests of each colony. Every state would favour using the most efficient and inexpensive lines to Johannesburg, for all systems would share in the combined project. Condemning the use of railways to increase government revenues, Selborne stipulated that the united system should run at cost. In his concern for the Rand, he neglected to specify how the coastal treasuries would recoup the loss of their railway receipts. However rosy the picture which

Selborne's scheme promised, the Cape and Natal were not likely to relish the immediate prospect of bankruptcy.

The high commissioner did realize that efficient railway management might be incompatible with democratic control. "It will be objected," he wrote,

that any system of railway unification must deprive the respective Colonial Parliaments of their proper control over the management of existing, and the development of future, railways running in their territory. That it will deprive them of the same immediate control as they now possess I admit at once, because unification is obviously impossible if exactly the same identical form of control, that is now exercised, is insisted upon; but my reply is that the present system of control is not the only possible system, and that I shall make it abundantly clear, in the course of this letter, that I recognise that unification, to be a practicable policy, must be made compatible with popular control.

As a solution to this conundrum, Selborne suggested entrusting general railway policy to a council composed of representatives elected from the participating governments. For the routine operation of the railways, he proposed a permanent commission. Essentially, Selborne's proposals amounted to an extension of the Intercolonial Council over all of British South Africa. And like the ICC, the united rail system was clearly designed first and foremost, to serve the Rand. In what was a veiled threat, Selborne added that the adherence by even one of the two coastal colonies to his scheme would enable it to go forward.

Throughout October and November, Selborne disseminated his message in public speeches in the Transvaal and Natal. Though sceptical, the Transvaal press endorsed his views, as did the *Natal Mercury*. Less enthusiastic, the Cape's *Eastern Province Herald* considered the suggestion that unification could be achieved piecemeal by two colonies uniting "positively mischievous," conjuring up as it did a CSAR-Natal union. The *South African News* suggested the destruction of the ICC as a preliminary step to railway amalgamation, while the *Cape Daily Telegraph* criticized the high commissioner for forcing the pace.[9] In any case, the matter slumbered for several months after the non-committal replies of the Cape and Natal governments.[10]

Selborne's contention that every new railway development in the interior would create serious trouble throughout South Africa was soon given ample proof. Under Milner's direction, the ICC had concluded two intercolonial accords. With the Cape it had agreed to build the Klerksdorp–Fourteen Streams line, and with Natal it had sanctioned the construction of a line from Bethlehem to Kroonstad. The completion of the first line in May 1906 placed the Cape in a favourable position to capture western Transvaal trade – at Natal's expense. Though discontented, Natal went no further than to issue a protest. It only had a month to wait before the completion of the Bethlehem-Kroonstad section evened the score. This enabled Natal to undercut its maritime neighbour in the southern Orange River Colony, previously the Cape's preserve. Not content with mere grumbling, the Cape threatened rebates on its ORC traffic. This brought the ICC into the fray, and its Railway Committee assured Natal that, if necessary, the CSAR would raise its rates to offset any Cape action. Failing to reach an agreement with its rival, the Cape appealed to the high commissioner.[11]

To avert a serious intercolonial conflict, Selborne entered into a vigorous correspondence with Sir Walter Hely-Hutchinson, the Cape's governor. Urging the justice of Natal's present claim, the high commissioner recounted the strenuous efforts he had made previously on behalf of the Cape and, more particularly, in support of the Jameson ministry. He could not, however, deny to Natal the advantages which, by agreement with the CSAR, it had a right to expect. The Cape premier, L.S. Jameson, this time was asking too much. The Cape's threatened rebates would, Selborne predicted, plunge South Africa into a disastrous rate war which could easily reach the "competitive zone" covered under the agreement with Portugal. In that event the CSAR would be forced to lower its rates on the Delagoa Bay line and, thereby, the ICC's revenues. To avert this eventuality, Selborne warned his colleague, he would authorize the CSAR to raise rates on its trunk lines from the Cape. In this way, he would nullify the effect of the Cape rebates and nip a rate war in the bud. He begged the Cape governor to convince his ministers to negotiate with Natal and promised to support any ensuing agreement.[12]

The Cape dashed these hopes when it made good its threat by advertising rebates on ORC traffic. Defending Jameson's action, Sir Walter wrote Selborne that he saw no reason for the CSAR's intervention. He further attempted to tie imperial considerations to the Cape's cause: "It is solely with a view to maintaining British interests in South Africa that he [Jameson] remains in office, and you may be quite sure that he would not have taken the step of granting the rebate if he had not considered it absolutely necessary in British interests (from the point of view of the necessity of maintaining a British ministry in power at the Cape) that he should do so." Selborne had anticipated this last contention in his previous letter, declaring then that "the weapon of the weakness of Jameson's Government has been strained to the breaking point, and the breaking point, I much fear, has now come."[13] However much Jameson needed imperial bolstering, imperial interests had other instruments besides Jameson or even the Cape.

Selborne continued his efforts to moderate the Cape and warned again of Transvaal retaliation. This led Hely-Hutchinson to threaten that he would, in such a contingency, protest to the British government. The high commissioner remained unconcerned by the prospect of a Cape appeal to London. He assured Sir Walter that he had already alerted Lord Elgin to this possibility and that "therefore the storm will not fall on my devoted head, but on that of the S. of S. [Secretary of State]."[14]

In fact, Selborne had informed Elgin only two days before of the crisis brewing. Strongly pushing Natal's case, he condemned the Cape for wrecking his arbitration attempt. As it stood, Natal would not negotiate until the Cape withdrew its rebates, which it steadily refused to consider. He reiterated these and other arguments he had used with Hely-Hutchinson, as he transmitted the CSAR's request to impose countervailing rates.

In its minute, the Railway Committee detailed the Cape's misconduct and roundly condemned its selfish greed, bad faith, and reckless hostility to Natal. Moreover, its precipitous action in granting rebates was a positive danger to the smooth operation of the existing communications system and its stable development in the future. Surprisingly, the Transvaal labour supply was not among the Railway Committee's worries, for even if a rate war reached the competitive zone, the CSAR could protect the agreement with Portugal by simply lowering its Delagoa Bay rates. What worried the committee was the consequent loss of revenue and its effect on the ICC budget. Moreover, the Cape's rebates had nullified the advantages Natal had expected from the Bethlehem-Kroonstad agreement with the ICC. Failure to check the Cape would discredit the Intercolonial Council and render its agreements worthless. Finally, if the Cape succeeded in unilaterally altering the railway rate structure, "the whole basis of the existing undertaking among the various administrations as to through rates would be destroyed." The Railway Committee therefore asked permission to impose countervailing rates against the Cape, and, in his cover letter, Selborne endorsed the request.[15]

The fears which Selborne and the committee expressed were not without foundation. If the Cape could single-handedly alter transport costs, nullify CSAR agreements with other colonies, bankrupt the ICC budget, and initiate rate wars, any colony could effectively reduce South Africa's rail network to chaos. The Transvaal and its mines would become hostage to the coastal colonies, with their endless quarrels. The imperial factor merely exacerbated the situation by encouraging a colony in the hope that it could break the status quo without retaliation. There is little doubt that the "appeal to Caesar" in this case encouraged the Cape's truculence. In the CSAR, however, the inland colonies did possess a potent weapon to foil the Cape – if only the colonial secretary would allow them to deploy it.

On 7 August Elgin informed Selborne that, while he recognized the seriousness of the situation, he could not authorize the imposition of countervailing rates until he had heard the Cape's version of events. Less than a week later, the colonial secretary received an angry response from the Railway Committee, which resolved that, "it is most undesirable that questions of this nature should be decided by Secretary of State for Colonies inasmuch as he can only come to decision after embarrassing delays and with necessarily imperfect knowledge of all the circumstances affecting the case."[16]

Even before he had received Elgin's 7 August telegram, Selborne set out to bring more peripheral pressure to bear on London. The previous week, in a message to the Natal governor, Sir Henry McCallum, the high commissioner suggested that Natal could strengthen his hand by threatening rebates itself. Then, as high commissioner, he could impose countervailing rates without appearing to favour either colony. Two weeks later the Natal ministers gave Selborne more than he had asked for by announcing their intention to grant rebates not only on ORC traffic but also on trade to the competitive zone (i.e., the Witwatersrand). When by August 25 Elgin had still received no appeal from the Cape, he authorized Selborne to act on the advice of the Railway Committee in order "to avoid a tariff war affecting the zone of Portuguese competition."[17]

Selborne acted immediately. Before the end of August, he intimated to Hely-Hutchinson that he could expect retaliatory action soon. A week later, Jameson's ministry was informed that countervailing rates against the Cape would come into force on ORC lines, effective 13 September. On receipt of this, the Cape pleaded for delay, at least until Jameson had arrived in England to present his case to the colonial secretary. After the high commissioner's prompt refusal, the Cape turned to London. On 10 September the colony's agent general there asked Elgin to prevent the CSAR from imposing these increased rates. The next day the sympathetic colonial secretary suggested by cable that the Cape's request be granted. Within twenty-four hours, Selborne telegraphed in reply that, as countervailing rates had already been published, it would prove impossible to retract them. He followed this up with another cable pointing out that the repudiation of his action would discredit him in the eyes of the Transvaal Executive Council and the Railway Committee. Furthermore, Natal would embark on a vicious rate war.[18]

The Colonial Office declined to overrule the high commissioner. In a minute, Elgin described the corner into which he had been driven:

"The H.C. is within his rights in saying that he was given authority to act. Whether when 'he laid everything before us' he really drew attention to all the material points, I am not quite sure. But I do not of course mean that he kept anything back – but in so complicated a business what was fully in the minds of those on the spot was not necessarily present to us. However we must deal with the case as we have it now."[19]

The Cape continued to press its views on Elgin. It sent petitions from chambers of commerce and even threatened to hold the CSAR legally responsible for any loss incurred from its countervailing rates. Elgin could only reply that his hands were tied and that he could not reverse the high commissioner's decision. Selborne provided evidence confirming the wisdom of his action when he cabled home that Natal had withdrawn all rebates threatened before.[20]

Meanwhile, Jameson had arrived in London where he pressed the Cape's case before the secretary of state. Shortly thereafter, Selborne sent his own emissary to London – Sir Hamilton Goold-Adams, governor of the Orange River Colony. On 2 October, Goold-Adams reported to Selborne a tentative arrangement he had reached with Jameson, whereby the Cape would withold payment of rebates, pending a general conference in South Africa. This constituted a significant climb down on the Cape's part. The stumbling block to a settlement was now Natal, which rejected Jameson's offer out of hand.[21]

Conditions in South Africa took a turn for the worse when, on 11 October, the Cape advertised further rebates. The CSAR immediately increased its rates accordingly. The Railway Committee's response irritated Fred Graham, who thought that it was abusing the authority Elgin had given it. The colonial secretary agreed, minuting, "I am not at all satisfied with the action of the Railway Committee. It is one of these bodies rather outside the ordinary constitutional status, which have to be held in check." He sarcastically noted the veracity of Selborne's observation that the CSAR's initial action came just in time to prevent a rate war spreading to the competitive zone; but he pointed out that Natal, not the Cape, had created this danger. In a telegram to Selborne, the colonial secretary coolly remarked, "I presume that [the] action of [the] Railway Committee has been approved by you on the ground that you were of opinion that the step was necessary in the interests of South Africa generally with the object of preventing a war of rates affecting the zone of Portuguese competition."[22]

The conflict smouldered on, as Selborne continued to urge Natal to negotiate with the Cape and Natal continued to resist all such promptings. Finally, both Selborne and the CSAR lost patience. The Cape had been brought to heel; now only Natal stood in the way of a settlement. In a later October telegram home, Selborne expressed his determination to convene a conference with or without Natal. "I should do my utmost to induce Governor [of] Natal to take part in such a Conference, but Railway Committee are of opinion that even if Natal refused to take part[,] Conference between Government of Cape of Good Hope and Central South African Railways should take place, and I agree with them."[23]

Elgin warmly approved this plan and suggested, as a basis of settlement, that Natal keep the advantages which the Bethlehem-Kroonstad agreement promised but make certain concessions to the Cape along the newly constructed Bethlehem-Modderpoort line. Selborne enthusiastically embraced this solution, replying "I was going to have made ... the very suggestion you here made." Isolated, having lost the support of the high commissioner and the csar, Natal saw fit to attend the conference, which adopted a settlement on the basis of Elgin's proposals. The Cape's rebates were removed along with the csar's countervailing rates. On 19 November, Selborne cabled home that the "railway difficulty is settled."[24]

Selborne was largely responsible for this result. He successfully exploited the Cape-Natal antagonism, shifting his weight to the former once it came into line. He possessed the highest card in the deck – the csar – and played it skilfully. He outmanoeuvred the secretary of state, prevented the Cape's unilateral revision of railway rates, and, finally, outflanked Natal's obstruction. And yet, as all knew, the dispute had dragged on for six months, and its settlement promised only temporary relief. The crux of the difficulty lay in the archaic political boundaries which divided an integrated economy. This was part of a larger problem: the absence of a polity strong enough, in the face of metropolitan obstruction, to stabilize economic activity and efficient enough to organize it into the most productive system possible.

It was the railway crisis that drove Selborne to embrace political unification as the only hope for South Africa's economic future. The Witwatersrand depended on the transportation network for its machinery, supplies, and food and so, indeed, did the entire business community. The constant threat of rate wars rendered the communications network unstable, which in turn made rational economic planning impossible. Moreover, any additional railway building would dislocate previous arrangements. Furthermore, the intercolonial rivalries constituted a serious threat to the political peace of British South Africa. In a lengthy telegram, he explained the political danger in detail:

It is on the railway question that the whole question of the future of South Africa really turns ... I will endeavour to put the situation in a nutshell. The railway interests of the Transvaal are diametrically opposed to those of all the other colonies, as long as South Africa is not federated. The Transvaal loses revenue in respect of every ton of goods that passes into the Transvaal by any other route except the Delagoa Bay route, and this loss of revenue aggregates hundreds of thousands of pounds annually. Now no State will sacrifice revenue on this scale for altruistic reasons or for reasons of patriotism. It is simply the old question of the closing of the drifts, which nearly brought about war in 1895, over again. Although it was in President Kruger's interest to do everything he could to conciliate the Orange Free State in those days, he simply could not afford the revenue involved and he only gave way at the point of the bayonet. No Responsible Government in the Transvaal will be able to do what President Kruger could not do in 1895, and you cannot present the point of the bayonet to Responsible Government in the Transvaal as Mr. Chamberlain did to President Kruger in 1895.[25]

There was, continued Selborne, only one remedy – the unification of all South African railways and ports, for then the Transvaal's revenue needs would no longer depend on Delagoa Bay. The high commissioner had contended so much a year before. Now, however, he added, "But unification is only possible under a Federal Government. The jealousies of the local Parliaments would make impossible control by any body which was not directly representative of all the people of British South Africa." The problem, he warned, required immediate attention, and the longer it remained unsolved, the more difficult its settlement would become. This long missive explains how Selborne had come to embrace political union. Without it, the interests of the Transvaal diverged dangerously from those of the other British colonies. Selborne's telegram starkly depicted the perils of the situation to the coastal states. In a future "drifts crisis" there would be no imperial bayonet to protect them.

What was not so apparent from this cable or from other messages he sent to the Colonial Office was the danger of the situation to the Transvaal. On this telegram, Churchill minuted, "Cheap living on the Rand is in itself of greater Imperial importance than Federation." And Selborne's old boss, Joseph Chamberlain, wrote to him the following year:

The crux of the position is the situation of the Transvaal and I should be disposed to think that Botha would not give up the position of vantage which he and his Government enjoy. They are the great consumers and Delagoa Bay is naturally the port for them. I find it difficult to see what they would gain by giving up this position and allowing the question of transport to slip from their hands and be undertaken by a central body on which they could only be inadequately represented."[26]

Many Transvaal capitalists had similar doubts.

These critical perspectives, however, neglect the crucial consideration of stability. With the vagaries of international diplomacy, sole reliance on a foreign port might prove a dangerous gamble. With the diplomatic situation in Europe and German intrigue in Southern Africa, this was no hollow fear. Moreover, the Rand still needed goods and produce from the coastal colonies, as well as markets. An unstable atmosphere, where transportation rates fluctuated unpredictably, where four states applied different laws and policies to commercial transactions, and where intercolonial relations evinced persistent acrimony, could only frustrate the accumulation of capital in every sector – mining, manufacturing, and commercial. The South African situation in 1906 made economic forecasting impossible.

Moreover, the Rand depended on outside capital. No investor would wish to plunge his pounds into a political whirlpool. In a letter to his old Admiralty colleague, Mr. Pretyman, on 13 January 1909, Selborne explained this crucial consideration:

How can you expect men not to hesitate investing capital in South Africa when every commercial transaction in the country is at the mercy of four different and often divergent sets of laws? How can one expect men not to hesitate in investing their capital when the whole basis of their calculations may be upset by a quarrel about customs or railway rates? I saw clearly that what I called jarring antagonisms of these four small governments was by far the most serious remaining obstruction to the development of South Africa. I saw that if those jarring antagonisms could be removed nothing that one South African Government could do could seriously obstruct development ... I saw that all the conditions of South Africa, political, economical, industrial, commercial, and legal, would become stable if we could get closer union. I saw that with stability must come capital, that with capital must come development, and that with development must come an increase of the British.[27]

While he considered mining the prime mover, Selborne sought to increase and spread its general spillover effects. Every economic sector required stability. Union, therefore, presented the perfect panacea which would reconcile and benefit all interests. The businessman would secure his markets, the coast its traffic, and, most important, the Rand its capital.

Selborne's reference to the British in his letter might suggest that, he was inspired, to some extent, by racial considerations. Some might argue that, like his predecessor, Selborne merely pressed economic development into the service of purely political ends, specifically the future swamping of Afrikaners by British immigrants. Not yet reassured by

Botha's moderation, the high commissioner, in March of 1906, presented a frightful possibility to Elgin: the emergence of "A United States of South Africa, republican, unconnected with the British Empire, with its own flag, and Boer in spirit and tradition." This, he warned, constituted "the permanent life ideal of Malan, Hertzog, and Smuts."[28] Six months later, Malan must have increased Selborne's fears when he wrote a series of articles urging unification.

Both logic and evidence suggest that fear of Boer domination formed a minor part of Selborne's motivation for union. One might wonder at the outset why he would hasten its coming by uniting Afrikanerdom himself. And what was to be gained by the immigration of British, whom he knew would invariably divide politically? Moreover in 1906, even before responsible government had come into effect, Selborne was writing to McCallum: "My deliberate opinion is that Federation or Unification is the thing we ought to go for. I would say this even if I knew that in a Federated or Unified South Africa the Dutch would be in a majority in the Parliament." These were strange words coming from a disciple of Milner. A little over a year later Selborne wrote in the same vein to Chamberlain.[29] What grounds were there for uniting South Africa under the leadership of Britain's late enemies?

The key to this puzzle lies in the meanings Selborne attached to "British supremacy" and "Boer spirit." He defined the former as progressive and the latter as retrogressive. An earlier chapter has explained how he came to praise Afrikaners such as Botha who, in time, embraced "the big thing." Indeed, the high commissioner's racialism was imbued with materialism. In 1909, he wrote to Sir Edward Grey:

You know by now of course that the great danger to the future of the Boers is the incapacity of the race, from 20 years old and upwards, to energise. There are of course many exceptions: but this is true of the race, and this is why they cannot profit by the industrial, mineral, or commercial development of the country. When a couple of generations have been properly educated, and have sufficiently felt the strain of the struggle for existence, they will rise to the crisis and regain the energy which is still latent in their nature. But our people have a start of at least two generations, and that is why I look forward to the political future with serene confidence.[30]

Selborne did not promote union simply to attract sufficient British settlers to swamp Afrikaners politically. What he feared in Afrikanerdom were unprogressive tendencies which the very erection of a modern state system would eradicate. Any institutional arrangement which encouraged material progress would by definition promote "British supremacy."

Imperial interests led Selborne to another reason for union – the liberation of the Empire from Liberal clutches. This proconsul did not identify imperialism with the "imperial factor." In fact, he considered Westminster a positive danger. To Selborne, the Radicals seemed bent on obstructing mining development at every turn. Still enraged over the Chinese labour issue and the J.B. Robinson affair, the governor feared that the Liberals were alienating British South Africans from the Empire. The Natalians resented imperial intervention, or the threat of it, during the Bambatha rebellion, while the Witwatersrand community blamed the imperial government for the severe depression throughout the country. The high commissioner emphasized this theme to Lord Salisbury, Lionel Phillips, and Chamberlain. To the last, he wrote:

We may, and I believe will, gain the full acquiescence of the Boers in their incorporation in the Empire, if the H. of C. will only let S.A. alone. If, on the other hand, the H. of C. goes on treating S.A. as the present one does, most surely it is the British in S.A. who will become disloyal to the Empire. They simply won't stand the treatment. So long as the S.A. Colonies are disunited and weak the malignant lunatics of the Home Rule Cobdenite party will intrude their baneful influence and interference whenever they have the opportunity, which will be whenever we are not in office in a high degree, and when we are in office in a less degree. But even these conceited ignorant and mischievous busy-bodies are afraid to lay hands or waggle tongues against an united Canada or Australia, and an united S.A. would by the act of its union be as it were automatically delivered from the curse of the H. of C.[31]

The Robinson and Gallagher concept of collaboration might prove useful here, for Selborne, no doubt, feared alienating the English in South Africa. One, however, should not take this argument too far or accept as fundamental the metropolitan-peripheral distinction. As the tone of the above illustrates, the high commmissioner's sympathies were fully with the British element in South Africa and not with Westminster. His attitude towards industrial problems, especially Chinese labour, demonstrated that his concerns went beyond mere British loyalty. He wanted material advancement and considered the British element essential to this. He desired not merely loyal collaborators but dynamic ones. In the railway tangle of 1906 Selborne's thinking began to crystallize, as did that of the Kindergarten and certain colonial statesmen. As Elgin occasionally sensed, the rail crisis involved much more than met the eye. The Witwatersrand trade which split South Africa politically was paradoxically becoming the basis of cooperation and union. In this dialectical transformation of centrifugal tendencies into centripetal ones, the Transvaal proved the crucial factor. From June to November of 1906, while the railway dispute was raging, this process intensified, involving at first the Transvaal and Natal and, by the end of the year, all four colonies. With tact, skill, and gentle prodding, they might be reined together so that they could pull in harness towards prosperity. If not, then the Transvaal would plod alone, at an unsteady pace and in dangerous directions.

8 Selborne's *Memorandum*: The High Commissioner Strikes Back

The political unification of South Africa had been cherished as an ideal by statesmen, both British and South African, long before the railway crisis. By 1906 it had become long-standing British policy to encourage the amalgamation of self-governing states within the various corners of the Empire. According to the orthodoxy of liberal imperialism, such consolidations strengthened the colonies involved and, in doing so, relieved the mother country of political responsibilities and financial burdens. The confederation of Canada in 1867 furnished an example for the rest of the self-governing colonies. The example had been repeated by the Australian colonies which federated into a commonwealth in 1901. Federation seemed the natural outcome of colonial evolution within a liberal empire.

As anxious as British statesmen were to replicate the Canadian model throughout the imperial world, they were reluctant to impose it from London, for to do so would violate the principle of self-government and perhaps even diminish the chance of success. The Canadian confederation itself had come from below, not above. According to the precepts of liberal imperialism, Britain should nurture colonial maturation, not force its growth.

The South African case, however, defied the idealized pattern of colonial evolution. From 1874 to 1880 the colonial secretary, Lord Carnarvon, tried to force confederation on the area. The attempt produced a political crisis with the Cape and eventually a military confrontation with the Transvaal Boers. The result was worse than failure, for imperial meddling had set back South African federation indefinitely. Carnarvon's blunders vindicated the Liberal policy of non-interference, and thereafter British politicians, Unionist and Liberal alike, avoided any action which could be construed as forcing federation from London. For the quarter-century after 1877, British imperialists retained Carnarvon's ideal, though not his methods or even motives.

With the Anglo-Boer War, the subject arose again but never advanced beyond the stage of speculation. While Unionist politicians sanctioned the remorseless application of imperial power to restructure the Transvaal, few proved willing to follow up conquest with confederation. Selborne certainly was not willing to do so, as he made clear in his 1899 memorandum, which advised letting "the question slumber." Whatever the risks in political amalgamation, he considered a union of customs and railways unobjectionable and, indeed, highly desirable for the sake of prosperity and British immigration.[1] Economic unification could be safely encouraged and might lay the groundwork for some sort of political union later.

After the war both the Unionist and Liberal governments envisioned eventual South African unification. In a 1906 cabinet memorandum, Lord Ripon, who had served as Gladstone's colonial secretary in the 1890s, advised his Liberal colleagues to abandon the Lyttelton Constitution on the grounds that it would give the Transvaal a constitution so different from the two coastal colonies as to hinder the smooth amalgamation of British South Africa.[2] At the same time, neither Balfour's government nor Campbell-Bannerman's wished to pursue the prospect actively.

As we have seen, even Milner recognized the difficulties in the way of union. He urged his successor simply to try to maintain intact the united CSAR system and the Intercolonial Council which administered it. Perhaps, in time, Milner hoped, this would lead to the fusion of all South African railways. Leaving political federation for the distant future, he held up to Selborne no more ambitious goal than the modest one of railway amalgamation.[3]

The vision of a united South Africa was not concocted by metropolitan politicians, nor was it the exclusive preserve of imperialists. For generations the ideal of confederation had inspired both Afrikaner and liberal British colonists. After the war, John X. Merriman, the Cape politician who had resisted imperial pressure strenuously since Carnarvon's time, proposed that the conquered republics be given self-government within a wider federation. A few years later, the Chinese labour controversy demonstrated to him that certain key decisions taken by one colony affected all the others in southern Africa. In 1906 he began a correspondence concerning union with M.T. Steyn, the former president of the Orange Free State, and J.C. Smuts. To the former, Merriman asserted in early 1906: "I want to do something to take the settlement of South African questions out of the hands of Downing Street, and at the same time to make us feel that we are members of one body – that the franchise [for non-whites] and Chinese questions are South African and not local affairs – and above all that ... safety lies in open discussion and not in heated one-sided meetings or in astute bargains." Although all three men, like many South Africans, envisioned union in the near future, they did not want the question raised while imperial authorities could comandeer it and create a union to serve British instead of local interests. For anti-imperialists, 1906 was an inauspicious time to open the matter. With the Transvaal and ORC under crown colony rule and with the infamous Dr Jameson installed as Cape premier, Merriman, Steyn, and Smuts would, like Selborne, "let the matter slumber."[4]

Selborne understood the danger of imposing union from above. It was therefore with great caution that he broached the matter in a speech at Pietermaritzburg in Natal in October 1905. Disavowing any attempt to force the pace, he declared that any movement for union must come from below. Nevertheless, he held the ideal before his audience and proclaimed that only by uniting could South Africa make the mark on the world that history had chosen for it. South Africa constituted, he avowed, one entity: "There never were States really more intimately connected with each other in their permanent interests, and it is impossible for a single State to suffer and all the others not to suffer with it. There never was a case in which the description in Corinthians more absolutely applied. 'Can the eye say to the mouth, I have not need of thee, or the head to the feet, I have not need of you? If one member suffer all the members suffer with it.'"[5] Though this speech had no immediate effect, it did help impress the ideal of union upon public consciousness in Natal. In June 1906 Ramsay Collins of the *Natal Mercury* commended the notion to Selborne, who endorsed it with the understanding that it originate from the people of the two colonies. The high commissioner suggested that the creation of local committees might popularize the cause.[6] In early August Selborne reported home that, for six months, he had noticed "the growth of a spontaneous movement both in Natal and the Transvaal towards closer union." Three weeks later he remarked on the rapid growth and strength of the movement for Transvaal-Natal amalgamation. Sceptical, the secretary of state expressed his fear that a partial federation might impede the complete unification of South Africa. Indeed, it might, he argued, force the Cape and Orange River Colony into their own union, under the leadership of the Bond, the Cape's powerful Afrikaner party.[7]

The momentum gathered force in September as J.G. Maydon, a prominent Natal politician and at the time the minister of railways and harbours for the colony, sent Selborne a memorandum prepared two months before. In this, Maydon argued for the political fusion of his colony and the Transvaal. This, he contended, would encourage, not hinder, the full unification of South Africa. A political union of this nature would, he argued, be easier to achieve than a general agreement on rail policy. From his proposal, Natal would acquire a share of the Transvaal's wealth, while the latter would gain access to a seaport of its own. Maydon also took the opportunity to aim some shots at the Liberals, especially in regard to their intervention in African policy:

Natal, although permitted territorially to absorb Zululand within the last three years has nevertheless been trammeled with conditions by the Imperial Government which are neither wise, nor just to the white Colonists. And, indeed, Natal's policy to the Native races as a whole is largely a consequence of the Reservations by the Home Government in regard to Native Legislation. At this very hour an Act has been kept a twelvemonth awaiting Imperial sanction because it contains clauses which empower Municipalities to regulate coloured traffic on the footpaths in the boroughs. A political party in England is clamouring that the new Constitution to be given to the Transvaal shall confer no power to control either her Natives or her foreign labour supply. Is it not self-evident that so long as we remain disunited we shall never quite successfully emancipate ourselves from this control which, never very wise is often, in these times of crisis in particular, wickedly foolish.[8]

Though Selborne shared Maydon's aims and desired to promote a Natal union, he did not wish to alienate the Cape irrevocably. By the time he received Maydon's memo he had become aware that certain sections of Cape opinion would welcome closer union. In his reply to Maydon, he alluded to this and expressed his relief that the Bethlehem-Kroonstad dispute had not poisoned his relations with the Jameson ministry. He told Maydon he could not, as high commissioner, move too far in advance either of local opinion or the imperial government. He confided to the Natal statesman, "I must be very cautious in what I do. There is nothing South Africans resent more than an attempt to move them from Downing Street. The real strength and promise of the present movement is that it is native born, that is, that it is South African. Be sure that I will do everything I possibly can to foster it; but I must always pose as the servant, not the promoter, of the movement. Do not think from this that I shall be timid. I think I can promise that I shall not be. I must only endeavour to be wise."[9] It would seem that Selborne's posturing was for the benefit of the Cape as well as London.

Meanwhile, as discussion on Transvaal-Natal amalgamation proceeded apace, some of Milner's disciples in the Kindergarten were formulating their own plans for unification on a South Africa-wide basis. These young men started working for closer union in June or July of 1906. No one knows how the project originated. Lionel Curtis, the Kindergarten member most active in the movement, claimed that his inspiration came from the publication in May 1906 of F.S. Oliver's biography of Alexander Hamilton. I would speculate, rather, that it might have been the Natal proposals that sparked the Kindergarten into action. The possibility of Natal's union with the Transvaal was under serious review by several important officials in each colony and was widely vented in the press. As for timing, Selborne's Pietermaritzburg speech shows that the issue was alive in Natal six months before Curtis and company had embraced it.

More is known about the idea's maturation. In August 1906 Curtis sent Milner a detailed account of the group's activities and requested a subsidy from the Rhodes Trust, for which Milner served as trustee. Though unenthusiastic, Milner reported back that the Trust was willing to advance £1,000 provided, first, that Lionel Curtis serve formally as organizing secretary for the project and, second, that Lord Selborne was kept fully informed of the proceedings.[10] The conditions were accepted, and the Kindergarten set about collecting material for a lengthy memorandum on the desirability of closer union.

Though Selborne had been apprised of Curtis's doings, he was not formally brought into Kindergarten counsels until September. The month before, he had informed the Colonial Office that Curtis had resigned from the Transvaal government. As Curtis recounted, this "was precipitated by the rapid manner in which things appeared to be moving towards union, and the need that was felt amongst us of doing something to guide and if possible hasten the movement." The Colonial Office was told nothing of these motives, but one official, Fred Graham, minuted suspiciously, "There is some mystery about this."[11]

Lord Selborne gave the group his full endorsement at an important meeting on 1 September. The two most prominent activists there, besides G.G. Robinson and Curtis, were Sir Patrick Duncan, still the Transvaal colonial secretary, and Lionel Hichens, the treasurer of both the Transvaal and the ICC. Also in attendance were Richard Feetham, now practising law in Johannesburg, and Sir Cecil Rodwell, the high commissioner's imperial secretary. Most of the meeting revolved around the Natal proposal and, on the strong recommendation of Duncan and Hichens, the group resolved not to let this opportunity slip by. They determined to make union, full or partial, the principal issue in the forthcoming Transvaal elections. Accordingly, the Kindergarten decided to approach the Progressives, and, in the meantime to prepare and issue a plan for union. On Selborne's suggestion, the conference also despatched Curtis to the Cape to survey opinion there and enlist the aid of Richard Jebb, an influential commentator on imperial affairs.[12]

Within weeks of the September meeting, Curtis began to nurse reservations about the Natal plan. He admitted the strength of pro-Transvaal feeling in that colony and attributed it to sagging revenues, a desire to cut into Cape trade, and gratitude for the Transvaal's support during the Bambatha rebellion. At the same time, he feared that a Transvaal-Natal union might embitter the Cape. "Any partial union," he wrote Selborne's private secretary, D.O. Malcolm, "will mean in practice bringing the recalcitrant Colony left out after, in one way or another, it has been brought to its knees and that to my mind is an evil in itself."[13]

The Kindergarten did not realize it at its September meeting, but a potent brew of pro-union sentiment was fermenting in the Cape. The rumours of a possible Transvaal-Natal union understandably alarmed F.S. Malan, member of the Cape Bond and editor of *Ons Land*. Fearing the isolation of his colony, he wrote a series of articles in which he promoted the full unification of South Africa. Appearing first in late August in *Ons Land*, these were reprinted by the *Johannesburg Star* in September. Behind the proposed Natal-Transvaal amalgamation, he saw Johannesburg politicians who desired to strengthen their ranks and Natalians who coveted an increased share of the lucrative Witwatersrand trade. Malan put forward union as a way of reconciling growth with democratic principles:

We believe that the pressure for federation will become irresistible not long after the establishment of responsible government in the neighbouring Colonies. Possibly this may happen sooner than many now think. In respect to finance, railways, and the administration of justice there already exists a strong inclination for a change in the political status of South Africa. The existence of the Customs Union, taken strictly, is in conflict with the fundamental principle of Parliamentary government, that the taxpayers themselves and alone should say what taxes they should pay. What right has Natal, for example, to say under the Customs Union what the import duties into the Transvaal shall be? This union is an unconstitutional institution, which we submit to because we cannot do otherwise now; but the sooner the taxpayers of South Africa can be placed on a constitutional basis the better.[14]

If parliamentary democracy was Malan's sole aim, there was no need for federation. The Cape could keep its parliament, withdraw from the customs union, and allow the Transvaal-Natal union to go forward without criticism. But, the vision of a Cape backwater, where people lived in parliamentary, poverty did not seem to inspire him. He therefore realized that "we cannot do otherwise now" than maintain such undemocratic institutions as the customs union.

The strength of pro-union feeling in the Cape took Curtis by surprise. He told Milner, that the calls for union emanated from many directions: from Malan of the Bond, Parkes of the *Cape Times,* and Colonel Crewe, the colonial secretary of the Cape. Curtis attributed this widespread enthusiasm to the intractable railway problem. He further predicted that Selborne would be forced into action by swelling opinion on the coast.[15]

Curtis now came out decidedly against the Transvaal-Natal union as redundant and harmful. It would only offend the Cape, which needed no persuading as to the desirability of union. From the tone of his letters, it would seem that Curtis trusted the Cape more than the Transvaal. No one could predict who would rule the latter in a year's time. Jameson, on the other hand, expected his ministry to last another two years – long enough to consummate union. Curtis agreed, but recognized the necessity of carrying along the Afrikaners from the start. "We cannot succeed or hope to succeed," he wrote Milner, "in any arrangement which would give the British population an advantage which they were not entitled to by their numbers. All we can do is to draw the line at any attempt of that kind which the Boers may make."[16] The Boer-British division, for Curtis, was neither fundamental nor relevant. "No doubt," he observed to Milner, "a good deal of ingenuity will be used to import the racial question into the question of Union, but for the present the feeling in favour of Union is running like a river of clear water across the muddy current of official politics."[17]

Curtis also reported that the Cape ministry desired a conference with the high commissioner as soon as possible. Accordingly, Colonel Crewe wrote Selborne and arranged for him to visit the Cape in November 1906 to confer with the ministry. In his meeting there, Selborne discussed the Kindergarten draft (though it is uncertain whether he actually had a copy on hand to show them) and came to an agreement whereby Jameson's ministry would formally request the high commissioner to furnish informational literature on union – in other words, the Kindergarten's memorandum.[18] This would enable the document to carry the prestige of the high commissioner's signature without the stigma that would attend the paper's uninvited release on Selborne's sole authority. To have issued the memorandum without local prompting would have conjured up in colonial minds memories of Carnarvon.

At the end of the month, the Cape government officially asked Selborne to "undertake a review of the situation," with a view to remedying the present "state of friction" and "mutual distrust."[19] Jameson hoped that the memorandum would come out before the Transvaal elections to prevent certain Progressive candidates from pledging themselves to a pro-Mozambique policy.[20] With its depleted treasury, the Cape pump needed little priming on the subject of closer union.

The prospect of having to share Rand booty with the Cape sapped some of Natal's enthusiasm for closer union. It was in late September 1906, after Malan's articles had appeared and after Curtis's trip to the Cape, that Maydon sent Selborne the memorandum on a Transvaal-Natal union which he had prepared in July. Though he looked forward to full union in the future, he still advocated his Transvaal-Natal scheme as a step in this direction. Early in 1907 Ramsay Collins, who had favoured his colony's amalgamation with the Transvaal, declined to support the broader movement, complaining to Selborne that full union would leave Natal only a small role to play. The previous December McCallum had warned that the moment was inopportune to introduce the issue. It would understandably reawaken loyalist fears of a united Afrikanerdom, a prospect which McCallum himself found alarming. Some would suspect Boer intrigue behind the movement. Moreover, the reaction might topple the weak Natal government.[21] It was in response to these fears that Selborne proclaimed his support for unification even if it meant an Afrikaner majority at the union polls. Though still unconvinced, McCallum reported three days later that the Natal prime minister, F.R. Moor, had grasped the nettle and come out for union. On 21 December, the high commissioner communicated the Cape's minute requesting a review of the situation to the Natal ministry, which expressed its full concurrence.[22] Despite the governor's misgivings, Natal could profitably do little else.

While the progress of the closer union movement exceeded the Kindergarten's expectations in the Cape, its future in the Transvaal caused Curtis grave concern. As early as 7 September, he expressed the hope that the Progressives would promptly endorse union before the Responsibles rushed in and stole their thunder. Five days later, he appeared still more anxious, remarking to Selborne that, "It would be to our eternal disgrace if the Dutch and responsibles declared for it and our people declared against. It is a blow from which they would never recover if to begin with they were found in the wrong camp."[23]

In a long letter to Milner, Curtis explained why he considered union essential to the Transvaal's economic health. Echoing Selborne's argument that it would create stable conditions for capital investment, he added a new dimension to the stability argument: migrant labour. "A change in the English Govt. may alter the whole conditions of labour supply." As long as the imperial factor remained a potent one in the regional situation, the labour supply would remain uncertain and so would investors. These arguments might constitute cogent inducements to the Randlords.

But our principal difficulty is this. The value of a form of Govt. to the mining industry which would introduce greater stability in political and therefore economic conditions can scarcely be disputed. But it is a [value?] to [be] felt not in this year or the next but in five or ten years. Like all measures which can be trusted to give any lasting relief to a distracted country it must be slow and gradual in its operation ... On the face of it the union of South Africa means great immediate sacrifice for the Transvaal. The benefit she is to obtain is diffused and postponed.[24]

The need to counter the Randlords' opposition reinforced the Kindergarten's original intention of publishing the memorandum before the Transvaal elections. At the meeting of 1 September, the object of prompt publication had been to enable the Progressives to initiate the movement. By the end of the month, the object was to prevent them from lagging behind. Worries about a Progressive wobble persisted, and in a late November letter to Maydon, Selborne stressed the importance of early publication. Certain Transvaal candidates, he feared, might, in ignorance of the union movement's strength, advocate closer ties with Delagoa Bay instead.[25]

There were grounds for concern. The ideal of union did not inspire all Randlords, much less all Transvaalers. Many Boer farmers wanted protection from coastal produce, and some sectors of capitalist opinion did in fact urge closer relations with Mozambique, which offered cheaper rail service than either the Cape or Natal. In early 1907, the *Transvaal Leader* took up this position. More politically minded, Sir Percy FitzPatrick worried about the position of the Transvaal British under a unified regime.[26]

There did exist, however, a substantial body of capitalist sentiment which favoured closer union. The *Johannesburg Star*, criticizing the *Leader*'s "policy of grovel" to Portugal, linked the issue of union to the Chinese labour controversy:

But the few men who look ahead ... are beginning to realise that even the question of Chinese labour is inextricably intertwined with the question of a United South Africa. Once our interests were obviously pooled, those "kith and kin" of ours at the Coast would prove a very serious obstacle to any hasty legislation likely to impair the prosperity of the Rand. On the other hand, the abolition of Chinese labour today would surely place union beyond the range of practical politics because it would drive the Transvaal into greater dependence than ever on the goodwill of her Portuguese neighbours.[27]

On 5 September 1906 *South African Mines Commerce and Industries* had argued on similar lines. It had also observed that federation would bolster South Africa's international credit and would free the country from Liberal meddling.

Perhaps long-term considerations of labour and capital eventually moved an increasing number of Randlords to Selborne's position, but so did the pace of the movement and the fear of being isolated. By December 1906 Selborne could report home that the Progressives had, as a whole, come out for union. Of course, by that time, so had the Responsibles and Het Volk.[28] However important union was to South Africa's economic future, the movement owed little thanks to the capitalists themselves, many of whom proved too short-sighted to embrace it. Not even Lionel Phillips, whose support Selborne had elicited early on, could be reckoned a strong ally. He told Wernher in January 1907 that he intended to contribute all of £100 to the movement so that he could obtain all printed material connected with it. He explained, "Although I do not intend to join any body that could be dragged into the political side of the federation question, it would not do for us to be entirely out of the matter, especially as material interests may be so vitally affected."[29] This was yet another case where the capitalists had to be led to a healthier future for enterprise.

There remained the imperial factor to be considered. At the end of September 1906 Selborne remarked to Elgin that the union movement was spreading in all directions and now the Cape as well as Natal were clamouring for federation. Citing the examples of the Boer general, C.F. Beyers, in the Transvaal and F.S. Malan in the Cape, he stated that this sentiment was shared by Boer and Briton alike. He also informed the secretary of state that the Cape ministers had already appealed to him privately for a conference to discuss how "the oldest colony" could initiate the movement formally. Predicting that he would be called upon to furnish informational material, he requested £1,500 for the increase in staff required to assemble it. He assured the colonial secretary, "I have always taken the line that it [federation] could only come from below – from the people. I must act as a servant of the people." Under the impression that Selborne only wished to furnish factual information, the Colonial Office, including Churchill, approved asking the Treasury for £1,000.[30]

Two months later, on 7 December 1906, Selborne cabled home that the Cape government would soon request him to publish a memorandum, which he had almost finished preparing. He proposed publishing it as soon as possible after the request. The approaching Transvaal elections made the matter urgent. Opinion at the Colonial Office was mixed. Noting the local enthusiasm for union and the fact that the request would come from a self-governing colony, Vernon and Graham would let Selborne do as he proposed. Just and Ommanney, however, reckoned that pre-election publication would involve too much interference on the high commissioner's part. Lambert termed Selborne's proposal dangerous but, in light of the local situation, would permit him to issue a colourless statement of facts. Churchill considered any publication undesirable without previous submission to the Colonial Office. "I trust S of S will not allow such a step to be taken without giving me an opportunity of expressing some private objections wh[ich] I feel." Drawing largely on Just's advice, Elgin refused to authorize publication of the memorandum before the Transvaal elections. Indeed, he doubted that such a document should issue from the high commissioner at all. "It will be better that you and HMG should not appear as endeavouring to promote the movement for federation, which should spring from below." Selborne, the message continued, should do no more than furnish information confidentially to the various governments on their invitation.[31]

Selborne replied that he had no intention of laying any scheme before South Africa. His memorandum would consist simply of an "historical exposition of the facts" and a neutral discussion of the railway and customs difficulty. It would "express no opinion and make no statement of fact of which His Majesty's Government would disapprove." As to alleged interference, he feared that the Colonial Office had misunderstood him. "I steadily adhered to my policy of letting the movement spring from below. The position is that it has sprung from below unprompted by me and quite spontaneously." The self-governing Cape Colony was making the request for a review of the intercolonial situation. Regrettably, there was no other agency which could undertake such a task, for no central South African institution existed. "In the High Commissioner alone all inter-Colonial questions and difficulties centre." The urgency of the matter arose from the Transvaal elections, in which many candidates might, out of ignorance, pledge themselves "to the simple, selfish Transvaal view of South African matters, and so handicap in advance the definite movement towards federation which will certainly be made next year or the year after by the Responsible Government[s] of South Africa."[32] His memo would not manipulate but rather enlighten.

At the Colonial Office, Graham adhered to his previous position while Ommanney and Just clung to theirs. Ommanney pointed out that, whatever its purpose, a published memorandum issued by the high commissioner would still appear an attempt to influence local politics. Just noted that Selborne's railway circular already existed to enlighten the Transvaal candidates. Moreover, he minuted, "The point at issue is, more particularly, whether Lord Selborne should publish his memorandum without its having been seen by HMG." Churchill, however, admitted "It is v[er]y hard to refuse L[or]d Selborne," although he still wished to see the document first. Selborne's request disturbed Elgin, who detected inconsistencies in his message. For example, the high commissioner contended that the movement had general support, yet he worried about the Transvaal's attitude. Nevertheless, the Liberal government, as Churchill realized, could not easily refuse the Cape's request for information. Accordingly, the colonial secretary informed Selborne that he could submit his memorandum confidentially to the Cape, with a view to subsequent publication. He repeated his reservations about issuing the document publicly before the Transvaal elections and instructed Selborne to let the British government see it beforehand.[33]

On hearing of Colonial Office obstruction, the outraged Kindergarten rejected Britain's right to prevent the memorandum's publication. The conflict involved much more than a question of timing or the Transvaal elections. It was fast becoming a question of the home government's prerogative, and a serious battle threatened to develop between the Liberal imperial factor and the avowedly imperialist Kindergarten which operated on the periphery. The Liberals at home learned nothing of the Kindergarten's resentment and remained unaware of the campaign mounted against them. On 24 December 1906 Duncan, Hichens, and Curtis wrote Selborne an angry letter in the name of all three. They did not want London even to see their work. "We always thought," they explained, "that if this document entered the official doors of the Colonial Office unpublished, they would close upon it and never open again." Winston Churchill, in particular, would never let it see the light of day. Moreover, to refuse to honour the Cape's request pending Britain's perusal involved a dangerous admission:

To admit to the Colonial Govt. that the memorandum which they have asked the High Commissioner to furnish [is] under the immediate and detailed direction of Downing Street is in itself calculated to awake the same jealousies as led to the miscarriage of Lord Carnarvon's attempt. It is the High Commissioner whom they know and trust and who is among them, whom they are asking to inform them on their own affairs, not the Colonial Office which to them represents the vexations rather than the privileges of the Imperial connection.

If the Colonial Office persisted in its attitude, the Kindergarten would tell all governments of South Africa that Britain had refused their request. Perhaps, then, leading colonial statesmen, such as Hull, Farrar, Botha, Smuts, Crewe, Jameson, Malan, Maydon, and Fraser, would want to issue the memorandum on their own account. The authors concluded with a bombshell: the suggestion that Selborne threaten London with his resignation.[34]

Provoked by this last suggestion, Selborne sent Hichens an indignant reply:

On all subjects on which you are entitled to advise me I welcome and value your advice in a high degree. But you signed a letter in which, in my opinion, advice was offered to me on two subjects on which no one except my wife is entitled unasked to advise me. Those two subjects were my relationship with the Secretary of State for the Colonies and the circumstances under which a High Commissioner ought or ought not to resign. For that reason I do not approve of your letter.[35]

In a meeting with Curtis, the high commissioner explained more calmly why he would not resign, except as a last resort. First of all, it would make federation a party question in England, and secondly his resignation would turn all South Africa against His Majesty's Government and possibly against the king himself. Moreover, Selborne upheld that the secretary of state did have a right to see the document, though not to mutilate it. Intractable, Curtis threatened to part company with Selborne and publish the draft himself on his own initiative. The high commissioner retorted that, while he could not stop publication of the original draft, he would himself issue an edited version of the same document. Then, scoffed Curtis, the governor would have to explain why two very similar statements had been issued from two different sources. Unabashed, Selborne sarcastically replied that he would simply tell the truth – that "loyal friends" had withdrawn their cooperation because he refused to resign on their decree. On the first day of 1907, he sent Curtis a letter reiterating that, without his signature, the memorandum would fall flat on its face. Curtis composed a letter formally asking for his draft back, but on the advice of Hichens and Duncan, he never posted it.[36]

Meanwhile, Selborne had been soliciting opinion from various quarters in South Africa as to the timing of publication. While Richard

Solomon urged publishing the memorandum before the elections, Smuts advised waiting until afterwards, not for fear of influencing local politics but because the elections would weaken its impact.[37] At the end of January the Cape ministers sent a minute urging immediate publication. Natal's ministry, on the other hand, would wait until after the Transvaal's political campaign. Before then, Selborne himself had decided it was better not to press further for immediate publication. He had told Curtis during their stormy meeting that he no longer regarded pre-election publication as essential. Perhaps the Kindergarten's impertinence had made it a point of honour for him to resist their demands. His correspondence with Sir Walter Hely-Hutchinson, the Cape governor, contains a more definite explanation. On 4 January 1907 Selborne remarked that no Transvaal candidates had so far brought up the subject of Delagoa Bay. Better, he considered, to withold the memorandum and let sleeping dogs lie.[38]

On 9 January, Selborne sent home a lengthy telegram explaining the complexities of the railway tangle and why some Progressive candidates might come out in favour of closer relations with Mozambique, which would constitute a statement against federation. He did not forecast, however, that his fears would necessarily materialize or that early publication would be required to prevent such a contingency. He did request discretionary power for early issue, if the situation demanded it. Though Ommanney considered the request quite reasonable, Churchill remarked in the minutes: "in our zeal for Federation and unification let us not forget the old maxim 'Divide et Imperia' [sic]. Do we want an ill-tempered confederation against Downing St. interference? By all means let us read Lord S's memo. But I shall view it with captious and apprehensive eye[s]. *We* cannot move too slowly in this."[39] In his reply, Elgin did not positively refuse Selborne's request but expressed his strong desire to see the document before publication. Selborne answered on 18 January that he would not at the moment press the point. By then, the matter had become academic, for the memorandum was due in London at any moment, copies having been sent out to the Cape, Natal, and England on 7 January.[40]

The *Selborne Memorandum* must be understood on the basis of what it did say and, thanks to Selborne's editing, on what it did not. The arguments put forward in the published version were genuine and important. They constituted a plea to bring the polity into line with the economy so as to foster stable conditions and a healthy business climate. Curtis confessed to Selborne, however, that he had deliberately placed a deeper message between the lines of his "factual" analysis. He articulated the real essence to the high commissioner:

The fundamental theme of the whole is simply this, that all attempts to regulate the domestic affairs of South Africa from England have failed and have led to the adoption of expedients which laid the foundation of the disunion which is at the root of South African troubles today ... The second point for consideration is in respect of the frank avowal of the weakness of our diplomatic position in dealing with any solid interest like Portugal or the shipping ring.[41]

Though this sounds odd coming from a self-styled imperialist, it becomes less so when one remembers that Curtis's England in 1906 was a Liberal one.

Even in the published copy, it did not take much reading between the lines to detect an anti-Liberal bent. Indeed, all South Africa's past troubles were laid at the door of the British government when the Liberals had controlled it. The high-handed way in which Liberal Britain had abolished slavery throughout the Empire had created the bitter division between Dutch and English. This decision caused the Great Trek, which in turn resulted in the formation of separate Boer states in the interior:

It can scarcely be doubted that if the inhabitants of Cape Colony had been consulted in the management of their own affairs, and invited to co-operate in the task of abolishing slavery, a matter affecting not merely the British Empire, but the civilised world, this passion to escape from Government control would never have possessed them [the Trekkers], and there would be but one government and one South African nationality at the present time.

In 1859 the Liberal government blocked Governor Sir George Grey's attempt to unite the Cape and the Orange Free State, both of which desired the union. By contrast, the Tory Carnarvon came in for only mild criticism for having "attempted to force upon her [South Africa] the gift of union which his predecessors in 1859 had withheld."[42] In 1906 lingering memories divided Boer from Briton and railway hostility split colony from colony. Presiding over this state of affairs was yet another Liberal government. The moral was clear.

More than a mere polemic against Westminster, the *Memorandum* constituted in some ways an economic policy paper. Almost a third of it, in fact, comprised a detailed history of the intercolonial railway conflicts. These had not only depleted coastal treasuries and embittered intercolonial relations but had also blinded each colony to the fundamental unity of the country. Instead of pulling together in harness, each colony struck out recklessly in its own direction and in doing so, threatened to overturn the entire cart:

The mischief of the situation lies in the fact that no one parliament assembles where members of the Transvaal can meet face to face with members from the coast, hear what the diversion of trade to Delagoa Bay means to the British South African ports and tell them what it would mean to the trade that industry creates if 90 per cent. of the natives employed underground were withdrawn, so that some plan to meet the difficulties of both could be devised."[43]

This little reminder to the maritime colonies of their dependence on the Rand might have wounded coastal pride, but it expressed the fundamental fact of their position.

Witwatersrand readers could not remain complacent for long; as they turned the pages, they encountered gloomy prophecies for gold mining unless investors could be tempted back. The South African economy was at present running in a vicious circle.

The management of the South African Railways in separate sections, each controlled by a different Government, has produced a system of rates which does not respond to the natural demands of trade, is highly unstable, and defeats the intention of the Customs Union. The general result is great uncertainty in the conditions of business so far as they are affected by rates and customs. But the markets themselves are in the highest degree unstable because they depend to a large extent on the mining industry, the development of which is checked for want of labour and of capital. This uncertainty as to the future of the mining industry is making itself felt in every business throughout the country, and not the least if the truth were known in the agricultural industry. But to what is the scarcity of capital due?

The last question was succinctly answered three paragraphs later: "In a word, fluctuations in political conditions mean constant destruction of capital." Without stability, the region's economy would remain speculative. Colonists, the author exhorted, must cease depending on fortuitous mineral discoveries and turn instead to the serious development of their country. South Africa, in short, must take control of its own resources and its own future.[44]

One resource to which the *Memorandum* made only fleeting reference was unskilled labour. The published version did remark that "Her local resources of labour cannot be turned by South Africa to the fullest use, until she is able to exercise some measure of general control over all parts of the country."[45] The readers, however, were not informed that the Kindergarten envisioned the continuation of imported labour for fifty years. From the original, Selborne struck out "*In about fifty years*" and inserted instead "*At any moment, the Transvaal is free to reconsider the question of imported labour.*"[46] The original draft urged the formation of a central government stable enough to give finality to any labour decision reached and strong enough to carry out the decision in the face of the British government's opposition. As it was, the colonies divided on the issue and left Britain as "the only will and brain where all those nerves meet." In this way, Britain usurped a function which should belong to South Africa. Again, the investor was involved. The uncorrected draft observed:

For the interests which ask for imported labour a decision in their favour is of little value except in so far as it can be regarded as final. It is not enough for an investor to feel that a supply of labour is available now. He must also have some measure of assurance that it will continue to be available until his money is repaid him with interest. So long as proposals affecting the value of his investments, made in one local Parliament, are liable to arouse opposition in neighbouring communites, the ultimate decision will often, in practice as well as in theory, rest with the Imperial Government. If interest in the matter is aroused in the United Kingdom, all sorts of new considerations are brought to bear and must be weighed by the supreme authority, and in any case the ultimate result is greatly postponed, and a period of mischievous uncertainty prolonged.

Selborne excised this and similar statements from the original.[47] Though sympathetic to the Kindergarten's views on this issue, he was well acquainted with prevailing sentiment at home on this question. Unlike Curtis, he did not spoil for a fight.

"Closely interwoven" with the labour question was the native problem, which provided another source of resentment towards the metropole. The *Memorandum* urged South Africa to assume responsibility for its own defence in the event of an African uprising.[48] Not altogether hidden in the published version was the implication, made explicit in the original, that so long as South Africa remained dependent on imperial troops, it would remain at the mercy of baneful Liberal policy. The authors, of course, held up the mission of uplift and civilization but about the franchise question they remained studiously vague. That was for a union parliament to decide. Unlike the final version, the original warned against any attempt to impose an African franchise on the "northern Colonies." As to coloureds, readers were enjoined to "extend the hand of sympathy."[49] The franchise excepted, the authors advocated the establishment of a "uniform native policy." The magnitude of the task necessitated united action. The presence of five or six different administrations made for inconsistent approaches to a problem which called for concerted action. Union would eradicate the present division of purpose. It would also eliminate the imperial factor, as readers of the published work could conclude, despite the omission of the following statement, which Selborne edited out: "All that need be said on this matter is this: – The most dangerous feature of South African disunion is its inevitable consequence in forcing on the Imperial Government and Parliament a close partnership in responsibility for handling the details of the native question, for it is really more difficult for them to deal with them aright than it would be for the colonies to find wise solutions for the problems of the United Kingdom in respect of religious education, trade disputes, or female franchise."[50] The *Memorandum*'s observations regarding African policy exuded an unmistakably proprietary tone. Interestingly enough, the authors discussed native and labour questions together in the same chapter. In a real sense, Curtis and company presented Africans as part of South Africa's natural wealth, the free utilization of which His Majesty's Government had no right to obstruct.

The *Selborne Memorandum* ended with a stirring appeal for both Boer and Briton to unite and develop a South African nationality which would constitute part of the Empire and a strength to it:

Every thoughtful South African looks forward to a fusion of thought, aim and blood between the British and Boer stock which will develop a national type as strong as all mixtures of the western peoples of Europe have ever proved. This, to me, is the true mission of the British Empire, to foster the growth of vigorous nations, adapted to the continent and country in which they live, distinguished by marked characteristics from the other peoples, who in the five continents are included in its magic bond of equal brotherhood under one Sovereign.[51]

The contents of the *Memorandum* exposed as ludicrous Liberal fears of imposing union from above. It was indeed the reverse: an appeal to unify despite London. In upholding the doctrine of non-interference, the Liberals were inadvertently interfering with local politics and aspirations. On reading the *Memorandum*, Colonial Office officals showed considerable surprise and uneasiness. Though previously willing to allow publication without prior submission home, R.V. Vernon appeared startled once he read the document:

I do not see how the prospect of its publication can be viewed without some apprehension. The real moral of the historical survey which forms the first section appears to me to be the expediency not of federation but of self-government – what Mr. Rhodes meant by the "elimination of the Imperial Factor" – and it seems doubtful whether the exposition of this doctrine comes best from the mouth of HM's High Commissioner. The recurrent references to

Washington ... appear to be curiously infelicitous. South African statesmen are quite likely to take George Washington as their model, but is it our place to suggest it?[52]

Nor did Lambert like having the government's hand forced by its own servant in South Africa. True, British governments had consistently favoured federation as an ultimate goal.

Lord Selborne's action in circulating this memo has however brought matters to an issue before the S of S wished. His memo is in the hands of all the Govts and is no doubt more or less known to all the leading men in public life (eg. Sir G. Farrar, who has just pronounced in favour of Federation). The question is whether if Lord Selborne desires suddenly to publish [he] is to be refused – I do not think in any case HMG should take responsibility for the memo as it stands. To refuse publication would no doubt be interpreted to mean that HMG disliked or at least were luke warm in the cause of Federation – and I incline to think that the best reply would be to effect that there is a good deal in the memo which HMG cannot endorse as expressing their considered opinion and that they would therefore prefer that the memo should not be published or at least that its publication should be postponed but that if and when Lord Selborne thinks that in view of its communication to the various Govts. it is not impossible [possible?] to resist the pressure to publish he may consent.[53]

H.W. Just, equally unhappy but realising the awkwardness of the situation, minuted "I do not however think that publication can well be objected to if the various South African Governments desire its publication, after the Transvaal elections are over, with the *caveat* proposed by Mr. Lambert."[54]

The observations of Just and Lambert illustrate the difficult situation in which Selborne's document had placed the Liberal government. It had come to power condemning Unionist attempts to extend British control over Southern Africa. The Liberals had presented themselves to the Empire and the House of Commons as the champions of colonial self-government. They had preached the doctrine of reconciliation between Boer and Briton and had given force to this vision by their "magnanimous gesture" to the Transvaal. How then could the Liberals suppress a document which the Cape and Natal had asked the high commissioner to write? They could not easily stifle the consummation of a long and cherished South African ideal – one which Malan supported as well as Jameson. To do so would have alienated South Africa from Liberal England and, with Selborne's resignation a likely result, would also have fed its enemies at home.

Churchill, for one, was not willing to court these risks. Throughout his previous correspondence on the subject he had shown himself jealously sensitive of the government's prerogatives in seeing the document before publication. Less than a month before its arrival in England, he had deprecated the creation of an "ill-tempered confederation," preaching instead the doctrine of "divide and rule." Now, curiously enough, after reading a document whose hostility to his government was obvious to all officials who read it, Churchill gushed:

The publication of this impressive and noble document can in my opinion be productive only of good. It contains truths the appreciation of which is indispensable to the progress and peace of South Africa. It is animated throughout by a lofty spirit of statesmanship and tolerance and expressed in language of grace and power wh[ich] in some passages achieve high literary quality. I desire to remark that from a House of Commons point of view the circulation of this memo. as a Parl. paper would be attended with great advantages. It would enlarge the outlook of every member upon S. African affairs. It would increase the confidence in the High Commissioner. It would point v[er]y clearly to the inspiring objective towards which events have long been irresistibly and are at last consciously moving.[55]

Why the change of heart? Unfortunately, aside from the powerful rhetoric, his minute contained no substantive reasons as to how the creation of an "ill-tempered confederation" had become an "inspiring objective." Perhaps the *Memorandum*'s "high literary quality" won Churchill over. Without reading his mind, one could also suggest that there was little else for him to do but paint the best face possible on the predicament Selborne had created for him. Not quite as euphoric but equally compliant, Elgin cabled Selborne that, as to publication, "The decision must now rest on your responsibility, and not on mine or His Majesty's Government."[56] In early 1906 the Liberals had overruled the high commissioner on the Chinese labour issue and had obstructed him on many others. Less than a year later, Selborne had succeeded in leading South Africa towards a prosperous future, breaking Liberal bonds as he did so. The Empire had struck back.

9 The Union of South Africa

Shortly after the *Selborne Memorandum* was released to the colonial governments, the Kindergarten prepared for further action. It decided that the next step should be to promote the cause through propaganda and through closer union societies, which would be established in each colony. Crucial to the campaign was the enlistment of representative Boers such as Botha and Smuts. Both were invited to a large dinner in January 1907, which the magnate Abe Bailey was holding to promote union. (Bailey had already made substantial contributions to the closer union movement.) With the Transvaal elections only a month away, the Boer politicians demurred from publicly supporting an imperialist initiative (by eating off a gold capitalist's plate)! Although Smuts maintained contact with the Kindergarten members, the refusal of the Afrikaner leaders to join their movement was a severe blow to the Kindergarten. Without Boer participation, their public campaign would appear partisan and imperialist. For this reason, Curtis decided to postpone the establishment of closer union societies. Instead, he and his friends would work quietly, collecting data and information pertinent to union.[1] Though behind the scenes, this research would prove indispensable in drawing up the specific provisions of any draft constitution for South Africa.

The Kindergarten's proposals became public in July of 1907 when the *Selborne Memorandum* was published. The document evoked a mixed reaction among South Africans, but few questioned the substance of its recommendations. There were, of course, some doubters in the press. While applauding closer union as a desirable goal, *South African Mines*

Commerce and Industries lamented that the Transvaal's dependence on Mozambique labour diminished its freedom of action and, in doing so, presented an obstacle to federation. Should any plan for political amalgamation threaten the *modus vivendi*, the Transvaal would find itself unable to participate without courting economic catastrophe. Of course, the editor bitterly reminded his readers, the retention of the Chinese would have obviated this problem. More sceptical of the ideal itself, the *Cape Argus*, representing mercantile interests in that colony, doubted that unification would end economic friction, and it questioned the *Memorandum*'s premise that these tensions sprang merely from boundary lines. The same divergence of interest would, it predicted, exist after union as before. Moreover, the depression diminished the bargaining power of the coastal colonies. "The States," it admonished, "should enter into the partnership full, so to speak of beans, full of spirits and strength, and not slide in shame-faced like a lot of poor relations."[2]

Most of the press throughout South Africa, however, commended the *Selborne Memorandum.* The *Transvaal Leader* and the *Johannesburg Star* praised its breadth of vision, while the *Rand Daily Mail* expressed its full concurrence with what it took to be the crux of Selborne's case: "The need for stability goes deeper than tariffs and railway rates. It is moral as well as economic. It is a handicap to that gradual up-building without which permanent prosperity cannot be obtained. It predisposes the community to speculation, as did the early land purchase regulations in Victoria. It induces a habit of risking everything to make money quickly, whilst favourable conditions last, because it holds out little hope of success by slower methods." Outside the Transvaal, the *Friend* endorsed the *Memorandum*'s claim that unification would benefit the agricultural interest by making all of South Africa one market. Even the *Natal Mercury* called Selborne's document "a great state paper."[3]

Politicians, especially those without mining affiliations, did not show such enthusiasm. However strongly they desired union, statesmen of an anti-imperialist bent were reluctant to praise the *Selborne Memorandum* too highly or too openly. The liberal J.X. Merriman, soon to become Cape prime minister, proved himself positively hostile to the Kindergarten initiative and attempted to prevent F.S. Malan from tabling the document in the Cape Parliament.[4] Though Merriman's efforts failed, he had cogent reasons for his opposition. He wrote privately to Smuts:

Now comes in Lord Selborne's windy effusion. Surely the price of flunkeyism can go no further than the attempt to compare it with Lord Durham's Report. I do not think that it will do much to help the cause of union forward, but it is useful as a warning of the spirit that is abroad that seeks to unite communities, not on the basis of national aspirations, but on that of material and trade interests with a strong imperial bias.[5]

Six months before, Smuts too expressed his distrust of the Kindergarten, but he exhorted Merriman to remember that "the thing itself is good." After the publication of the *Memorandum*, he enjoined caution but affirmed: "My own position is that federation or rather unification is a good and wise ideal; it is the only alternative to Downing Street which is a most baneful factor."[6] For his part, M.T. Steyn, the old Free State president, roundly criticized the document and, in mockery, discerned the thrust of Selborne's argument without realizing it:

The whole pamphlet is crude, full of rhetoric and bad history. If I understand him [Selborne] correctly then his main reason for federation is to prevent Imperial interference, to which he ascribes all our past evils, but what he seems to forget is that Imperial interference only came in support of the demand for such interference from Imperial servants in South Africa. There may always be this demand as long as we retain those servants, thus if Lord Selborne draws his reason to its logical conclusion he must advocate cutting the painter.[7]

Essentially, this was precisely what Selborne advocated.

Whatever misgivings Smuts reported to Merriman about the Kindergarten initiative, he was at least sympathetic enough to offer Selborne advice as to publication. He never lost his faith in "the thing itself," and after publication he attempted to counter Merriman's increasing scepticism. Repeating the usual arguments that union would eliminate intercolonial friction as well as Downing Street interference, he added a new note of urgency. The forthcoming customs and railway conference presented, he suggested, a perfect time for action, and he warned that failure to seize this chance would result in the further estrangement, perhaps irretrievably, of the British South African colonies. Of course, he assured the Cape politician, he would take no definite steps until after the imminent elections in the Cape Colony and the ORC.[8]

The outcome of both these political contests fully justified Smuts's optimism, for early 1908 found Merriman installed as Cape premier and Abraham Fischer, founder of the Orangia Unie, as head of the Orange River Colony. Thus the Afrikaner parties or their allies controlled three of the four colonial governments in South Africa, a fact which helped remove suspicion as a potential obstacle to union. Moreover, the existence of three sympathetic governments made it possible to exert concerted pressure on Natal, which, though wary of the present closer union movement, would find it difficult to stand alone. When the colonial premiers assembled at Pretoria in May 1908 for the Intercolonial Customs and Railway Conference, they readily resolved that the separate legislatures be asked to appoint delegates to a National Convention for the purpose of constituting a united South Africa.

It is easy to exaggerate the importance of ideology or the role of personalities in bringing the separate colonies to the National Convention. While certain historians represent union as the triumph of Liberal magnanimity, others stress regional ideologies, whether colonial nationalism or the Boer desire for a united Afrikanerdom.[9] Leonard Thompson assigned prominence of place to Merriman and Smuts, as the local politicians who led the unification movement to eliminate imperial influence.[10]

It is clear that the drive to union was propelled by the needs of the South African economy. The Witwatersrand required cheap transport, cheaper labour, and most important, large injections of foreign capital, and all of these depended on political and economic stability. The impoverished coastal colonies, in turn, needed Witwatersrand trade for their economic survival, and, throughout the proceedings, the Transvaal held the upper hand. The Cape and Natal governments approached the convention with deficits of £3,630,216 and £1,507,143 respectively, and they could see no relief in sight, as their railway revenues continued to plummet.[11]

Early in 1907 the Transvaal gave the Cape still more cause for alarm by announcing its intention to withdraw from the Customs and Railway Union. Both politicians and press fully appreciated these stark facts. As Merriman described the Pretoria conference, "The general idea among all parties to the Conference is that we must either unite or break. The social and economic conditions of the inland Colonies are so different from the coastal ones that it is almost impossible, except as one people, to frame a tariff that can be of general application. And the same applies to the railway tariffs." A week earlier he had summarized the Cape's position in succinct terms: "It is playing a game with all the trumps in your opponents' hands."[12]

The *Transvaal Leader* offered this interpretation of the Intercolonial Conference: "With Treasuries depleted; with existent or prospective deficits which must appal the stoutest hearted; with uncertainty in enterprise; with many of our best assets – our men and women – leaving the country, and, worst of all, with hope gradually deserting many who remain – with these grim facts before them, the statesmen in session in our Capital could not but feel that an exhausted people required an inspiring lead." Even critics of the Pretoria gathering understood the motives which had prompted its resolutions. The *Cape Argus*, for example, complained, "As a pauper, it [the Cape] submissively accepts the dictation of the Transvaal, and it went deliberately to the Conference, stripped and in tatters – why? In order that a compact of partnership should be forced upon her people."[13]

The Transvaal did not feel the economic pinch as severely as its neighbours. While the high cost of living in Johannesburg was a serious grievance, it was not unendurable, nor did union seem the only way to bring costs down. There was always the shorter Delagoa Bay route. Predictably, not all elements in the Transvaal shared the ardour for union which impelled Selborne or Smuts. Three months before the Pretoria conference an isolationist movement gained momentum in the Transvaal, especially among farmers who wanted protection from coastal competitors. Though not a dominant force, the growth of this separatist tendency provided a major reason for Smuts's haste in pushing union.[14] Nor did the British interest, even in Johannesburg, line up solidly behind the Pretoria resolutions. Sir Percy FitzPatrick worried that a united South Africa would ensure perpetual domination by the Afrikaners. *South African Mines Commerce and Industries* echoed these fears, while the more conciliatory *Rand Daily Mail* stated, as the magnate George Farrar had, that much would depend on the selection of delegates to the National Convention.[15] Farrar was in no hurry to amalgamate what he termed the "high grade" Transvaal with its "low grade" neighbours.[16]

The Transvaal's economic needs may not have demanded immediate fulfilment, but sort of political amalgamation would become essential to the colony's prosperity over the long term. For this reason, the more far-sighted of the politicians and magnates favoured taking advantage of the present opportunity lest it be lost indefinitely. As Selborne wrote to Patrick Duncan of the Kindergarten, "Those who urge delay about Federation on the grounds of the present political preponderance of the Dutch are the most short-sighted. While the general instability of South Africa continues, all real prosperity will be impossible and all expansion, and the Dutch will continue to preponderate ad eternam ...: there can be no expansion without stability; and there can be no stability without Federation. Q.E.D."[17] In a similar vein, the high commissioner rebutted Farrar's criticism of amalgamating with the "low grade" coast; Selborne pointed out that however "high grade" the Transvaal was, it still required capital, which would not come until political consolidation had brought stability.[18]

Assisted by Botha's tact and the government's conciliatory offer that the opposition appoint three members to the eight-man Transvaal delegation, the "broad view" triumphed, and the reluctant Progressives came into line. On the eve of the National Convention, the *Rand Daily Mail* summed up the high feelings of the moment when it promoted "the big thing." "For 'the big thing' means progress all round. It means that South Africa will take her true place in the world. It means increased confidence in Europe, which must make for greater development in all parts of South Africa. We think the time is ripe for 'the big thing'."[19]

The time was also ripe for the Kindergarten to carry its program to the public. Soon after the Pretoria conference, Lionel Curtis set about to galvanize public sentiment, establishing a journal, *The State*, to popularize the cause of union. In addition, he founded closer union societies in various localities to channel the movement. In the same month that the National Convention commenced its work, these separate branches created a central coordinating body, which elected as consecutive presidents the respected Cape liberal, W.P. Schreiner, and the former president of the Orange Free State, M.T. Steyn. Consciously non-racial, these societies boasted a membership which included prominent Boers as well as Britons. However imperialist the origins of the closer union movement, it projected an ideal that generated wide appeal throughout white South Africa among both Dutch and English.

The National Convention opened in Durban on 12 October 1908. With the largest delegation at twelve members, the Cape Colony was ably represented. Indeed, Sir Henry de Villiers, the convention's president was chosen from its ranks. Half of its members were from the recently formed South African Party which, led by Merriman, included both British liberals and Afrikaners. Of the remaining Cape delegation, two were independent and four were Unionists. (An imperialist party, the latter included Dr Jameson.) The eight-person Transvaal team contained four members of Het Volk (including Smuts and Botha), three Progressives, and Henry Hull, a Nationalist. The Progressives chose as their representatives Sir Percy FitzPatrick, Sir George Farrar, and an obscure solicitor, Henry Lindsay. Needless to say, the Afrikaners dominated the ORC contingent. Four of its five members belonged to the Orangia Unie party, including its leader, Abraham Fischer. Natal's six members were all English speakers.

After the Durban session, the convention's draft constitution went before the colonial legislatives, which issued instructions to the delegates for their guidance at the Bloemfontein session of the convention in April 1909. By the next month all four colonial governments had approved the draft bill, which thereupon went to England, where it readily passed the House of Commons. The Union of South Africa was formally proclaimed on 31 May 1910.

The fundamental basis for the South African constitution had been agreed to by all parties but Natal before the National Convention assembled in October 1908. About the specific terms of the act, however, serious disagreements arose. The selection of the capital, for example, evoked an acrimonious quarrel which the delegates could only resolve by splitting it between Pretoria and Cape Town. A previous chapter has discussed the tenuous compromise worked out to break the deadlock over the African franchise. Despite these tensions, the convention managed to complete its work rapidly and conclude its labours with a remarkable unanimity.

Thompson attributed this harmony to three factors. First of all, he cited the economic homogeneity of the delegates, with farming interests predominant among them. "Mining, banking, and commerce," he observed, "were comparatively poorly represented, and the manufacturing industries and white labour were not represented at all – nor were the non-Europeans. However significant the interracial and intercolonial rivalries may have been, therefore, the convention could be counted on not to neglect the interests or to ignore the prejudices of the white farmers of South Africa."[20] This point seems a dubious one, for the agricultural interests of each colony clashed with those of another. The Transvaal's protection was the Cape's poison. And the major feature which all farmers shared, at least those who were not absentee cultivators, was a common dependence on Witwatersrand prosperity.

More valid was the second explanation Thompson offered for the convention's harmonious conclusion: the paradoxical workings of lingering racialism. The fatuous confidence among both Dutch and English that their "race" would ultimately triumph in a united South Africa encouraged the delegates from each group to suppress differences and to bring on union, confident of ultimate success. This smugness certainly pervaded Selborne's attitude. It is difficult, however, to dissociate this ideological factor from its material context, for, it will be remembered, Selborne predicated his criteria for evaluating a race on its adaptability to modern economic conditions. He distinguished the Afrikaner race by its inability to energize and the British by its instinct for progress. In large measure, he defined British supremacy in terms of material development. Given his assumptions, Selborne's faith in the British future of South Africa was not entirely misplaced.[21]

Finally, exponents of the conventional wisdom stress the crucial role played by moderate personalities, especially Smuts and Botha, who both believed in conciliation and who together possessed the political weight to bring it about. In Thompson's words: "The unanimous signing of the final, as well as the first, report of the Convention was indeed an act of courage and restraint on the part of every delegate, a vindication of the chairmanship of Sir Henry de Villiers, and above all, a triumph for the statesmanship of Botha and Smuts – a realization of their political ideals on a grand scale."[22] No doubt, the generals' moderation assuaged Progressive worries, while their political prestige as leaders in war and peace delivered a united Afrikanerdom to the union.

While Botha, Smuts, and de Villiers occupied centre stage, the successful production involved the efforts of countless individuals behind the scenes. Moreover, it was the Kindergarten who had written the play. The fact that, by 1908, many of Milner's young men were without office left them considerable time to master all the information regarding union. As Merriman's biographer, Phyllis Lewsen, observed: "Ultimately, because Merriman was so busy and because his Kindergarten helpers were so able and skilled, it was they who drew up the detailed blueprint for the Convention." At Smuts's side throughout 1908 and 1909 was the Kindergarten's Robert Brand. Also advising Smuts was Patrick Duncan. Of all the politicians at the National Convention, Smuts was, in the words of Walter Nimocks, "the principle architect of the South African constitution."[23]

Thompson's analysis gave short shrift to one potent factor which made for unanimity at the convention: the Transvaal's economic dominance. Yet even he went so far as to admit that "Transvaal preparation, Transvaal brains, Transvaal teamwork, and Transvaal economic strength prevailed on most issues in the convention."[24] He might have added that it was Transvaal economic strength that generated union in the first place and ensured that the final product would be conducive to capital accumulation.

Fully alive to the Transvaal's preponderant power, Selborne, when pressed, proved himself quite prepared to deploy it. In several letters to his Unionist friends, he discussed the upcoming convention and the constitutional provisions he regarded as vital. He told Lyttelton in May 1908 that "there seems to me to be only one thing which really matters fundamentally, and that is that the basis of representation should be one vote, one value ... and automatic redistribution." If that were not agreed to, he continued, the British South Africans should refuse to enter union.[25]

The high commissioner's logic shows lingering traces of racial distrust and conforms to Thompson's picture of fatuous racialism. Industrial progress would attract British settlers, who would give the British element a political preponderance – under the right system of representation. To cite Selborne's attitude as an example of autonomous idealism would, however, be misleading. If, as Selborne knew, the British would always divide among themselves, how could he anticipate British political supremacy, however large their immigration? The solution to this problem becomes clear when one realizes that Selborne's conception of British supremacy was not strictly political. The materialist assumptions behind his racialism have already been referred to often above, and during the National Convention he articulated them clearly. In his rebuttal to the claim that rural areas deserved over-representation because they had a more stable and permanent population, Selborne argued that urban dwellers paid a greater share of taxes and contained a more highly educated population. He admitted in 1909 to Alfred Lyttelton that the towns might contain a large floating population: "But it is also true that in the country districts are found at least as large a proportion of men who are at least equally valueless to the country, men sunk in abysmal sloth and ignorance, who have never done and never will do an honest day's work in their lives, mere parasites on the country."[26]

However divided it was, the British element shared a common commitment to modernity. But, while superior in this respect, it remained vulnerable to the Afrikaners, who possessed political skills which made them powerful adversaries. As he told his old cabinet colleague St. John Brodrick, "In its standard of government, in its conception of society, and in its power of developing a modern civilisation, the Dutch Africander race is quite distinctly inferior to the British, but in its capacity of politics it is, I confess with humiliation, quite distinctly superior." The Progressives' selection of the colourless Lindsay as one of their convention delegates underscored their political ineptitude. And all-British Natal was even worse, nominating a Dutchman to their delegation. "How," asked the exasperated high commissioner, "can you help people that are such colossal idiots?"[27] Nonetheless, Selborne was determined to try by rallying the British behind the voters' basis. If progress could be adequately represented, it could frustrate any obscurantist attempt to stop the clock.

Initially, it seemed that Selborne's fears would not materialize. The Progressive leaders and the Rand press came out strongly for the voters' basis, making its adoption an essential prerequisite for Johannesburg's participation in the federation proceedings.[28] Though Smuts's early constitutional proposals prescribed the population basis, Fitz-Patrick's insistence on one man, one vote induced the Transvaal colonial secretary to modify his drafts. In their final form, the proposals which Smuts presented to the convention embodied not only the voters' basis but also proportional representation, which, by giving more political weight to rural English-speakers, gave the South African British more than they had asked for. The Durban session of the National Convention adopted Smuts's provisions but, to appease the farming interest, made it permissible to overload sparsely populated areas by 15 per cent and to under-represent urban areas by the same margin.[29]

Selborne, however, was not completely satisfied that "equal rights" were adequately safeguarded under the draft act passed at Durban, and in February 1909 suggested to Farrar that these clauses be entrenched.[30] Events two months later confirmed his fears when the Cape parliament, with the urging of Jan Hofmeyer, the leader of the Afrikaner Bond, resolved on making the 15 per cent margin (for overloading rural districts) mandatory instead of merely permissive. Throughout April the high commissioner wrote furiously to Transvaal political leaders, both Progressive and Het Volk, urging that they make no concession to the Cape on this score.

Selborne did more than simply cheer the Progressives on; he coached them as to strategy and could barely resist taking the ball himself. He supplied Farrar with arguments to use in debate against the proposed amendments. The high commissioner congratulated the Progressive delegates on their threat to wreck union if any amendments were made. "I give you my opinion clearly," he reassured Farrar, "that Hofmeyr and Co. will *at the last point* give away and not wreck union on those clauses, and that if you put your back to the wall and stand firm you will win a splendid victory." If the Cape did stand out, the other three colonies could join without her, and Pretoria would become the sole capital. He promised the magnate, "you may rely on my support in this matter to the very last extremity."[31] He intimated that Farrar should circulate his letter to FitzPatrick and the other Progressives.

Whether prompted by this advice or not, a letter from FitzPatrick appeared in the *Cape Times* two days later. Without impugning the Bond's motives, he warned that, "if their [the Bond leaders'] aim had been the worst possible, if they had meant to wreck union and to destroy the spirit of trust and comradeship between the races, the most devilish ingenuity could not have devised a better way." Equally adamant, Farrar vowed to Selborne that he would sacrifice union rather than whittle down equal rights. He agreed, however, that the Cape was bluffing. The Kindergarten also entered the fray, mobilizing the *State* for the purpose. The April edition warned that tinkering with the draft act would destroy "the delicate balance of concession and compromise and, in doing so, imperil the 'big thing'."[32]

The High Commissioner also despatched several letters to the Transvaal prime minister. On 8 April, he assured Botha of his support in upholding the equal rights clauses. He again held out the bait that, if the Cape refused to submit, Pretoria would become the indivisible capital of the Union. Botha agreed that "we will have to be very firm and stand by our guns."[33] By the end of the month, Selborne added a note of menace, advising Botha that the Liberal government, as the champions of equal electoral rights, would find it difficult to sanction a constitution which violated this principle. As for himself, "If ... Mr. Hofmeyr succeeded in his opposition to your declared policy in this matter there is no sacrifice or effort which I would not ... make to prevent the consummation of an Union which I know would bring disaster and not happiness to South Africa."[34]

At the Bloemfontein session of the convention, Abraham Fischer of the Orange River Colony moved to amend the equal rights clauses in the direction of the Cape proposals. Though only the ORC and some of the Cape delegates supported it, Merriman and his Cape colleague, J.W. Sauer, warned that failure to modify these clauses would probably result in the Cape's rejection of the constitution. FitzPatrick countered that the Transvaal would do the same if the convention altered voting provisions in any way. De Villiers broke the stalemate with a proposal eliminating proportional representation but retaining the rest of the articles. The Orangia Unie, the South African Party, and the Het Volk members of the Transvaal readily accepted the compromise but the Progressives refused unless the clauses were entrenched, a demand which the rest of the convention could not entertain.[35]

Mystery still surrounds the Progressive conference of 6 May which Lord Selborne attended. By Selborne's account, he urged the Progressives to accept Curtis's advice and settle for the reservation rather than the entrenchment of the voters' basis; he also warned them on no account to break with Botha. Since it was Selborne who first suggested entrenchment, his advice two months later to accept reservation instead probably carried weight with the Progressives. In any case, they came around to his view. On the morning of the 7th, the high commissioner explained his controversial intervention to Botha and later that day, the convention adopted both de Villiers' compromise and the reservation of these clauses.[36]

However vague the details of Selborne's involvement, one may reasonably conclude that his previous letters to both Botha and Farrar helped stiffen the Transvaal's stance and solidify that of the Progressives. He gave Farrar and his colleagues a lead, coordinated their activities, and moderated their posture once essentials had been secured. The Progressives clearly carried the day, for they surrendered only proportional representation, which they had never even asked for in the first place. Most important is the fact that before de Villiers' compromise, the Transvaal was willing to force some sort of union through the teeth of the Cape's opposition. How long this colony could have stayed out of a united South Africa remains problematic. What is certain is that the Transvaal had the power and determination to unify without the Cape.

It was admittedly a close call, for not only did most ORC delegates support the SAP on this issue, the Natal representatives were threatening to boycott union on another score. The negotiations between the Transvaal and Mozambique had engendered distrust in Natal despite the

Transvaal's pre-convention assurances that the resultant treaty would effect an improvement for Natal and that, in any case, the Botha government would consult the coastal colonies before signing any treaty.[37] At the Durban session, the Transvaal purchased Natal's acquiescence to a draft treaty by concluding a separate agreement guaranteeing Natal 30 per cent of the rail traffic to the competitive zone. Neverthless, the publication of the final treaty, which did not differ substantially from the draft, evoked widespread indignation in that colony. That this occurred at the same time that the Cape parliament was assaulting the equal rights articles caused particular concern. In the same letter to Botha in which he urged unification with or without the Cape, Selborne declared that "At all costs we must stop Mr. Maydon and Mr. Green [Natal politicians] from becoming opponents of Union."[38]

Three days earlier Selborne had presented a cogent argument to J.G. Maydon, the Natal minister for railways and harbours. He pointed out that Natal would benefit from the new arrangement, which would guarantee the colony more trade than it presently carried. Moreover, the coastal colonies, if unified to the Transvaal, could exert more influence over future negotiations with Portugal. Natal's abstention from union would, he warned, bring disaster to its people.[39] These arguments failed to convince Maydon, who came out actively against closer union.

Lionel Curtis worried not so much about Natal's dissatisfaction as about the British government, which he hoped would endorse union whatever the dissident little colony decided to do with itself. If it did not, it "would produce a state of feeling in the three other colonies which one can scarcely picture." Selborne reassured Curtis that he was quite certain the Liberals would not obstruct union on account of Natal.[40]

Throughout the Bloemfontein session, the Transvaal refused to amend the treaty. Sir Matthew Nathan, the governor of Natal, had estimates prepared which predicted that, even with Maydon's opposition, the colony's referendum would pass union by 10,600 votes to 8,400. A week later, Nathan was more optimistic, now estimating that two-thirds of the Natal electorate would favour it. For his part, Selborne informed Crewe that he, as colonial secretary, might have to decide whether to sanction the South Africa Bill if Natal stood out. "It is imperative that the answer should be clearly and unmistakably in the affirmative." Any other answer might encourage the separatists in that colony.[41] Of course, with the equal rights deadlock broken, Selborne's hand was considerably stronger.

Events fully justified Nathan's optimism, for three-quarters of the Natal electorate endorsed the convention's draft. One may safely attribute this result to the economic facts of life. However meagre Natal considered its share of traffic would be within union, its share outside would have been far smaller. On the other hand, it might be argued that, as strong as the Transvaal's position was, concerted action by Natal, the Cape, and the ORC could have generated decisive pressure on it. The interests of the coastal colonies, however, were divergent, and if, say, the Cape had stood aside, the Transvaal could have bribed Natal by transferring to it some of the Cape's share of the Rand's traffic. After all, as Maydon's protest demonstrated, Natal could be bought. In light of the Witwatersrand's clout, the National Convention's "harmonious conclusion" seems hardly surprising.

The unitary form the constitution took has attracted much attention from political historians. As early as 1906 Merriman favoured a unitary as opposed to a federal structure. Though Smuts did not come around to this view until later, he had accepted it well before the Pretoria conference, and his draft constitutions were built on unitary premises. The Kindergarten shifted more markedly. In 1906 Richard Feetham prepared a paper in which he assumed that, however desirable union seemed in theory, the vast distances in South Africa rendered it impossible. During the next two years, however, the Kindergarten moved towards the unitary ideal.[42] Indeed, their shift can be seen in the two-volume *Government of South Africa*, which Curtis released in 1908. While the first part of the work assumes federation, the latter part advocated a highly centralized union. According to Nimocks, the shift occurred because Afrikaner opinion had come to favour it. It might be added that unification (as opposed to federation) fitted more logically with the Kindergarten's aims of efficiency, effectiveness, and control. By July 1908 Selborne too had embraced this basis. He wrote Northcote, "Certainly, if it comes off every effort will be made to avoid the Australian blunders and to keep the States in their proper place."[43]

Once committed to the unitary scheme, the Kindergarten launched an effective propaganda campaign to promote it. Through the closer union societies and the press, Curtis and his friends mobilized educated opinion in favour of union rather than federation. In the *State*, distinguished scholars such as Sir Perceval Laurence presented sophisticated arguments against federalism. In the same journal, H.A.L. Fisher declared: "The more rapidly society progresses, and with every multiplication of ties with the outer world, the more acutely will the relative rigidity of the federal form be felt."[44] This propaganda campaign ensured that the opposite point of view was seldom heard.

Well before this press campaign, Smuts produced drafts which embodied the unitary essentials of the future South Africa constitution. The first of these, drawn up in August 1908, prescribed a supreme Parliament but left vague the precise relationship between the central and provincial governments. This imprecision evoked criticism from not only Merriman and Sir Henry de Villiers, but also R.H. Brand, a Kindergarten member in Smuts's full-time service. Under Brand's guidance, Smuts prepared a new draft, the substance of which the National Convention came to adopt as the basis of the constitution. The provinces were now left with only those powers specifically enumerated, such as public works and municipal regulations, and even these were subject to the cabinet's veto. Moreover, the central parliament might make the provinces responsible for the execution of any national law.[45] Thus, the local legislatures became merely administrative agencies for the central government.

The Union took over all of South Africa's rail lines, which were integrated into one system and managed by a permanent commission, independent of Parliament. Financially, the convention accepted the Transvaal's proposals whereby the central government assumed all provincial assets and liabilities. Thereafter, the provinces depended on Pretoria for subsidies. As R.H. Brand astutely observed in *The Union of South Africa*, "All government centres in finance. There is no doubt that the Convention, whether deliberately or not, has by means of the financial provisions of the Constitution sealed the authority of the Union Government over the provinces. they are held in a vice and the former has simply to turn the screw in order to secure its ends."[46]

The creation of union generated a spirit of optimism, but this represented more than merely effusive idealism. To be sure, the sentiment of reconciliation was often displayed, especially in the speeches of Smuts and Botha.[47] Other motives appeared besides goodwill. Throughout the Transvaal press, forward-looking commentators castigated as shortsighted the "little Transvaal" complaint that the colony would become the milch cow for the insolvent coastal states. With all the enthusiasm of a convert, Sir George Farrar assured a Progressive congress that the Transvaal would receive handsome repayment for its beneficence in sharing its assets with its bankrupt neighbours. A plethora of articles and speeches offered more precise details as to the value and form of this repayment. Despite the misgivings of the Johannesburg Chamber of Commerce, most analysts asserted that commerce would benefit from the cheaper transportation and stability that union would bring. A so-called expert, writing for the *Rand Daily Mail*, nicely encapsulated the commercial argument:

Undoubtedly the advantages of uniformity of administration and of regulations, etc., in the public services of South Africa are immense, and every business man realises to the point of irritability, the impossibility under present conditions of bringing about many reforms and increased facilities by reason of the fact that, even after convincing the Minister or departmental head in this Colony, of the importance and urgency of certain provisions, it is found that the consent of every other colony is needed, and an official of conservative tendencies in any one of these can effactually bar any progress. This is particularly so in regard to railway and customs matters and Government departmental policy and regulations of various kinds. The entire South African commercial community will hail with immense gratification the prospect of the codification of laws and regulations affecting trade, which at present are so complex as to be a constant source of annoyance.[48]

Transvaal public opinion was riding a high wave of optimism indeed, but it was buoyed up by sound economic logic.

These socio-economic themes were accompanied by a sense of independence, a new South African nationalism which was self-assured but outward-looking. Botha envisioned expansion to the Congo. The *State* stressed South Africa's reliance on the world economy for markets, capital, and foodstuffs. This fact made South Africa especially dependent on the sea for transport and consequently on the British navy for protection. The journal warned its readers that the world was divided into four competing empires: the British, American, Russian, and German, the last being the most dangerous.[49]

The inclusion of South Africa in the British Empire in no way entailed its subordination. Indeed, Selborne looked to the periphery to influence the metropole. In a dinner at the Carlton Club, he sang the praises of union and lamented the divisions in English society. England, he claimed, had always been cursed by enemies within such as Charles James Fox. Presently, men of this cast were rending Britain asunder.

Englishmen are subjected to these cleavages of opinion arising from social questions which manifest themselves among almost all civilised nations. In addition our religious struggles have developed further lines of cleavage, perhaps in a greater degree than any other civilised race. But I would ask you, gentlemen, this question – ... no nation can escape its national history, but why – why when we leave England do we carry our weaknesses as well as our strength into other parts of the earth? We talk of the Colonies. That is a familiar expression – younger partners in the British Empire – and the daughters of England that are now her partners. These colonies have received from time to time many a great advantage from the strength and the influence of England. But in the years that are to come I believe, from my heart, that the daughters are going to repay their mother a hundredfold. And I know they are going to repay her more than this, that it is by their influence they are going to restore to England that unity against the foreigner which she once had but which she partially lost.[50]

To Selborne, the periphery of the Empire was more solid than the
core.

Subsequent events have confirmed the predictions of both advocates
and critics of union in 1909. Materially, South Africa expanded greatly
after union. Agricultural production increased from a value of £26 million in 1910–11 to £41.2 million in 1917–18. During the same period
the value of mining output rose from £32.5 million to £37.4 million,
manufacturing from £10 million to £22.5 million, and commerce
from £15 million to £30 million.[51]

More than this, the outset of union saw a boom in capital investment,
which jumped from a paltry £1.8 million in 1907 to £13.2 million in
1909.[52] Union also facilitated the coordination and organization of labour recruitment. It made possible the systematic dispossession of Africans who were eventually left with nothing to sell but their labour. The
constitution also helped stabilize the communication network which fed
Johannesburg and spread its spill-over. There is strong circumstancial evidence that South Africa's exuberance in 1909 was not misplaced.

Of course, union alone did not cause these results. The First World
War greatly increased the volume of trade. The boom in capital investment in 1909 might have resulted as much from optimistic speculation as from deliberate calculation, and it predated union. Moreover,
investment fell off after 1909, and as late as 1938, Schumann was still
bewildered by the unpredictability of South African business cycles.[53]
As to the labour question, some proponents of union envisioned a
white labour solution rather than the one which South Africa actually
adopted. But, if the constitution's framers did not create an instrument for instant wealth, they did erect a framework which facilitated
the control and development of resources, both capital and labour. In
doing so, they fostered capital accumulation. History since union has
fulfilled both the optimistic vision of a prosperous future as well as the
pessimistic fear of a coercive state.

It cannot be claimed that material conditions alone caused the closer
union movement or determined the specific features of the constitution. It has, however, been suggested that material factors did influence
the National Convention, both directly and indirectly. Indirectly, Witwatersrand wealth gave the coastal colonies a strong inducement for union
and provided the Transvaal with the strength to dominate the convention. A union could come into being without the Cape or Natal but not
without the Transvaal. To be sure, the Transvaal did not hold all the
cards, but it held the high ones, and Merriman knew it as well as Smuts.

Economic considerations influenced the drafting of the constitution
in a more direct way – through the agency of the Kindergarten. Sel-

borne, Curtis, and their allies perceived that South Africa required an efficient, well-organized state to control its resources and channel its productive energy, to stabilize conditions and so make South Africa safe for capital investment. Thanks to their propaganda efforts and to Selborne's persuasion, both official and personal, reluctant capitalists such as FitzPatrick and Farrar were moved to embrace "the big thing." The influence of this intelligentsia did not stop there. Through long study of South African problems, the Curtis coterie proved itself better prepared than active politicians to draft clauses in the constitution, especially those relating to finance and administration. R.H. Brand came to Smuts's side well before the convention opened. The railway clauses were the work of Kerr. In a sense, Thompson's preoccupation with political questions, such as the franchise or the location of sovereignty, led him to minimize the significance of the constitution's administrative and railway clauses, and these, as Brand noted, sealed the fate of the provinces. The Kindergarten must take considerable responsibility for the autocratic system of government that South Africa chose. The constitution made the central government supreme but not necessarily Parliament, whose authority was circumscribed by administration.

Quite pleased with the constitution, Selborne was sanguine about the future. Not all of his Unionist comrades shared his exuberance. They failed to understand his thinking or the prominent part materialism played in it, cleaving as they did to race as the only sure foundation of British supremacy. In March of 1908 Chamberlain voiced anxiety on this score. Would not the unification of the Dutch, he asked, enhance their political strength and place the entire country at their disposal? Lord Salisbury expressed similar doubts:

And yet I have great doubts as to its [unification's] wisdom. I quite understand the fiscal difficulties in South Africa, and I can well believe that the friction as to the railways and the customs union there may be of such a dangerous character that anything may be better. But I cannot conceal from myself that from a British point of view the sum total of the policy which ends in unification inspires me with great misgivings, for I suppose two results are assured: there will be no balance of power henceforward in South Africa and the Dutch element will dominate the united strength of the whole sub-continent. This Dutch supremacy may have what laws they like. No limitations which may be inserted as a condition of unification can be relied upon, for we never could go to war again, especially as it would be with the whole of South Africa.[54]

The remaining Milnerites refused to follow Milner's doctrine in the direction Selborne was carrying it. Milnerism had unsuccessfully tried to combine both racialism and materialism. By 1909 the contradictions in this doctrine were fully exposed. It became clear that one could not have both British political supremacy and material progress, at least not for the foreseeable future. Union, needed to expedite the latter, might conceivably put the Afrikaners in a stronger political position. Was South Africa to be British or prosperous?

Vere Stent, whom Milner had made editor of the *Pretoria News*, came down decidedly on the side of race. It was time to abandon the magnates, who had become a positive danger to British interests. "I cannot," he wrote Milner, "work up any enthusiasm for Closer Union, for I feel that we shall bring into being political trusts as powerful and as dangerous as the gold trust of Lionel Phillips which he has striven to create in Johannesburg. When the gold trust and the Dutch political trust are in power together the ordinary Englishman will be worse off than before the War." Rudyard Kipling interpreted Milnerism in the same light as Stent. In reply to Selborne's sanguine assertion that Milner's work was imperishable, Kipling retorted: "As regards Lord Milner's work, it seemed to me that these are early days to *assume* that any of it will survive *in the intention for which it was created* ... As I see it, Lord Milner was sent out to do certain work, on certain lines, in furtherance of certain principles. Later on, the English abandoned those principles, obliterated the main lines of Lord Milner's work, and handed over absolute control of the details to another race." And Milner himself recoiled from the direction Selborne was going. "I think," he wrote Chaplin, "the Constitution *per se* is not so bad. Seeing what the cards were, which the respective parties held, no better result could be expected. But I have steadily refused all suggestions that I should gush over it ... All the power is with the boers, and will remain with them. But I cannot see that it is anything to raise paens over. The British attitude on the whole question is so astounding, to my mind so absolutely idiotic, that it simply makes me mute."[55]

Selborne interpreted Milnerism in quite a different light. He summarized his reflections on the constitution in a letter to L.S. Amery:

The natural richness of S.A. is such that the stream of development ought to flow in a strong broad deep and continuous current. Kruger dammed it and dammed it effectually. Milner blew up that dam with dynamite. Then the current began to flow. Certain obstructions and snags however remained. All these the unification will remove. Then the current will flow in its natural strength breadth depth and regularity. This current will bear on its waters more and more British. It cannot bear anything else because the Boers are by the influence of history and the absence of education incapable even of embarking on the current. I speak of the race as a race, the exception only proves the rule. This will change I am glad to say by education and changed environment but we have at least two generations start of them. And in no other way could the British population have been made to increase. Now nobody and nothing can stop or even check their increase. This is the fundamental simple fact. Nothing else matters. This alone is essential: Constitutions, governments, retrenchments, and all else are non-essentials, affecting the fundamental fact in an infinitesimal degree only. I do not even mention the attitude of the Boers. Much of much interest might be said about it, but it is also a nonessential. – It is no longer in their power to dam the stream or even to check its current after unification has been accomplished. Botha sees this and deliberately welcomes the "big thing." Hofmeyr sees it and squirms and writhes and loathes it.[56]

The high commissioner wrote in similar terms to his old British Unionist friends, and in every letter he modestly presented union as the culmination of Milner's work. In fact, Milner undertook the task half-heartedly and eventually lost heart completely. Selborne, however, devoted all his energy single-mindedly to the creation of a modern state to foster material progress. Milner might have succeeded better than he knew, but Selborne succeeded better and knew what he was doing. And unlike his predecessor, Selborne confronted a hostile government at home, politically powerful Afrikaners in South Africa, and Progressive defectors within his own ranks. It was Selborne's vision, Selborne's tact, and Selborne's determination which carried union through these obstacles to bring it to reality.

10 Conclusion

Lord Selborne sailed from Cape Town for the last time on 18 May 1910, shortly before the jubilant ceremonies which inaugurated union. Although he had finished his work in South Africa, a serious battle with the Liberals awaited him at home and, as soon as he reached London, he took up the cause of the House of Lords.

The first issue that confronted Selborne on his return was the constitutional crisis surrounding the House of Lords. The far-reaching nature of the taxation provisions in Lloyd George People's Budget in 1909 brought the Lords to reject the measure, despite their longstanding policy of not obstructing money bills. As a result of their boldness the House of Commons introduced a Parliament Bill to curtail their authority. This rescinded the Lords' veto on money bills and circumscribed their powers over other legislation. A bill passed by three successive sessions of the House of Commons (after being twice rejected by their Lordships) would become law, provided that two years had elapsed since the original introduction of the bill. After acrimonious negotiations, fierce debates, and two elections, the Parliament Bill finally passed the House of Lords in 1911 by 131 votes to 114. What had persuaded the majority of their Lordships was the promise which Asquith secured from Edward VII and from his successor, George V, to create new peers if necessary to force the measure through the upper house. As the voting count showed, a substantial number of peers refused to yield to the threat of creation. Selborne was one of these "ditchers" who fought the Liberal measure to the bitter end. Finishing the debate in the House, he declared rhetorically, "The question is, shall we perish in the dark, slain by our own hand, or in the light, killed by our enemies."[1]

Despite his dogged opposition to the Parliament Act, Selborne was no mere reactionary. As he recounted in his Reminiscences, he considered the tax provisions of the People's Budget "wholly mischievous."[2] Moreover, as he often noted, this was no simple money bill but the first instalment of a wide-ranging social program, which the House of Lords certainly had the right, indeed duty, to address. Not content with having imposed this baneful measure on the nation, the Commons was proceeding to eliminate effectively the second chamber from the machinery of government. The attempt, Selborne considered, was unconstitutional and revolutionary. It was for this reason that he wished to force the creation of peers. As he wrote to F.S. Oliver early in 1911, "The reason why I think the Parliament Bill the very worst possible solution is that it is a veiled revolution which, to my mind, is far more dangerous than a naked revolution."[3] What the Parliament Act had created was a single-chamber tyranny. With the House of Commons in sole control of England, the nation and its empire would, in time, fragment into chaos.

Before and after the Parliament Act had passed, Selborne worked assiduously for the reform of the second chamber so that it could remain a vital and effective part of the constitution. Although he presented many options on the composition and selection of the upper house, he favoured having it chosen by men and women over thirty years of age. Once reconstructed, the second chamber should have its powers restored, indeed enhanced. Should a deadlock arise between the two houses, Selborne proposed, after the South African fashion, a joint conference. If that failed to break the impasse, the voters should decide the issue in a referendum. Selborne carried on the work for constitutional reform well after the Parliament Act had passed. In 1911 he felt a pressing necessity to find some way of prying England from the grasp of "malignant lunatics" in the House of Commons.[4]

While one constitutional question simmered on, another boiled over onto the English scene. The campaign for women's suffrage, which had been gathering force for the first decade of this century, took a militant turn after 1910. Lord and Lady Selborne became ardent proponents for the rights of women. For Lord Selborne it was not only justice to confer the franchise on women but also a practical way of balancing the volatile impulses of young men with what he thought would be the more conservative sentiments of women. On hearing of a proposal in 1916 to enfranchise all men in uniform, he expressed his reservations to Lord Salisbury: "Personally, I think it would be most unjust to women and dangerous to the State to enfranchise the adult fighting men and no women. Dangerous to the state because I firmly believe in the steadying influence of the women voters in essentials in the long run. Unjust to the women because I believe that the interests of labour, women, and of the women's view of certain social matters would be ruthlessly sacrificed."[5] In 1918 the Selbornes' wishes were realized to a degree when the Representation of People's Act enfranchised all males over twenty-one and women over thirty who met a low property qualification.

No sooner had the Lords controversy abated then the perennial question of Irish Home Rule erupted with a vengeance – this time, with a Tory vengeance. As the elections of 1910 had left the Liberals without a strong majority, they were forced to rely on the Irish members to pass the Parliament Act. The price was a new Home Rule Bill. In 1912 Asquith introduced a measure which would confer autonomy on Ireland in internal affairs. Foreign and defence matters would stay within the responsibility of the imperial Parliament, which would remain the supreme authority. In return for this devolution of power, Irish representatives at Westminster would be reduced from eight-four to forty-two.

The inclusion of Ulster proved a fatal flaw, as armed Ulstermen started drilling to resist the measure. More serious still, they were supported by the British army in Ireland and by the Conservative party in England. In early 1914 the Home Rule Bill passed the House of Commons for the third time after being twice rejected by Lords; it included a provision for any county's exclusion for six years. The concession failed to satisfy Ulster, whose Volunteers continued to drill, as did the rival Irish Volunteers. Should the Liberals ever attempt to implement Home Rule, it seemed certain that they would face a bloody civil war in Ireland, which could spill back to England.

Not surprisingly, Selborne roundly condemned the bill. He charged that it roused the implacable opposition of Ulster without satisfying the nationalists in the south. Nonetheless, unlike many of his peers, Selborne recoiled from the prospect of civil war. He urgently pressed the government to hold a referendum or election on the issues. He warned Sir Edward Grey that, if the Liberals refused, "I do not see how your conflict with Ulster can be avoided, and, if that once begins, God in heaven knows where it will end."[6] Yet, at the same time, he attempted to assuage the fervour of his Unionist colleagues. He explained to Thomas Platt, a young back-bencher:

I will never say that it is always wrong to take up arms. I should myself take up arms without any hesitation for the Monarchy against a republic, and I have already said that I think Ulster is wholly justified in her present attitude. But civil

war is the ultima ratio and the last party in the world that ought to turn to arms
if it can possibly avoid it or go outside legal and constitutional forms is the
Conservative and Unionist Party.[7]

It was around this time that Lord Selborne became a convert to the
devolutionist ideas of F.S. Oliver, a friend to many Unionists and author of an influential biography of Alexander Hamilton in 1906. Various schemes for devolution, federation, and home rule all around had
been in circulation since the mid-nineteenth century. When the Irish
problem flared up again during the Edwardian crisis, discussion about
constitutional alternatives became frequent and intense. In late 1910
the Round Table held moots on the subject at Blackmoor, the Selborne estate. Lionel Curtis saw home rule all round as a prelude to imperial federation. While Selborne never lost sight of the imperial
aspects of the question, it seems that it was the domestic situation
which drove him to embrace Oliver's ideas. Many thoughtful statesmen, such as Oliver, proposed making provisions for the devolution of
power onto the other components of the United Kingdom, as well as
Ireland. By late 1913 Selborne was proselytizing the cause. If Ireland
received self-government, he would make sure that Wales, Scotland,
and England got the same treatment. In the event of Irish Home Rule
he continued, "I should become a devolutionist before everything else
and subordinate all my politics the one aim of securing the control of
exclusively English affairs to the English."[8]

By fostering the disintegration of the United Kingdom into English,
Welsh, and Scottish components, many devolutionist plans made necessary consolidation at a larger level, which, Selborne mused, might
lead to imperial federation. He hoped that the perilous international
situation would convince the dominions to participate in a truly imperial parliament. He elaborated on his ideas in a memorandum:

And supposing the Dominions ever do consent to join us for imperial purposes, which is the ideal to which many of us look forward (and which some of
us think will be the only possible way not only of main- taining the British Empire, but of preventing the Mother Country and the Dominions alike of sink-
ing to a position of comparative unimportance in the world, considering what
the size and strength of the United States, of the German Empire, and of Russia will be in the future), we shall bind ourselves in this position. Four parliaments, an English, a Scottish, an Irish, a Welsh, concerned only with the local
affairs of those parts of the United Kingdom. A fifth Parliament for the United
Kingdom concerned only with affairs common to all parts of the United Kingdom, but which are not imperial affairs. And a sixth Parliament concerned
only with imperial affairs common to all parts of the Empire.

The Empire's parliament could treat imperial matters, foreign affairs, and defense policy. While Selborne did not detail the allocation of powers among the various levels of government, he confidently predicted to Sir Edward Grey that the difficulties were much less than commonly supposed.[9]

Selborne's plans, the implementation of Irish Home Rule, and mercifully, the plunge towards civil war were all cut short when Germany invaded Belgium in August 1914. As for many families in the British Empire, the First World War was a personal as well as a national tragedy for Lord and Lady Selborne. In January of 1916, while serving with the Hampshire Regiment in Mesopotamia, their second son, Robert Palmer, was killed in action.

The year before, Lord Selborne had dutifully accepted the presidency of the Board of Agriculture and Fisheries in Asquith's war cabinet. To him was entrusted the vital task of maintaining Britain's wartime food supply. To prepare for the possibility of submarine attacks, Selborne commissioned Lord Milner to investigate how Britain could increase its food production. In July of 1915 Milner's committee issued an interim report, which called for a government subsidy to secure for farmers a guaranteed price of 45 shillings per quarter of wheat. This measure would at least raise the proportion of home-grown wheat from one-fifth of Britain's total consumption to one-third. Acknowledging that his proposal amounted to government interference in the free market, Milner assumed that Selborne did not object to "reasonable socialism."

Selborne backed the scheme wholeheartedly. With a strong social conscience that, on this occasion, overrode the claims of private property, he wrote to Vaughan Nash, the secretary of the Ministry of Reconstruction:

Agriculture must in fact be protected from such a fall in prices as would make it again wholly unrenumerative and destroy its capital. But, if the State intervenes for this purpose, it must clearly intervene also to see that the wages of labour never fall to the old level, and it must also intervene to see that the land is not wasted, that bad farming is not tolerated, and that the landowner makes the best use of his land to the national advantage. In fact landowners must be shown that the possession of agricultural land is a great national trust.

Selborne proposed this not merely as an emergency war measure; he advocated that it become a permanent feature of British agriculture.[10]

He urgently pressed Asquith to consent to the subsidy and to do so promptly so that farmers could begin ploughing in September. The imperturbable prime minister seemed unconcerned. "In my opinion," he wrote Selborne, "there is not the least fear that any probable or conceivable development of German submarine activity can be a serious menace to our food supply." When Selborne kept pressing, Asquith replied that his proposal was "quite impossible," as the subject was a "highly contentious one."[11]

Selborne soon had even greater cause for exasperation. In Easter 1916 an Irish insurrection broke out in Dublin. The government promptly suppressed the rebellion and placed Ireland under martial law. Although the cabinet authorized Lloyd George to act as a mediator between Ulster and the southern nationalists, the irrepressible minister exceeded his instructions without the full cabinet's knowledge. He arranged a deal whereby Home Rule would be implemented immediately for all Ireland but the six countries of Ulster, whose fate would be settled by an imperial conference after the war. Although the agreement foundered, Selborne was outraged by Lloyd George's doings, which came as a complete surprise. In forceful terms he told Asquith "Not only have I never agreed to any such proposal [Lloyd George's deal] but I have never had it made to me, nor have I ever heard it discussed."[12] Selborne felt that these proceedings constituted a breach of trust so serious that he resigned from the cabinet. Not only did he nurse grave reservations about extending self-government to a rebellious region in the middle of a desperate war; he also felt completely frustrated by the cabinet's ineffectual, incompetent, and irresponsible leadership.

After the peace, Selborne's views on domestic politics mellowed. Even before the war ended, he told Salisbury that he did not fear a large electorate nor a Labour government:

On the whole I should prefer the Labour government now [rather than a Liberal one]. Before the war I should have been more afraid of their attitude on imperial questions. I am not afraid of that now. Of course things will be done which I shall vehemently dislike, but these things were already being done before the war; and the war has confirmed the intense belief which I have had now for a good many years in the instincts and intentions of my fellow-countrymen and women.

Reluctantly, he came to embrace democracy: "There is no form of Government which looks more ludicrous on paper than democracy, and for most nations democracy is a very bad form of Government, but on the whole I believe it to be the best form for our race in the 20th century."[13] These words themselves, coming as they did from an aristocratic "ditcher," gave proof that class tensions had diminished.

Selborne continued to work for constitutional reform and the construction of an imperial federation. In September 1916 he was writing to Salisbury: "I think this [imperial federation] is a great ideal to work for because the British Empire will replace the United Kingdom so far as international relations and national defence is concerned, we shall have a Power which will be most potent to keep the peace of the world and will not be aggressive and we shall be able to keep England for the English uncontaminated and unrevolutionised by the Celtic fringes." In 1917 Selborne elaborated on his scheme for the allocation of powers among the various levels of imperial government. Of course, defence, foreign, and imperial policy would fall within the ambit of the imperial parliament, while the kingdom parliaments would treat domestic matters. As for industrial questions, Selborne expressed ambivalence but was inclined to assign these subjects to the kingdoms. Residual powers should, he believed, reside with the imperial parliament.[14]

Selborne felt that imperial consolidation would strengthen the Empire's defence, foreign stature, commerce, and industry. "Also," he continued, "I regard it as the only way by which the problem of reconstruction in domestic affairs can possibly be dealt with and, therefore, as the greatest safeguard against revolution." The danger of rebellion, he now felt, would arise not so much from labour strife as from the electorate's impatience with the House of Commons.[15]

In retrospect, the failure of such schemes for imperial federation might seem inevitable. In the five years following the First World War, however, in the wake of extensive imperial cooperation during the conflict, and in the flux in imperial relations created by the Irish troubles, the Empire might indeed have taken a different shape from the one which it did assume.

When the Conservatives regained power in 1922, Lord Selborne informed Bonar Law that he could not take up a cabinet seat. His reasons were personal. First, he had developed a chronic throat condition which prevented him from speaking at any great length. And second, he had received, since 1916, several valuable corporate directorships, which he would be obliged to relinquish on entering cabinet office. Without these, he would have to give up his estate at Blackmoor. After much thought and prayer, he decided to sacrifice his career so that he could keep Blackmoor "as a home and rallying place for all my children and grandchildren." He, of course, still worked for imperial consolidation, constitutional reform, and industrial peace. Though he continued to resist socialist measures, he came to see the need for strong state involvement in the economy and for the equitable distribution of profits between labour, management, and capital.[16]

Selborne's retirement from politics gave him the time to enjoy his home and family. He did continue to serve on the boards of various corporations. What occupied the remainder of his public life was his service to the Church of England. In 1924 he became chairman of the House of Laity for the Church Assembly. Though Selborne remained inactive politically during the decade of appeasement, war would again bring tragedy for his family. In 1942 his eldest grandson was killed on active service in the Hampshire Regiment. Lord Selborne himself died in the same year.

Epilogue

With Lord Selborne's departure from South Africa in 1910, the imperial factor, as a political force in the region, vanished. Superficially, it would seem that Selborne's high commissionership represented merely the exhaust fumes of imperialism, that he presided over an imperial retreat. If he had any influence at all, so the argument runs, it was in preserving the loyalty of Britain's collaborators, in gracefully devolving power to the Afrikaners, and in following the orders of the Liberal government once it overruled his own recommendations, as it usually did. By this logic, Selborne's importance lay in facilitating the transfer of power from metropole to periphery.

The thesis of imperial retreat, however, fails to explain Selborne's buoyant optimism in 1909, nor does it account for the work the high commissioner actually performed in South Africa. To be sure, his superiors overruled him on responsible government, but they came to accept the voters' basis for the constitution, to which Selborne attached much greater importance. And after reprimanding the governor for interfering in the West Ridgeway proceedings, the Liberal government accepted his advice. Admittedly, local opinion regarding the African franchise, prevailed over Selborne's more liberal views. But the course of union policy towards Africans has not been determined by local ideology alone. For one thing, the Afrikaner rulers inherited sophisticated bureaucratic machinery from the imperial regime. Appreciating the usefulness of this apparatus of control, Selborne attempted to extend it so that Africans would be ruled by "experts" instead of by white politicians. Though his ideas failed to gain acceptance in 1909, their influence outlasted his high commissionership, and subsequent politicians instituted many of his suggestions.

Moreover, African policy was constructed in the context of industrialization, and this Selborne vigorously promoted. He appreciated the Rand's need for labour and the racist lines which structured the workforce. His assistance to the Witwatersrand went far beyond mere sympathy. In 1907 he persuaded Botha to deploy imperial troops against white miners striking against industry's attempt to deskill them. Although he failed to secure Chinese importation on a permanent basis, he protected the labour supply from drastic Liberal action and bought precious time for replacements to be found. In addition, he successfully struggled with the home authorities to retain the Importation Ordinance which, if it failed to meet all of his expectations, at least effectively maximized labour productivity. With the serious tensions between management and workers on the mines, this network of control proved essential. It is important to note that the period from 1905 to 1906 was a critical one for capital accumulation. Without Selborne at the helm, the Rand industry might well have crashed.

More than this, the high commissioner assisted the industry by deploying political power on its behalf. Often this entailed taking measures which many capitalists were too short-sighted to recognize as conducive to long-term prosperity. He promoted agricultural projects, such as the land bank, which not only encouraged the growth of capitalist farming but also incorporated progressive Afrikaners into the reconstructed Transvaal. Also, in the face of Liberal hostility, he frustrated J.B. Robinson's offensive against the Witwatersrand Native Labour Association in Mozambique, thereby protecting the magnates from themselves. In 1906 he extinguished the rate war which had flared up along the railways, and which the Liberal government inadvertently fanned. Most important, Selborne instigated the constitutional change which provided the country with political and administrative stability, and consequently, it was hoped, more favourable business conditions. The high commissioner publicly promoted the cause of union in 1905 in a speech which, unexpectedly, set off the movement to closer union. Thereafter, Selborne manipulated developments, first courting Natal and then luring in the Cape. On this issue, he outflanked London. And while local statesmen drafted the constitution's political clauses, the Kindergarten designed the essential administrative and financial provisions of the act. Selborne, in short, carried forward and completed the work which Milner had barely begun – the construction of a modern South African state.

Thus, the conclusions of this book tend to diverge from the peripheral line and to confirm the findings of radical historians.[1] First, it is clear that the economic development of the Rand constituted Selborne's foremost objective in South Africa. It even took precedence over the political aim of denying power to the Boers. Chinese labour meant more to the high commissioner than saving the Lyttelton Constitution, and his work for closer union sprang not from a desire to outflank the Afrikaners politically but from his firm commitment to economic progress. Largely for the sake of capital accumulation, he wished to end the political instability engendered by the four bickering colonies. Moreover, he wanted to forge a state powerful and efficient enough to administer a capitalist economy. In this sense, the present work carries the conclusions of Marks and Trapido into the post-Milner period. Without being reductionist, one must note that Selborne's ideological beliefs mitigated but also reinforced his economic objectives; his social Darwinism, for example, accorded well with capitalist needs.

While the study associates Selborne closely with the Randlords, it dissociates him completely from the Liberals, except on African policy, where there was broad agreement. It posits a clear divergence between the parties, which no doubt reflected the socio-political tensions that Dangerfield discussed over fifty years ago in the *The Strange Death of Liberal England*. Though Hyam noted that the Liberals diverged with the Unionists on Chinese labour, he minimized this disagreement in light of the similarities in political aims – the maintenance of British supremacy in South Africa. Yet Selborne considered the Chinese issue more crucial than the constitutional settlement. And far from converging towards the Liberals on the question of union, Selborne was, in fact, striking back. The object in his mind was not to preserve British influence in South Africa but to banish it. The reason? Quite simply because he viewed the Liberals as a greater threat to imperial interests than the Afrikaners. Throughout his tenure in South Africa, Selborne associated imperial interests closely with material progress.

Related to the above is the third contention of this study – that Selborne's career in South Africa demonstrates the questionable value of conceiving imperialism as metropolitan dominance over periphery. Though an imperialist, Selborne did not identify "imperial interests" with the "imperial factor." Indeed, he felt that Britain's late enemies in South Africa were more trustworthy than the Liberals as guardians of the Empire.[2] In this light, Leonard Thompson's view stands in need of qualification. He underestimates the importance of the imperialists in designing union, and he minimizes the role of economic factors. Finally, confusing imperialism with the imperial factor, he interprets the closer union movement as anti-imperial, whereas in the eyes of Selborne and his political allies, it was precisely the opposite. Thus, Selborne's policies in South Africa may be characterized as economic, anti-Liberal, and neither metropolitan nor peripheral but cosmopolitan.

These themes bring us to a final consideration of Selborne's mature conception of empire. During his high commissionership, his beliefs had evolved from what they had been a decade before when he penned his dire state paper about a United States of South Africa.[3] In that 1896 memorandum he attributed Britain's deteriorating position in South Africa to the mineral discoveries in the interior. Once the Empire had extended its jurisdiction to the Witwatersrand, its mineral wealth became a precious imperial asset rather than a danger. Selborne came to appreciate this within three months of landing in South Africa. In 1908 he was writing as if economic growth had constituted a *casus belli* in 1899. As he wrote to Joseph Chamberlain, Vereeniging had made possible not only British supremacy but also the reconstruction of South Africa into "an united, progressive modern State."[4] By the time he left southern Africa, his imperialism had come to include material progress through large-scale capitalist enterprise and world-wide expansion.

Some historians, however, would contend that Selborne encouraged material development simply to promote British immigration, which would, in turn, strengthen British influence. Admittedly, he commended this argument in his 1899 minute on war aims and in subsequent letters when high commissioner.[5] It is misleading, however, to minimize progress by casting it as merely an instrument for British supremacy. For one thing, as he stated in his 1896 memorandum, Selborne did not consider English immigration as likely to help the fate of the Empire in South Africa. Indeed, the dreaded United States of South Africa would be created by the British majority which he anticipated in the Transvaal.[6] Moreover, to posit simply an instrumental connection between material progress (as means) and British supremacy (as end) is to ignore the close relationship which Selborne saw between them. Through his social Darwinism, he fused the two together in such a way that progressiveness became a defining characteristic of what British meant.

That an Edwardian statesman should hold racist views towards non-whites comes as no shock to modern readers, but it is often overlooked that Selborne's Darwinism applied to ethnic white groups as well. Even in the 1896 document, he mused that "though sprung from the same stock, the two races [Boer and British] do not amalgamate. It shews what a lot of Celtic and Norman blood must be infused in us." He developed these beliefs much more fully while in South Africa and arrived at the conclusion that the key difference between the English and the Afrikaner was the latter's genetic inability to energize. Thus, he predicted that "if there is industrial and commercial progress, the

British and the British alone can profit by it."[7] Though competition
with the English would regenerate Boer stock, by then the British
would have a long head start. To miss Selborne's social Darwinism is to
neglect an essential feature of his imperialism. In contrast to Kruger's
obscurantist South African Republic, the British Empire was the embodiment of all things progressive.[8]

Selborne carried this attitude into his relations with Africans. Here,
too, it is impossible to dissociate his ideology from the material context
in which it operated. Hard work and individual competition would, he
predicted, improve the black species. While confident of European racial superiority, he feared that racist restrictions such as employment
colour bars would enervate the white race by coddling it. Although his
paternalism towards Africans did not coincide perfectly with capitalist
imperatives, there was considerable overlap. The civilization test he
proposed for admitting Africans into the white socio-political order
evinced a strong materialist aspect, such as private property and a reasonable standard of living.

Of course, Selborne's conception of empire involved more than materialism or social Darwinism. Complementing these elements was a political component. As governor of the Transvaal, he appreciated that
only a well-organized and efficient state could provide the stability required for prosperity. His chief preoccupation as high commissioner
was the consolidation of South Africa into a strong, unified state. The
political unification of the Empire followed as the logical end in Selborne's view. He agreed with Lionel Curtis in 1907 that, as South Africa
needed unification, the Empire itself required a "clear and coherent
scheme."[9] The erection of an imperial super-state would create a formidable block of power and wealth. Political integration would also facilitate the global exchange of finance and trade.

These economic, ideological, and political imperatives, brought Selborne into sharp collision with the Liberal party, as well as the radicals
and socialists who supported it. He regarded imperialism as the vital issue for Great Britain. "Radicalism," he wrote to the *Morning Post* in
1912, "is a dying creed ... Imperialism and Socialism are living creeds
and when Radical Ministers seek for ideas which will move the minds
of men they have to turn to one or the other of them." In this article,
he elaborated on the domestic aspects of Unionist policy:

Unionists believe in the nation and Unionist policy should be always national
as opposed to the sectional policy of the Radicals. They oppose disestablish-
ment because it would remove the national recognition of the truth of Christianity, and most of us believe that a national policy not based on the faith of
Christ is a political edifice founded in the quicksands ... They uphold the right

to own private property and the right of a man to *work*, because they believe that the strength and moral health of the nation is dependent on the liberty of the individuals of which it is composed. They are opposed to unbridled collectivism because it is incompatible with the liberty of the nation, and to uncontrolled individualism because it is incompatible with the happiness of the nation. They know that all men are not equal and that a political system founded on the theory of equality must fail, but they believe that all men and women have a right to the best opportunity which can be afforded them of using their gifts to the best advantage, and therefore they are prepared to use the power of the nation to assist the individual and thus adjust the balance between individualism and collectivism."[10]

As Selborne preached unity for Great Britain, he envisioned a coherent Greater Britain, which would synthesize metropole and periphery into a larger whole. The Empire was not, in his view, a web of bilateral relationships all centring in London. Nor would Great Britain exercise a dominant influence in Selborne's empire. At no time, not even in his 1896 memorandum, did he urge the resurrection of British power in Southern Africa. He thought in broader terms – in terms of Empire, not Britain. The war did not decide whether Britain should remain a decisive factor in the country but "whether South Africa was to remain secluded and isolated in one of the world's ruts or whether it was going to play the great part that it could play in the Empire." The same logic applied to England itself, and Selborne stressed to Lord Curzon the importance of "enlarging our mind from the U.K. to the Empire." His imperialism was broad enough to subsume colonial nationalism, which he fully welcomed. "I have always," he confided to Sir Matthew Nathan, governor of Natal, "believed that the best chance for its [the Empire's] future lies in fostering what Jebb calls colonial nationalism." Indeed, as he told Lord Salisbury, he considered his colonial brethren much sounder on imperial issues than people at home. The real threat to the Empire, he believed, lay in the House of Commons.[11]

It was the House of Commons that directly challenged every tenet of Selborne's imperialism: economic development, political consolidation, social Darwinism, domestic cohesion, and imperial holism. It would be facile and reductionist to claim that these were interlocking components of British capitalism in the late nineteenth century. It is not too much, however, to claim that these five aspects of Selborne's imperialism were complementary and mutually reinforcing. Political consolidation would foster stability which would promote economic growth, as would the effacement of parochial boundaries between metropole and periphery. The appeal for domestic unity came as a response to the dangerous class strife which rocked the foundations of profitability – private property. And finally, Darwinism could be used to explain, rationalize, and legitimate competition on an individual or (more likely in the early twentieth century) corporate basis – whether between peoples, races, nations, or empires. In short, these five inter-connected features in Selborne's vision of empire justified capitalism and assisted its operation and survival during the perilous time of the Edwardian crisis.[12]

Besides encouraging capitalism in the Empire, Selborne defended the rights of private property against the claims of socialism at home. And his efforts to solidify the Empire would certainly have helped to provide British capital with a stable and expansive field of investment and enterprise. Yet this summation of Selborne's political life lacks something. It misses the transcendent aspect of his imperialism, his faith in the righteousness of the imperial cause. He believed deeply in the Empire and served it well in peace and war. In his person he blended patrician qualities from three centuries. He embodied the ef-ficiency of the twentieth century, the honour and probity of the nine-teenth, and the pluck of the eighteenth. The situations he confronted demanded such qualities. In him were reconciled the cross-currents of his age. A gentleman and a capitalist, he was a provincial notable but also a member of an imperial class. He identified with Hampshire, with England, and with the Empire without any division of loyalties. After all, for this imperial gentleman, they were merely three different views of the same thing.

Appendix

BIOGRAPHICAL NOTES

This list identifies people who figured prominently in Selborne's life during the time he was high commissioner, from 1905 to 1910. Thus, the relevant periods of their careers have been emphasized.

ABDURAHMAN, Abdullah (*c.* 1872–1940), Cape coloured leader and doctor. First non-white elected to Cape Town city council. Became president of African Political (later People's) Organisation in 1905; led deputation to England to obtain provision for coloured franchise in new constitutions, 1906. On W.P. Schreiner's mission to Britain in 1909 to protest colour bar in Union constitution. A strong believer in improvement through education, Abdurahman actively sought to extend school facilities for non-whites. Elected to Cape Provincial Council in 1914. Attempted to establish a united non-white front, convening mass conferences for this purpose in 1927, 1930, 1931, and 1934. Optimistic and moderate, Abdurahman never worked outside constitutional channels. His moderation failed to inspire younger, more radical generations of coloured intellectuals.

ALBU, Sir George (1857–1935), Rand capitalist. On arrival in South Africa in 1876, entered Kimberley diamond business. Moved to Johannesburg where he established General Mining and Finance Corporation in 1895.

AMERY, Leopold (1873–1955), statesman and journalist. *Times* correspondent in Boer War. Under Milner's influence became a passionate imperialist. Entered British House of Commons as Conservative in 1911. Opposed Parliament Bill and Home Rule. Intelligence officer in First World War. First Lord of Admiralty, 1922–4. Colonial secretary, 1924–9. India Office, 1940–5.

ASQUITH, Herbert Henry (1st Earl of Oxford and Asquith) (1852–1928), Liberal prime minister. Educated at Oxford. Called to bar, 1876. Liberal MP, 1886–1918. Home secretary, 1892–5. Joined Liberal-Imperial wing of party during Boer War. Chancellor of exchequer, 1905–8. Prime minister, 1908–16; faced successive crises over budget of 1909, Parliament Bill of 1911, Home Rule, and First World War.

BAGOT, Walter Lewis (1864–1927), corporate manager. Member of British military administration in Johannesburg during Boer War. General manager, Chamber of Mines Labour Importation Agency.

BAILEY, Sir Abraham (Abe) (1864–1940), Rand capitalist and politician. Originally a stockbroker, he invested in mining and founded the South African Townships, Mining and Finance Corporation. Member of Cape Legislative Assembly, 1902–5; Transvaal Legislative Assembly, 1907–10; Union Assembly, 1915–24.

BAIN, James Thompson (1859–1919), engineer and labour leader. Came to South Africa in 1887. Played major role in founding unions in Cape and Transvaal. Editor of Johannesburg *Witness*. Secretary of Transvaal Federation of Trades, 1911. One of the most militant leaders during the industrial unrest of 1913–14.

BALFOUR, Arthur James (1848–1930), philosopher and statesman. Conservative MP, 1874–1922. First lord of treasury and leader of Commons, 1891–2, 1895–1902. Prime minister, 1902–5. Tried to hold together a party badly divided over tariff reform. Set up Committee of Imperial Defence. Resigned as Tory leader when his advice to concede on Parliament Bill was rejected. In inner cabinet of Coalition government during First World War; foreign secretary, 1916–19.

BAMBATHA (1865–1906), leader of 1906 Zulu rebellion. Chief of small branch of Zulu in northern Natal. Clashed with Natal administration over fiscal matters and was officially deposed in 1906; fled north into Zululand and organized resistance to poll tax. Conducted guerilla campaign for two months before being killed.

BEIT, Alfred (1853–1906), Rand capitalist. Entered diamond business on arrival in South Africa in 1875. Became partner of Jules Porges, on whose retirement he co-founded Wernher, Beit and Co. Gave substantial backing to

Rhodes for De Beers amalgamation in 1888. After gold discoveries, founded Johannesburg firm of H. Eckstein and Co.

BLACKWOOD, Lord Basil (1870–1917), administrator. Assistant colonial secretary, Orange River Colony, 1901–7. Colonial secretary, Barbados, 1907–9.

BOTHA, General Louis (1862–1919), statesman and soldier. Sheep farmer in youth; involved in creation of New Republic, 1884; on its dissolution, moved to SAR. Elected to Volksraad, 1897. Played prominent part in Boer guerilla operations against British, 1899–1902. Founded Het Volk party after war; acknowledged leader of Boer people. Transvaal prime minister, 1907–10. Prime minister of Union, 1910–19. Proponent of reconciliation and acceptance of South Africa's inclusion in Empire. Suppressed Boer rebellion in 1914.

BRAKHAN, Gottfried Heinrich Amandus (1856–1923), Rand capitalist. Arrived in South Africa in 1892. Entered firm of A. Goerz and Co.; appointed managing director, 1898.

BRAND, Robert Henry (1878–1963), Kindergarten member. Educated at New College, Oxford. Joined Milner's staff in South Africa, 1902. Made permanent secretary to Intercolonial Council, 1904; remained an employee of Transvaal government after Afrikaners gained power in 1907. Smuts's secretary at National Convention, 1908–9. Returned to England, 1909. On editorial board of *Round Table*. Joined Lazard Brothers (banking house). His expertise often sought in international monetary conferences. Publications include *The Union of South Africa* (1909) and *Why I Am not a Socialist* (1923).

BRODRICK, William St. John, [9th Viscount Midleton and 1st Earl of Midleton] (1856–1942), statesman. Educated at Eton and Oxford. Conservative MP, 1880–1906. Secretary of state for war, 1900; instrumental in creation of Committee of Imperial Defence. Secretary of state for India, 1903–5. A close personal friend of Selborne.

BROWNE, Albert (1860–1923), politician and civil servant. Came to South Africa in 1891. Assistant imperial secretary, South Africa, 1901–7. Colonial treasurer, Orange River Colony, 1907–10. Constitutionalist delegate to National Convention, 1908–9.

BRUCE, Victor Alexander [9th Earl of Elgin and 13th Earl of Kincardine] (1849–1917), statesman. Viceroy of India, 1893–8. Chairman of royal commission which inquired into military preparations of Boer War, 1902. Secretary of state for colonies, 1905–8. Though he treated Selborne considerately, he never gained his high commissioner's respect.

CAMPBELL-BANNERMAN, Sir Henry (1836–1908), Liberal prime minister. Entered Commons as Liberal, 1868. Chief secretary for Ireland, 1884–5. Secretary for war, 1886 and 1892–5 under Gladstone and Rosebery. Member of Committee of Inquiry into Jameson Raid. Leader of Liberal party, 1898. Denounced Unionist war efforts as "methods of barbarism"; advocated conciliation with Boers and prompt concession of self-government. Prime minister, 1905–8; ended importation of Chinese labour and granted responsible government to conquered colonies.

CARTWRIGHT, Albert (1868–1956), journalist. Pro-Boer during war. Secretary of Conciliation Committee. Editor of *Rand Daily Mail*, 1905, and *Transvaal Leader*, 1907.

CECIL, James Edward [4th Marquess of Salisbury] (1861–1947), Conservative statesman. At Oxford with Selborne. Conservative MP, 1885–1903. Commanded 4th Bedfordshire battalion in South Africa, 1899–1900. President of Board of Trade, 1905. Recognized as leader of "old Conservatives." Opposed Finance Bill (1909) and Parliament Bill (1911). Continued to work with Selborne for Lords' reform after First World War. Leader of Lords, 1925–9. Leader of opposition in Lords, 1929–31.

CECIL, Lady Maud [Countess of Selborne] (1858–1950), Conservative feminist. Eldest child of 3rd Marquess of Salisbury. By Selborne, whom she married in 1883, had three sons and one daughter. Prominent in movement for women's suffrage before First World War. Selborne was a devoted husband and often discussed important matters of political policy with Lady Selborne.

CECIL, Robert Arthur Talbot Gascoyne [3rd Marquess of Salisbury] (1830–1903), statesman and diplomatist. Conservative MP, 1853–68. Prime minister and foreign secretary, 1885, 1886–92, 1895–1902 (resigned latter portfolio in 1900). Selborne's father-in-law.

CHAMBERLAIN, Joseph (1836–1914), Statesman. Mayor of Birmingham, 1873–5. Entered Commons shortly after as a Liberal radical keenly interested in social reform. Served in several Gladstone cabinets. Split party in 1886 over home rule; brought his Unionist wing into alliance with Conservatives. Secretary of state for colonies, 1895–1903. Resigned post to lead tariff reform movement. Working closely with Chamberlain at the Colonial Office (1895–1900), Selborne developed great respect and affection for "the chief."

CHAPLIN, Sir Francis Drummond Percy (1866–1933), Rand capitalist and politician. After arrival in South Africa (1895), he joined Consolidated Gold Fields and soon became manager, serving in this capacity until 1914. President of the Chamber of Mines, 1905–6. Member of Transvaal Legislative Assembly, 1907–10. Member of Union Assembly, 1910–14. Administrator of Rhodesia, 1914–23. Re-entered Union Assembly, 1924.

CHURCHILL, Winston Spencer (1874–1965), soldier and statesman. Educated at Harrow and Sandhurst. Entered army in 1895; took part in various military expeditions, 1895–9. War correspondent in South Africa for *Morning Post*, 1899–1900; taken prisoner but escaped. Entered Commons as Conservative in 1900 but crossed floor in 1904. Liberal undersecretary of state for colonies, 1906–8; spokesman for Colonial Office in Commons. President of Board of Trade, 1908–10. Home secretary, 1910–11. First Lord of Admiralty, 1911–15. While working under him in South Africa, Selborne considered Churchill reckless and radical.

CRESWELL, Frederick Hugh (1866–1947/8), mining engineer and labour leader. Became manager, Durban Deep Mine in 1894 and later of Village Main Reef Mine. Took up cause of white labour. Elected to Union Parliament, 1910; leader of South African Labour Party. Minister of labour, 1924–5 and 1929–33.

CREWE, General Charles P. (1858–1936), politician and soldier. Member of Cape Legislative Assembly after 1899. Fought with imperial forces during Boer War. Colonial secretary in Jameson's ministry, 1904–8. Unionist member of Union Assembly.

CREWE-MILNES, Robert Offley Ashburton [2nd Baron Houghton and Marquess of Crewe] (1858–1945), statesman. Viceroy of Ireland, 1892–5. Lord President of the Council, 1905–8. Secretary of state for colonies, 1908–10; worked with Selborne on Act of Union and provisions for protectorates. Secretary of state for India, 1910–15. Leader of House of Lords, 1908. Though representing a Liberal minority in the upper chamber, Crewe fought to carry out the Liberal program of Lords' reform, 1909–11.

CURTIS, Lionel George (1872–1955), Kindergarten member. Secretary to Milner, 1900. Johannesburg town clerk, 1901–3. Made assistant colonial secretary to organize municipal government, 1903. Primary author of *Selborne Memorandum*. Left government service in 1907 to start closer union societies. With friends, founded Round Table. With British delegation at Paris Peace Conference, 1919. Expressed his belief in Commonwealth and world unity in *Civitos Dei* (1934–7).

CURZON, George Nathaniel [Marquess Curzon of Kedleston] (1859–1925), statesman. Struck up friendship with Selborne at Oxford. Entered Commons as Conservative, 1886. Viceroy of India, 1899–1905; initiated controversial reforms; undertook unpopular partition of Bengal; met resistance from British cabinet over his forward policy in Persian Gulf. In 1911, led moderates in Lords who accepted Parliament Bill. Foreign secretary, 1919–23.

DE JONGH, Jacobus Nicholas (1858–1911), president of Chamber of Mines, 1906–7.

DE VILLIERS, Jacob Abraham Jeremy [Jaap] (1868–1932), jurist and politician. State attorney, Orange Free State; resigned in 1898. Commando during Boer War; captured by British and sent to Bermuda. Member of Transvaal Legislative Assembly, 1907–10. Attorney general and minister of mines in Transvaal government. Appointed chief justice of Union, 1929.

DE VILLIERS, Johan Hendrik [Baron De Villiers of Wynberg] (1842–1914), jurist and statesman. Entered Cape Assembly, 1867; held various cabinet posts. Chief justice of Cape, 1873–1914. An advocate of confederation since 1870s. Urged conciliation on Kruger to avert war. President of National Convention, 1908–9. First chief justice of Union.

DINUZULU (c. 1870–1913), Zulu chief. With Boer assistance, consolidated his position as Zulu king. Resisted British annexation of Zululand, 1887; tried for treason and banished to St Helena; allowed to return in 1897 as local chief. Protested loyalty when Bambatha rebellion broke out in 1906 but was tried by special court in 1909 and sentenced to four years imprisonment, which he served until Botha, as Union prime minister, released him.

DUNCAN, Sir Patrick (1870–1943), Kindergarten member. Milner's private secretary at Inland Revenue. At Milner's request, came to South Africa in 1901. Colonial secretary for Transvaal, 1903–7. Member of Railway Committee of Intercolonial Council and Transvaal Legislative Council until 1907. Entered politics as Progressive. Pushed for closer union; helped draft Selborne Memorandum; co-edited State. Legal adviser on Transvaal deputation to National Convention 1908–9. Active in Union politics, holding cabinet posts under Smuts and Hertzog. Prominent in bringing about fusion of parties which led to founding of United Party. Governor General of Union of South Africa, 1936–43.

ECKSTEIN, Sir Friedrich Gustav Jonathan (1856–1930), Rand capitalist. Joined H. Eckstein, 1888. Partner in Wernher, Beit and Co. in London, 1902–10. Became director, Central Mining and Investment Corp., 1911; chairman, 1912–14.

EVANS, William (1882–1936), administrator. In British civil service, Straits Settlement. Superintendent of Foreign Labour Department, 1904–5.

FARRAR, Sir George Herbert (1859–1915), Rand capitalist and politician. Chairman of Anglo-French Exploration Co. and of the East Rand Proprietary Mines. Member of Reform Committee, 1895. Became leader of Progressive party in 1904. Member of Transvaal Legislative Assembly, 1907–10. Delegate to National Convention, 1908–9. Member of Union Assembly, 1910–11.

FEETHAM, Richard (1874–1965), Kindergarten member. Educated at New College, Oxford. Came to South Africa in 1901. Town clerk of Johannesburg, 1903–5. Legal adviser to Lord Selborne and member of Transvaal Legislative Council, 1907–10. Early proponent of union. Elected to Union Legislative Assembly, 1915. Appointed to South African Supreme Court, 1923. Made chancellor of University of Witwatersrand, 1949. Opposed apartheid in higher education and general policy of Nationalist regime after 1945.

FITZPATRICK, Sir James Percy (1862–1931), politician. Went to South Africa, 1884. Joined H. Eckstein and Co., 1892; partner, 1902–7. Member of Transvaal Legislative Assembly, 1907–10. Delegate to National Convention, 1908–9. Member of Union Assembly, 1911–20. Selborne knew him as a zealous Progressive politician. South Africans know as the author of their most famous adventure story, *Jock of the Bushveld.*

FISCHER, Abraham (1850–1913), politician. Prime minister of Orange River Colony, 1907–10. Delegate to National Convention. Minister of lands and interior, 1910–13.

FRASER, Sir John George (1840–1927), lawyer and politician. Held several posts in Orange Free State government. Chairman of Volksraad, 1884. Defeated by M.T. Steyn in presidential election of 1896. Opposed Free State participation in Boer War. Occupied many official positions during crown colony regime; member of nominated Legislative Council and Intercolonial Council. After responsible government, founded Constitutional Party in opposition to Orangia Unie. Member of ORC's Legislative Assembly, 1907–1910. Appointed delegate to National Convention but withdrew on grounds of health. Union senator, 1910–20.

GREY, Sir Edward [3rd Baronet and Viscount Grey of Fallodon] (1862–1933), statesman. Educated at Winchester with Selborne, then Oxford. Liberal MP, 1885–1916. Parliamentary undersecretary, Foreign Office, 1892–5. Joined Liberal-Imperialist wing of party during Boer War. Liberal foreign secretary, 1905–16; continued Lansdowne's policy of rapprochement with France; brought Britain into First World War. Chancellor of Oxford University, 1928–33.

GOOLD-ADAMS, Sir Hamilton John (1858–1920), soldier and administrator. Went to South Africa with British army in 1884; on Warren expedition. Subsequently with Bechuanaland Border Police. Resident commissioner, Barotse-land, 1896–7. Resident commissioner, Bechuanaland Protectorate, 1897–1901. Besieged at Mafeking during Boer War; commanded Town Guard. Lieu-tenant-governor of Orange River Colony, 1901–7, and governor, 1907–10. Carried out work of postwar repatriation, reconstruction, and agricultural de-velopment. Left South Africa in 1910.

HALDANE, Richard Burdon [Viscount Haldane] (1856–1928), statesman and philosopher. Liberal MP, 1885–1911. A Liberal-Imperialist during Boer War. Liberal secretary for war, 1905–12; initiated major reforms in army. Lord chancellor, 1912–15. Consolidated small number of Labour peers into official Opposition in House of Lords, 1925–8.

HICHENS, Lionel (1874–1940), Kindergarten member. Educated at Winches-ter and New College, Oxford. Volunteered for service in Boer War, 1899. Ac-cepted administrative post under Cromer in Egypt, 1900. Returned to South Africa to join Milner's administration, 1901. Town treasurer of Johannesburg, 1901. Colonial treasurer of Transvaal, 1902. Treasurer of Intercolonial Coun-cil, 1903–7. Returned to England in 1907 after grant of self-government to Transvaal. Entered business, which occupied the rest of his life.

HOFMEYR, Jan Hendrik (1845–1909), Cape statesman. Newspaper editor; ad-vocated equal language rights for Cape Dutch. Entered Cape Parliament, 1879. Started farmers' associations which coalesced into Afrikaner Bond (1883), the only organized party in Cape Parliament until 1898. Led Bond, but held cabinet rank only six months, preferring role of king-maker. Allied with Rhodes until Raid. Tried to prevent war in 1899. Encouraged reconcilia-tion after war. At National Convention, strongly supported Cape franchise.

HOPWOOD, Sir Francis [Lord Southborough] (1860–1947), official. Perma-nent secretary, Board of Trade, 1901. On West Ridgeway Committee. Perma-nent undersecretary at Colonial Office, 1907–11.

HULL, Henry Charles (1860–1932), politician. Member, Transvaal Legislative As-sembly, 1903–7. Treasurer of Transvaal under Botha, 1907–10. Delegate to Na-tional Convention, 1908–9. Minister of finance in first Union cabinet, 1910–12.

JABAVU, John Tengo (1859–1921), African spokesman. Founded newspaper *Imvo Zabantsundu (Bantu Opinion)*, 1884. Publicized African grievances; con-demned curtailment of African political and civil rights throughout South Africa. Prominent in promoting African education. Worked through white po-litical parties and used moderate tactics, which, in time, alienated more radi-cal black leaders.

JAMESON, Sir Leander Starr (1853–1917), South African politician. Went out as a doctor to South Africa in 1878. Became associated with Rhodes; undertook negotiations with Lobengula, Matabele chief, to secure mineral concessions for BSAC. Administrator of Mashonaland, 1891. Took part in Matabele War, 1893. Administrator of Matabeleland, 1897. Led infamous raid across Transvaal border, 1895; arrested by Boer officials and handed over to British authorities who sentenced him to a brief term in jail. Entered Cape Parliament in 1900; leader of Progressive party. Prime minister of Cape, 1904–8. Played important part in closer union movement. Delegate at National Convention, 1908–9. Elected to Union Parliament; became leader of opposition, 1911.

JAMIESON, J.W. (dates unknown), administrator. British commercial attaché in Peking (before 1904). Superintendent of Foreign Labour Department, 1905–8.

JEBB, Richard (1874–1953), imperial theorist. Travelled round world, 1897–1901. Wrote influential *Studies in Colonial Nationalism* (1905), which sought to reconcile imperial membership with colonial nationalism.

JUST, Hartman W. (1854–1929), official. Entered Colonial Office 1878; chiefly concerned with South Africa. Assistant undersecretary, 1907–16.

KEITH, A.B. (1879–1944) – Official. Entered Colonial Office, 1901. Secretary to Crown Agents, 1903. Called to bar, 1904. Returned to Colonial Office, 1905. Author of many books on imperial affairs.

KERR, Philip Henry [11th Marquess of Lothian] (1882–1940), Kindergarten member. Educated at New College, Oxford. Went to South Africa in 1904 as private secretary to Sir Arthur Lawley, then lieutenant-governor of Transvaal. Assistant-secretary of Intercolonial Council and of Railway Committee, 1905–8. Secretary of Transvaal Indigency Commission, 1907. Promoted closer union movement; edited *The State*. Helped found the *Round Table* and became its first editor, 1910. As Lloyd George's private secretary, drew up preface to Treaty of Versailles.

LAGDEN, Sir Godfrey Yeatman (1851–1934), administrator of African affairs. Appointed resident commissioner of Basutoland in 1893. Commissioner for native affairs in Transvaal, 1901–7. Chairman of South African Native Affairs Commission, 1903–5. On Executive and Legislative Councils of Transvaal during crown colony period; became disenchanted with Milner and advocated responsible government. Retired to England in 1907.

LAMBERT, H.C.M. (b. 1868), official. Entered Colonial Office, 1892. 1st class clerk, 1898, principal clerk, 1907.

LANGERMAN(N), Sir Jan Willem Stuckeris (1853–1929), manager on Rand and politician. Managing director for J.B. Robinson mines and for Randfontein Estates. Member of Transvaal Assembly, 1907–10 and of Union Assembly.

LAWLEY, Arthur [6th Baron Wenlock] (1860–1932), colonial official. Administrator of Matabeleland, 1898–1901. Lieutenant-governor of Transvaal, 1902; Milner's devoted deputy during reconstruction. Governor of Madras, 1905–11.

LONG, Walter Hume [1st Viscount Long of Wraxall] (1854–1924), politician. Conservative MP, 1880–1921. Visited South Africa, 1909. Opposed Finance Bill (1909), Parliament Bill (1911), and Home Rule. Competed with Austen Chamberlain for Tory leadership in 1911; both deferred to Bonar Law to avoid split. Secretary of state for colonies, 1916. Confidant of Selborne.

LOREBURN, Lord [Sir Robert Reid] (1846–1923), statesman. Entered Parliament as Liberal, 1880. Attorney general, 1894. Lord chancellor, 1905–12.

LOVEDAY, R. Kelsey (1853–1910), politician. Member of SAR Volksraad. On Transvaal Legislative Council and Intercolonial Council during crown colony period. Founded Pretoria Political Association, 1906. Member of Transvaal Legislative Assembly, 1907–10, and Union Parliament after 1910.

LUCAS, Sir Charles P. (1853–1931), official. Entered Colonial Office, 1877. Assistant undersecretary, 1897. Head of Dominions Department, 1907–11.

LYTTELTON, Alfred (1857–1913), politician. Entered Parliament as Liberal Unionist, 1895. Chairman of commission to inquire into concessions granted by Kruger. Secretary of state for colonies, 1903–5.

MALAN, François Stephanus (1871–1941), politician. Editor of *Ons Land*, 1895–8. Member of Cape Assembly, 1900–10; Union Assembly, 1910–27. Held various cabinet posts. An early advocate of closer union and a delegate to National Convention.

MALCOLM, Sir Dougal Orme (1877–1955), economist. Entered Colonial Office, 1900. Went to South Africa in 1905 as private secretary to Selborne. A director of BSAC, 1913–54. Became a director of De Beers Consolidated Mines and Consolidated Gold Fields of South Africa.

MAYDON, John George (1857–1919), Natal politician. Member of Natal Legislative Council, 1893–7. Elected member of Legislative Assembly, 1901. Colonial secretary, 1903. Minister of railways and harbours, 1904. Resigned from Parliament, 1906. Elected to Union Parliament, 1910.

MCCALLUM, Col. Sir Henry E. (1852–1919), soldier and official. Governor of Lagos (1897), Newfoundland (1898), Natal (1901–7), and Ceylon, 1907.

MERRIMAN, John X. (1841–1926), Cape politician. Member of Cape House of Assembly, 1869–1910 and of Union Assembly, 1910–24. Treasurer, 1890–3 and 1898–1900. Prime minister, 1908–10. Delegate to National Convention, 1908–9.

MILNER, Alfred [Viscount Milner] (1854–1925), imperial statesman. Educated at King's College, London, and Oxford. Took part in formation of Liberal Unionist Association, 1886. Held various administrative offices in Egypt. Chairman, Board of Inland Revenue, 1892–7. High commissioner for South Africa, 1897–1905; pursued aggressive policy towards Kruger which led to war; undertook immense reconstruction of Transvaal after war. His crown colony regime and his Chinese labour policy aroused keen opposition in England and South Africa. After returning to England, he opposed Lloyd George's budget (1909), the Parliament Bill (1911), and Home Rule. Cooperated with Selborne during First World War in efforts to increase food production. Secretary of state for colonies, 1918–1921. Selborne held Milner in high esteem.

MOOR, Frederick Robert (1853–1927), politician. Member of Natal Assembly, 1886–1910. Minister of native affairs, 1893–7 and 1899–1903. Prime minister and minister of native affairs, 1906–10. Delegate to National Convention, 1908–9.

NATHAN, Lt.-Col. Sir Matthew (1862–1939), soldier and official. Governor, Gold Coast (1900), Hong Kong (1903), Natal (1907–9).

NEUMANN, Sir Sigismund (1856–1916), Rand capitalist. Founded S. Neumann and Co.; often collaborated with H. Eckstein and Co.

NIVEN, A. Mackie (1854–1928), Rand financier. Imprisoned by Kruger for activities with Reform Committee, 1895–6. Member of Johannesburg Town Council, 1902–6. Chairman of 1903 Labour Commission. Close friend of Fitz-Patrick. Chairman of inaugural meeting of Transvaal Progressive Association.

NORTHCOTE, Henry Stafford [Baron Northcote of Exeter] (1846–1911), statesman. Conservative MP, 1880–99. Chairman of Associated Chambers of Commerce; became well-known in business circles. Governor of Bombay,

1900–4. Governor general of Commonwealth of Australia. A close and regular correspondent with Selborne.

OMMANNEY, Sir Montagu F. (1842–1925), imperial official. Entered Colonial Office, 1874. Crown agent, 1877–1900. Permanent undersecretary, 1900. Retired in 1907.

ORPEN, Joseph Millerd (1828–1923), surveyor. Emigrated to South Africa in 1848. Served terms in Free State Volksraad, Cape Legislative Assembly, and Legislative Council of Southern Rhodesia. Though he fought Africans in several frontier wars, he vigorously upheld Basuto rights; chief mediator between Moshoeshoe and British government during negotiations which resulted in Britain's annexation of Basutoland. Went to Cape in 1870 and was appointed British resident of Griqualand East. During preparation for union, openly advocated liberal franchise towards non-whites.

PERRY, J.F. [Peter] (d. 1935), business administrator. Arrived in South Africa, 1900. Milner's imperial secretary, 1900–3. Chairman of Witwatersrand Native Labour Association, 1903–10.

PETTY-FITZMAURICE, Henry Charles Keith [5th Marquess of Lansdowne] (1845–1927), statesman. Governor general of Canada, 1883–8. Viceroy of India, 1888–94. Secretary of state for war, 1895–1900. Secretary of state for foreign affairs, 1900–5; concluded alliance with Japan (1902) and entente with France (1904). Leader of Conservatives in Lords, 1903. Abstained on Parliament Bill, 1911. Joined War Cabinet, 1914; resigned after publication of his unpopular peace memorandum.

PHILLIPS, Sir Lionel (1855–1936), Rand capitalist. Partner in H. Eckstein and Co. Pioneered deep-level mining. President of Chamber of Mines, 1893–6. Arrested for activities with Reform Committee, 1895–6. Elected to Union Parliament as a Progressive, 1910.

PRETYMAN, Rt. Hon. Ernest George (1860–1931), politician. Conservative MP, 1895–1906. Civil Lord of Admiralty, 1900–3. Secretary to Admiralty, 1903–6. Parliamentary secretary, Board of Trade, 1915–16. Civil Lord of Admiralty, 1916–19. Worked closely with Selborne on naval reform, 1900–5.

QUINN, John W. (1864–1916), public figure. A baker by trade. On Uitlander Council in 1899. Appointed to Johannesburg Town Council, 1901 and continued serving on it after it became elective. On 1903 Labour Commission but refused to sign majority report. President of Johannesburg Chamber of Commerce, 1905–6. Leading member of Responsible Government Association but broke away in 1906. Member of Transvaal Assembly 1907–10. Unionist member of Union Assembly.

REYERSBACH, Louis Julius (1869–1927), Rand capitalist. Partner in H. Eckstein and Co., 1902–9. Appointed participating director of Central Mining and Investment Corp., 1910.

RIDGEWAY, Sir Joseph West (1844–1930), statesman and soldier. Indian Army until 1889. Undersecretary for Ireland, 1887–92. Governor of Ceylon, 1896–1903. Chairman of Committee of Inquiry in Transvaal and Orange River Colony, 1906. Chairman, Tropical Diseases Research Fund Committee.

RIPON, Lord (1827–1909), politician. Entered Parliament as Liberal in 1853. Secretary for war, 1863–6. Lord President of Council, 1868–73. Viceroy of India, 1880–4. Secretary of state for colonies, 1892–5. Lord Privy Seal, 1905–8 and leader of Liberal party in Lords.

RISSIK, Johann Friedrich Bernhard (1857–1925), surveyor and politician. Appointed surveyor general of South African Republic, 1895. Served with Botha in Boer War. Minister of native affairs and of lands, 1907–10. Played important part in negotiating Mozambique Convention, 1908–9. Commissioner of railways and harbours, 1917.

ROBINSON [later Dawson], George Geoffrey (1874–1944), Kindergarten member. Official in Colonial Office, 1898–1901. Milner's private secretary, 1901–5. Editor of *Johannesburg Star*, 1906–10. Editor of *The Times* of London, 1912–19, 1923–41.

ROBINSON, Sir Joseph Benjamin (1840–1929), Rand capitalist. Entered diamond industry at Kimberley. Subsequently, with Alfred Beit and M. Marcus, formed Robinson Syndicate on Witwatersrand. On its dissolution, Robinson founded Randfontein Estates which Johannesburg Consolidated Investment Co. bought in 1916. A Het Volk supporter after the Boer War. Was regarded with suspicion by fellow magnates and contempt by Selborne.

RODWELL, Sir Cecil Hunter (1874–1953), Kindergarten member. Served with British military in Boer War. Imperial secretary to high commissioner, 1903–11. Governor of Southern Rhodesia, 1928–34.

SAMUEL, Herbert (1870–1963), politician. Entered Parliament, 1902. Undersecretary at Home Office, 1905–9. Took an active interest in South African affairs after Boer War.

SCHREINER, Olive (1855–1920), author, feminist, and public figure. Her novel *The Story of an African Farm* received wide acclaim when it first came out in 1883. Her condemnations of jingoistic tendencies in British policy after 1895 made her appear pro-Boer. A strong supporter of African rights, she publicly attacked white injustice to black whenever she saw it. She took on Rhodes himself for brutality in Mashonaland. Also devoted herself to women's suffrage. She was one of the few who, during the union negotiations, pointed out the dangers of a unitary constitution.

SCHREINER, Theophilus Lyndall (1844–1920), statesman. Staunch upholder of African rights. Represented Tembuland in Cape and subsequently in Union Assembly. In 1914 he replaced his brother William as senator in Union Parliament to oversee African interests.

SCHREINER, William Philip (1857–1919), jurist and statesman. Younger brother of Olive. After brilliant legal career, entered Cape Parliament, becoming attorney general in Rhodes's 1893 ministry. Broke with Rhodes after Jameson Raid. Prime minister of Cape, 1898. After unsuccessful efforts to prevent war, reluctantly took Cape into conflict. Resigned under pressure from Milner, 1900. Advocated liberal African policy. Resigned membeship of National Convention to defend Dinuzulu at trial. Led mission to England against South Africa Act, particularly its unitary form and franchise clauses. Appointed Union senator to look after African interests.

SEELY, Colonel J.E.B. (1868–1947), soldier and politician. Served in Boer War. Entered Parliament in 1901 as Conservative but crossed floor in 1903. Undersecretary of state for colonies, 1908–1911. Undersecretary at War Office, 1911–12. Secretary of state for war, 1912–14.

SMUTS, Field-Marshall Jan Christian (1870–1950), premier of Union of South Africa. Studied law at Cambridge. State attorney for Kruger, 1898. Joined Boer forces in Boer War, distinguishing himself as daring general. One of Het Volk leaders after war. Colonial secretary and minister of education in Botha cabinet, 1907–10. A major architect of union constitution. Minister of defence, mines, and interior in Botha's Union cabinet. Served in Britain's War Cabinet during First World War. Prime minister of Union, 1919–26; defeated at polls because of his severe repression of white miners' strike in 1922. After reunion of parties (1933), became deputy prime minister under Hertzog. Prime minister, 1939–1948.

SOLOMON, Edward Philip (1845–1914), lawyer and politician. Johannesburg attorney, 1890–1905. Member of Reform Committee. Founder and president of Responsible Government Association. Elected to Transvaal Legislative Assembly in 1907; served in Botha's cabinet as minister of public works. Union senator, 1910–14. Elder brother of Richard.

SOLOMON, H.W. [Harry] (1858–c. 1920), businessman. Chairman of Johannesburg Stock Exchange, 1895–1903. In 1903 he was nominated to Transvaal Legislative Council. Elected to Legislative Assembly in 1907 as a National Association candidate.

SOLOMON, Sir Richard (1850–1913), lawyer and politician. Left legal practice to enter politics as a member of Cape Legislative Assembly. Attorney general in Schreiner's ministry, 1898. Became Transvaal attorney general in 1902 and twice acted as lieutenant-governor. Hoped to lead a coalition ministry after self-government but was defeated in 1907 election. Served as agent-general for Transvaal in London, 1907. High commissioner for Union of South Africa, 1910–13.

STEYN, Marthinus Theunis (1857–1916), jurist and statesman. Appointed chief justice of Orange Free State, 1889. Elected president, 1896 and 1901. Arranged Bloemfontein Conference between Milner and Kruger to stave off war, but when hostilities commenced, Steyn joined the Boer forces in the field. Though he disapproved of the *Selborne Memorandum*, he promoted closer union and represented his colony as a delegate to the National Convention, 1908–9.

STRANGE, Harold Fairbrother (1861–1911), Rand capitalist. Manager of Mining Department of the Johannesburg Consolidated Investment Co. Ltd. President of Chamber of Mines, 1904–5.

VERNON, Roland Venables (d. 1942), imperial official. Entered Colonial Office, 1900. Served in various administrative capacities throughout Empire.

WERNHER, Sir Julius Charles (1850–1912), Rand capitalist and international financier. Went to South Africa in 1871 as agent for Jules Porges and Co. of Paris. In 1889 entered partnership with Alfred Beit and Max Michaelis, establishing firm of Wernher, Beit, and Co. A prominent force in the amalgamation of the Kimberley diamond companies, he was made a life governor of De Beers Consolidated Mines in 1889. Returning to London shortly thereafter, he later became chairman of Central Mining and Investment Corporation, 1905–12.

WHITESIDE, Peter (1870–1929), Labour leader. Came to Transvaal from Australia in 1892. Elected to executive of Engine Drivers' Society. Served with British military during Boer War. Nominated by Milner to Johannesburg Town Council. Strong opponent of Chinese importation. Labour member of Transvaal Legislative Assembly, 1907–10. Union senator.

WOLMARANS, Frederik Gerhardus Hendrik (1835–1921), politician. Member of South African Republic's Volksraad, 1890–1900; served twice as its chairman. Regarded by Selborne as an extreme "irreconcilable" after Boer War.

WOOLLS SAMPSON, Sir Aubrey (1856–1924), soldier and politician. Served with imperial forces in campaigns against Sekhukhune, Zulus, and Transvaalers (1878–81). Convicted and unrepentent member of Reform Committee, 1896. Founded and commanded Imperial Light Horse during Boer War; severely wounded. Unionist member of Union Legislative Assembly. To Selborne, Woolls-Sampson typified the Transvaal colonial loyalist.

Notes

Preface

1 Fieldhouse, "Humpty-Dumpty," 10, 21, and passim.
2 When I speak of radical, I imply a criticism of capitalism often from a marxist perspective. Of course, one can be a radical-peripheralist, who posits that, while capitalism supplied the dynamics of imperial expansion, the particular capitalist interests involved emerged from the periphery. (An in-

sightful analysis of "peripheral capitalism" was offered by Donald Denoon in *Settler Capitalism*.) Conversely, one can be a multi-causal metropolitanist, who locates the source of British overseas activity within Britain itself but who finds, at the same time, many causes at work. And, further confusing the issue, two recent scholars, P.J. Cain and A.G. Hopkins, offer an interpretation of imperialism which, though metropolitan and economic, does not criticize capitalism. For these reasons, I have attempted to be precise when describing the two main historiographical traditions currently in the field.

I often use the term peripheralist as a shorthand to describe Ronald Robinson and John Gallagher, as well as their disciples. The radical-metropolitanists are often designated as simply radicals for the sake of brevity. I also deploy the terms peripheralist and metropolitan according to customary usage to distinguish broadly between historians who confer causal primacy to the colonial areas and those who attach most significance to Great Britain. The sense in which I use these terms will be clear from the context.

One final note concerns Cain and Hopkins. While not radical, their interpretation does place importance on the metropolitan economy. They can therefore be grouped with the radical-metropolitanists for present purposes, even if only as associate members. For an insightful discussion of the difficulties in classifying theories of imperialism, see Kubicek, *Economic Imperialism*, ch. 1.

3 Robinson and Gallagher, "Imperialism of Free Trade," 1–15.

4 Robinson and Gallagher, *Africa and the Victorians*.

5 Hobson's articles were collected together and published in 1900 as *The War in South Africa*. For his mature theory, see his *Imperialism: a Study*, especially ch. 6, "The Economic Taproot of Imperialism."

6 Lenin, *Imperialism*, 88 and passim. The original edition came out in 1917.

7 For a summary of underdevelopment theory, see Brewer, *Marxist Theories of Imperialism*, 152–80. See also Wallerstein, "Three Stages of African Involvement," 30–57.

8 Warren, *Imperialism*, 9 and passim. A recent study by Sandbrook and Barker suggests that, despite First World pressure, African states could break out of dependency, given the appropriate political institutions and the will. Thus, the authors modify the picture of metropolitan omnipotence. See Sandbrook and Barker, *The Politics of Africa's Economic Stagnation*.

9 Quoted in Marks and Trapido, "Lord Milner," 52–3.

10 Some historians have diminished the gap. Donald Denoon, in *Settler Capitalism*, writes from a radical perspective but attempts to show how international capital was mediated by regional factors. From the other side, D.K. Fieldhouse emphasizes the dynamic role of economic factors in creating local crises. The gap, nonetheless, remains. To Denoon, settler capitalism ultimately depended on the metropolitan economy, whereas, to Fieldhouse,

the metropole had little impact on local crises. See Denoon, *Settler Capitalism*, passim; Fieldhouse, *Economics and Empire*, passim.

11 Davis and Huttenback, *Mammon and the Pursuit of Empire*, 38. One might argue that, since most of these economic developments concerned foreign as opposed to colonial areas, the official mind of imperialism need not have taken cognizance of the increasing scale of British capital exports. This line of argument rests on a dubious distinction between imperial and diplomatic considerations; in fact, the two were interrelated. Britain's international relations affected its actions towards the Empire and vice versa. Moreover, British statesmen often served in both imperial and diplomatic capacities throughout their careers.

12 An interesting attempt to bridge the gap was made by John MacKenzie in *Propaganda and Empire*, 1–12. He points out that while only a small elite circle was well acquainted with imperial affairs, there was a pervasive consciousness of Empire and pride in it at all levels of society. MacKenzie attributes this wide identification with the Empire to propaganda pumped out by certain interests which favoured imperialism. Unfortunately, apart from suggesting that imperial patriotism inhibited the development of working-class consciousness, MacKenzie is rather vague on the material interests which gained from imperial activity. In a more recent book, MacKenzie reiterates these points but appears less certain that imperial enthusiasm was generated by propaganda; he admits that it might have reflected the genuine sentiments of the working class. See MacKenzie, ed., introduction to *Imperialism and Popular Culture*, 1–10.

13 Cain and Hopkins, "Political Economy of British Expansion," "Gentlemanly Capitalism," 2 parts; see also *British Imperialism*, especially 1:3–52.

14 Cain and Hopkins, "Gentlemanly Capitalism," I and II; see also their *British Imperialism*, I:34.

15 Cain and Hopkins, "Gentlemanly Capitalism;" II:19 and *British Imperialism*, passim; A.N. Porter, " 'Gentlemanly Capitalism' and Empire," 269, 280.

16 Hyam, *Elgin and Churchill*, 425.

17 Thompson, *Unification of South Africa*, 64, 67. The staying-power of Thompson's thesis was demonstrated recently by Deryck Schreuder, who, in a chapter on South Africa from 1902 to 1910, offered an interpretation of union which was almost identical to Thompson's. See Schreuder, "Colonial Nationalism," 215.

18 It is interesting that two recent specialists in African history have remarked on the need for more attention to human agency in southern African history, especially to the European agents of domination. According to Jean and John Comaroff, in their *Of Revelation and Revolution*, historiography has shown a growing interest in human agency, but

in practice, this seems almost exclusively to involve a concern with (1) the reaction and resistance of blacks to the faceless forces of colonization and

control or (2) the efforts of the "African working class to 'make itself.'"
Thompson (e.g., 1975) might have taken care, in the English case, to
demonstrate that it is as important to account for the motivation of rulers
as it is to understand those of the ruled. With few exceptions (e.g., Ranger
1987), however, comparable attention has not been paid in southern Africa to the consciousness and intentionality of those identified as 'agents'
of domination. Quite the reverse: their actions continue to be seen largely
as a reflex of political and economic processes. An ironic inversion, surely
of the distortions of an earlier liberal historiography! (1:9).

Chapter One

1 B. Porter, *Lion's Share*, 140; P. Kennedy, *Rise and Fall of the Great Powers*, 228;
Lee, *British Economy*, 219; and Mathias, *First Industrial Nation*, 383.

2 C.H. Lee believes that Britain's growth was much more gradual, averaging
1 per cent in the eighteenth century, rising to 2–2.5 per cent during the
first seventy years of the nineteenth century, and then declining again after
1870. See Lee, *British Economy*, 4.

3 P. Kennedy, *Anglo-German Antagonism*, 292–3. One recent historian, Sidney
Pollard, finds conventional accounts of Britain's decline greatly exaggerated. Its consistent expertise in shipbuilding confounded the notion of
English backwardness, as did its superb record of wartime innovation. In
absolute, per capita terms, Pollard reminds us, "Britain was still the most
successful economy in Europe in 1913, only the United States having
overtaken her income and output levels and in their case it was recognised
that the resource base was very different from that of the European countries." See *Britain's Prime and Britain's Decline*, 6.

4 Mathias, *First Industrial Nation*, 375–93; see also Sked, *Britain's Decline*,
11–13, 39; Wiener, *English Culture and Decline*, 157–66; Hobsbawm, *Industry
and Empire*, 190–3.

5 Lee, *British Economy*, 1–10. The financial sector invested capital in various
enterprises and also provided banking services, such as discounting bills of
exchange. In the later Victorian period, the service sector grew to include
such additional activities as shipping and insurance. These interrelated
concerns, taken together, are termed the City interest or, more briefly, the
City. The proceeds from these activities are known as invisibles, to distinguish them from the visible trade in commodities.

6 B. Porter, *Lion's Share*, 69; Lee, *British Economy*, 53–4; and Pollard, *Britain's
Prime and Britain's Decline*, 61. See also Davis and Huttenback, *Mammon and
the Pursuit of Empire*, 37–8.

7 Ingham, *Capitalism Divided*, 40–1.

8 Hobsbawm, *Industry and Empire*, 192; Lee, *British Economy*, 70; Ingham, *Capitalism Divided*, 62–78. On the other hand, Davis and Huttenback con-

cluded that industry enjoyed abundant capital. A fair retort would suggest that, without the City, it might have received more.

9 Pollard, *Britain's Prime and Britain's Decline*, 110, 256–9; Davis and Huttenback, *Mammon and the Pursuit of Empire*, 12.

10 Davis and Huttenback, *Mammon and the Pursuit of Empire*, 310–17. For the Egyptian case, see Hopkins, "Victorians and Africa," 363–91.

11 Hobsbawm, *Industry and Empire*, 149.

12 Drummond, *Gold Standard*, 17. Shula Marks and Stanley Trapido hit the point squarely on the head in their article "Lord Milner and the South African State," 56: "Fundamental to Britain's position in the late nineteenth century was its place at the heart of the international money market."

13 Speech by Lord Salisbury to the Primrose League in London, 4 May 1898, quoted in Grenville, *Lord Salisbury*, 165–6.

14 Barnett, *Collapse of British Power*, 27–8.

15 Though Richard Price argued that the working class was, at best, indifferent to the war, recent evidence confirms the older view that there was a strong popular jingo current. See Price, *An Imperial War*, passim; see also Blanch, "British Society and the War," in Warwick, ed., *South African War*, 210–38.

16 "The crisis was predominantly one between the classes of capital and labour, in which the government became reluctantly involved, by no means wholly on the side of capital, but it was complicated by the co-existence of three other crises [the suffrage question, the Tory rebellion, and Ireland], any one of which was a potentially violent challenge to the entrenched order." See Perkin, *Rise of Professional Society*, 172.

17 Dangerfield, *Strange Death of Liberal England*, 219.

18 For a succinct discussion of migratory labour in Africa, see Stichter, *Migrant Laborers*, passim.

19 Richardson and Van-Helten, "Gold Mining Industry," 22, 14.

20 Milner to Haldane, 11 July 1901, *Milner Papers*, ed. Headlam, 2:264.

21 See Mendelsohn, "Blainey and the Jameson Raid," 157–70.

22 A.N. Porter, "British Imperial Policy," 45.

23 See A.N. Porter, "South African War: Context and Motive Reconsidered," 52–5; see also his, *Origins of the South African War*, passim.

24 Both Milner and Kruger assumed that Uitlander numbers were sufficient to swamp the Boers at the polls. According to Wilde, it was believed that there were 60,000 male Uitlanders, compared with 30,000 burghers (adult male Afrikaners). As only adult males could vote, it seemed as if the enfranchisement of the Uitlanders was tantamount to giving them the country. See Wilde, *Joseph Chamberlain and the South African Republic*, 113.

25 Stokes, "Milnerism," 52–3.

26 Denoon, *Grand Illusion*, 210–11, 252. By the Vereeniging Treaty of 1902, Britain agreed to provide £3 million for the resettlement of the bitter-enders. A further £2 million was handed out to the hands-uppers. In addition,

the British army had distributed £4.5 million as compensation. Finally, a development loan earmarked £4 million to assist Afrikaners. See Denoon, *Grand Illusion*, 63. Despite the substantial sums provided for rehabilitation, it was doubtful that Milner could have eradicated Afrikaner bitterness. War memories, especially of the misery and death suffered by women and children in the concentration camps, created deep animosity, which Boer religious leaders stirred up. These resentments would contribute to the growth of Afrikaner nationalism before the First World War and after.

27 Kendle, *Round Table Movement*, 11; for an excellent background on the Kindergarten, see 22–45.

28 Denoon, *Grand Illusion*, 209–14.

Chapter Two

1 When Louis Napoleon emerged as French leader after the revolution of 1848, Marx is supposed to have remarked that history repeats itself; it appears first as tragedy and a second time as farce.

2 Cannadine, *Decline and Fall*, 251.

3 Selborne Papers, MS 191, Reminiscences, 15–17.

4 William St John Brodrick, 1st Earl of Midleton (1855–1942), was a Conservative MP from 1880 to 1906. Appointed secretary of state for war in 1900, he was made secretary of state for India three years later. George Nathaniel Curzon, Marquess Curzon of Kedleston (1854–1925), was viceroy of India from 1899 to 1905. Both Brodrick and Curzon had been close friends of Selborne since Oxford. Selborne might have been an old boy, but he was a new kind of peer.

5 Boyce, ed., introduction to *Crisis of British Unionism*, ix.

6 Ibid.

7 Chamberlain Papers, JC 10/1011, Selborne's memorandum on drifts crisis, 29 October 1895.

8 Selborne Papers, MS 15, fols. 3–5, minute by Selborne, 10 October 1895; Wilde, "Joseph Chamberlain and the South African Republic," 12.

9 A.N. Porter, "British Imperial Policy," 43–4; see also by the same author, "South African War," 52–7, and *Origins of the South African War*; Chamberlain Papers, JC 10/1/48, Selborne's notes, 6 June 1896.

10 The document can be found in the Selborne Papers, MS 15, fols. 80–7. Inscribed upon it is an estimated date: 11 November 1896. Although unsigned, the author is clearly Selborne. The memorandum refers to the editor of the *Daily News* as a schoolmate. In 1896 the editor in question, Edward Cook, had indeed attended Winchester when Selborne was there. In addition, there exist, in both the Selborne and Chamberlain collections, papers containing virtually identical arguments to those in the memorandum. Two such documents were signed by Selborne and dated October

1896. See Selborne Papers, MS8, fols. 91–4, Selborne to Chamberlain, 6 October 1896, and Chamberlain Papers, JC 10/1/73, Selborne to Chamberlain, 18 October 1896; see also Robinson and Gallager, *Africa and the Victorians* 434–7. Further treatment of this controversial document will be offered below.

11 Selborne Papers, MS15, fols. 110–11, undated memorandum in Selborne's hand, with date pencilled in at top "early 1897?"; see also same collection, MS8, fols, 91–4, Selborne to Chamberlain, 6 October 1896; and MS8, fols. 107–10, Selborne to Chamberlain, 18 October 1896. In Selborne's own view there was no contradiction between the Conventions and Britain's right as paramount power to intervene on behalf of the Uitlanders in the SAR. What resolved the contradiction was the suzerain status which, in Selborne's view, both conventions conferred on Britain. The republic maintained that since the term was only used in the Pretoria agreement and did not reappear in the London Convention, the said "suzerainty" ceased to hold force. Selborne countered that, if such were the case, then the republic's existence ceased too, for the London document made no explicit mention of Transvaal independence. See minute on CO 417/218/11502, [n.d.].

12 CO 417/214/3428, High Commissioner to Secretary of State, 27 January 1897, minute by Selborne; see also, Selborne Papers, MS14, fols. 192–5, Selborne to Greene, 9 April 1897.

13 Selborne Papers, MS15, fols. 102–4, Selborne to George Grey, 5 April 1897.

14 MS8, fols. 162–3, Selborne to Chamberlain, 3 March 1897.

15 Wilde, "Joseph Chamberlain and the South African Republic," 63–4; CO 417/242/5747, Milner to Chamberlain, 23 February 1898.

16 Selborne to Milner, 22 March 1898, *Milner Papers*, ed. Headlam, I:229–30.

17 Selborne Papers, MS11, fols. 81–8, Milner to Selborne, 9 May 1898.

18 Milner Papers, dep. 205, fols. 202–6, Selborne to Milner, 28 June 1898; Selborne Papers, MS15, fol. 155, Selborne's minute on the South African situation, 2 June 1898.

19 Milner Papers, dep. 205, fols. 123–4, Selborne to Milner, 25 March 1898; CO 417/217/8667, Milner to Chamberlain, 7 April 1897, Selborne's minute of 5 May; CO 417/247/28526, Milner to Chamberlain, 29 November 1898, Selborne's minute of 28 December; CO 417/259/7376, Milner to Chamberlain, 8 March 1899, Selborne's minute of 7 April; and Selborne Papers, MS11, fols. 115–6, Selborne to Milner, 8 February 1899.

20 CO 417/259/5710, Milner to Chamberlain, 5 March 1899 (telegram), Selborne's minute of 8 March; see also Selborne Papers, MS15, fol. 162, Selborne to Beit, 15 March 1899. For quotations, see Selborne Papers, MS9, fols. 36–8, Selborne to Chamberlain, 15 March 1899.

21 Milner to Chamberlain, 4 May 1899, *Milner Papers*, I:349–53; Curzon Papers, MS5 Eur. F 111–229, fols. 9–12, Selborne to Curzon, 7 May 1899.

22 CO 417/262/14983, Milner to Chamberlain, 10 June 1899, Selborne's minute, 12 June. Nor did the Cape's anti-war sentiment move Selborne, who was fully convinced by Percy FitzPatrick that this criticism of Milner reflected pro-Boer propaganda in the colony. Selborne Papers, MS9, fols. 56–9, Selborne to Chamberlain, 3 July 1899.

23 Milner Papers, dep. 183, fols. 166–9, Selborne to Milner, 28 June 1899.

24 Selborne Papers, MS11, fols 166–73, Selborne to Milner, 22 July 1899; CO 417/263/1701, Milner to Chamberlain, 2 July 1899, minutes by Selborne, 3 July and Chamberlain, 3 July; Balfour Papers, ADD. MS5. 49707, fols. 45–7, Selborne to Balfour, 20 July 1899; and Milner Papers, dep. 211, fols. 48–53, Selborne to Milner, 27 July 1899.

25 Selborne Papers, MS11, fols. 172–9, Milner to Selborne, 12 July 1899.

26 "The Position after the War," minute by Selborne, 16 November 1899. A copy can be found in the Selborne Papers, MS9, fols. 86–92.

27 Curzon Papers, Eur. F111–229, fols. 59–60, Selborne to Curzon, 11 October 1900; Chamberlain Papers, JC 11/32/1, Selborne to Chamberlain, 28 September 1900.

28 Marder, *Dreadnought to Scapa Flow*, I:49.

29 Boyce, ed., *Crisis of British Power*, 106 n5.

30 Cabinet memorandum by Lord Selborne: The Navy's Estimates and the Chancellor of the Exchequer's Memorandum on the Growth of Expenditure, 16 November 1901, quoted in *Crisis of British Power*, ed. Boyce, 129–36.

31 Memorandum by Lord Selborne: Balance of Naval Power in the Far East, 4 September 1901, quoted in ibid., 123–6.

32 Selborne's Cabinet Memorandum of 16 November 1901, *Crisis of British Power*, ed. Boyce, 129–36; Balfour Papers, ADD. MSS. 49707, fols. 105–6, Selborne to Balfour, 4 April 1902; Curzon Papers, MSS. Eur. F111–229, fols. 77–84, Selborne to Curzon, 4 January 1903; Cabinet Memorandum by Lord Selborne, 26 February 1904, quoted in *Crisis of British Power*, 171. See also Marder, *Dreadnought to Scapa Flow*, I:49; McDermott, "Committee of Imperial Defence," 264–72

33 Selborne Papers, MS15, fols. 80–7, memorandum by Selborne, 11 November 1896. To Robinson and Gallagher, this memorandum reveals Selborne's fear that peripheral pressures were pushing South Africa away from metropolitan control. The reader will see that my interpretation of this document is rather different.

34 *The Times* (London), 31 May 1899.

35 Curzon Papers, MSS. Eur. F111–229, fols. 89–93, Selborne to Curzon, 21 October 1903.

36 CO 417/250/15550, Foreign Office to Colonial Office, 18 July 1898, Selborne's minute, 20 July 1898.

37 The closest Selborne came to associating imperial interests with the imperial factor was in his 1899 minute on war aims. Here the undersecretary was clearly under Milner's intoxicating influence. This wore off by 1905, especially after the sobering effect of the Liberal landslide victory.

38 Curzon Papers, Eur. F111–229, fols 84–92, Selborne to Curzon, 21 October 1903.

39 Balfour Papers, MSS. ADD. 49775, fols. 27–30, Lyttelton to Balfour, 20 January 1905.

40 Milner Papers, dep. 10, fols. 108–9, Lyttelton to Milner, 9 April 1905; dep. 176, fols. 210–11, Milner to Balfour, 27 March 1905.

41 Milner Papers, dep. 222, fols. 229–263, Milner to Selborne, 14 April 1905 (Milner's emphasis).

Chapter Three

1 Richardson, *Chinese Mine Labour*, 188–9.

2 Johnstone, *Class, Race and Gold*, 21–5, 71–7; Wilson, *Labour in the South African Gold Mines*, 34–40; and TMIC, *Report*, p. 18, sec. 199.

3 From 96,704 in 1899 the number of unskilled labourers had dropped to 42,587 in 1902, and though the figure increased the following year to 64,454, it remained considerably below prewar levels. See Van der Horst, *Native Labour in South Africa*, 164–6.

4 Denoon, "Transvaal Labour Crisis," 487–8.

5 Richardson, *Chinese Mine Labour*, 166–72; Denoon, "Transvaal Labour Crisis," 491.

6 Van der Horst, *Native Labour in South Africa*, 230–1; Richardson, *Chinese Mine Labour*, 100 (table A. 9).

7 *Rand Daily Mail*, 24 May 1905, leader.

8 Selborne Papers, MS71, fols. 171–84, Selborne to Pretyman, 13 January 1909.

9 See Selborne to Grey, 13 January 1906 in Grey Papers, FO 800/111. See also, Selborne to Milner, 14 March 1904, in Milner Papers, dep. 188, fols. 171–81.

10 Grey Papers, FO 800/111, Selborne to Grey, 24 November 1905.

11 CO 291/88/2258, Selborne to Elgin, 30 December 1905; enclosure: memorandum by F. Perry, 21 November 1905. The Witwatersrand Native Labour Association (WNLA) was the chamber's agency for African labour recruitment. It conducted most of its operations in Mozambique.

12 Ibid., Selborne's cover letter. The high commissioner still clung to this explanation in 1909 when he attributed Botha's success with labour problems to the general depression. See marginal comment by Selborne, 21 December 1909, on a copy of his letter to Grey, 24 November 1905 in Selborne Papers, MS54, fol. 45. The reasons why, after 1910, South Africa

experienced both mining prosperity and general recovery can be debated at length, but it is true that, from 1903 to 1909, the country saw the rapid advance of the gold industry accompanied by a prolonged depression. See Schurmann, *Structural Changes and Business Cycles*, 93. It is also generally recognized that the depression did in fact help free labour for the gold fields before Union. This was precisely the situation Selborne hoped to avoid.

13 Selborne Papers, MS 48, fols. 169–73, Selborne to Elgin, 26 January 1906.

14 Actually, Selborne had been misled, for the Chinese were primarily employed on producing mines. See Richardson, *Chinese Mine Labour*, 168. (New development work was crucial to offset the inevitable exhaustion of old mines.)

15 Grey Papers, FO 800/111, Grey to Selborne, 22 December 1905; Selborne to Grey, 13 January 1906.

16 CO 291/88/2257, Selborne to Elgin, 30 December 1905.

17 *Rand Daily Mail*, 2 January 1905; *South African Mines Commerce and Industries*, 13 January, 26 May 1906.

18 Selborne Papers, MS54, fols. 91–106, Selborne to Churchill, 2 March 1906; Grey Papers, FO 800/111, Selborne to Grey, 24 November 1905.

19 CO 291/85/35815, Selborne to Lyttelton, 18 September 1905; Grey Papers, FO 800/111, Selborne to Grey, 24 November 1905.

20 CO 291/88/2258, Selborne to Elgin, 30 December 1905, despatch and enclosures.

21 *Transvaal Leader*, 15 December 1906, letter from Cresswell.

22 Selborne Papers, MS54, fols. 139–58, Churchill to Selborne, 16 June 1906.

23 Hyam, *Elgin and Churchill*, 73.

24 Grey Papers, FO 800/111, Selborne to Grey, 24 November 1905; Selborne Papers, MS48, fols. 169–73, Selborne to Elgin, 26 January 1905.

25 CAB 37/81/183, memorandum: "Chinese Labour in the Transvaal: the Question of its Continuation," 18 December 1905.

26 Hyam, *Elgin and Churchill*, 65–6.

27 CAB 37/82/23, memo by Elgin, 16 February 1906; CO 879/106/807, Elgin to Selborne, 16 February 1906.

28 Selborne Papers, MS71, fols. 17–19, Haldane to Selborne, 25 January 1906.

29 Cited in Hyam, *Elgin and Churchill*, 75–7. Churchill wrote this on 24 February 1906.

30 CO 291/88/44878, Elgin to Selborne, 20 December 1905.

31 Milner Papers, dep. 191, fols. 17–21, Selborne to Lawley, 15 January 1906.

32 Selborne Papers, MS54, fols. 121–4, Selborne to Churchill, 8 April 1906.

33 There is evidence that Selborne's optimism was not misplaced. True, many Boers did oppose the introduction of the Chinese. But, as Het Volk's joint resolution with the Responsibles in March 1905 showed, they did not dogmatically oppose it. The white working class split on this issue. Though the

many pro-importation signatures garnered by force or fraud along the Rand furnish inadequate testimony of white worker sentiment, support for Chinese labour was no doubt widespread. David Buchanan of the Independent Labour Party lent credence to this conclusion when he publicly cautioned workers against co-option by the "capitalists." See *Transvaal Leader,* 14 May 1906. Donald Denoon remarks that little overt pressure was needed to gain support for Chinese labour from the white workforce. After all, it would have been inconceivable if "white miners generally failed to recognize the power of their employer." See Denoon, "Capital and Capitalists," 130.

34 *South African Mines Commerce and Industries,* 20 January 1906. See also Neumann's remarks in the *Transvaal Leader,* 2 January 1906.

35 CO 291/88/45427, Selborne to Elgin, 23 December 1905.

36 CAB 37/82/3, memorandum, 2 January 1906.

37 Asquith MSS. 10, Campbell-Bannerman to Asquith, 28 December 1905; CO 879/106/807, Elgin to Selborne, 5 January 1906.

38 *Transvaal Leader,* 9 January 1906, leader; *Johannesburg Star,* 10 January 1906, leader.

39 CAB 37/82/2, memo by Herbert Samuel, 22 December 1905.

40 Ibid., enclosure: Elgin's memo on Samuel's proposal, 2 January 1906; CO 879/106/807, Elgin to Selborne, 6 January 1906. For Selborne's admission that some coolies did not understand the terms of the contract when they signed, see CO 291/85/35815, Selborne to Lyttelton, 18 September 1905.

41 CO 879/106/807, Selborne to Elgin, 21 January 1906. In a further letter, Selborne protested that the Chinese would misinterpret the offer as an order to leave; some might even consider it a breach of contract. See Selborne Papers, MS48, fols. 219–27, Selborne to Elgin, 18 March 1906.

42 CO 829/106/807, Elgin to Selborne, 8 March 1906; Selborne Papers, MS48, fols, 247–56, Elgin to Selborne, 25 April 1906.

43 Selborne Papers, MS54, fols, 109–12, Churchill to Selborne, 11 March 1906; ibid., fols. 127–8, Churchill to Selborne, 28 April 1906.

44 CO 879/106/807, Selborne to Elgin, 17 April 1906.

45 *PP,* lxxx (1906), Cd. 3025, pp. 570–3, Selborne to Elgin, 16 April 1906; enclosure from the Chamber of Mines, April 4, 1906. The Chamber argued lamely that, though the coolies were satisfied, many would find the offer too tempting to resist.

46 Selborne Papers, MS62, fols. 6–7, Farrar to Selborne, 4 April 1906.

47 Phillips to Eckstein, 7 May 1906, *All that Glittered,* eds. Jeeves and Fraser, 154; *South African Mines Commerce and Industries,* 4 February 1906.

48 CO 291/97/11338, Selborne to Elgin, 31 March 1906.

49 CO 879/106/807, Selborne to Elgin, 28 May 1906; CO 291/99/19157, Selborne to Elgin, 28 May 1906.

50 *Manchester Guardian*, 15 June 1906.

51 Selborne Papers, MS54, fols. 139–58, Churchill to Selborne, 16 June 1906; ibid., fols. 159–66, Selborne to Churchill, 5 July 1906. CO 879/106/807, Selborne to Elgin, 21 July, 15 August 1906; Elgin to Selborne, 12 September 1906; Selborne to Elgin, 23 October 1906 and Elgin to Selborne, 11 November 1906; Selborne to Elgin, 1 July 1907.

52 Richardson, "Coolies and Randlords," pp. 151–77.

53 CO 291/83/22915, Selborne to Lyttelton, 12 June 1905.

54 See CO minute by Just, 19 February 1906 in 879/830.

55 *PP*, lxxx (1906), Cd. 3025, pp. 579–82, Selborne to Elgin, 10 April 1906.

56 Annual Report of the Foreign Labour Department, 1904–5 in *PP*, lxxx (1906), Cd. 3025, Appendix IV, p. 683.

57 Cohen, "Resistance and Hidden Forms of Consciousness," 8–22, passim. See also Stichter, *Migrant Laborers*, 134–5.

58 Annual Report of the Foreign Labour Department, 1904–5 in *PP*, lxxx (1906), Cd. 3025, Appendix IV, p. 683; ibid., enclosure in no. 30, p. 538, Selborne to Elgin, 12 March 1906.

59 CO 291/85/35815, Selborne to Lyttelton, 18 September 1905. Natal Governor McCallum corroborated Selborne's opinion. Without telling the high commissioner, he paid a surprise visit to the Witwatersrand Deep Mine and reported enthusiastically that the living conditions were "clean and commodious," the food was "savoury," "fresh," and issued in "super-abundance," while the general treatment was "ultra-luxurious." "The main impression which I have taken away from the Transvaal," he gushed, "is that mineowners must indeed have been in despair about labour to have induced them to go in for what appears to me to be an expensive, troublesome, and elaborate system." See CO 291/95/4007, Selborne to Elgin, 15 January 1906; enclosure: McCallum to Selborne, 10 January 1906.

60 Selborne Papers, MS100, fols. 61–2, Lord Selborne to Lady Selborne, 2 June 1905; Grey Papers, FO 800/111, Selborne to Grey, 29 November 1905.

61 CO 879/106/807, Elgin to Selborne, 14 November 1906; Selborne to Elgin, 15 November 1906.

62 Grey Papers, FO 800/111, Selborne to Grey, 13 January 1906.

63 Ibid., Selborne to Grey, 24 November 1905; Selborne Papers, MS71, fols. 171–84, Selborne to Pretyman, 13 January 1909.

64 Selborne Papers, MS48, fols. 169–73, Selborne to Elgin, 26 January 1906.

65 *Journal of the Chemical, Metallurgical and Mining Society of South Africa*, April 1906; *Transvaal Leader*, 2 February 1906.

66 *South African Mines Commerce and Industries*, 14 July 1906.

67 Selborne Papers, MS48, fols. 196–205, Elgin to Selborne, 22 February 1906.

68 Samuel, Speech to the House of Commons, 27 July 1905, *Parliamentary Debates*, Commons, 4th ser., vol. 150 (1905), cols. 671–2.

69 Grey Papers, FO 800/111, Selborne to Grey, 24 November 1905.

70 CO 291/85/35815, Selborne to Lyttelton, 18 September 1905. So suspicious was he of white miners abusing authority that, when he told his wife that a white miner had been killed in a Chinese "row," he commented that he would be "very surprised if it does not turn out to have been the miner's fault." See Selborne Papers, MS100, fols. 64–6, Lord Selborne to Lady Selborne, 11 June 1905.

71 Grey Papers, FO 800/111, Selborne to Grey, 24 November 1905.

72 CAB 37/80/160, enclosure: Selborne to Lyttelton, 7 August 1905.

73 Evans Papers, MSS Af.s.1587, Evans to Lyttelton, 22 April 1906.

74 CAB 37/80/160, enclosure: Selborne to Lyttelton, 22 April 1906; Lawley to Chamber of Mines, 13 June 1905; Selborne to Lyttelton, 7 August 1905.

75 Ibid., Milner to Lyttelton, 8 October 1905.

76 CO 291/84/30852, Lyttelton to Selborne, 24 October 1905.

77 Milner Papers, dep. 190, fols. 86–7, Selborne to Milner, 21 August 1905.

78 Selborne Papers, MS57, fols. 3–4, Selborne to Lawley, 8 June 1905.

79 CAB 37/80/160, enclosure: Selborne to Lyttelton, 7 August 1905.

80 CO 291/85/35815, Selborne to Lyttelton, 18 September 1905.

81 Ibid. Where a jail sentence was imposed, the attorney general would review the case. The lieutenant-governor would review all collective fines imposed, and the Supreme Court would do the same for flogging sentences.

82 CO 291/84/30852, Lyttelton to Selborne, 24 October 1905.

83 CO 291/83/26882, Selborne to Lyttelton, 10 July 1905.

84 CO 291/85/35815, Selborne to Lyttelton, 18 September 1905; Selborne Papers, MS57, fols. 36–9, Lt. Governor to Chaplin, 21 July 1905.

85 CO 291/87/45324, Selborne to Lyttelton, 4 December 1905; enclosure; Superintendent, FLD to Mine Managers (form letter), 20 November 1905; Selborne to Lyttelton, 4 December 1905; enclosure: Jamieson's instructions to inspectors, 23 November 1905.

86 Evans Papers, MSS Afr.s.1587, Bagot to Evans, 31 July 1907.

87 Selborne Papers, MS57, fols. 29–30, 36–9, Selborne to Lawley, 20 and 21 July 1905.

88 Selborne Papers, MS57, fols. 38–9, Selborne to Lawley, 10 July 1905.

89 See the case of Witthauer in *PP*, lxxx (1906), Cd. 3025, pp. 550–3, Selborne to Elgin, 2 April 1906, enclosure by Jamieson. Also in CO 879/106/807, Selborne to Elgin, 22 April 1906. For Selborne's 'intimidation' by the Chinese police, see CO 291/95/5639, Selborne to Elgin, 29 January 1906. In January 1906, desertion figures more than doubled, totalling 809 for that month. High rates continued for the rest of the year. See *PP*, lxxx (1906), Cd. 3025, p. 538, Selborne to Elgin, 12 March 1906.

90   Certain capitalists exploited even this dismal situation. On 10 May 1906, the *Transvaal Leader* carried an advertisement for Wood's Great Peppermint cure. The ad conjectured that the Chinese deserters were simply seeking Wood's cure. The advertisement exhorted: "Talk to a Chinese in his own language, or display something to him that he can read, such as the inside wrapper of Wood's Great Peppermint cure bottle, and he will easily be persuaded you are a friend. Better still, give him a bottle of cure he reverences and you are absolutely safe with him."

91   CO 291/85/35008, Selborne to Lyttelton, 11 September 1905, enclosure; CO 291/84/30852, Lyttelton to Selborne, 24 October 1905.

92   *PP,* lxxx (1906), Cd. 3025, enclosures in no. 101, pp. 587–93, Selborne to Elgin, 7 May 1906.

93   CO 291/99/20606, Selborne to Elgin, 21 May 1906; enclosure: Botha to Selborne, 10 May 1906.

94   Ibid. Eight months before, Selborne had considered that the outrages had been committed by wandering Chinese who had lost their way. At that time he did not consider it necessary to restrict the Chinese more tightly to the compounds. See CO 291/85/35815, Selborne to Lyttelton, 18 September 1905.

95   *PP,* lxxx (1906), Cd. 3025, no. 124, p. 647, Elgin to Selborne, 10 June 1906.

96   Selborne Papers, MS62, fols. 8–11, Selborne to Farrar, 3 May 1906.

97   Phillips to Selborne, 22 March 1906, reprinted in *All that Glittered,* eds. Jeeves and Fraser, 156–8.

98   Selborne Papers, MS72, fols. 98–9, Selborne to de Jongh, 14 July 1906.

99   *PP,* lxxx (1906), Cd. 3025, pp. 593–611, Report of the Special Committee, 2 May 1906, enclosure in Selborne to Elgin, 7 May 1906; ibid., p. 646, Elgin to Selborne, 11 June 1906.

100 *PP,* lxxx (1906), Cd. 3025, pp. 608–10, Selborne to Elgin, 7 May 1906, enclosure: annexure to Report of Special Committee; see memo by Bagot, 1 May 1906; ibid., pp. 606–8, enclosure: Letter from Jamieson to Bagot, 4 December 1905.

101 Milner Papers, dep. 192, fols. 3–7, Selborne to Milner, 7 May 1906.

102 Selborne Papers, MS59, fols. 180–3, Selborne to Northcote, 15 February 1906.

Chapter Four

1   Selborne, like his superiors, came to favour self-government but for very different reasons. While, as Ronald Hyam demonstrates, the Liberals sought to preserve the influence of the imperial factor, Selborne wanted to extirpate it from South Africa. See Hyam, *Elgin and Churchill,* 172.

2 "The Position after the War," minute by Selborne, 16 November 1899. A copy can be found in the Selborne Papers, MS9, fols. 86–92.

3 Selborne Papers, MS9, fols. 150–65, Selborne to Chamberlain, 27 February 1908.

4 Selborne did not seek material development alone. Indeed, he noted that several progressive Afrikaners, such as Smuts, cherished the ideal of a Dutch United States in South Africa. For these men, the South African Republic provided "the only possible fulcrum from which to work for the realisation of their ideal ..." As antipathetic as they were towards Kruger, they opposed Britain more.

5 Selborne Papers, MS71, fols. 171–84, Selborne to Pretyman, 13 January 1909. To Lyttelton in 1906 Selborne listed only two instances in which he would resign: if the Chinese were repatriated en bloc, and if the population basis were adopted. This will be discussed more fully below. See Selborne Papers, MS59, fols. 188–92, Selborne to Lyttelton, 4 August 1906; enclosure in Selborne to Northcote, 7 August 1906, fols. 186–7.

6 Denoon, *Grand Illusion*, 36.

7 Johnstone, *Class, Race, and Gold*, 55–6. Among these unions can be counted the Amalgamated Society of Carpenters (formed in 1881), Amalgamated Engineering Union (1886), Witwatersrand Mine Employees and Mechanics Union (1892), and the South African Engine Drivers' Association (1898).

8 See Denoon, "Capital and Capitalists," 130.

9 Two of these, Louis Botha and Jan Smuts, assumed control of the Het Volk party, which claimed to speak for all Afrikaners. Although no deep fissures emerged before 1910, the Afrikaners did not achieve unity as an ethnic group until well after union. In the judgment of Giliomee, it was not until the interwar years that Boer intellectuals and predikants managed to unite Afrikanerdom and thereby mobilize ethnic power. See Giliomee, "Beginnings of Afrikaner Ethnic Consciousness," 47–9.

10 Denoon, *Grand Illusion*, 59–61. Many of these *bywoners* drifted to the rapidly growing cities. During Selborne's tenure, the Transvaal's urban population grew by 58 per cent. In 1904, 55 per cent of Transvaal whites lived in the cities, particularly in the Witwatersrand area, where 123,000 Europeans made their home. Some of the poor whites turned to such enterprises as driving cabs or selling illicit liquor, but soon these opportunities closed up. These hapless victims of Transvaal growth swelled the ranks of the unemployed. Their numbers eventually increased to the extent that they became a major social and political problem. With poverty, crime, and racial mixing, Johannesburg presented a danger to white society which the state could not ignore. These troubles were in the cauldron when Selborne arrived. See Van Onselen, *New Babylon*, 24–6; also Johnstone, *Class, Race and Gold*, 53; and Keegan, "The Making of the Rural Economy," 42–50.

11 Selborne Papers, MS52, fol. 97, reported in Richard Solomon to Selborne, 8 February 1906.

12 Milner Papers, dep. 222, fols. 229–63, Milner to Selborne, 14 April 1905, (Milner's emphasis).

13 Selborne Papers, MS3, fols. 50–7, Selborne to Brodrick, 1 July 1908; ibid., MS9, fols. 150–65, Selborne to Chamberlain, 24 February 1908. "Fitz-Patrick is the typical Irish fighting politician, and he supplies the element of pugnacity, which is a little wanting in Farrar. But Farrar is much the best political tactician of the two, and his judgment is the sounder and steadier."

14 Ibid., MS62, fols. 17–18, Farrar to Selborne, 2 March 1907.

15 Milner Papers, dep. 191, fols. 79–92, FitzPatrick to Wernher, 19 February 1906. In a more personal note, FitzPatrick characterized Selborne as "a conceited ass." See FitzPatrick to his wife, 7 July 1906, eds. Duminy and Guest, *FitzPatrick*, 465–7. (Wernher was a senior partner with the firm, Wernher, Beit and Co., which had invested heavily in the Witwatersrand.)

16 Milner Papers, dep. 191, fols. 210–17, G. Robinson to Milner, 31 March 1906.

17 Ibid., dep. 222, fols. 229–63, Milner to Selborne, 14 April 1905. While Milner considered F.D.P. Chaplin, George Farrar, Abe Bailey, and J.P. FitzPatrick loyal to the core and public-spirited enough to take government office, he predicted that other trustworthy magnates of the Mackie Niven stripe would shy away from active politics. On the other hand, he described Harold Strange, George Albu, Louis Reyersbach, and Amandus Brakham as "political neutrals" and willing to work with any government. Worse still, J.W.S. Langerman was an "out and out Boer, and rather a poisonous one at that."

18 Selborne Papers, MS3, fols. 50–7, Selborne to Brodrick, 1 July 1908.

19 Ibid., MS9, fols. 106–17, Chamberlain to Selborne, 24 March 1908.

20 Ibid., MS71, fols. 14–16, Selborne to Pretyman, 4 August 1905.

21 Ibid., MS59, fols. 172–3, Selborne to Northcote, 21 August 1905; fols. 174–7, Selborne to Northcote, 23 November 1905.

22 Milner Papers, dep. 189, fols. 162–3, Selborne to Milner, 19 May 1905.

23 Selborne Papers, MS71, fols. 30–42, Selborne to Asquith, 22 February 1906.

24 Keegan, "Agrarian Class Relations," 234–54.

25 Selborne Papers, MS162, fols. 213–5, Selborne to Elgin, 14 May 1906.

26 CO 291/87/40852, Selborne to Lyttelton, 14 November 1905; Lyttelton to Selborne, 17 November 1905; CO 291/87/41642, Selborne to Lyttelton, 22 November 1905.

27 CO 291/87/44555, Selborne to Lyttelton, 27 November 1905.

28 Ibid., minute by Ommanney, 19 December 1905.

29 Milner Papers, dep. 192, fols. 277–94, FitzPatrick to Milner, November 1906 [no day given].

30 CO 291/88/44104, minute by Churchill, 18 December 1905.

31 Grey Papers, FO 800/111, Grey to Selborne, 22 December 1905; also Selborne Papers, MS71, fols. 34–7, Asquith to Selborne, 27 March 1906; ibid., fols. 65–8, Haldane to Selborne, 11 April 1906.

32 CAB 37/82/23, copy of letter, Roderick Jones to Baron de Reuter, 8 February 1906.

33 See above and Selborne Papers, MS59, fols. 188–92, Selborne to Lyttelton, 4 August 1906; fols. 186–7, enclosure in Selborne to Northcote, 7 August 1906.

34 Milner Papers, dep. 222, fols. 404–7, Milner to Selborne, 10 February 1906.

35 Grey Papers, FO 800/111, Selborne to Grey, 24 November 1905.

36 Selborne Papers, MS71, fols. 30–42, Selborne to Asquith, 22 February 1906.

37 CO 291/88/1604, memo from Selborne to Elgin, 13 December 1905.

38 CO 291/95/197, Selborne to Elgin, 1 January 1906.

39 Selborne Papers, MS58, fol. 97, R. Solomon to Selborne, 8 February 1906.

40 Ibid., fols. 76–8, R. Solomon to Selborne, 19 January 1906.

41 Ibid., MS59, fols. 188–92, Selborne to Lyttelton, 4 August 1906; fols. 186–7, enclosure in Selborne to Northcote, 7 August 1906.

42 CO 291/95/1648, Selborne to Elgin, 13 January 1906.

43 Selborne Papers, MS59, fols. 180–3, Selborne to Northcote, 10 February 1906.

44 *South African Mines Commerce and Industries*, 3 February 1906; ibid., 20 January 1906.

45 CO 291/96/4253, Selborne to Elgin, 3 February 1906; Selborne Papers, MS48, fols. 219–27, Selborne to Elgin, 28 March 1906.

46 *South African Mines Commerce and Industries*, 3 February 1906.

47 CAB 37/81/182, memo by Elgin, 16 December 1905; CAB 41/30/36, 20 December 1905.

48 CO 879/106/807, Elgin to Selborne, 6 January 1906.

49 CO 291/95/941, Selborne to Elgin, 7 January 1906; CO 291/95/4050, Selborne to Elgin, 15 January 1906.

50 CO 291/96/6472, Selborne to Elgin, 22 February 1906; *Transvaal Leader*, 23 February 1906, report on Chamber of Mines' general meeting of 22 February 1906; CO 879/116/807, Selborne to Elgin, 10 March 1906; CO 291/97/7912, Selborne to Elgin, 10 March 1906.

51 CAB 37/82/4, minute by Churchill, 2 January 1906. For a complete discussion of Liberal policy-making, see Hyam, *Elgin and Churchill*, 98–152.

52 CAB 37/82/14, minute by Churchill, 30 January 1906. In this objective, the Liberals were closer to Selborne than they thought. He too wished to build the Transvaal polity on a broad foundation, but not for the purpose of imperial influence but for economic expansion.

53 CAB 37/82/4, minute by Churchill, 2 January 1906.

54 Elgin Papers, Loreburn to Elgin, 21 January 1906.

55 CAB 41/30/37, 3 January 1906; CAB 41/30/41, 13 February 1906; CO 291/111/6082, Elgin to Selborne, 18 February 1906.

56 In Churchill's memo of 30 January, he declared that, coming to the scene fresh, the Liberals were free from the Progressives, Boers, or the Lyttelton legacy. The new government was in the position of "a Grand Elector" – "independent, uncompromised, [and] free to hold the scales even." See CAB 37/82/14.

57 Selborne Papers, MS71, fols. 65–8, Haldane to Selborne, 11 April 1906.

58 Selborne Papers, MS71, fols. 69–78, Fred Graham to Selborne, 12 May 1906.

59 To Haldane, Selborne warned, "I will therefore serve the Cabinet as long as I possibly can; but I could not take any responsibility for handing the country, bound hand and foot, over to the Boers, simply because they happen to have more women and children in the country than the British." See Selborne Papers, MS71, fols. 43–53, Selborne to Haldane, 5 March 1906. He wrote in similar terms to his Unionist friends; the voters' basis and the Chinese were the only two matters on which he would resign.

60 CO 291/88/1604, Selborne to Elgin, 23 December 1905.

61 Ibid., minute by Keith, 15 January 1906; also minute by Just, 16 January.

62 Selborne Papers, MS48, fols. 167–8, Selborne to Elgin, 7 January 1906.

63 CO 291/95/3409, Selborne to Elgin, 29 January 1906. Keith remarked sceptically, "The Progressives know the value of meetings and agitation. It is curious that the Governor sends us nothing of the views of the other side, just as he has never sent us officially the views of the miners as to Chinese labour." See minute by Keith, 30 January 1906. Selborne's depiction of the British attitude had some basis in fact. F. Perry, chairman of the WNLA, observed to Milner that the most enthusiastic supporters of the voters' basis were the non-capitalist British of the Woolls Sampson type. He regretted, in fact, that several magnates took no stand on the issue. George Albu, for example, was advising them "to keep quiet and shut our eyes and open our mouth and see what a good Liberal Government has got us." In the February pact between the Responsibles and Het Volk, the former held out for the voters' principle. See Milner Papers, dep. 191, fols. 34–45, F. Perry to Milner, 12 February 1906, and Selborne Papers, MS58, fol. 97, R. Solomon to Selborne, 8 February 1906.

64 Selborne Papers, MS48, fols. 180–7, Elgin to Selborne, 2 February 1906.

65 Ibid., fols. 193–5, Selborne to Elgin, 22 February 1906; fols. 213–18, Selborne to Elgin, 17 March 1906.

66 Ibid., MS71, fols. 30–42, Selborne to Asquith, 22 February 1906.

67 CO 291/96/9441, Selborne to Elgin, 23 February 1906; CO 291/97/ 14035, Selborne to Elgin, 2 April 1906; CO 291/100/22460, Selborne to Elgin, 21 June 1906.

68 CO 291/96/9374, memo by Fred Graham, 3 April 1906.

69 CAB 37/82/4/14/21/33, memos by Churchill, 2 and 30 January, 4 February 1906, 15 March 1906. Loreburn's draft constitution also envisioned the voters' principle. See CAB 37/82/16, 31 January 1906.

70 CAB 37/82/23, memo by Elgin, 12 February 1906.

71 CO 291/111/6082, Elgin to Selborne, 18 February 1906.

72 Selborne Papers, MS54, fols. 117–20, Churchill to Selborne, 24 March 1906; CO 879/106/807, Elgin to Selborne, 6 April 1906; Milner Papers, dep. 222, fols. 408–10, Milner to Selborne, 1 April 1906; Selborne Papers, MS71, fols. 54–7, Asquith to Selborne, 27 March 1906; ibid., fols. 65–8, Haldane to Selborne, 11 April 1906.

73 Selborne Papers, MS58, fols. 104–6, Selborne to R. Solomon, 14 February 1906.

74 Ibid., fols. 259–68, memo by Selborne, n.d. but note says end of 1906.

75 Milner Papers, dep. 191, fols. 95–102, G. Robinson to Milner, 25 February 1906; ibid., fols. 128–36, Chaplin to Milner, 4 March 1906; ibid., dep. 192, fols. 14–42, FitzPatrick to Wernher, 7 May 1906.

76 See CO 879/106/829, memo by West Ridgeway, 27 May 1906.

77 CAB 37/83/51, "Secret and 'Private and Personal' telegrams relating to the Proceedings of the Transvaal Committee of Inquiry, to the 28th May," West Ridgeway to Elgin, 12 May 1906; CAB 37/83/53, West Ridgeway to Elgin, 14 May 1906.

78 CO 879/106/820, memo by West Ridgeway, 27 May 1906.

79 Selborne Papers, MS48, fols. 276–81, Selborne to Elgin, 21 May 1906. In a letter to Balfour, Selborne asserted that on hearing of West Ridgeway's proposal, he sent for the Progressive delegates. See ibid., MS64, fols. 139–41, Selborne to Balfour, 13 June 1908.

80 CO 879/106/820, memo by West Ridgeway, 27 May 1906; Selborne Papers, MS64, fols. 113–16, Progressive Executive to West Ridgeway, 15 May 1906.

81 CAB 37/83/51, West Ridgeway to Elgin, 15 May 1906; Elgin to Selborne, 16 May 1906; Selborne to Elgin, 19 May 1906. See also, Selborne Papers, MS48, fols. 276–81, Selborne to Elgin, 21 May 1906.

82 CAB 37/83/51, Elgin to Selborne, 23 May 1906. For this episode and for the West Ridgeway proceedings, see Hyam, *Elgin and Churchill*, 137–52.

83 Selborne Papers, MS49, fols. 42–52, Selborne to Elgin, 3 August 1906.

84 CO 291/100/28777, Selborne to Elgin, 16 June 1906; minute by Churchill, 11 August 1906.

85 CO 291/99/1810, Selborne to Elgin, 19 May 1906; minute by Lambert, 21 May; and minute by Graham, 21 May (Just was more critical of Sel-

borne's intervention); CAB 37/83/51, Elgin to West Ridgeway, 23 May 1906.

86 Milner Papers, dep. 192, fols. 172–6, Selborne to Milner, 24 June 1906.

87 Africa (S), No. 853, in CO 879/106 (Report of West Ridgeway Commission, Transvaal).

88 Milner Papers, dep. 192, fols. 196–9, Selborne to Milner, 25 August 1906; Selborne Papers, MS49, fols. 42–52, Selborne to Elgin, 3 August 1906; ibid., MS1, fols. 83–98, Selborne to Balfour, 13 June 1908.

89 See CO 291/83/22917, Selborne to Lyttelton, 12 June 1905, and CO 291/96/6752, Selborne to Elgin, 5 February 1906.

90 Selborne admitted this to Walter Long in a letter of 21 December 1907; see Selborne Papers, MS71, fols. 151–3.

91 Milner Papers, dep. 218, fols. 138–9, Chaplin to Milner, 25 February 1907.

92 See XXXIX (b) of the Letters Patent of 1906 (Transvaal), copy in Selborne Papers, MS175; the substance of the Letters Patent was reported to Selborne by Elgin on 31 July 1906, see Selborne Papers, MS162, fol. 101.

93 CO 291/106/47998, Selborne to Elgin, 10 December 1906; Milner Papers, dep. 191, fols. 17–21, Selborne to Lawley, 15 January 1906.

Chapter Five

1 Jeeves, *Migrant Labour,* 59–60.

2 In Davies's terms, at stake were both the powers of ownership and of possession. See Davies, *Capital, State, and White Labour,* 221.

3 See Jeeves, *Migrant Labour,* 225.

4 Negotiated as a temporary instrument pending the conclusion of a permanent treaty, the *modus vivendi* of 1901 granted the Transvaal recruiting privileges in Mozambique and accorded the latter a schedule of railway rates which undercut those of the British colonies. The agreement also stipulated that in the event of alteration in Cape or Natal rail charges, those on the Delagoa Bay line would be adjusted accordingly. The agreement could be denounced by either party, but while the railway clauses would remain in force for a year after denunciation, labour recruiting would cease immediately. See Van der Poel, *Railway and Customs,* 221.

5 Williams, ed., *Selborne Memorandum,* 176 (diagram in Appendix B). From 35 per cent in 1902, the Cape's share of Johannesburg traffic declined to 21 per cent in 1903, 16 per cent in 1904, and 15 per cent in 1905. Even in absolute terms, the "oldest colony" saw its railway revenue shrink from £5.6 million in 1902–3 to £4 million two years later. See D.M. Goodfellow, *Economic History of South Africa,* 197. Though Natal's proportion of the Johannesburg traffic increased from 35 per cent in 1902 to 44 per cent in 1903, it declined the following year to 41 per cent and to 36 per cent in 1905. From 1904 to 1905, its railway revenue fell from £2.5 million to £1.9

million. The customs receipts of these colonies followed the course of their railway revenues. As could have been predicted, the Portuguese lines had captured almost half of railway business by 1905. See Van der Poel, *Railways and Customs*, 110–17.

6 CO 879/81/776, Milner to Chamberlain, 6 April 1903.

7 CO 527/11/38793, Selborne to Elgin, 1 October 1906. In this missive, Selborne urged the Foreign Office to turn the screw on Portugal. He recommended informing Lisbon that so long as the arrangement operated, Britain must act on the opinion of its legal authorities. Though he would in no way adopt any policy which might jeopardize the Transvaal's labour supply, the high commissioner reminded London that the Portuguese too profited from the labour clause and were not likely to denounce it. Besides his recognition of the value to Portugal, Selborne's new boldness can also be attributed to the deterioration of intercolonial relations within British South Africa. Moreover, as his advice anticipated action from the metropole, he doubtless figured that London, unlike Pretoria, could afford to be brave. See also CO 527/11/35646, Selborne to Elgin, 27 September 1906 and CO 879/106/807, Elgin to Selborne, 3 November 1906.

8 Selborne Papers, MS164, fols. 16–17, Copy of *modus vivendi*, 1901.

9 Jeeves, *Migrant Labour*, 190, 199. In South Africa, the Chamber's monopsony had collapsed altogether between 1906 and 1909. See Jeeves, 58, 87–9.

10 CO 417/427/8491, Selborne to Elgin, 19 February 1906; enclosures: Coutinho to Selborne, 22 November 1905; Selborne to Coutinho, 6 December 1905.

11 Selborne Papers, MS167, fols. 137–40, Selborne to Elgin, 2 April 1906; enclosures: Wilson (TMLA) to Selborne, 28 March 1906; C.H. Rodwell (imperial secretary) to Wilson, 29 March 1906; TMLA to Selborne, 29 March 1906; TMLA to Selborne, 30 March 1906; Rodwell to TMLA, 31 March 1906; TMLA to Selborne, 2 April 1906; Rodwell to TMLA, 2 April 1906.

12 Ibid., fol. 141, Selborne to Elgin, 23 April 1906; enclosures: circular letter from TMLA to Eckstein, Farrar, Barnato, JCIC, Goerz, GMFC, Neumann, Robinson, and Consolidated Goldfield Mining Groups, 14 April 1906.

13 CO 291/97/13985, Selborne to Elgin, 2 April 1906; enclosures: P. W. Dix (Secretary, WNLA) to High Commissioner's Office, 22 March 1906; minute by Churchill, 17 May.

14 CO 291/114/14965, J. B. Robinson to Colonial Office, 27 April 1906.

15 Selborne Papers, MS49, fols. 29–33b, Selborne to Elgin, 4 July 1906.

16 CO 291/114/14965, minutes by Just, 1 May, and Ommanney, 5 May 1906; Selborne Papers, MS167, fol. 144, Elgin to Selborne, 7 May 1906.

17 CO 291/98/16623, Selborne to Elgin, 10 May 1906.

18 Ibid., see minutes of Lambert, 11 May; Just, 11 May; and Graham, 14 May 1906.

19 Ibid., minute by Churchill, 15 May. The undersecretary remarked sardoni-
cally, "I think we should certainly support the TMLA at Lisbon, according to
our original inclination, now that we know that it is 'a matter of perfect indifference' to Lord Selborne." See also ibid., Elgin to Selborne, 17 May 1906.

20 CO 291/99/18098, Selborne to Elgin, 19 May 1906; minutes by Lambert,
21 May; Graham, 22 May; and Churchill, 22 May.

21 CO 291/99/19005, Selborne to Elgin, 26 May 1906.

22 To be sure, the humanitarian aspect of the question constituted a genuine
concern for the governor. And evidence suggests that, contrary to
Churchill's prognosis, free recruiting in other areas did present serious
problems of control and did spawn abuses which the absence of one responsible agency made difficult to eradicate. (See Jeeves, *Migrant Labour*,
88.) Even here, however, the control which WNLA provided did not operate solely for the Africans' benefit. Indeed, Mozambique's defence of the
monopsony reflected deep-seated fears that free recruiting would stimulate
African unrest. Portugal had 'pacified' the interior barely a decade before
and, not even by 1910 did the administration exercise effective control.
Moreover, the colony's hold over its labour resources was feeble at best.
(See Vail and White, *Capitalism and Colonialism in Mozambique*, 110, 178–
83.) In fact, in its recruiting areas, WNLA exerted a more powerful presence than the government itself. (See Jeeves, *Migrant Labour*, 190.) Mozambique authorities were not merely posturing when in November 1906 they
warned their British counterparts that the governor general "is much
afraid that the simultaneous operations of the two rival organisations might
result in conflicts and struggles, which would make difficult the work of recruiting and would increase the price of labour, as well as be a source of disturbance amongst the natives themselves" (CO 291/104/47341, Selborne
to Elgin, 3 December 1906; enclosure: S. Ribeiro [Sec.-Genl.] to HMG's
Consul-General Lourenço-Marques, 26 November 1906).

The Chamber of Mines recognised this danger and in a letter of 15 May,
made Selborne aware of it, if he had not been already. (See CO 291/99/
20627, Selborne to Elgin, 21 May 1906; enclosure: Chamber of Mines to
Governor, 15 May 1906.) There was more behind Selborne's praise of
WNLA as an instrument of control than simply African interests.

23 CO 291/99/19005, minute by Churchill, 1 June.

24 Ibid., minute by Elgin, 2 June.

25 CO 291/114/20738, J.B. Robinson to Colonial Office, 8 June 1906.; ibid.,
/20878, J.B. Robinson to Colonial Office, 11 June 1906; ibid., /21320, J.B.
Robinson to Colonial Office, 14 June 1906; ibid., /22803, J.B. Robinson to
Colonial Office, 18 June 1906.

26 CO 291/114/20738, minute by Churchill, 11 June.

27 Selborne Papers, MS54, fols. 139–58, Churchill to Selborne, 11 June 1906.

28 CO 291/99/20627, memorandum on interview with Robinson.

29 CO 291/100/27373, Selborne to Elgin, 5 July 1906; ibid., /24373, Elgin to Selborne, 7 July 1906.

30 CO 291/114/34111, J. B. Robinson to Colonial Office, 14 September 1906; ibid., /41502, Selborne to Elgin, 22 October 1906; enclosures: Malcolm to Consul-General, Lourenço Marques, 22 September 1906; Baldwin (Consul-General, Lourenco Marques) to Selborne, 26 September 1906; Baldwin to Selborne, 16 October 1906; Baldwin to Selborne, 8 October 1906; Ribeiro (Sec.-Genrl., Mozambique) to Baldwin, 13 October 1906.

31 CO 291/103/38905, Selborne to Elgin, 28 September 1906; ibid., /36825, Selborne to Elgin, 5 October 1906; CO 879/106/807, Elgin to Selborne, 3 October 1906; and ibid., Elgin to Selborne, 18 October 1906.

32 CO 291/104/42568, Selborne to Elgin, 29 October 1906; enclosure from WNLA, 25 October 1906. CO 291/105/43515, Selborne to Elgin, 5 November 1906; enclosures: almost identical letters from WNLA groups, dated from 24 October to 2 November. In fact the only free recruiting in Mozambique to date was by Robinson, who had been expelled from the Chamber.

33 CO 879/106/807, Elgin to Selborne, 7 November 1906.

34 CO 291/115/5603, Selborne to Elgin, 13 February 1907; see minutes: Hopwood, 15 February, Churchill, 15 February, and Elgin, 18 February.

35 Selborne Papers, MS167, fol. 204, Selborne to Elgin, 8 April 1907; enclosure: Ministers to Governor, 3 April 1907. CO 291/116/12150, Selborne to Elgin, 5 April 1907; see minutes, Churchill, 8 April and Elgin, 9 April. Elgin relented hesitantly, remarking, "I do not think we can do otherwise nor do I wish it. But I agree with Mr. Lambert that there may be difficulties ahead."

36 CO 291/119/33759, Selborne to Elgin, 28 August 1907; minutes by Lambert, 24 September; see also Selborne Papers, MS167, fol. 211, Acting Governor to Elgin, 16 September 1907; enclosure: Ministers to Governor, 12 September 1907.

37 Selborne Papers, MS50, fols. 147–8, Selborne to Elgin, 14 December 1907.

38 Katzenellenbogen, *South Africa and Southern Mozambique*, 98–8.

39 Selborne Papers, MS54, fols. 109–12, Churchill to Selborne, 11 March 1906; ibid., fols. 167–78, Churchill to Selborne, 2 January 1907.

40 CO 291/106/2454, Selborne to Elgin, 31 December 1906; minutes by Churchill, 8 February; see also, Hyam, *Elgin and Churchill*, 84.

41 Selborne Papers, MS100, fols. 105–6, Lord Selborne to Lady Selborne, 3 April 1907; ibid., fol. 96, Lord Selborne to Lady Selborne, 30 March 1907.

42 CAB 37/88/55, minute by Churchill, 28 April 1907.

43 Cf. discussion in Hyam, *Elgin and Churchill*, 89–93. In his paraphrases of Churchill's paper, Hyam neglected to mention the financial proposal the undersecretary was making.

44 Selborne Papers, MS100, fols. 129–31, 159–60, Selborne to Lady Selborne, 12 May, 15 June 1907.

45 Milner Papers, dep. 194, fols. 162–86, FitzPatrick to Milner, 3 August 1907.

46 *Rand Daily Mail*, 15 June 1907.

47 Selborne Papers, MS50, fols. 132–7, Selborne to Elgin, 25 November 1907.

48 Jeeves, *Migrant Labour*, 81, 84, 120.

49 Selborne Papers, MS54, fols. 38–45, handwritten note, dated 21 December 1909, inscribed on back of his letter to Grey, 24 November 1905.

50 Jeeves, *Migrant Labour*, 31.

51 Davies, *Capital State and White Labour*, 61–4, Jeeves, *Migrant Labour*, 66.

52 *TMIC, Evidence*, I:94 (Reyersbach).

53 Ibid., I:152 (Way); ibid., IV:1467 (Chaplin).

54 *TMIC, Report*, p. 24, sec. 261.

55 Selborne Papers, MS54, fol. 159–66, Selborne to Churchill, 5 July 1906. It is not surprising that, even on this issue, the high commissioner was at odds with his Liberal superiors.

56 Ibid., fols. 157–64, memorandum by Selborne to L. Phillips, 15 January 1906; also, Phillips's reply to Selborne, n.d.

57 Smuts Papers, 187/61/1908, Selborne to Smuts, 1 September 1908; enclosure: "Notes on a Suggested Policy towards Coloured People and Natives."

58 Ibid.

59 Selborne Papers, MS100, fols. 123–6, Lord Selborne to Lady Selborne, 3 May 1907.

60 Yudelman, "Lord Rothschild," 258; Davies, *Capital and White Labour*, 70–1.

61 Selborne Papers, MS100, fols. 141–2, Lord Selborne to Lady Selborne, 18 May 1907; ibid., MS50, fols. 61–2, Selborne to Elgin, 23 May 1907.

62 Ibid., MS70, fols. 77–9, Selborne to Churchill, 25 May 1907.

63 CO 291/117/18380, Selborne to Elgin, 23 May 1907; minute from Vernon, 24 May; Selborne Papers, MS100, Lord Selborne to Lady Selborne, 27 May 1907.

64 Yudelman, "Lord Rothschild," 269; see also Davies's discussion in *Capital, State and White Labour*, 115–18, as well as Katz, "White Workers' Grievances," 129–32.

65 Johannesburg *Star*, 27 May 1907, leader.

66 Selborne Papers, MS70, fols. 77–9, Selborne to Churchill, 25 May 1907.

67 CO 291/117/18380, minute by Churchill, 25 May 1907.

68 Selborne Papers, MS71, fol. 42, Selborne to Asquith, 22 February 1906. Note on back in Selborne's hand, 21 December 1904.

Chapter Six

1 D. Goodfellow, *Economic History of South Africa*, 188–9.

2 In the Cape, two-thirds of the African population resided in the reserves and, of the remaining third outside, most occupied white-owned land, while a few did enjoy freehold tenure. Though not yet as overcrowded or impoverished as they would become a generation later, inhabitants within the reserves could by 1905 feel the pinch of land shortage. It was perhaps indicative of the increasing land pressure that at the turn of the century some Africans attempted to purchase land communally outside of the areas designated for them. Unlike the Cape, until 1905 the Transvaal refused to recognize the legal right of Africans to own land at all, outside of a few minuscule locations. As in Natal, African holdings in the Transvaal were registered in the name of a government trust. Most of the Africans in the northern colony had no recognized holdings anyway, and resided instead on crown lands or white-owned property. To be sure, black tenants enjoyed considerable autonomy as squatters under white landlords, whose exactions were not intolerably onerous. Indeed, the development of the South African economy after the mineral discoveries stimulated African agricultural production, which grew impressively – often with squatting arrangements. In return for a portion of the crop or cash payment, African tenants (or squatters) could occupy white-owned land and farm it as they wished. In the last quarter of the nineteenth century an increasing number of blacks found these arrangements quite profitable; as squatters, they could produce enough for subsistence and for sale on the market. Whether one classifies these people as petty-bourgeois, peasants, or proto-proletarian, their fortunes were on the rise until the first decade of the century. Thereafter, they lost ground. The Transvaal as well as the Cape had passed various laws designed to restrict the practice of squatting, and, though largely unenforced before Union, these measures were on the books for landlords to use at their convenience. Tim Keegan has stressed that the transition from sharecropping to tenancy arrangements was quite gradual, continuing throughout the interwar years. See Keegan, "Making of the Rural Economy," 50–6. See also annexures 7 and 8 of SANAC, *Report*, 27–8; Davenport and Hunt, eds., *Right to the Land*, 31; D. Goodfellow, *Economic History of South Africa*, 152–8; Lacey, *Working for Boroko*, 15; Bundy, *South African Peasantry*, 21.

3 Van der Horst, *Native Labour in South Africa*, 161–2.

4 See Stichter, *Migrant Laborers*, 24–5, 81–7. See also Beinart, *Political Economy of Pondoland*, passim. For the harmful consequences that migratory labour had on agricultural production, gender relations, family life, and the traditional authority of elders, see Stichter, 61–3.

5 Warwick, "Black People and the War," 207. See also *PP,* xlv (1903), Cd. 1551, p. 419, Report by S.W.J. Scholefield, Native Commissioner of Water-berg, 18 February 1903.

6 *PP,* xlv (1903), Cd. 1551, pp. 405–9, Interim Report, Native Affairs Dept., 12 December 1901; see also *PP,* lxii (1904), Cd. 2025, pp. 143–9, 155–8, 160, Annual Report by Commissioner for Native Affairs for year ending 30 June 1903.

7 Lagden had under him five district commissioners, who in turn were as-sisted by twenty-three sub-commissioners. The commissioners' central duty was the maintenance of law and order, and they were endowed with certain judicial powers as well as the authority to inflict punishment by fines not ex-ceeding £5. See *PP,* lxii (1904), Cd. 2025, pp. 145–7, annual Report by the Commissioner for Native Affairs for Year ending 30 June 1903; *PP,* xlv (1903), Cd. 1551, pp. 394–6, Report by Commissioner for Native Affairs for Year 1902.

8 *PP,* lxii (1904), Cd. 2025, p. 144, Annual reports by Commissioner for Na-tive Affairs for year ending 30 June 1903; *PP,* xlv (1903), Cd. 1551, p. 406, Interim Report, Native Affairs Dept., 12 December 1901. The Department instructed its commissioners "to encourage native labour in all reasonable ways, but not to recruit it, except for Government purposes or public works."

9 SANAC, *Report,* p. 35, sec. 193; p. 96, sec. 443; and p. 97, sec. 446.

10 Johnstone, *Class, Race, and Gold,* passim.; see also Davies, *Capital, State, and White Labour,* 72–84; and Bozzoli, *Political Nature of a Ruling Class,* 105.

11 Bundy, *South African Pesantry,* chapter 4, passim; Lacey, *Working for Boroko,* 4–7.

12 This echoes the recent view put forth by Saul Dubow. "My own understand-ing of segregation ... [is] that the relationship between segregation and capitalist development should be interpreted in the 'weak' sense of pre-serving the existing social structure under conditions of rapid industrial growth. Further, it may be argued that segregation worked in the long-term interests of capitalism by helping to secure the social conditions for the re-productions of capitalism as a system. However, this is not to say that segre-gation was the best, most efficient or indeed the only way to secure capitalist development. Rather, it is to suggest that segregation had at least as much to do with the ideological legitimation of white domination as with the requirements of capital accumulation." See Dubow, *Racial Segregation,* 2–3.

13 CO 291/84/32457, Selborne to Lyttelton, 21 August 1905; see minute by Keith, 13 September 1905.

14 SANAC, *Report,* pp. 64–5, sec. 321. A particularly insightful discussion of Tswana Zionists was offered by Jean Comaroff, who explained how Africans appropriated European symbols and practices for their own construction

of the spiritual universe. "In appropriating core signs from Protestant orthodoxy and the secular culture that bore it, Zionism resituated them in its own holistic landscape and, by extending them into the mundane 'nooks and crannies' of everyday life, naturalized them as the captured bearers of alien power." See J. Comaroff, *Body of Power*, 197.

15 Denoon, "Transvaal Labour Crisis," 481–94, passim.

16 *PP*, xlv (1903), Cd. 2024, p. 403, Report for Commissioner of Native Affairs, 1902.

17 Chanaiwa, "African Humanism in Southern Africa," 33–5.

18 See Beinart and Bundy, *Hidden Struggles*, 34–7.

19 Marks, *Reluctant Rebellion*, xv–xvii, 121–2, and 132–4.

20 CO 291/97/13144, Selborne to Elgin, 26 March 1906; CO 417/428/32516, Selborne to Elgin, 13 August 1906.

21 Selborne Papers, MS71, fols. 25–9, Lagden to Selborne, 11 February 1906.

22 CO 417/428/32516, Selborne to Elgin, 13 August 1906.

23 Selborne Papers, MS50, fols. 141–6, Selborne to Elgin, 13 December 1907; CO 879/106/820, Selborne to Elgin, 10 September 1907; enclosure: Selborne to Nathan, 4 September 1907.

24 Selborne Papers, MS1, fols. 99–111, Selborne to Balfour, 25 June 1909.

25 Nathan's predecessor, Sir Henry McCallum, did not consider Dinuzulu the instigator of the revolt and his attitude no doubt explains Selborne's early exoneration of the chief. The day before he sent his despatch of August 1906, the high commissioner received a letter from Sir Henry McCallum, who discounted the notion that Dinuzulu or any individual had engineered the Natal rebellion. Rather, McCallum attributed the disturbances to an abstract principle and "that abstract is Ethiopianism" (see Selborne Papers, MS56, fols. 138–45, McCallum to Selborne, 12 August 1906). It is not surprising that the rebellion bewildered European witnesses. By the twentieth century Africans in Natal faced increasing land shortages, as well as intensified white pressure to coerce them into labour relations. Though subject to traditional Zulu authority, they also experienced new influences such as Ethiopianism. These pressures and influences transformed social, economic, and political relationships. In the process, ethnic identity was re-forged, blending the old and new. Thus, although prone to exaggeration, the European commentators did discern different facets of a complex and changing sense of ethnicity, in which Zulu traditions merged with "Ethiopian" tendencies. Although this process had barely begun in 1906, it matured in the inter-war years. Indeed, Zulu ethnic consciousness is still strong today, which demonstrates the modernity of ethnicity. See Marks, "Patriotism, Patriarchy and Purity," 216–25.

26 CO 291/97/13144, Selborne to Elgin, 26 March 1906. There were a few grains of truth in this paternalistic analysis. Migratory labour had created considerable tension between the young male migrants and the elders, who

found it increasingly difficult to retain their control. It is also true that the eradication of warfare and raiding brought structural unemployment. See Stichter, *Migrant Laborers*, 10–12.

27 CO 291/97/13144, minute by Lambert, 2 April 1906; CO 417/428/32516, Selborne to Elgin, 13 August 1906; minute by Vernon, 4 September 1906. Contemporaries attributed the uprising to Ethiopianism and the mission-educated "Kolwa." Shula Marks, however, has concluded that, while some African Christians did figure conspicuously in the revolt, the pattern of participation cut along traditional cleavages. It was the rebellion itself which stimulated African consciousness and engendered a new spirit. See Marks, *Reluctant Rebellion*, 310–13, 335, 365.

28 CO 291/97/13144, Selborne to Elgin, 26 March 1906.

29 Selborne Papers, MS1, fols. 99–111, Selborne to Balfour, 25 June 1908.

30 CO 417/428/32516, Selborne to Elgin, 13 August 1906; CO 291/97/13144, Selborne to Elgin, 26 March 1906.

31 CO 291/96/6752, Selborne to Elgin, 5 February 1906.

32 Ibid., minutes by Keith, 18 April; Graham, 30 April; and Elgin, 15 May 1906.

33 CO 291/96/5406, minute by Churchill, 3 March 1906.

34 Africa (S), No. 853 in CO 879/853 (Report of West Ridgeway Commission), p. 25, sections 101–3. When Selborne actually proposed his nominations to the Legislative Council, he cited Lionel Phillips, Lionel Curtis, Richard Feetham, and Lionel Hichens as especially sympathetic to Africans. None of these men had much acquaintance at all with African affairs, but they were all imperially minded and, most important, highly respected for their administrative talent. See CO 879/106/874, Selborne to Elgin, 7 February 1907; C. O. 879/106/875, Selborne to Elgin, 10 February 1906.

35 CO 291/97/13144, Selborne to Elgin, 26 March 1906; minutes by Keith, 18 April; Lambert, 21 April; Graham, 30 April; Ommanney, 5 May; and Elgin, 15 May 1906.

36 CO 291/119/32853, Selborne to Elgin, 26 August 1907; enclosure: copy of Native Administration Amendment Bill. Under the proposed bill, the paramount chief could depose any chief or headman, amalgamate tribes, and relocate any tribes or members thereof. Moreover, he could stipulate the powers and responsibilities of headmen and prescribe conditions under which marriages could be validly contracted. While Africans might appeal specific judgments of chiefs, "No court of law in this Colony shall have jurisdiction to review or declare invalid or unlawful any act order or direction of the Paramount Chief purporting to be done made or given in the exercise of the powers on him conferred."

37 CO 879/94/866, Selborne to Elgin, 19 August 1907.

38 CO 291/119/32934, Selborne to Elgin, 26 August 1907.

39 CO 291/119/32853, Selborne to Elgin, 26 August 1907; enclosure: extract of trial: *Mathibe* v. *Lt. Gov.*, 28 June 1907.

40 Hammond-Tooke, *Command and Consensus*, 34–5.

41 CO 879/94/866, Selborne to Elgin, 19 August 1907.

42 Selborne's ideas emerged again, albeit in stunted form, with Smuts's Native Affairs Act of 1920 (see Tatz, *Shadow and Substance*, 34–5). To be sure, the engrossment of administrative control over Africans and the simultaneous diminution of parliamentary power over them was a long-standing South African aim well before Selborne's time. The practice of styling a governor supreme chief originated with Shepstone in Natal. The process of differentiating African policy from white was well advanced in the Cape by 1905 (see Brookes, *History of Native Policy*, 109–18). At the very time Selborne was writing, the commission reporting on the recent disturbances in Natal was similarly recommending that native policy be removed from settler control (see Marks, *Reluctant Rebellion*, 343). It might seem, then, that Selborne's attitude on African policy merely reflected tendencies which had been moving in the direction of differentiation well before he had even landed in South Africa and which would continue long after he had left. Though not inaccurate, the picture above obscures important differences between the Cape's treatment of the Transkei and Selborne's plans for the Transvaal.

   In the former case, the resilience of African society had frustrated the Cape's "civilising mission" and had thrown it back, to some degree, on African laws and customs. To a large extent, of course, the Transvaal in practice ruled through traditional authorities. But, as has been shown, the only reference Selborne made to native law was the incorrect conclusion that, as paramount chief, the governor had despotic powers. While African resistance in Basutoland had inclined the Cape to leave Africans to themselves, the Bambatha disturbance impressed on Selborne the necessity of increasing white control through the autocratic powers of state. Though he recognized the dangers of interfering too suddenly or too ruthlessly with African culture, he also saw tribalism itself as a threat and had no intention of shoring it up. As he wrote Smuts in 1908, one of the objects of native policy was "to ensure the gradual destruction of the tribal system, which is incompatible with civilisation" (Smuts Papers, 187/61/1908, Selborne to Smuts, 1 September 1908; enclosure: "Notes on a Suggested Policy towards Coloured People and Natives"). Out of Shepstonian paternalism and Cape liberalism, Selborne forged a conception of African policy which might be termed administrative statism – enlightened, but despotic.

43 Davenport and Hunt, eds., *Right to the Land*, Document No. 65, 40.

44 CO 291/84/28897, Selborne to Lyttelton, 24 July 1905; CO 291/84/29963, Selborne to Lyttelton, 31 July 1905; CO 879/88/779, Mr. Rubusana and Mr. Williams to Colonial Office, 14 November 1905.

45 CO 291/84/29963, Selborne to Lyttelton, 31 July 1905; CO 291/86/ 38479, Selborne to Lyttelton, 9 October 1905 (Selborne's emphasis).

46 CO 291/86/42937, minutes by Keith, 12 July; Ommaney, 2 September; and Churchill, 2 December 1905; ibid., Elgin to Selborne, 22 February 1906.

47 CO 879/97/897, Methuen (Deputy Governor) to Crewe, 20 October 1908; see enclosure: Selborne's "Notes."

48 Smuts Papers, 187/61/1908, Selborne to Smuts, 1 September 1908. Before the bill in question was introduced, some of its intended provisions leaked out and became the subject of searching questions in the House of Commons. In South Africa the bill was modified so as to exclude any vested interests from its operation. As amended, the measure was sent on to London without comment by Lord Methuen, the deputy governor. Taking note of the modifications, Crewe informed the Transvaal that he would not disallow the bill. See CO 879/97/897, Methuen to Crewe, 28 October 1908; CO 879/106/900, Crewe to Selborne, 28 December 1908.

49 CO 291/127/27072, Selborne to Crewe 6 July 1908; see enclosure.

50 CO 879/97/897, Selborne to Crewe, 22 July 1908; enclosure: Native Affairs Society (Transvaal) to Acting Secretary of Native Affairs, 13 May 1908. The mining industry itself tended to fear that the eviction of squatters would raise the already high cost of living on the Rand by destroying this inexpensive and efficient source of agricultural production. Moreover, by forcing some tenants to evacuate the colony altogether, the act would rob the Rand of potential labourers. See Trapido, "Landlord and Tenant," 37, 45–7, 55. The Randlords' diffuse posture towards this issue demonstrates that, however "imperative" the destruction of the peasantry was to capitalism, immediate exigencies prevented the capitalists themselves from acting consistently in their long-term interests.

51 The issue of kaffir farming was, it might be noted, a burning one among South African whites. Many large landholders, particularly companies, found it preferable to let land to blacks for a share of the crops produced. SANAC strongly condemned the practice for fostering absentee landlordism to the detriment of white commercial farming. The commission further criticized squatting for restricting the supply of labour. In a more humanitarian vein, Lagden also noted that the practice made African tenure insecure. See SANAC, *Report*, 30–3, sec. 167–83.

52 CO 291/126/22370, Selborne to Secretary of State, 1 June 1908.

53 CO 291/126/24315, Selborne to Secretary of State, 15 June 1908; enclosure: Selborne to Rissik, 30 May 1908.

54 Smuts Papers, 187/61/1908, Selborne to Smuts, 1 September 1908; see enclosure: Selborne's "Notes." Selborne never set forth full proposals for the permanent and comprehensive settlement of the land question in South Africa. Thus, he offered no coherent policy regarding the principle

of territorial segregation. Nevertheless, from his specific proposals, it is clear that he would not accept legal prohibitions on individual African land purchase in urban areas. He did, however, oppose racial mixing in slum areas. As for non-urban areas, white pressure inclined him to accept territorial segregation, and concomitantly, he urged the creation of adequate reserve areas. To speculate on Selborne's personal views on this large issue (i.e., if he had been able to formulate policy alone, without South African whites or British Liberals), it would seem that he would not in principle debar blacks from owning land anywhere in the country. He would, however, consign the following groups to separate areas, whether reserves or urban locations: (a) blacks living under communal ownership arrangements (including those he identified as tribal Africans); (b) black squatters on white farms; and (c) detribalized blacks (or Indians) who were unwilling or unable to adopt a European standard of living. In short, the only non-whites Selborne would permit in European areas would be middle-class already or respectable enough to accept the bourgeois rules of the game. In either case, their numbers would amount to a handful of South Africa's non-white population.

55 It is interesting that the Colonial Office did not share Selborne's misgivings and was prepared to sanction the measure. As officials observed, the principle of territorial segregation, whether in town or country, accorded fully with the recommendations of SANAC. Only Just suggested awaiting a final report from the high commissioner before approving the bill. See minutes of CO 291/126/24315, Selborne to Crewe, 15 June 1908; also CO 291/126/22370, Selborne to Secretary of State, 1 June 1908, minutes by Keith, 30; Lambert, 7 August; Just, 3 August. The issue of African urban residence was not insignificant. Less than fifteen years after Selborne had left South Africa, this matter aroused the anxious concern of gold and maize, both afraid that towns would attract workers away from farm and compound. Responding to this pressure, the state in 1923 enacted the first measure in a long series of influx control acts. According to Marian Lacey, the growth of towns threatened not only the supply of labour but its structure too and indeed the racial ordering of society. The city conjured up to white minds the image of detribalized, perhaps educated, blacks packed together with poor whites, whom they could out-compete for employment. Such a spectre, which in the twenties actually began to materialize, struck panic into white hearts, even the hardened ones of the Rand magnates (see Lacey, *Working for Boroko*, 267–8). Yet Selborne in 1908 welcomed this prospect of African advancement in the city and did what he could to bring it about. With his enthusiasm for black progress and his contempt for poor whites, it is doubtful that developments fifteen years later would have changed his mind.

56 Smuts Papers, 187/61/1908, Selborne to Smuts, 1 September 1908; see enclosure: Selborne's "Notes."

57 CO 879/88/779, Selborne to Lyttelton, 9 October 1905.

58 CO 291/96/11334, Selborne to Elgin, 12 March 1906.

59 Selborne Papers, MS58, fols. 156–61, Selborne to R. Solomon, 9 April 1906.

60 Ibid., fols. 108–10, R. Solomon to Selborne, 15 February 1906; fols. 183–6, copy of tax ordinance, and fols. 189–91, Selborne to R. Solomon, 28 May, 1906. See also CO 879/97/897, Selborne to Secretary of State, 6 July 1908.

61 South Africa Native Congress to Chamberlain, quoted in Karis and Carter, eds., *Protest and Hope*, 18–29.

62 Extracts of Minutes of Evidence, SANAC, quoted in ibid., 34–9.

63 Selborne Papers, MS58, fols. 203–6, Selborne to R. Solomon, 14 June 1906; ibid., fols. 200–2, memo from Lagden, 5 June 1906.

64 *PP*, lvii (1907), Cd. 3528, pp. 556–7, Annual Report of Native Affairs Department, 1 July 1905 to 30 June 1906.

65 Smuts Papers, 187/61/1908, Selborne to Smuts, 1 September 1908; see enclosure: Selborne's "Notes." In evidence before SANAC, Rev. Kumalo incisively criticized the sort of industrial education Selborne was proposing: "And in regard to industrial education, it is only training to go and plough and sow seed. The Natives do all that. Every native knows how to plough ground, and to sow seed, and how to do all that kind of thing. That is not what is wanted. They must be taught to study the soil, and they must be enabled to study everything, so that they can improve … When they know these things, they must learn how to make contracts, and they must know all the other branches of work which will make them skilled workers" (see Extracts of Minutes of Evidence, SANAC, quoted in Karis and Carter, eds., *Protest and Hope*, 34–9). This last eventuality was precisely what Transvaal ministers dreaded, and Selborne knew it.

66 Selborne Papers, MS58, fols. 129–35, Lagden to Selborne, 30 December 1905, and fols. 108–10, R. Solomon to Selborne, 15 February 1906.

67 CO 879/89/800, Selborne to Elgin, 16 July 1906; enclosure from Executive Committee of Transvaal Native Congress.

68 Smuts Papers, 187/61/1908, Selborne to Smuts, 1 September 1908; see enclosure: Selborne's "Notes."

69 CO 291/97/13144, Selborne to Elgin, 26 March 1906.

70 CO 291/83/21858, Selborne to Lyttelton, 5 June 1905; enclosure: meeting of APO, 31 May 1905; CO 879/89/800, Dr Abdurahman to Colonial Office, June 18, 1906; enclosure: Petition of Coloured British Subjects to King Edward VII.

71 CO 291/97/13144, Selborne to Elgin, 26 March 1906; Elgin's minute of 5 April. See also Africa (S), No. 853 in CO 879/106 (Report of West Ridgeway Commission), 32–3, sec. 144.

72 CO 879/89/800, Selborne to Elgin, 5 February 1906.

73 *Selborne Memorandum*, 112-3. Though Selborne did not author this document, the views which it expressed on this issue more similar to Selborne's own.

74 CO 879/97/897, Selborne to Crewe, 24 October 1908; CO 879/97/897, Selborne to Crewe, 22 February 1908; enclosure: Imperial Secretary to J.M. Orpen, 31 January 1908; ibid., 3 February 1908; enclosure: extract from *Natal Mercury*, 21 January 1908.

75 Smuts Papers, 187/61/1908, Selborne to Smuts, 1 September 1908; see enclosure: Selborne's "Notes."

76 Lacey, *Working for Boroko*, 278.

77 Smuts Papers, 187/61/1908, Selborne to Smuts, 1 September 1908. Paul Rich has delineated many currents of racial thinking in early twentieth-century Britain. Though still alive, the old evangelical goal of assimilation through conversion and civilization had given way to a new belief in differentiation. This assumed different forms: a romantic racism, scientific social Darwinism, or cultural relativism as espoused by Mary Kingsley. In the 1920s, these were all overshadowed by the multiracial Commonwealth ideal, which would extend self-government to all "civilised" races under the rubric of British institutions. See Rich, *Race and Empire*, 1-70, passim. John Kendle has explained how in the 1920s even Kindergarten members, such as Philip Kerr and Lionel Curtis, came to embrace eventual dominion status for India. See Kendle, *Round Table Movement*, 226-7, 245-7. To situate Selborne in this context, we must first note that he showed traces of all these racial views. Fundamentally, however, he was an assimilationist in that his ultimate aim was the incorporation of all South Africans into one civilization. Although differentiation was only a temporary expedient, it would last several generations, during which Selborne would consign all 'uncivilised' blacks to the benevolent despotism of white administrators. Even so, Selborne's aim was always incorporation and the chief agency of progress towards this was, in his Darwinistic thinking, inter-racial contact and competition. He might, therefore, be termed a Darwinistic assimilationist.

78 An anti-imperialist liberal, J.X. Merriman was, at the time, prime minister of the Cape.

79 Thompson, *Unification of South Africa*, 212-17.

80 CO 879/106/927, Selborne to Crewe, 24 October 1908; enclosure: Selborne to De Villiers, 22 October 1908. The colonial secretary endorsed Selborne's reply, adding only the qualification that he might "incline perhaps in [the] direction of [the] Cape system more than you do" (see CO 879/106/900, Crewe to Selborne, 27 October 1908). This, in fact, was the gravest objection the Colonial Office saw with the governor's civilization test. Lambert hoped that its implementation would not deprive any Cape voters of existing rights, while Lucas lamented that HMG had not declared itself more strongly for the Cape system at the outset. See CO 417/459/

41744, Selborne to Elgin, 24 October 1908, minutes by Lambert, 25 October; and Lucas, 24 October.

81 Petitions were received from the South African Native Convention, the Transvaal Native Union, the African Political Organisation, the Orange River Colony Native Association, and even the conservative Transkeian General Council. White liberals joined their non-European countrymen in castigating the new constitution. Prominent Cape politicians from both benches petitioned England, and W.P. Schreiner led a delegation there to mount a public campaign. Schreiner's delegation, along with the rest of the appeals, all came to nothing. Crewe appreciated who held the South African cards in 1909. See CO 879/100/927, Selborne to Crewe, 5 April 1909; enclosure: Resolution of South African Native Convention, sent 27 March 1909; Methuen (Deputy Governor, Transvaal) to Crewe, 6 May 1909; enclosure: Resolution of Transvaal Native Union, 8 March 1909; Crewe to Selborne, 20 August 1909; enclosure: Petition of Executive Committee of Orange River Colony Native Association, 21 June 1909; Hely-Hutchinson (Governor, Cape) to Crewe, 1 July 1909; enclosure: Resolution of General Council of Transkeian Territories, 21 June 1909. See also Hely-Hutchinson to Crewe, 10 June 1909; enclosures: Appeal from J. Gordon Sprigg, W.P. Schreiner, et al., and Prime Minister to Governor, 10 June 1909.

82 Ibid., Selborne to Crewe, 15 February 1909.

83 *The State*, May 1910, "The Month: Lord Selborne's Farewell."

Chapter Seven

1 The Intercolonial Council financed its routine operations out of railway revenue, but relied, for new construction, on sums earmarked for the purpose in the guaranteed loan. In addition, its yearly deficits were made good by contributions from the two colonies, subject to the secretary of state's approval. Though it could contract with private companies, the council could not borrow on the open market. Reflecting the crown colony regime which had spawned it, the council had a fully nominated membership. As it stood in 1905 after several modifications by orders-in-council, the ICC consisted of eight official members (four from each colony) and ten unofficial ones (six from the Transvaal and four from the ORC). The high commissioner appointed eight of the unofficial members and the colonial secretary two. The specific task of devising railway policy fell to the three- to nine-man standing committee and its appointed chairman. See CAB 37/82/1, memo on the Intercolonial Council prepared by the Colonial Office, 1 January 1906.

2 Denoon, *Grand Illusion*, 209–15; Selborne Papers, MS164, fol. 38, Selborne to Lyttelton, 16 September 1905 (despatch); and CO 879/88/779, Lyttelton to Selborne, 7 December 1905.

3 For Het Volk's position, see CO 879/88/779, Selborne to Lyttelton, 7 August 1905.

4 Selborne Papers, MS164, fols. 47–9, Selborne to Lyttelton, 20 November 1905 (despatch).

5 Ibid., MS170, fols. 59–63, memorandum by Selborne, 1 August 1905. CO 879/88/779, Selborne to Lyttelton, 7 August 1905; Selborne Papers, MS164, fols. 47–9, Selborne to Lyttelton, 20 November 1905 (despatch). In attendance were Richard Solomon, Sir Hamilton Goold-Adams, Patrick Duncan, Lionel Hichens, Albert Browne, and Lord Basil Blackwood.

6 A copy of the new constitution can be found in the Selborne Papers, MS175. See section xlix of Transvaal Letter Patent. This can also be found in *PP*, lxxx, (1906), Cd. 3250, p. 713.

7 Selborne Papers, MS49, fols. 72–7, Selborne to Elgin, 30 August 1906; CO 291/120/42753, Selborne to Elgin, 6 December 1907; CO 879/106/900, Selborne to Elgin, 27 May 1908.

8 CO 417/413/35818, Circular letter from Selborne to the various South African governments, 15 September 1905; enclosure in Selborne to Lyttelton, 18 September 1905. For a full discussion of the railway tangle, see Ellsworth, "British South African Colonies."

9 See leaders in *Johannesburg Star*, 17 October 1905 and 22 November 1905. See also *Natal Mercury* of 22 November 1905 (quoted the next day in the *Transvaal Leader.*) On 23 November 1905 the *Leader* carried the articles cited from the *Eastern Province Herald*, the *South African News*, and the *Cape Daily Telegraph*.

10 Selborne Papers, MS164, fols. 31–2. See Cape's reply of 30 October and Natal's of 8 November.

11 Van der Poel, *Railways and Customs*, 132–3; CO 527/10/28334, Selborne to Elgin, 1 August 1906.

12 Selborne Papers, MS55, fols. 35–41, Selborne to Hely-Hutchinson, 11 July 1906.

13 Ibid., fols. 42–51, Hely-Hutchinson to Selborne, 14 July 1906; fols. 35–41, Selborne to Hely-Hutchinson, 11 July 1906.

14 Ibid., fols. 53–5, Selborne to Hely-Hutchinson, n.d.; fols. 62–9, Hely-Hutchinson to Selborne, 24 July 1906; fols. 78–82, Selborne to Hely-Hutchinson, 3 August 1906.

15 CO 527/10/28334, Selborne to Elgin, 1 August 1906; ibid., /31503 Selborne to Elgin, 6 August 1906; enclosure from the Railway Committee, n.d.

16 CO 879/106/807, Elgin to Selborne, 7 August 1906; CO 527/10/29937, Selborne to Elgin, 13 August 1906.

17 Selborne Papers, MS56, fols. 132–5, Selborne to McCallum, 2 August 1906; CO 527/10/30375, enclosure in Selborne to Elgin, 16 August 1905; Elgin to Selborne, 25 August 1906.

18 CO 879/106/807, Hely-Hutchinson to Selborne, 8 September 1906: see enclosure; CO 527/10/33712, Selborne to Elgin, 11 September 1906; enclosure: Selborne to Hely-Hutchinson, 9 September 1906; CO 879/106/807, Elgin to Selborne, 11 September 1906; CO 527/11/34405, Selborne to Elgin, 13 September 1906.

19 CO 527/10/33822, Selborne to Elgin, 12 September 1906. See Elgin's minute, n.d.

20 CO 879/106/807, Hely-Hutchinson to Elgin, 15 September 1906; CO 879/106/807, Hely-Hutchinson to Elgin, 13 September 1906; enclosure: minute from Ministers, 12 September 1906; CO 879/106/807, Elgin to Hely-Hutchinson, 15 September 1906; CO 879/106/807, Selborne to Elgin, 17 September 1906.

21 CO 527/11/34405, Elgin to Selborne, 19 September 1906; CO 879/106/807, Goold-Adams to Selborne, 2 October 1906; CO 879/106/807, Brand to Goold-Adams, 10 October 1906; enclosure from Natal Ministers, 10 October 1906.

22 CO 879/106/807, Hely-Hutchinson to Elgin, 11 October 1906; CO 527/11/37723, Selborne to Elgin, 12 October 1906; see minutes of Graham, 13 October and Elgin, 14 October. See also CO 879/106/807, Elgin to Selborne, 15 October 1906.

23 CO 527/11/37577, Selborne to Elgin, 11 October 1906, and CO 527/11/38210, Selborne to Elgin, 15 October 1906; CO 527/11/39432, Selborne to Elgin, 25 October 1906.

24 CO 879/106/807, Elgin to Selborne, 27 October 1906; CO 879/106/807, Selborne to Elgin, 30 October 1906; Selborne Papers, MS55, fols. 98–101, Selborne to Hely-Hutchinson, 20 November 1906; CO 527/11/42768, Selborne to Elgin, 19 November 1906.

25 Selborne Papers, MS49, fols. 129–36, Selborne to Elgin, 23 October 1906.

26 CO 417/442/1330, Selborne to Elgin, 9 January 1907; see Churchill's minute, n.d.; Selborne Papers, MS9, fols. 172–6, Chamberlain to Selborne, 15 April 1908.

27 Selborne Papers, MS71, fols. 171–84, Selborne to Pretyman, 13 January 1909.

28 Ibid., MS48, fols. 219–27, Selborne to Elgin, 28 March 1906. In addition, Selborne told Mrs Lyttelton that no factor had influenced him more than the irreconcilable "ORC, and its miserable Government," which he hoped the Union would suffocate. This, of course, appeared four years after Union in a letter whose purpose was to praise the former colonial secretary and vindicate his suspicions of Afrikanerdom (see Selborne Papers, MS72, fols. 40–8, Selborne to Mrs Lyttelton, August 1914.) Nowhere in his pre-Union correspondence did Selborne mention the ORC factor.

29 Selborne Papers, MS56, fols. 60–2, Selborne to McCallum, 12 December 1906; MS9, fols. 150–65, Selborne to Chamberlain, 24 February 1908. In

this letter he wrote: "I most ardently support federation or unification on Imperial grounds and my support would be just as strenuous if I knew for certain that the Boers would have a secure advantage in the S.A. Parliament."

30 Grey Papers, FO 800/111, Selborne to Grey, 28 February 1909.
31 Selborne Papers, MS9, fols. 150–65, Selborne to Chamberlain, 24 February 1908. See also Phillips to Wernher, 28 January 1907, Jeeves and Fraser, eds., *All that Glittered*, 171–4; and Selborne Papers, MS6, fols. 1–12, Selborne to Salisbury, 22 August 1908.

Chapter Eight

1 Selborne Papers, MS9, fols. 86–92, "The Position after the War," minute by Selborne, 16 November 1899.
2 CAB 37/81/185, "Constitution of the Transvaal," memo by Ripon, 26 December 1906. An authority on the Kindergarten, Walter Nimocks, has indicated the great difficulties in terminology which attend this question. The terms "federation" and "union" were used interchangeably until the eve of the National Convention, when it became important to specify the constitutional shape of the amalgamated colonies. See Nimocks, *Milner's Young Men*, 75, n1. Like Nimocks, I follow traditional usage; in the following account, federation, unification, closer union, and union all designate some form of political amalgamation without denoting its precise form. When discussing events in 1908 and after, I use these terms with more deliberation and precision.
3 *Milner Papers*, 2:550–8, Milner to Selborne, 14 April 1905.
4 The quotation and the other information in this paragraph can be found in Lewsen, *John X. Merriman*, 235, 286–7.
5 *Johannesburg Star*, 13 October 1905, report of Selborne's speech at Pieter maritzburg.
6 Selborne Papers, MS65, fols. 3–4, R. Collins to Selborne, 20 June 1906 and Selborne's reply, 1 July 1906.
7 Selborne Papers, MS49, fols. 42–51, Selborne to Elgin, 3 August 1906; fols. 65–8, Selborne to Elgin, 25 August 1906; fols. 82–9, Elgin to Selborne, 6 September 1906.
8 Ibid., MS65, fols. 27–36, Maydon to Selborne, 27 September 1906; enclosure: memorandum dated 22 July 1906.
9 Ibid., fols. 37–9, Selborne to Maydon, 1 October 1906.
10 See Kendle, *The Round Table Movement*, 22–7; Nimocks, *Milner's Young Men*, 75–81.
11 Milner Papers, dep. 192, fols. 204–15, Curtis to Milner, 10 September 1906; CO 291/102/32521, Graham's minute, 24 September 1906 on Selborne to Elgin, 13 August 1906.

12 Milner Papers, dep. 192, fols. 204–15, Curtis to Milner, 10 September 1906.

13 Selborne Papers, MS65, fols. 5–9, Curtis to Malcolm, 7 September 1906.

14 *Johannesburg Star,* 17 September 1906.

15 Milner Papers, dep. 192, fols. 204–15, Curtis to Milner, 10 September 1906.

16 Selborne Papers, MS65, fols. 15–25, Curtis to Selborne, 23 September 1906; Milner Papers, dep. 192, fols 222–39, Curtis to Milner, 29 September 1906.

17 Milner Papers, dep. 192, fols. 204–15, Curtis to Milner, 10 September 1906.

18 Selborne Papers, MS65, fols. 37–9, Selborne to Maydon, 1 October 1906; fols. 40–1, Selborne to Maydon, 22 November 1906. Curtis had prepared the groundwork for this. See Kendle, *Round Table,* 23.

19 Selborne to Elgin, 7 January 1907; enclosure: minute from Cape Ministers, 28 November 1906, *Selborne Memorandum,* 1–6. (The *Selborne Memorandum* can also be found in the *PP,* lvii (1907), Cd. 3564. The document itself was sent to London in Selborne's despatch to Elgin of 7 January 1907, CO 417/42/3463. In the following, my citations to the published document are from the Williams edition.)

20 Selborne Papers, MS54, fols. 189–94, Selborne to Hopwood, 18 January 1907.

21 Ibid., MS65, fols. 27–8, Maydon to Selborne, 27 September 1906; fols. 238–9, Collins to Selborne, 18 March 1907; MS56, fols. 156–9, McCallum to Selborne, 10 December 1906.

22 Ibid., MS56, fols. 60–2, Selborne to McCallum, 12 December 1906; fols. 163–8, McCallum to Selborne, 15 December 1906; Selborne to McCallum, 21 December 1906, and McCallum to Selborne, 29 December 1906.

23 Ibid., MS65, fols. 5–9, Curtis to Milner, 7 September 1906; fols. 13–14, Curtis to Selborne, 12 September 1906.

24 Milner Papers, dep. 192, fols. 222–39, Curtis to Milner, 29 September 1906.

25 Selborne Papers, MS65, fols. 40–1, Selborne to Maydon, 22 November 1906.

26 See *Johannesburg Star*'s criticism of the *Leader*'s posture in the *Star*'s leader, 15 January 1907; Milner Papers, dep. 194, fols. 162–86, FitzPatrick to Milner, 3 August 1907.

27 *Johannesburg Star,* 27 November 1906 and 15 January 1907, leaders.

28 CO 241/106/48042, Selborne to Elgin, 10 December 1906.

29 Phillips to Wernher, 28 January 1907, eds., Jeeves and Fraser, eds., *All that Glittered* 171–4.

30 CO 417/428/39075, Selborne to Elgin, 29 September 1906.

31 Ibid., 45222, Selborne to Elgin, 7 December 1906; see minutes of Vernon, 8 December; Graham, 10 December; Just, 10 December; Ommanney, 12 December; Lambert, 10 December; Churchill, 11 December; and Elgin's reply to Selborne, 13 December 1906.

32 Ibid., 46563, Selborne to Elgin, 15 December 1906.

33 Ibid., see minutes of Graham, 20 December; Ommanney, 20 December; Just, 19 December; Churchill, 26 December; Elgin, 26 December; and Elgin's reply to Selborne, 29 December 1906.

34 Selborne Papers, MS65, fols. 69–104, Duncan, Hichens, and Curtis to Selborne, 24 December 1906. As their focus is more on the closer union movement than on Selborne, Kendle and Nimocks allude but briefly to the friction between the Kindergarten and Selborne. See Kendle, *Round Table Movement*, 28, and Nimocks, *Milner's Young Men*, 83–4. In my view, this friction signifies the deep animosity between these Milnerite imperialists and the Liberal imperial factor.

35 Selborne Papers, MS65, fols. 140–4, Selborne to Hichens, 1 January 1907.

36 Ibid., MS66, fols 112–15, Selborne's notes on his meeting with Curtis. The notes were dated Dec. 20th, which must be incorrect for they refer to the joint letter of the 24th; see also MS65, fols. 131–8, Selborne to Curtis, 1 January 1907; fol. 146, letter in Curtis's hand, n.d. On this draft was written that Hichens and Duncan had dissuaded him from sending it.

37 Ibid., MS65, fol. 201, R. Solomon to Selborne, 15 January 1906; fol. 200, Smuts to Selborne, 12 January 1907. Privately, Smuts told Merriman that while he considered federation itself desirable, he would watch the present movement carefully. There were, he warned, "sinister influences at work." See Hancock and Van der Poel, eds., *Selections from the Smuts Papers*, 2:321, Smuts to Merriman, 25 January 1907.

38 Selborne Papers, MS65, fols 215–6, minute from Cape Ministers, 30 January 1907; fol. 219, McCallum to Selborne, 2 February 1907; fols. 188–90, Selborne to Hely-Hutchinson, 4 January 1907. I am indebted to Ron Ellsworth for drawing my attention to this document and this point.

39 CO 417/442/1330, Selborne to Elgin, 9 January 1907. See minutes of Ommanney, 11 January 1907 and Churchill (n.d.).

40 CO 879/106/874, Elgin to Selborne, 16 January 1907; 874, Selborne to Elgin, 18 January 1907; CO 417/442/3463, Selborne to Elgin, 7 January 1907.

41 Selborne Papers, MS65, fols. 42–68, Curtis to Selborne, 3 November 1906. Nimocks argued that Selborne edited out material likely to offend "either of the two dominant white groups." See Nimocks, *Milner's Young Men*, 83. I would contend that, in his excisions, the high commissioner was not as concerned about local feeling as he was about the sensibilities of the Liberal government in London.

42 *Selborne Memorandum*, 34, 43–4.

43 Ibid., 93–4.

44 Ibid., 126–30, 134–7, 155.

45 Ibid., 114.

46 Proofs of the *Selborne Memorandum*; this can be found in Rhodes House, Oxford under Curtis, L., 610.13 r.40, hereafter referred to as Proofs (*SM*). For this particular citation, see pp. 109–10.

47 Proofs (*SM*), 111–12, 124.

48 *Selborne Memorandum*, 108–14.

49 Proofs (*SM*), 92–5, 170–3. Compare with published version in *Selborne Memorandum*, 112–14.

50 Proofs (*SM*), 103.

51 *Selborne Memorandum*, 173.

52 CO 417/442/3463, Selborne to Elgin, 7 January 1907; see Vernon's minute of 30 January.

53 Ibid., see Lambert's minute of 31 January.

54 Ibid., see Just's minute of 2 February. The reception which the *Selborne Memorandum* received in London renders Leonard Thompson's interpretation of Kindergarten motives (i.e., that Curtis and co. sought to shore up British influence in South Africa) rather questionable. See Thompson, *Unification of South Africa*, 82. Also questionable is the claim offered recently by Deryck Schreuder that, for the success of closer union, "it was circumstantially vital that a new Liberal administration was massively elected to power in Great Britain from early 1906, with Lord Elgin and the young Winston Churchill being placed in charge of colonial affairs. A major mandate of that administration was to end the awful embroglio of South African entanglements, on firm Liberal lines of devolution, while still looking to crucial British interests in strategy and investment" ("Colonial Nationalism," 215).

55 CO 417/442/3463, Churchill's minute of 15 March 1907.

56 CO 879/106/874, Elgin to Selborne, 19 February 1907.

Chapter Nine

1 Kendle, *Round Table Movement*, 33–5.

2 *South Africa Mines, Commerce, and Industries*, 6 July 1907; *Cape Argus*, 4 July 1907, leader.

3 See leaders in *Transvaal Leader, Johannesburg Star*, and *Rand Daily Mail*, all on 4 July 1907; *Friend*, 11 July 1907, leader; *Natal Mercury*, 4 July 1907, leader.

4 Thompson, *Unification of South Africa*, 76.

5 Merriman to Smuts, 7 July 1907, Hancock and Van der Poel, eds. *Selections from the Smuts Papers*, 2:347.

6 Ibid., 2:321, 355.

7 Steyn to Merriman, 11 September 1907, Lewsen, ed., *Correspondence of John X. Merriman*, 4:49.

8 Selborne Papers, MS65, fol. 200, Smuts to Selborne, 12 January 1907. See also Smuts to Merriman, 28 September 1907, 2:355–6.

9 Pyrah, *Imperial Policy and South Africa*, 230–3; Davenport, *Afrikaner Bond*, 270–1.

10 Thompson, *Unification of South Africa*, 71. Despite the Kindergarten initiative for closer union, Thompson believes that Steyn, Merriman, and Smuts took the movement over and directed it to their own ends. In his words, "These three men determined the timing of the unification movement. They prevented it from becoming dynamic before their parties had assumed office in all three colonies, and directly that political swing had been completed in February 1908 they accelerated and controlled it, while the members of the Kindergarten adopted the subordinate role of expert advisers and propagandists."

11 Ibid., 54.

12 Merriman to Sir Somerset French, 3 June 1908, *Correspondence of John X. Merriman*, 4:78–9.

13 *Transvaal Leader*, 6 May 1908, leader; *Cape Argus*, 5 May 1908, leader.

14 Thompson, *Unification of South Africa*, 81.

15 *South African Mines Commerce and Industries*, 9 May 1908; *Rand Daily Mail*, 12 May 1908, leader.

16 Selborne Papers, MS62, fols. 28–31, Selborne to Farrar/FitzPatrick, 21 July 1908.

17 Selborne to Duncan, 30 November 1907, cited in Thompson, *Unification of South Africa*, 80. Unfortunately, Thompson does not fully discuss the significance of this advice.

18 Selborne Papers, MS62, fols. 28–31, Selborne to Farrar/FitzPatrick, 21 July 1908.

19 *Rand Daily Mail*, 12 October 1908, leader.

20 Thompson, *Unification of South Africa*, 175.

21 Ibid., 175–6.

22 Ibid., 334.

23 Nimocks, *Milner's Young Men*, 104–5; Lewsen, *John X. Merriman*, 104.

24 Thompson, *Unification of South Africa*, 180.

25 Selborne Papers, MS71, fols. 163–5, Selborne to Lyttelton, 15 May 1908.

26 Ibid., MS52, fols. 125–8, Selborne to Crewe, 29 April 1909; MS66, fols. 163–5, Selborne to Lyttelton, 29 April 1909.

27 Selborne Papers, MS3, fols. 50–7, Selborne to Brodrick, 1 July 1908.

28 See Farrar's speech reported in the *Johannesburg Star*, 13 May 1908; also, Chaplin's in *Star*, 15 May.

29 Thompson, *Unification of South Africa*, 133, 231–8, 369–70. Proportional representation was dropped from the final draft.

30 Selborne Papers, MS62, fols. 48–9, Selborne to Farrar, 12 February 1909.

31 Ibid., fols. 50–57, Selborne to Farrar, 8 April 1909 (Selborne's emphasis).
For example, Selborne gave Farrar full particulars of the Australia Commonwealth Electoral Act of 1902 and the English Government Act of 1888,
both of which furnished precedents against such overloading as the Cape
advocated.

32 Copy of letter as it appeared in *Transvaal Leader,* 10 April 1909; Selborne
Papers, MS62, fols. 59–60, Farrar to Selborne, 15 April 1909; *State,* April
1909.

33 Selborne Papers, MS60, Selborne to Botha, 8 April 1909; MS52, fol. 131,
Botha to Selborne, 12 April 1909; enclosure in Selborne to Crewe,
29 April 1904, fols. 125–8.

34 Ibid., MS52, fols. 132–4, Selborne to Botha, 29 April 1909.

35 Thompson, *Unification of South Africa,* 368–72.

36 Selborne Papers, MS60, note of 7 May 1909.

37 Thompson, *Unification of South Africa,* 167.

38 Selborne Papers, MS60, Selborne to Botha, 8 April 1909.

39 Ibid., MS66, fols. 152–6 Selborne to Maydon, 5 April 1909.

40 Ibid., fols. 161–3, Curtis to Selborne, 8 April 1909; Selborne to Curtis,
10 April 1909.

41 Ibid., MS56, fols. 239–40, Nathan to Selborne, 27 May 1909; fol. 247,
Nathan to Selborne, 4 June 1909; MS53, fol. 200, Selborne to Crewe,
1 June 1909.

42 Thompson, *Unification of South Africa,* 100–3. See also Nimocks, *Milner's
Young Men,* 100–3.

43 Selborne Papers, MS59, Selborne to Northcote, 13 July 1908.

44 Sir Perceval Laurence, "Problems of Closer Union," *State,* January 1909;
H.A.L. Fisher, "The American Union," ibid., May 1909.

45 Thompson, *Unification of South Africa,* 8.

46 Brand, *Union of South Africa,* 90–1.

47 Speaking to a large meeting in Pretoria, Smuts termed the draft constitution
"the final treaty of peace between the white people of South Africa," while
Botha implored the same audience "to extend the hand of brotherhood
across the graves of those who have unfortunately fallen in the past." Smuts
went so far as to claim that the constitution "bore the impression of a higher
hand." See *Rand Daily Mail,* 25 February 1909. *The Friend* was so caught up in
these "good feelings" that it now wondered what had kept the white races divided for so long. See *The Friend,* 10 February 1909, leader. Inspired by a different vision, Steyn declared to a Unie congress that the constitution
signified the fulfilment of a dream for which Afrikaners had fought and suffered since Voortrekker days. See *Rand Daily Mail,* 5 March 1909.

48 *Rand Daily Mail,* 11 February 1909. See also leader in same journal for
12 March 1909.

49 *Rand Daily Mail,* 25 February 1909; *State,* July 1909.

50 *Rand Daily Mail,* 27 April 1909.
51 Schumann, *Structural Change and Business Cycles,* 222.
52 Frankel, *Capital Investment,* 94.
53 Schumann, *Structural Change and Business Cycles,* 376–85.
54 Selborne Papers, MS9, fols. 166–71, Chamberlain to Selborne, 24 March 1908; MS5, fols. 213–20, Salisbury to Selborne, 19 July 1908.
55 Milner Papers, dep. 196, fols. 27–31, Stent to Milner, 20 January 1909; dep. 34, fols. 51–2, Kipling to Selborne, 17 March 1908; enclosure in Kipling to Milner, March 1908; and dep. 196, fols. 80–1, Milner to Chaplin, 17 April 1909.
56 Selborne Papers, MS66, fols. 187–94, Selborne to Amery, 2 April 1909.

Chapter Ten

1 Dangerfield, *Strange Death of Liberal England,* 64.
2 Selborne Papers, Reminiscences, fol. 61.
3 Selborne to F.S. Oliver, 30 March 1911, in Boyce, ed., *Crisis of British Unionism,* 55–6.
4 See *The Times* (London) for reports on his speeches of 28 February 1911, 19 March 1911, and 21 March 1911.
5 Selborne to Salisbury, 25 August 1916, in Boyce, ed., *Crisis of British Unionism,* 195.
6 Selborne to Robert Palmer, 16 April 1912, in ibid., 81–2; Selborne Papers, MS77, fols. 96–9, Selborne to Grey, 3 April 1914.
7 Selborne Papers, MS77, fols. 18–22, Selborne to Platt, 19 September 1912; MS77, fols. 106–7, Selborne to Lansdowne, 1 May 1914.
8 The authoritative account of the constitutional proposals put forward during this period to solve the Irish difficulty is provided by Kendle in *Ireland and the Federal Solution,* 1–3, 107–18 and 166–7. As Kendle notes, "federation," "devolution," and "home rule all round" were used interchangeably, though what most British politicians had in mind was not federation (which would undermine the sovereignty of the British Parliament) but home rule all round, in which Westminster would devolve certain powers onto regional or "national" bodies. See also Kendle's *Round Table Movement and Imperial Union,* 143–5 and 162–3. The quotation comes from Selborne Papers, MS77, fols. 101–3, Selborne to Curzon, 9 April 1914.
9 Selborne to Grey, 3 April 1914, in Boyce, ed., *Crisis of British Unionism,* 107.
10 Cabinet memorandum by Selborne, 21 July 1915, enclosure in Selborne to Asquith, 22 July 1915, in ibid., 135–41; Milner Papers, dep. 350, fols. 196–9, Milner to Selborne, 7 July 1915; and Selborne Papers, MS83, fols. 3–10, Selborne to Nash, 15 May 1916.
11 Asquith to Selborne, 16 July 1915, in Boyce, ed., *Crisis of British Unionism,* 141.

12 Selborne to Asquith, 16 June 1916 in ibid., 178. The complicated political manoeuvrings surrounding this episode, especially Lloyd George's duplicity, are recounted lucidly in Kendle, *Walter Long*, 97–118. In the event, it was Walter Long, soon to be colonial secretary, who derailed the deal.

13 Selborne Papers, MS6, fols. 174–6, Selborne to Salisbury, 25 August 1916; MS6, fols. 185–91, Selborne to Salisbury, 12 September 1916.

14 For details see Kendle, *Ireland and the Federal Solution*, 179–87.

15 Selborne Papers, MS6, fols.185–9, Selborne to Salisbury, 12 September 1916; Boyce, ed., introduction to *Crisis of British Unionism*, xv–xvi; and Selborne to Salisbury, 17 June 1918, ibid., 218–21.

16 Selborne Papers, MS191, fol. 36 and MS192, fols, 226–7, Reminiscences, finished in 1937; Selborne to Salisbury, 26 October 1922, in Boyce, ed., *Crisis of British Unionism*, 241.

Epilogue

1 In its pluralistic assumptions about causality, its focus on politics and policy, and its emphasis on human agency, this book has deployed a liberal approach throughout. Its findings, however, are in accordance with those of the neo-Marxist interpretation. In this case, a liberal methodology has led to a radical conclusion. For a perceptive explanation of modern liberal historiography about South Africa, see Butler and Schreuder, "Liberal Historiography since 1945," 149.

2 Many years ago, Carl Berger brought the metropole/periphery distinction into question in his seminal study, *The Sense of Power*. In this, he argued that there was no conflict between Canadian nationalism and imperialism, that indeed "Imperialism was one form of Canadian nationalism." Canadian patriots believed that participation in a wide-ranging world empire enhanced Canadian international status and esteem (see *Sense of Power*, 259 and passim). Thus, it would seem that Selborne's faith in his colonial brethren was not misplaced, although he diverged with them on one point. While material considerations infused Selborne's conception of empire, the Canadian imperialists were complete idealists. Economic factors found no place in their imperialism.

3 Robinson and Gallagher cite this document to support their claim that the imperial factor was hostage to the complex interplay of local forces on the periphery. See Robinson and Gallagher, *Africa and the Victorians*, 462–72. I have argued, to the contrary, that Selborne appreciated that what fuelled local dependence was metropolitan capital.

4 Selborne Papers, MS9, fols. 150–65, Selborne to Chamberlain, 24 February 1908.

5 "The Position after the War," minute by Selborne, 16 November 1899. A copy can be found in the Selborne Papers, MS9, fols. 86–92.

6 Selborne Papers, MS15, fols. 80–7, unsigned, undated memorandum. On the document, an estimated date is given as 11 November 1896. Robinson and Gallagher consider that this is "clearly Selborne's work" and I would agree. Robinson and Gallagher, *Africa and the Victorians*, 434–7, see especially 434 n.1.

7 Selborne Papers, MS71, fols. 171–84, Selborne to Pretyman, 13 January 1909.

8 Ibid., fols. 131–4, Selborne to Curtis, 11 November 1907.

9 Ibid. For the Kindergarten's work to solidify the Empire after 1910, see Kendle, *Round Table Movement.*

10 Drafts in the Selborne Papers, MS79, fols. 80–92; published in the *Morning Post* in two parts on 29 and 31 July 1912.

11 Ibid., MS71, fols. 171–84, Selborne to Pretyman, 3 January 1909; Curzon Papers, Eur. F111–229, fols. 84–92, Selborne to Curzon, 21 October 1903; Selborne Papers, MS56, fols. 194–7, Selborne to Nathan, 13 May 1908; MS5, fols. 158–62, Selborne to Salisbury, 18 May 1907. One strong influence on Selborne was Richard Jebb, a respected imperial theorist who visited South Africa extensively during Selborne's tenure there. Selborne's enthusiasm for colonial nationalism was no doubt sparked or at least stoked by Jebb. Like Selborne, Jebb assumed that British colonists, wherever they went, were inherently more industrious, able, and progressive than any other group. Both these men attached great importance to economic factors in forging the ties of empire. However, while Jebb envisioned the Empire becoming a set of alliances between independent states, Selborne believed strongly in imperial consolidation. See Jebb, *Studies in Colonial Nationalism*, 272–302. See also Schreuder, "Colonial Nationalism and 'Tribal Nationalism,' " 192–204.

12 Selborne's conception of empire bears a resemblance to the "ideological cluster" delineated by John MacKenzie. This was "made up of a renewed militarism, a devotion to royalty, an identification and worship of national heroes, together with a contemporary cult of personality and racial ideas associated with social Darwinism. Together these constituted a new type of patriotism, which derived a special significance from Britain's unique mission. That the mission was unique in scale was apparent to all. That it was also unique in its moral content was one of the principal propagandist points of the age. Empire had the power to regenerate not only the 'backward' world, but also the British themselves, to raise them from the gloom and apprehension of the later nineteenth century, and by creating a national purpose with a high moral content lead to class conciliation." See MacKenzie, *Propaganda and Empire*, 2. Selborne fits well into MacKenzie's picture except in one important respect. His close association with the colonial elite, which figured prominently in his imperial ideas, takes him beyond the confines of MacKenzie's England-centred construction of the imperial creed.

Bibliography

PRIMARY SOURCES

Unpublished material

GOVERNMENT DOCUMENTS (PUBLIC RECORD OFFICE, LONDON, UK)

Colonial Office Records
CO 96 (Gold Coast)
    Vol.: 291 (Apr. 1897)
CO 224 (Orange River Colony)
    Vol.: 18 (Nov.-Dec., 1905)
CO 267 (Sierra Leone)
    Vols.: 434; 438; 450 (Dec. 1897–May 1898)
CO 291 (Transvaal)
    Vols.: 83; 84; 85; 86; 87; 88; 95; 96; 97; 98; 99; 100; 101; 102; 103; 104; 105; 106; 111; 113; 114; 115; 116; 117; 118; 119; 120; 125; 126; 127; 128; 129; 131; 132 (June 1905-Dec. 1908).
CO 417 (South Africa)
    Vols.: 152; 160; 164; 177; 179; 180; 181; 182; 183; 184; 185; 192; 197; 203; 214; 215; 217; 218; 220; 223; 242; 243; 244; 245; 246; 247; 249; 250; 259; 260; 261; 262; 263; 264; 265; 269; 413; 422; 424; 426; 427; 428; 439; 440; 441; 455; 458; 459; 470; 471 (Dec. 1895–Dec. 1899); (Sept. 1905–May 1909)
CO 446 (Northern Nigeria)
    Vols.: 1; 3 (Mar.–Oct. 1898)

CO 527 (South Africa, Inter-Colonial Council)
   Vols.: 5; 10; 11; 14 (June 1905-Jan. 1907)
CO 879 (South Africa, Confidential Print)
   Vol.: 84–Nos. 744, 746, 747
   Vol.: 85–Nos. 752, 755, 756, 757, 760, 761, 762
   Vol.: 86–Nos. 763, 764, 765, 766
   Vol.: 87–No. 773
   Vol.: 88–No. 779
   Vol.: 89–Nos. 795, 796, 796A, 796B, 796C, 797, 798, 799, 800, 801
   Vol.: 90–Nos. 715, 716, 743, 747, 760, 765, 795
   Vol.: 91–Nos. 802, 804, 805, 807, 808, 809, 810, 811, 812, 813, 814, 815
   Vol.: 92–Nos. 816, 817, 818, 819, 820, 821, 822, 823, 824, 825, 826, 827,
   828, 829, 830, 833, 834, 837, 8837A, 838, 840, 842, 843
   Vol.: 93–Nos. 847, 849, 851, 852, 853, 854, 857, 858, 859, 860, 860A, 863
   Vol.: 94–Nos. 866, 867, 868
   Vol.: 95–Nos. 871, 872, 874
   Vol.: 96–Nos. 880, 887, 890
   Vol.: 97–Nos. 891, 892, 893, 897, 898
   Vol.: 98–Nos. 899, 900, 901, 907
   Vol.: 99–No. 920
   Vol.: 100–Nos. 925, 927
   Vol.: 101–No. 931
   Vol.: 102–Nos. 932, 933, 934, 936
   Vol.: 103–Nos. 943, 944A, 946
   Vol.: 104–Nos. 947, 948, 952
   Vol.: 105–No. 957
   Vol.: 106–Nos. 807, 820, 834, 853, 854, 874, 900, 925, 934, 952
   (Jan. 1904–Dec. 1910)

Cabinet Records
CAB 37 (Memoranda printed for the use of the Cabinet)
   Vol.: 49–No. 26
   Vol.: 80–No. 160
   Vol.: 81–Nos. 178, 179, 180, 181, 182, 183, 184, 185
   Vol.: 82–Nos. 2, 3, 4, 5, 10, 11, 12, 14, 16, 18, 19, 21, 22, 23, 31, 33, 34
   Vol.: 83–Nos. 49, 51, 53, 67, 68, 69
   Vol.: 85–Nos. 83, 84, 86, 87, 105
   Vol.: 88–No. 55
   Vol.: 89–Nos. 91, 92
   Vol.: 90–No. 93
   Vol.: 94–No. 110
   Vol.: 97–Nos. 4, 6, 22 Vol.: 98–Nos. 35, 48, 52

Vol.: 99–No. 66

(Mar. 1899; Oct. 1905–Apr. 1909)

CAB 41 (Prime Minister's letters to Sovereign)

Vol.: 26–Nos. 2, 5, 23, 27, 28

Vol.: 27–Nos. 2, 3, 23, 31, 38, 39

Vol.: 28–Nos. 10, 14, 20, 25, 26

Vol.: 29–Nos. 2, 17, 18, 26, 27, 28, 29, 30, 32, 33, 34, 35, 36, 37, 38, 39

Vol.: 30–Nos. 36, 37, 39, 41, 42, 46, 48, 49, 51, 57, 58, 59, 60, 63, 66, 69, 70, 75, 77

Vol.: 31–Nos. 39, 65

Vol.: 32–No. 25

(Feb. 1901-July 1909)

War Office Records

Vol.: 32–No. 7116 (Nov. 1908)

PRIVATE PAPERS AND MISCELLANEOUS MANUSCRIPTS

Bodleian Library, Oxford, UK

Asquith Papers,

Lionel Curtis Papers

Milner Papers

Round Table Papers (listed under Curtis)

Selborne Papers

British Library, London, UK

Balfour Papers

Ripon Papers

Hatfield house, Hatfield, UK

Salisbury Papers (3rd Marquess)

India Office Library, London, UK

Curzon Papers

Public Record Office, London, UK

Sir Edward Grey Papers

Landsdowne Papers

Rhodes House Library, Oxford, UK

Feetham Papers

Lagden Papers

Nathan Papers

Selborne Memorandum, proofs (listed under Curtis, L.)

William Evans Papers

Transvaal Archives Depot, Pretoria, Republic of South Africa

Smuts Papers (courtesy of John Bottomley)

University of Birmingham Library, Birmingham, UK
   Joseph Chamberlain Papers

Published material

PARLIAMENTARY DEBATES

South Africa
Orange River Colony
   1907–8 (Legislative Assembly and Legislative Council)
   1909   (Legislative Council)
Transvaal
   1904–5 (Legislative Council)
   1908   (Legislative Council)
   1909   (Legislative Assembly and Legislative Council)
   1910   (Legislative Assembly and Legislative Council)

United Kingdom
Hansard, 4th series
   1905 – Vols. 141–2, 146, 150
   1906 – Vols. 152, 154–5, 158, 162, 165, 167
   1907 – Vols. 169–70, 174, 176–7
   1908 – Vols. 183, 186, 188, 193
Hansard, 5th series, House of Commons
   1909 – Vols. 1–2, 4, 5, 8–9
   1910 – Vol. 18
Hansard, 5th series, House of Lords
   1909 – Vols. 1–2
   1933 – Vols. 88 and 90

BRITISH SESSIONAL PAPERS (PARLIAMENTARY PAPERS) –
COMMONS

1903 Vol. xlv:
   Cd. 1531 – Correspondence relating to labour recruitment in British Central Africa
   Cd. 1641 – Papers relating to Inter-Colonial Council
   Cd. 1684 – Despatch from Transvaal Governor regarding position of British Indians
1904 Vol. xxxix:
   Cd. 1896 – Report of Transvaal Labour Commission, 1903.
   Vol. lxi:
   Cd. 1844 – Report by Mr. Henry Birchenough on prospects of British trade in South Africa

Cd. 1895 – Further correspondence regarding affairs in the Transvaal and Orange River Colony

Cds. 1898, 1899, 1941, 1986 – Further correspondence regarding the Transvaal Labour Ordinance and amendments

Cd. 2103 – Census returns for British South Africa, 1904

Cd. 2104 – Further correspondence regarding affairs in the Transvaal and Orange River Colony

Vol. lxii:

Cd. 1945 – Further correspondence regarding the Transvaal Labour Ordinance and amendments

Cd. 1950 – Correspondence relating to labour recruitment in British Central Africa

1905 Vol. lv:

Cd. 2400 – Despatch transmitting Letters Patent and Order- in-Council providing for constitutional changes in the Transvaal

Cd. 2401 – Further correspondence regarding the Transvaal Labour Ordinance and amendments

Cd. 2479 – Papers relating to constitutional changes in the Transvaal

Cds. 2482, 2563 – Further correspondence regarding affairs in the Transvaal and the Orange River Colony

Vol. lvi:

Cd. 2239 – Correspondence regarding the position of British Indians in the Transvaal

1906 Vol. lxxx:

Cds. 2786, 2788, 2819, 3025, 3028 – Further correspondence regarding affairs in the Transvaal and Orange River Colony (especially Chinese labour)

Cd. 3250 – Letters Patent and Instructions regarding the Transvaal; also the Swaziland Order-in-Council

Cd. 3251 – The Asiatic Law Amendment Ordinance, No. 29 of 1906

1907 – Vol. lvii:

Cd. 3308 – Correspondence regarding legislation affecting Asiatics

Cd. 3338 – Annual Report of the Foreign Labour Department, 1905–6

Cd. 3405 – Correspondence regarding the introduction of Chinese labourers in excess of licenses issued

Cd. 3526 – Letters Patent and Instructions regarding the Orange River Colony

Cd. 3528 – Further correspondence regarding affairs in the Transvaal and Orange River Colony

Cd. 3564 – Papers relating to the Federation of the South African Colonies (The Selborne Memorandum)

1908 Vol. lxx:

Cd. 4119 – Report on African Education by E.B. Sargant (Part III – education in the Protectorates)

Vol. lxxiii:

Cds. 3887, 3892 – Correspondence regarding legislation affecting Asiatics in the Transvaal

Cd. 3994 – Correspondence regarding the Indentured Labour Laws Temporary Continuance Act, 1907

Cd. 4327 – Correspondence regarding legislation affecting Asiatics in the Transvaal

1909 Vol. lx:

Cd. 4525 – Report of Convention delegates, 1908–9 with copy of South Africa Constitution Bill, 1909

Cd. 4721 – Second report of delegates, with copy of South Africa Constitution Bill, as finally passed by the Convention

Vol. lxi:

Cd. 4584 – Correspondence regarding legislation affecting Asiatics in the Transvaal

1910 Vol. lxvi:

Cd. 5363 – Correspondence regarding legislation affecting Asiatics in the Transvaal

REPORTS

South African Native Affairs Commission, 1903–5, *Report*
Transvaal Indigency Commission, 1906–8, *Report*
Transvaal Mining Industry Commission, 1907–8, *Report* and *Evidence*

PUBLISHED CORRESPONDENCE, COLLECTED DOCUMENTS, AND CONTEMPORARY BOOKS

Anonymous [Curtis, Lionel]. *The Government of South Africa.* 2 vols. Cape Town: Central News Agency 1908.

Brand, R.H. *The Union of South Africa.* Oxford: The Clarendon Press 1909.

Boyce, D. George, ed. *The Crisis of British Power: The Imperial and Naval Papers of the Second Earl of Selborne, 1895–1910.* London: The Historian's Press 1990.

– *The Crisis of British Unionism: the Domestic Political Papers of the Second Earl of Selborne, 1885–1922.* London: The Historian's Press 1987.

Churchill, Randolph, ed. *Winston Churchill.* 6 vols. London: Heinemann 1969.

Davenport, T.R.H., and K.S. Hunt, eds. *The Right to the Land.* Cape Town: David Philip 1974.

Duminy, A.H., and W.R. Guest, eds. *FitzPatrick: South African Politician, Selected Papers, 1888–1906.* Johannesburg: McGraw-Hill 1976.

Hancock, W.K., and Jean Van der Poel, eds. *Selections from the Smuts Papers.* 7 vols. Cambridge: Cambridge University Press 1966–73.

Headlam, Cecil, ed. *The Milner Papers: South Africa, 1897–1905.* 2 vols. London: Cassell 1931.

Houghton, D. Hobart, and Jenifer Dagut, eds. *Source Material on the South African Economy: 1860–1970.* 3 vols. Cape Town: Oxford University Press 1972–3.

Jebb, Richard. *Studies in Colonial Nationalism.* London: Edward Arnold 1905.

Jeeves, Alan, and Maryna Fraser, eds. *All that Glittered: Selected Correspondence of Lionel Phillips, 1890–1924.* Cape Town: Oxford University Press 1977.

Karis, Thomas, and Gwendolen M. Carter, eds. *From Protest to Challenge: a Documentary History of African Politics in South Africa, 1882–1964.* 4 vols. Vol. 1: *Protest and Hope, 1882–1934.* Stanford, Calif.: Hoover Institution Press 1972.

Lagden, Sir Godfrey. *The Basutos: the Mountaineers and their Country.* 2 vols. London: Hutchinson 1909.

Lewsen, Phyllis, ed. *Selections from the Correspondence of J.X. Merriman, 1870–1924.* 4 vols. Cape Town: Van Riebeeck Society 1960–9.

Lord Milner. *The Nation and the Empire: Speeches and Addresses: with an Introduction by Lord Milner.* London: Constable 1913.

Phillips, Lionel. *Transvaal Problems: some Notes on Current Politics.* London: John Murray 1905.

Praagh, L.V. *The Transvaal and Its Mines: The Encyclopedia History of the Transvaal.* London: Praagh and Lloyd 1906.

Schreiner, Olive. *Closer Union: A Letter on the South African Union and Principles of Government.* London: A.C. Fifield 1909.

Walton, Sir Edgar H. *The Inner History of the National Convention of South Africa.* New York: Longmans, Green 1912.

Williams, Basil, ed. *The Selborne Memorandum: A Review of the Mutual Relations of the British South African Colonies in 1907.* London: Oxford University Press 1925.

NEWSPAPERS AND PERIODICALS

South Africa
Cape Argus, 1905–9
The Friend, 1907–9
Johannesburg Star, 1905–9
Journal of the Chemical, Metallurgical, and Mining Society, 1906–8
Natal Mercury, 1907, 1909
Pretoria News, 1906
Rand Daily Mail, 1905–9
South African Mines Commerce and Industries (formerly *South African Mining Journal*), 1905–9
The State, 1909–10
Transvaal Leader, 1905–9

United Kingdom
Contemporary Review, 1905–10
Empire Review, 1906–10

Fortnightly Review, 1905–10
Manchester Guardian, 1905–10
Morning Post, 1912
National Review, 1905–10
Nineteenth Century, 1905–10
Review of Reviews, 1905
Round Table, 1910–11
The Times (London), 1905–10

SECONDARY SOURCES

Arrighi, Giovanni. "Labour Supplies in Historical Perspective: A Study of the Proletarianization of the African Peasantry in Rhodesia." In *Essays on the Political Economy of Africa,* edited by Giovanni Arrighi and John S. Saul. London: Monthly Review Press 1973.

Arrighi, Giovanni, and John S. Saul, eds. *Essays on the Political Economy of Africa.* London: Monthly Review Press 1973.

Atmore, A., and S. Marks. "The Imperial Factor in South Africa in the Nineteenth Century: Towards a Reassessment." *Journal of Imperial and Commonwealth History* 3 (1974): 105–39.

Barnett, Corelli. *The Collapse of British Power.* Atlantic Heights, NJ: Humanities Press 1972.

Beinart, William, and Colin Bundy. *Hidden Struggles in Rural South Africa: Politics and Popular Movements in the Transkei and Eastern Cape, 1890–1930.* Middletown, Conn.: Wesleyan University Press 1987.

Beinart, William. *The Political Economy of Pondoland, 1860–1930.* Cambridge: Cambridge University Press 1982.

Benyon, John. *Proconsul and Paramountcy in South Africa: The High Commission, British Supremacy and the Sub-Continent, 1806–1910.* Pietermaritzburg: University of Natal Press 1980.

Berger, Carl. *The Sense of Power: Studies in the Ideas of Canadian Imperialism, 1867–1914.* Toronto: University of Toronto Press 1970.

Blainey, G. "Lost Causes of the Jameson Raid." *Economic History Review* (2nd series) 18 (1965): 350–66.

Blanch, M.C. "British Society and the War." In *The South African War: the Anglo-Boer War, 1899–1902,* edited by Peter Warwick. Harlow, Essex: Longman 1980.

Booth, Alan R. "Lord Selborne and the British Protectorates, 1908–1910." *Journal of African History* 10 (1969): 133–48.

Bozzoli, Belinda. *The Political Nature of a Ruling Class: Capital and Ideology in South Africa, 1890–1933.* London: Routledge and Kegan Paul 1981.

Bozzoli, Belinda, ed. *Labour, Townships, and Protest: Studies in the Social History of the Witwatersrand.* Johannesburg: Ravan Press 1979.

– . *Town and Countryside in the Transvaal: Capitalist Penetration and Popular Response.* Johannesburg: Ravan Press 1983.

Brewer, Anthony. *Marxist Theories of Imperialism: A Critical Survey.* London: Routledge and Kegan Paul, 1980.

Brookes, Edgar H. *The History of Native Policy in South Africa (from 1830 to the Present Day.)* Cape Town: Nasionale Pers 1924.

Bundy, Colin. "The Emergence and Decline of a South African Peasantry." *African Affairs* 71 (1972): 369–88.

– . *The Rise and Fall of the South African Peasantry.* London: Heinemann 1979.

Butler, Jeffrey. *The Liberal Party and the Jameson Raid.* Oxford: The Clarendon Press 1968.

Butler, Jeffrey, Richard Elphick, and David Welsh, eds. *Democratic Liberalism in South Africa: Its History and Prospect.* Middletown, Conn.: Wesleyan University Press 1987.

Butler, Jeffrey, and Deryck Schreuder. "Liberal Historiography since 1945." *Democratic Liberalism in South Africa: Its History and Prospect,* edited by Jeffrey Butler, Richard Elphick, and David Welsh. Middletown, Conn.: Wesleyan University Press 1987.

Cain, P.J., and Hopkins, A.G. *British Imperialism: Innovation and Expansion, 1688–1914.* 2 vols. London: Longman 1993.

– . "Gentlemanly Capitalism and British Expansion Overseas: I. The Old Colonial System, 1688–1850." *Economic History Review* 39 (1986): 501–25.

– . "Gentlemanly Capitalism and British Expansion Overseas: II. New Imperialism, 1850–1945." *Economic History Review* 40 (1987): 1–26.

– . "The Political Economy of British Expansion Overseas, 1750–1914." *Economic History Review* 33 (1980): 463–90.

Cambridge History of the British Empire (eds. A.P. Newton, E.A. Benians, and E. A. Walker). 2nd ed. 8 vols. Vol. 8: *South Africa, Rhodesia, and the Protectorates.* Cambridge: Cambridge University Press 1963.

Cannadine, David. *The Decline and Fall of the British Aristocracy.* New York: Doubleday 1990.

Chanaiwa, David. "African Humanism in Southern Africa: The Utopian, Traditionalist, and Colonialist Worlds of Mission-Educated Elites." In *Independence without Freedom: The Political Economy of Colonial Education in Southern Africa,* edited by Agrippah T. Mugomba and Mougo Nyaggah. Santa Barbara: ABC-Clio 1980.

Cell, John W. *The Highest Stage of White Supremacy: The Origins of Segregation in South Africa and the American South.* Cambridge: Cambridge University Press 1982.

Cohen, Robin. "Resistance and Hidden Forms of Consciousness amongst African Workers." *Review of African Political Economy* 19 (1980): 8–22.

Comaroff, Jean. *Body of Power, Spirit of Resistance: the Culture and History of a South African People.* Chicago: University of Chicago Press 1985.

Comaroff, Jean and John. *Of Revelation and Revolution: Christianity, Colonialism, and Consciousness in South Africa.* Vol. 1. Chicago: University of Chicago Press 1991.

Cooper, Frederick. "Africa and the World Economy." *African Studies Review* 24 (1981): 1–86.

Coplan, David. "The Emergence of an African Working-Class Culture." In *Industrialisation and Social Change in South Africa: African Class Formation, Culture, and Consciousness, 1870–1930*, edited by Shula Marks and Richard Rathbone. Harlow, Essex: Longman 1982.

Dangerfield, George. *The Strange Death of Liberal England, 1910–1914*. New York: Capricorn Books 1935.

Davenport, T.R.H. *The Afrikaner Bond: The History of a South African Political Party, 1880–1911*. Cape Town: Oxford University Press 1966.

– "The Cape Liberal Tradition to 1910." In *Democratic Liberalism in South Africa: Its History and Prospect*, edited by Jeffrey Butler, Richard Elphick, and David Welsh. Middletown, Conn.: Wesleyan University Press 1987.

– *South Africa: A Modern History*. 3rd ed. Toronto: University of Toronto Press 1987.

Davies, Robert H. *Capital, State and White Labour in South Africa, 1900–1960: An Historical Materialist Analysis of Class Formation and Class Relations*. Atlantic Highlands, NJ: Humanities Press 1979.

Davis, Lance, and Robert Huttenback. *Mammon and the Pursuit of Empire: the Political Economy of British Imperialism, 1860–1912*. Cambridge: Cambridge University Press 1986.

Denoon, Donald. "Capital and Capitalists in the Transvaal in the 1890s and 1900s." *Historical Journal* 23 (1980): 111–32.

– . "'Capitalist Influence' and the Transvaal Government during the Crown Colony Period, 1900–1906." *Historical Journal* 11 (1968): 301–31.

– . *A Grand Illusion: The Failure of Imperial Policy in the Transvaal Colony during the Period of Reconstruction, 1900–1905*. London: Longman 1973.

– . *Settler Capitalism: the Dynamics of Dependent Development in the Southern Hemisphere*. Oxford: Clarendon Press 1983.

– . "The Transvaal Labour Crisis, 1906–7." *Journal of African History* 7 (1967): 481–94.

Drummond, Ian. *The Gold Standard and the International Monetary System, 1900–1934*. London: Macmillan 1987.

Dubow, Saul. *Racial Segregation and the Origins of Apartheid in South Africa, 1919–36*. London: Macmillan 1989.

Duminy, A.H. *The Capitalists and the Outbreak of the Anglo-Boer War*. Research Monograph No. 3. Natal University 1977.

– . *Sir Alfred Milner and the Outbreak of the Anglo-Boer War*. Research Monograph No. 2. Natal University 1976.

Ellsworth, Ronald Thomas. "The British South African Colonies and the Imperial-Transvaal Conflict: Competition and Collaboration in the Late Nineteenth Century." M.A. thesis, Queen's University, Kingston 1979.

– . "Economic Regionalism, Political Centralism and South African Union." Research essay, Queen's University, Kingston, 1981.

Etherington, Norman. *Theories of Imperialism: War, Conquest and Capital.* London: Croom Helm 1984.

– . "Theories of Imperialism in Southern Africa Revisited." *African Affairs* 81 (1982): 385–407.

Fieldhouse, D.K. *Economics and Empire, 1830–1914.* Ithaca, NY: Cornell University Press 1973.

– . "Can Humpty-Dumpty be put together again? Imperial History in the 1980s." *Journal of Imperial and Commonwealth History* 12 (1984): 9–23.

– . "'Imperialism': An Historiographical Revision." *Economic History Review* (2nd series), 14 (1961): 187–209.

Frankel, S. Herbert. *Capital Investment in Africa: Its Course and Effects.* London: Oxford University Press 1938.

– . *The Railway Policy of South Africa: An Analysis of the Effects of Railway Rates, Finance and Management on the Economic Development of the Union.* Johannesburg: Hortors 1928.

Fredrickson, George M. *White Supremacy: A Comparative Study in American and South African History.* New York: Oxford University Press 1981.

Gann, L.H. and Peter Duignan. *Burden of Empire: An Appraisal of Western Colonialism in Africa South of the Sahara.* London: Frederick A. Praeger 1967.

– . *The Rulers of British Africa: 1870–1914.* Stanford, Calif.: Stanford University Press 1978.

– . "'Het Volk': The Botha-Smuts Party in the Transvaal, 1904–11." *Historical Journal* 9 (1966): 101–32.

Giliomee, Hermann. "The Beginnings of Afrikaner Ethnic consciousness, 1850–1915." In *The Creation of Tribalism in Southern Africa,* edited by Leroy Vail. London: James Currey 1989.

Goodfellow, Clement Francis. *Great Britain and South African Confederation, 1870–1881.* Cape Town: Oxford University Press 1966.

Goodfellow, D.M. *A Modern Economic History of South Africa.* London: Routledge 1931.

Greenberg, Stanley B. *Race and State in Capitalist Development: Comparative Perspectives.* New Haven: Yale University Press 1980.

Grenville, J.A.S. *Lord Salisbury and Foreign Policy: The Close of the Nineteenth Century.* London: Athlone Press 1970.

Hailey, Lord. *The Republic of South Africa and the High Commission Territories.* London: Oxford University Press 1963.

Hammond-Tooke, W.D. *Command or Consensus: The Development of Transkeian Local Government.* Cape Town: David Philip 1975.

Hancock, W.K. *Smuts.* 2 vols. Vol. 1: *The Sanguine Years, 1870–1919.* Cambridge: Cambridge University Press 1962.

Hobsbawm, E.J. *Industry and Empire: An Economic History of Britain since 1750*. London: Weidenfeld and Nicolson 1968.

Hobson, J.A. *Imperialism: A Study*. New York: James Pott 1902.

– . *The War in South Africa: Its Causes and Effects*. London: James Nisbet 1900.

Hopkins, A.G. *An Economic History of West Africa*. London: Longman 1973.

– . "The Victorians and Africa: a Reconsideration of the Occupation of Egypt, 1882." *Journal of African History* 27 (1986): 363–91.

Hyam, Ronald. "African Interests and the South Africa Act, 1908–1910." *Historical Journal* 13 (1970): 85–105.

– . *Elgin and Churchill at the Colonial Office, 1905–1908: The Watershed of the Empire-Commonwealth*. New York: St. Martin's Press 1968.

– . "Smuts and the Decision of the Liberal Government to Grant Responsible Government to the Transvaal, January and February, 1906." *Historical Journal* 8 (1965): 380–98.

Inabinett, Kay Risher. "Lord Selborne in South Africa, 1905–1910." Ph.D. thesis, University of South Carolina 1977.

Ingham, Geoffrey. *Capitalism Divided? the City and Industry in British Social Development*. London: Macmillan 1984.

Jeeves, Alan. "The Control of Migratory Labour on the South African Gold Mines in the Era of Kruger and Milner." *Journal of Southern African Studies* 2 (1975): 3–29.

– . *Migrant Labour in South Africa's Mining Economy: The Struggle for the Gold Mines' Labour Supply, 1890–1920*. Kingston: McGill-Queen's University Press 1985.

– . "The Rand Capitalists and the Coming of the South African War, 1896–1899." *Canadian Historical Papers* 1973.

Johnstone, Frederick A. *Class, Race and Gold: A Study of Class Relations and Racial Discrimination in South Africa*. London: Routledge and Kegan Paul 1976.

Katz, Elaine. "White Workers' Grievances and the Industrial Colour Bar, 1902–1913." *South African Journal of Economics* 42 (1974): 127–56.

Katzenellenbogen, Simon E. *South Africa and Southern Mozambique: Labour, Railways and Trade in the Making of a Relationship*. Manchester: Manchester University Press 1982.

Keegan, Timothy. "The Making of the Rural Economy: from 1850 to the Present." In *Studies in the Economic History of Southern Africa: South Africa, Lesotho, and Swaziland*, edited by Z. Konczacki, J. Parpart, and T. Shaw. Vol. 2. London: Frank Case 1991.

– . "The Restructuring of Agrarian Class Relations in a Colonial Economy: The Orange River Colony, 1902–10." *Journal of Southern African Studies* 5 (1979): 234–54.

Kendle, John Edward. *Ireland and the Federal Solution: the Debate over the United Kingdom Constitution, 1870–1921*. Kingston: McGill-Queen's Press 1989.

– . *The Round Table Movement and Imperial Union*. Toronto: University of Toronto Press 1975.

– . *Walter Long, Ireland, and the Union, 1905–1920.* Kingston: McGill-Queen's Press 1992.

Kennedy, Paul. *The Rise and Fall of the Great Powers: Economic Change and Military Conflict from 1500 to 2000.* London: Unwin Hyman 1988.

– . *The Rise of the Anglo-German Antagonism, 1860–1914.* London: Ashfield Press 1987.

Kennedy, W.P.M., and H.J. Schlosberg. *The Laws and Customs of the South African Constitution: A Treatise on the Constitutional and Administrative Law of the Union of South Africa, the Mandated Territory of South-West Africa, and the South African Crown Territories.* London: Oxford University Press 1935.

Keppel-Jones, Arthur. *Rhodes and Rhodesia: The White Conquest of Zimbabwe, 1884–1902.* Kingston: McGill-Queen's University Press 1983.

Konczacki, Z., J. Parpart, and T. Shaw, eds. *Studies in the Economic History of Southern Africa: South Africa, Lesotho, and Swaziland.* Vol. 2. London: Frank Cass 1991.

Koss, Stephen, ed. *The Pro-Boers: The Anatomy of an Antiwar Movement.* Chicago: University of Chicago Press 1973.

Kubicek, Robert V. *The Administration of Imperialism: Joseph Chamberlain at the Colonial Office.* Durham, NC: Duke University Press 1969.

– . *Economic Imperialism in Theory and Practice: The Case of South African Gold Mining Finance, 1886–1914.* Durham, NC: Duke University Press 1979.

– . "The Randlords in 1895: A Reassessment." *Journal of British Studies* 11 (1972): 84–103.

Lacey, Marian. *Working for Boroko: The Origins of a Coercive Labour System in South Africa.* Johannesburg: Ravan Press 1981.

Langer, William L. *The Diplomacy of Imperialism, 1890–1902.* New York: Alfred A. Knopf 1960.

Lee, C.H. *The British Economy since 1700: a Macroeconomic Perspective.* Cambridge: Cambridge University Press 1987.

Le May, G.H.L. *British Supremacy in South Africa, 1899–1907.* Oxford: The Clarendon Press 1965.

Lenin, V.I. *Imperialism: The Highest Stage of Capitalism.* Moscow: Foreign Languages Publishing House, n.d. (originally published 1916).

Lewsen, Phyllis. "The Cape Liberal Tradition – Myth or Reality?" University of London, Institute of Commonwealth Studies, *Collected Seminar Papers on the Societies of Southern Africa in the 19th and 20th Centuries* 1 (1969–70): 72–88.

– . *John X. Merriman: Paradoxical South African Statesman.* New Haven: Yale University Press 1982.

Lipton, Merle. *Capitalism and Apartheid: South Africa, 1910–84.* Totowa, NJ: Rowman and Allanheld 1985.

Louis, William Roger, ed. *Imperialism: the Robinson and Gallagher Controversy.* London: New Viewpoints 1976.

MacKenzie, John, ed. *Imperialism and Popular Culture.* Manchester: Manchester University Press 1986.

– .*Propaganda and Empire: the Manipulation of British Public Opinion, 1880–1960.* Manchester: Manchester University Press 1984.

Magdoff, Harry. *Imperialism: From the Colonial Age to the Present.* London: Monthly Review Press 1978.

Marais, J.S. *The Fall of Kruger's Republic.* Oxford: The Clarendon Press 1961.

Marder, Arthur J. *From the Dreadnought to Scapa Flow: the Royal Navy in the Fisher Era, 1904–1919.* 5 vols. Vol. 1: *The Road to War, 1904–1914.* London: Oxford University Press 1961.

Marks, Shula. "Patriotism, Patriarchy and Purity: Natal and the Politics of Zulu Ethnic Consciousness." In *The Creation of Tribalism in Southern Africa,* edited by L. Vail. London: James Curry 1989.

– . *Reluctant Rebellion: The 1906–8 Disturbance in Natal.* Oxford: The Clarendon Press 1970.

– . "Review Article: Scrambling for South Africa." *Journal of African History* 23 (1982): 97–113.

Marks, Shula, and Richard Rathbone, eds. *Industrialisation and Social Change in South Africa: African Class Formation, Culture, and Consciousness, 1870–1930.* Harlow, Essex: Longman 1982.

Marks, Shula and Trapido, Stanley. "Lord Milner and the South African State." *History Workshop* 8 (1979): 50–80.

Mathias, Peter. *The First Industrial Nation: an Economic History of Britain, 1700–1914.* London: Methuen 1983.

Matthew, H.C.G. *The Liberal Imperialists: The Ideas and Politics of a Post-Gladstonian Elite.* London: Oxford University Press 1973.

Maylam, Paul. *Rhodes, the Tswana, and the British: Colonialism, Collaboration, and Conflict in the Bechuanaland Protectorate, 1885–1899.* Westport, Conn.: Greenwood Press 1980.

Mawby, A.A. "Capital, Government and Politics in the Transvaal, 1900–1907: A Revision and a Reversion."*Historical Journal* 17 (1974): 387–415.

McDermott, W.J. "The Immediate Origins of the Committee of Imperial Defence: A Reappraisal." *Canadian Journal of History* 7 (1972): 253–72.

Mendelsohn, Richard. "Blainey and the Jameson Raid: The Debate Renewed." *Journal of Southern African Studies* 6 (1980): 157–70.

Miles, Robert. *Capitalism and Unfree Labour: Anomaly or Necessity?* London: Tavistock 1987.

Monger, George. *The End of Isolation: British Foreign Policy, 1900–1907.* London: Thomas Nelson 1963.

Moodie, Dunbar. "Mine Culture and Miners' Identity on the South African Gold Mines." In *Town and Countryside in the Transvaal: Capitalist Penetration and Popular Response,* edited by Belinda Bozzoli. Johannesburg: Ravan Press 1983.

Morony, Sean. "Mine Married Quarters: the Differential Stabilisation of the Witwatersrand Workforce, 1900–1920." In *Industrialisation and Social Change in South Africa: African Class Formation, Culture and Consciousness, 1870–1930*, edited by Shula Marks and Richard Rathbone. Harlow, Essex: Longman 1982.

Mugomba, Agrippah T., and Mougo Nyaggah, eds. *Independence without Freedom: The Political Economy of Colonial Education in Southern Africa*. Santa Barbara: ABC-Clio 1980.

Nimocks, Walter. *Milner's Young Men: The 'Kindergarten' in Edwardian Imperial Affairs*. Durham, NC: Duke University Press 1968.

O'Meara, Dan. *Volkskaptialisme: Class, Capital and Ideology in the Development of Afrikaner Nationalism, 1934–1948*. Cambridge: Cambridge University Press 1983.

Owen, Roger, and Bob Sutcliffe, eds. *Studies in the Theory of Imperialism*. London: Longman 1972.

Pakenham, Elizabeth. *Jameson's Raid*. London: Weidenfeld and Nicolson 1960.

Palmer, Robin, and Neil Parsons, eds. *The Roots of Rural Poverty in Central and Southern Africa*. Berkeley: University of California Press 1977.

Perkin, Harold. *The Rise of Professional Society: England since 1880*. London: Routledge 1989.

Pillay, Bala. *British Indians in the Transvaal: Trade, Politics and Imperial Relations, 1885–1906*. London: Longman 1976.

Platt, D.C.M. "Economic Factors in British Policy during the 'New Imperialism'." *Past and Present* 39 (1968): 120–38.

– . "The Imperialism of Free Trade: Some Reservations." *Economic History Review* (2nd series) 21 (1968): 296–306.

– . "The National Economy and British Imperial Expansion before 1914." *Journal of Imperial and Commonwealth History* 2 (1973): 3–14.

Pollard, Sidney. *Britain's Prime and Britain's Decline: the British Economy, 1870–1914*. London: Edward Arnold 1984.

Porter, Andrew. "British Imperial Policy and South Africa, 1895–9." In *The South African War: the Anglo-Boer War, 1899–1902*, edited by Peter Warwick. Harlow, Essex: Longman 1980.

– . "'Gentlemanly Capitalism' and Empire: the British Experience since 1750?" *Journal of Imperial and Commonwealth History* 18 (1990): 256–95.

– . *The Origins of the South African War: Joseph Chamberlain and the Diplomacy of Imperialism, 1895–99*. Manchester: Manchester University Press 1980.

– . "Sir Alfred Milner and the Press, 1897–99." *Historical Journal* 16 (1973): 323–39.

– . "The South African War (1899–1902): Context and Motive Reconsidered." *Journal of African History* 31 (1990): 43–57.

Porter, Bernard. *The Lion's Share: A Short History of British Imperialism, 1850–1970*. London: Longman, 1975.

Price, Richard. *An Imperial War and the British Working Class: Working-Class Atti-tudes and Reactions to the Boer War, 1899–1902*. London: Routledge and Kegan Paul 1972.

Pyrah, G.B. *Imperial Policy and South Africa, 1902–10*. Oxford: The Clarendon Press 1955.

Ranger, Terrence. "The People in African Resistance: A Review." *Journal of Southern African Studies* 4 (1977): 125–46.

Reeves, J.A. "Chinese Labour in South Africa, 1901–1910." M.A. thesis, University of Witwatersrand 1954.

Rich, Paul. " 'Milnerism and a Ripping Yarn': Transvaal Land Settlement and John Buchan's Novel 'Prester John' 1901–10." In *Town and Countryside in the Transvaal: Capitalist Penetration and Popular Response*, edited by Belinda Bozzoli. Johannesburg: Ravan Press 1983.

– . "The Origins of Apartheid Ideology: The Case of Ernest Stubbs and Trans-vaal Native Administration, c. 1902–1932." *African Affairs* 79 (1980): 171–94.

– . *Race and Empire in British Politics*. Cambridge: Cambridge University Press 1986.

– *White Power and the Liberal Conscience: Racial Segregation and South African Lib-eralism, 1921–60*. Manchester: Manchester University Press 1984.

Richardson, Peter. *Chinese Mine Labour in the Transvaal*. London: Macmillan 1982.

– . "Coolies and Randlords: the North Randfontein Chinese Miners' 'Strike' of 1905." *Journal of Southern African Studies* 2 (1976): 151–77.

Richardson, Peter, and Jean Jacques Van-Helten. "Labour in the South African Gold Mining Industry, 1886–1914." In *Industrialisation and Social Change in South Africa: African Class Formation, Culture, and Consciousness, 1870–1930*, ed-ited by Shula Marks and Richard Rathbone. Harlow, Essex: Longman 1982.

Robinson, Ronald. "Non-European Foundations of European Imperialism: A Sketch for a Theory of Collaboration." In *Studies in the Theory of Imperialism*. edited by Roger Owen and Bob Sutcliffe. London: Longman 1972.

Robinson, Ronald, and John Gallagher. "The Imperialism of Free Trade." *Eco-nomic History Review* (2nd series) 6 (1953–4): 1–15.

Robinson, Ronald, and John Gallagher, with Alice Denny. *Africa and the Victori-ans: The Climax of Imperialism*. Garden City, NY: Doubleday 1961.

Rose, Kenneth. *The Later Cecils*. London: Weidenfeld and Nicolson 1975.

Rotberg, Robert, with Miles Shore. *The Founder: Cecil Rhodes and the Pursuit of Power*. New York: Oxford University Press 1988.

Roxborough, Ian. *Theories of Underdevelopment*. London: Macmillan 1979.

Sandbrook, Richard, with Judith Barker. *The Politics of Africa's Economic Stagna-tion*. Cambridge: Cambridge University Press 1985.

Schreuder, Deryck. "Colonial Nationalism and 'Tribal Nationalism': Making the White South African State, 1899–1910." In *The Rise of Colonial National-*

ism: Australia, New Zealand, Canada and South Africa first assert their Nationalities, 1880–1914, edited by John Eddy and Deryck Schreuder. Sydney: Allen and Unwin 1988.

– . *The Scramble for Southern Africa, 1877–1895: The Politics of Partition Reappraised*. Cambridge: Cambridge University Press 1980.

Schumann, C.G.W. *Structural Changes and Business Cycles in South Africa, 1806–1936*. London: P.S. King 1938.

Semmel, Bernard. *Imperialism and Social Reform: English Social-Imperial Thought, 1895–1914*. Garden City, NY: Anchor Books 1968 (originally published by Allen and Unwin in 1960).

Sked, Alan. *Britain's Decline: Problems and Perspectives*. Oxford: Basil Blackwell 1987.

Stichter, Sharon. *Migrant Laborers*. Cambridge: Cambridge University Press, 1985.

Stokes, Eric. "Late Nineteenth-Century Colonial Expansion and the Attack on the Theory of Economic Imperialism: A Case of Mistaken Identity?" *Historical Journal* 12 (1969): 285–301.

– . "Milnerism." *Historical Journal* 5 (1962): 47–60.

Sundkler, B.G.M. *Zulu Zion: and Some Swazi Zionists*. London: Oxford University Press 1976.

Tatz, Colin Martin. *Shadow and Substance in South Africa: A Study in Land and Franchise Policies Affecting Africans, 1910–1960*. Pietermaritzburg: University of Natal Press 1962.

Thompson, L.M. *The Unification of South Africa, 1902–10*. Oxford: The Clarendon Press 1960.

Thornton, A.P. *The Imperial Idea and Its Enemies: A Study in British Power*. London: Macmillan 1959.

Trapido, Stanley. "Landlord and Tenant in a Colonial Economy." *Journal of Southern African Studies* 5 (1978): 26–58.

Vail, Leroy, and Landeg White. *Capitalism and Colonialism in Mozambique: A Study of Quelimane District*. Minneapolis: University of Minnesota Press 1980.

Vail, Leroy, ed. *The Creation of Tribalism in Southern Africa*. London: James Currey 1984.

Van den Berghe, Pierre L. *South Africa: A Study in Conflict*. Middletown, Conn.: Wesleyan University Press 1965.

Van der Horst, Sheila T. *Native Labour in South Africa*. London: Frank Cass, 1971 (originally published in 1942).

Van der Poel, Jean. *The Jameson Raid*. London: Oxford University Press 1951.

– . *Railways and Customs Policies in South Africa, 1885–1910*. London: Royal Empire Society 1933.

Van-Helten, J.J. "British Capital, the British State and Economic Investment in South Africa, 1886–1914." University of London, Institute of Commonwealth Studies, *Collected Seminar Papers on the Societies of Southern Africa in the 19th and 20th Centuries* 9 (1977–8): 1–17.

— . "German Capital, the Netherlands' Railway Company, and the Political Economy of the Transvaal, 1886–1900." *Journal of African History* 19 (1978): 369–90.

— . "Milner and the Mind of Imperialism." University of London, Institute of Commonwealth Studies, *Collected Seminar Papers on the Societies of Southern Africa in the 19th and 20th Centuries* 10 (1978–9): 42–56.

— . "Review Article: Mining and Imperialism." *Journal of Southern African Studies* 6 (1980): 230–55.

Van Onselen, Charles. *Chibaro: African Mine Labour in Southern Rhodesia, 1900–1933.* London: Pluto Press 1976.

— . *Studies in the Social and Economic History of the Witwatersrand, 1886–1914.* 2 vols. Vol. 1: *New Babylon.* Vol. 2: *New Nineveh.* Harlow, Essex: Longman 1982.

Walker, Eric A. *Lord De Villiers and his Times: South Africa, 1842–1914.* London: Constable 1925.

Wallerstein, Immanuel. "The Three Stages of African Involvement in the World-Economy." In *The Political Economy of Contemporary Africa,* edited by Peter C. W. Gutkind and Immanuel Wallerstein. Beverly Hills, Calif.: Sage Publications 1976.

Walshe, Peter. *The Rise of African Nationalism in South Africa: The African National Congress, 1912–1952.* Los Angeles: University of California Press 1971.

Warren, Bill. *Imperialism: Pioneer of Capitalism.* London: Verso 1980.

Warwick, Peter. "Black People and the War." In *The South African War: The Anglo-Boer War, 1899–1902.* Edited by Peter Warwick. Harlow, Essex: Longman 1980.

Warwick, Peter, ed. *The South African War: The Anglo-Boer War, 1899–1902.* Harlow, Essex: Longman 1980.

Weiner, Martin. *English Culture and the Decline of the Industrial Spirit, 1850–1980.* Cambridge: Cambridge University Press 1981.

Welsh, David. *The Roots of Segregation: Native Policy in Colonial Natal, 1845–1910.* Cape Town: Oxford University Press 1971.

Wilde, Richard H. "Joseph Chamberlain and the South African Republic, 1895–1899: A Study in the Formulation of Imperial Policy." *Archives Year Book for South African History,* vol. 1 1956.

Wilson, Francis. *Labour in the South African Gold Mines, 1911–1969.* Cambridge: Cambridge University Press 1972.

Yudelman, David. *The Emergence of Modern South Africa: State, Capital, and the Incorporation of Organized Labor on the South African Gold Fields, 1902–1939.* Westport, Conn.: Greenwood Press 1983.

— . "Lord Rothschild, Afrikaner Scabs and the 1907 Strike: A State-Capital Daguerrotype." *African Affairs* 81 (1982): 257–69.

Index

Abdurahman, Abdullah, 22, 116, 119

Admiralty, 93; Selborne as first lord of, 3, 34–5

African franchise: in Cape, 13, 24, 101, 103; Selborne's views on, 104–5, 120–5, 189; and South African unification, 120–3, 158, 168; withheld at Vereeniging, 22, 38–9, 119–20; *see also* African policy; Africans; colour prejudice among South African whites; Selborne, policy towards non-whites

African labour, 149, 190; as argument for union, 157–9, 177; and Chinese labour, 42, 44, 46; as cause for unrest, 24, 106–8; conditions on mines, 13–14, 22, 47, 52; on farms, 114, 117–19; migratory form of, 13, 102–3, 237n4; in Mozambique, 84–92, 234n22; possibility of advancement, 96–8; recruitment of, 85, 87–95, 234n22, 238n8; shortage of, 22, 41–2, 221n3; ultra-exploitability of, 41, 101–2

African policy, 32; bureaucratic rule, 13, 22–4, 101–23, 158–9, 189–90, 237n2, 238n7, 241n42; and capitalism, 101–4, 113–14, 117–19, 121–5, 190, 193, 238n12; "civilization" as aim, 104, 116–18, 121, 193, 241n42; conquest and suppression, 11–13; education, 116–17, 244n65; pass system, 118–19;

taxation, 116–17; territorial segregation, 22, 103, 112–16, 242–3n54, 243n55

African Political Organisation, 22, 119

Africans, 68; disabilities, 13, 22, 24, 101–5, 118–19; educated elite, 104–5, 112–15, 119–24; land dispossession and restriction, 13, 24, 101, 103, 106–7, 112–16, 237n2; political protest, 112, 119, 123; proletarianization, 13, 101–3, 117–18, 177, 190, 237n2; religion, 105, 108, 238–9n14, 239n25, 240n27; subjugation, 11–13; unrest, 24, 105–9, 121–4, 158, 239n25, 240n27

Afrikaner Bond, 25, 116, 144, 147–8, 171; *see also* Afrikaners, Cape

Afrikaner nationalism, 227n9; embittered by Anglo-Boer War, 21, 217–18n26; South African unification, 147, 165, 168–9; threat to British Empire, 9, 21, 68, 139

Afrikaners, 191; and Anglo-Boer War, 18–19, 21; Chinese labour, 20–1, 48, 60–3, 73, 93–4; colour prejudice of, 104, 116; divisions amongst, 20–1, 66, 227n9; hostility to British, 17, 38, 71–2, 139, 156; political strength during reconstruction period, 19–21, 23–5, 33–4, 65, 80–2; rapprochement with